Keeper of the Wild

Keeper of the Wild

THE LIFE OF
Ernest Oberholtzer

JOE PADDOCK

MINNESOTA HISTORICAL SOCIETY PRESS

www.mnhs.org/mhspress

Manufactured in the United States of America

10 9 8 7 6 5 4 3 2 1

∞ The paper used in this publication meets the minimum requirements of the American National Standard for Information Sciences — Permanence for Printed Library materials, ANSI Z39.48-1984

International Standard Book Number
0-87351-409-2 (cloth)

Library of Congress Cataloging-in-Publication Data

Paddock, Joe.
    Keeper of the wild : the life of Ernest Oberholtzer.
        p. cm.
    ISBN 0-87351-409-2 (cloth : alk. paper)
    1. Oberholtzer, Ernest C. (Ernest Carl), 1884–1977.
    2. Conservationists—United States—Biography.
    I. Minnesota Historical Society Press.

QH31.O23 P34 2001
333.72′092—dc21
    [B]   2001032659

For Jean Sanford Replinger,
a tireless worker for the Oberholtzer legacy,
without whose inspiration and continuing support
this book would never have come into being.

Keeper of the Wild

Acknowledgments

Throughout his life Ernest Oberholtzer attracted exceptional people in support of his goals, and upon embarking on the writing of this book, I soon found that nothing had changed. It's been wonderful that so many have come forth to selflessly aid in my effort to bring the Oberholtzer story back into the light. There are those whose continuing help requires that their names appear more than once in the acknowledgments below.

My sincere thanks then to the board of directors of the Ernest C. Oberholtzer Foundation for their continuing work in preserving the Oberholtzer legend and for permission to use the Oberholtzer materials in my collaborative approach to writing this book. Current board members are Jim Davis, Delores DeLaittre, John Delanoy, Ted Hall, Mary Holmes, Charles A. Kelly, Robin Monahan, Jean Sanford Replinger, Mary Alice Smith, Harry Sweatt, and Douglas Wood. I also include in my thanks honorary board member Marnee Monahan.

My sincere thanks as well to the Minnesota Historical Society for its ongoing and unfailingly generous support of my effort. Special thanks here to Jim Fogerty, who offered every courtesy in orienting me to the society's Oberholtzer collections. And special thanks, too, to Lucile Kane, who in the 1960s conducted most of the society's oral history interviews with Oberholtzer and who wrote the biographical sketch introductory to those interviews that has proven so important to the first chapter of this book. Thanks as well to those other interviewers—George and Gene Monahan, Russell Fridley, Pete Heffelfinger, Evan Hart, and others—who helped with the taping of the Oberholtzer story.

My thanks to the Koochiching County Historical Society and its director, Ed Erichbauer, for opening their files and copying for me materials that could not have been found elsewhere.

And then there are those friends of Oberholtzer who patiently, even enthusiastically, sat through hours of probing oral history interviews. Without their memories and insights, it would have been very difficult for me to develop the living image of Ober that I hope I've achieved. These patient and supportive individuals were Ray Anderson, Harry "Pinay" Boshkaykin, Barbara Breckenridge, Charlene Erickson, Dr. Harry Henderson, Bob Hilke, Don "Buck" Johnson, and Kerttu Macki. Mallard Island Program Director Jean Sanford Replinger must be thanked here as well for an interview that was rich with insight into the life of a man she had only come to know after his death.

My thanks again to Barbara Breckenridge for her superb job of transcribing the above interviews and for the use of the series of letters she wrote to her mother while working for Ober as Mallard Island cook during the summer of 1955.

Sincere thanks must go as well to Alicia Johnson for the summary of her interview with Marnee Monahan and to Marnee herself, whose memories of Ober provided angles of insight I have discovered nowhere else.

Then there were individuals whose simple presence, often on Ober's Mallard Island, has proven a continuing inspiration and source of information for me. These engaging storytellers include Ray Anderson, Lauren Erickson, Ted Hall, Bob Hilke, Edith and John Rylander, and Allen Snowball.

Ted Hall must be thanked again for his abundant and wonderful writing about Ober from which I have so often quoted. And Edith Rylander for her wonderful piece, "All the Different Obers," which I've included in its entirety in chapter one. And Kevin Proescholdt for information on key moments along the road to the present-day status of protected areas within the Quetico-Superior region. And Betty Gorshe for information relating to Ober's childhood in Davenport, Iowa. And Charles Woodard for his many fine suggestions for improvement of the nearly completed manuscript. And thanks to Bill Holm for his magnificent depiction of the presence of music on Mallard Island and in the life of Oberholtzer. My sincere thanks as well to R. H. Cockburn for his knowledgeable and richly detailed article, "Voyage to Nutheltin," which proved incredibly helpful in my effort to envision and depict Ober and Billy's great journey. And my sincere thanks to R. Newell Searle for his book *Saving Quetico-Superior.* Had he not gone before me, unraveling the complex threads of the early struggle for preservation of the Rainy Lake watershed would have proven difficult for me indeed.

How can I adequately thank the photographers who have given so much in support of this work? Ray Anderson was so kind as to print dozens of Oberholtzer photographs at my request. Bill Schaefer copied for me many of the images held within the Oberholtzer collections on Mallard Island. (For additional photographs in this collection, see *Toward Magnetic North: The Oberholtzer-Magee 1912 Canoe Journey to Hudson Bay,* published by the Oberholtzer Foundation, 2000.) And those famous, yes, great, photographers, Dalton Muir and John Szarkowski, have been incredibly generous in providing so much of their work in support of the Oberholtzer story.

My sincere thanks as well to the staff of the Minnesota Historical Society Press, its director, Greg Britton, its book designer, Will Powers, and especially to my editor, Shannon M. Pennefeather, for her continuing clarity and tireless work enhancing and perfecting the manuscript.

I cannot possibly thank enough my wife, Nancy Paddock, for her patience, insight, and continuing support through these long years of research and writing.

There are, of course, many Mallard Island friends who must go unnamed here whose insights, support, and enthusiasm have buoyed me along the way. And finally, it would be a mistake not to mention and thank as well Mallard Island itself and the spirits that dwell in that beautiful place.

Introduction

We have too few environmental heroes to allow one so important as Ernest Oberholtzer to slip from our collective memory. In a time when only fragments of our wild heritage remain and many of us are uncertain as to whether or not these too must be sacrificed to maintain our material well being, the story of Ernest Oberholtzer's life reminds us that there is another way. It reminds as well that the other way, that of the keeper and, yes, creator of Edens, might lead to even more abundant life than is to be found along a path of practical materialism. As you will discover, the life of Ernest Oberholtzer was indeed an abundant one, rich in adventure, culture, friendship, and accomplishment.

In the late 1980s, a decade after Oberholtzer's 1977 death, my friends Bill Holm and Jean Replinger introduced me to the Oberholtzer story. Jean is the program director for Mallard Island, Oberholtzer's long-time home on Rainy Lake, and she invited me to spend time on the island. It had been suggested that I might find parallels between my interests and those of the man everyone called Ober. Mallard Island is a magical place on which the presence of the man whose home it was for fifty years still hovers strong. He is there in the design and arrangement of the many small buildings, in the collections of books, artifacts, and memorabilia. He is there in the Native American presence. He is there especially in the minds and memories of his old friends who often return to the island and tell stories of him. And, yes, I did find that my interests paralleled those of the man I discovered there.

As a regional poet for southwest Minnesota and later a founding member of the Land Stewardship Project, I had maintained what I thought of as a "soft activism," cultural and environmental, though sometimes situations led to hard confrontations. It was easy for me, then, to imagine the joys and miseries of Ober's forty years of activism on behalf of North American wilderness. On the island, I discovered as well something for which I, and I think most of us, had long yearned: an integration of nature and culture through which we are able to experience something of our fullness. In part at least, Ober had gone to the wilderness to heal himself. I, too, in my youth had turned to nature to heal, not a heart but a life, and I spent much of a six-year period living in an unimproved cabin on Minnesota's wild Kettle River. I did, then, feel close to the man I discovered on

Mallard Island, and after repeated visits there, I found that, despite other long-held plans, I intended to tell his story.

My first entry in the first of several notebooks filled while planning this book contains what was to be my central and continuing approach in the writing of it: "The idea to let it be, as much as possible, Ober's book, his voice, his writing, his photos. . . . To write as well and insightfully as I am able when necessary and appropriate, but otherwise to be transparent, to get out of the way and allow Ober's life to emerge from his own words and works." Along the way, I found that to follow my vision and understanding of the story I had to tell more of it than I had imagined, but, as the book developed, my original concept held, and I hope and believe that these pages themselves, overflowing with the very alive voice of Ernest Oberholtzer, will prove ample justification for my unusual and experimental approach.

This then is not a conventional historical biography, nor is it anything like a complete history of the long struggle to preserve the wilderness character of the Quetico-Superior region. It is instead the story of a fascinating life.

For a time my working title was *Legend.* In part, this had to do with one meaning of the name the Ojibwe gave Ober, but there is also what I have come to think of as the Oberholtzer legend, that is, the story or sequence of stories that Ober and those who knew him told over and over again about his life. In large part, then, this book is the telling of that legend, narrated as fully as possible in the words of Oberholtzer himself. Enough historical background has been provided to sustain the story, the legend, but this is far less historical essay than lively narrative. In Ober's writing and oral history telling, there is a richness of detail that will provide the reader with much the same sensuous satisfaction one finds in descriptive fiction, and the book is, in fact, somewhat novelistic in its technical approach. It is my belief that the intelligent general reader will find this book a fascinating "read" and that the specialist in Quetico-Superior history will benefit as well from this first introduction to the life of the man who was the central figure through the early years of the struggle for preservation of the border lakes region.

At the start I believed it would be easier for me to allow Ober, through his writing and oral history interviews, to tell his own story. In truth, however, the effort to integrate my writing with his voice and to make of our "collaboration" a seamless web has proven to be the most difficult technical challenge of a rather long writing career. In addition, interesting material proved so abundant as to sometimes be overwhelming. There are hundreds of pages of oral history, an endless series of journals, and many thousands of letters, reports, articles, and stories written by Ober in the collection devoted to him at the Minnesota History Center. And this is to say nothing of the collection maintained on Ober's Mallard Island and the plentiful materials held by so many of his kind and helpful friends.

The quality of Ober's voice had much to do with my choice to use it so generously. It's a voice that expresses warmth and enthusiasm, intelligence and openness, humor, modesty, niceness, respect. Indeed, Ober's voice is a rather full expression of his self, and since such expression is what this work is about, why not then go to the source? In the deeper sense of the word, Ober's voice *charmed* many during his lifetime, and will, I believe, continue to do so.

My decision to let Ober tell his own story also had much to do with the fact that he was a storyteller. In fact, one of the meanings of "Atisokan," the name given Ober by the Ojibwe, is "storyteller," and through the years, as has already been suggested, he wove the strands of his life into legend. His long-time friend Bob Hilke told me in an interview that Ober was the "best storyteller, bar none, that I've ever heard. Ober could go into town on the simplest errand and come back with a story, just so funny, made up of things that had happened that most people would never have thought about or noticed. . . . Or the Indian stories that he told. He finally got a feel for these to the point that it was as if he was living it as he was telling it. As a young boy, I couldn't help but just be enthralled."[1]

Further down that first page in my first notebook, I find: "I think of Ober remorsing in his journals that he did not write enough." It wasn't, however, that he didn't write enough—he seems to have written, especially letters, nearly every day of his life—but that he had not written a book or *the* book. One can only be amazed at how often in his journals the subject comes up. And just below the above-quoted line from my notebook, I find: "I think of Aldo Leopold who in life never knew what his writing was to mean to us . . . [so much of it edited, collected and arranged] after his death by his son Luna." Leopold was a friend of Ober's. In 1935, they were among eight founding members of the Wilderness Society. At mid-century, Ober, as president of the Quetico-Superior Council, may well have been the more famous environmentalist of the two. His long struggle with Edward Backus had received a great deal of publicity. But, with the publication of Leopold's significant books, his influence and reputation have greatly expanded. Ober's, however, have waned, until today his name is recognized by only a few.

As well as the story of a life, then, it is hoped that this work will prove to be something of a resurrection. In part at least, it is the resurrection and fulfillment of Ober's dream to write a book. Should it prove unworthy of him, it is not, of course, his fault. More importantly, it is hoped that this work will be the vehicle to resurrect the Oberholtzer legend into the consciousness of our new century. There is ever so much in it that will nourish us. It was hard for me to take on the burden—though often a joyous one—of writing this book. It was not in my life plan. But, as mentioned earlier, I felt a great affinity for the man and his story. In addition, I had come to believe that Ober's might just be the greatest uncelebrated environmental story in North American history, and that something had to be done about it. Surely an empowering starting point for any writer.

Guardedly, I continue to believe that my original intuition as to the importance of the Oberholtzer story was on the mark. Interestingly, however, no matter how significant Ober's visionary and activist role in laying the foundation for what were to become the Boundary Waters Canoe Area Wilderness, Quetico Provincial Park, and Voyageurs National Park, no matter how exciting his nine-year standoff with the last of the great lumber barons, Edward Wellington Backus, it has been the personality of Ober as an individual that has most fascinated me. On the one hand, he was a kind and nurturing caretaker of people and places. On the other, he richly manifested the archetype of the hero, first, as a youthful adventurer and, later, as a mature man willing to sacrifice self, no matter how harshly the choice worked against the grain of his hopes, for what he believed to be the greater good. It is at this point, among others, that his spiritual dimension is revealed.

Stories about Ober sometimes lean toward the mystical, and I will finish with one such of my own. With the manuscript of this book nearly complete, my wife, Nancy, and I made a pilgrimage to Ober's grave in Davenport, Iowa. In a soft slow rain, we searched for hours in the haunting gloom of the "rarely beautiful and wild cemetery" where Ober and his family lay buried.[2] Finally, in the oldest section of the cemetery, near the top of a hill crowned by a mausoleum, Nancy discovered the graves. They were framed by a square made of heavy lengths of eight-inch marble. This frame contained as well a life-sized statue of what I took to be an earth goddess of antiquity, perhaps Demeter or Kore. She was barefoot and her hair and robes were long and flowing. She held a wreath of roses in her left hand. Her right hand was missing. Then there were the graves of Ober, his mother Rosa, his grandparents, Ernest and Sarah Carl, two children of theirs who had died in infancy, and Ober's brother Frank, who had died at age five. Ober's grave was a bit sunken, and the hollow contained a wet carpet of oak leaves. Overwhelmed for a moment at being so close to his remains and by the impossibility of ever really knowing him, I heard my voice say:

"Ober, if I thought I could talk with you, I would dig you up."

And then the very strange thing happened: from all corners of that dark and lovely wooded cemetery, crows rose from wet branches. Cawing and black wings flapping, they began to pour in on us through the soft rain. They settled in the branches of gnarled oaks in a semicircle above us, surely a hundred of them, and they cawed mightily there for long minutes. And I dearly hoped I was receiving a message of thanks.

JOE PADDOCK
Litchfield, Minnesota

Keeper of the Wild

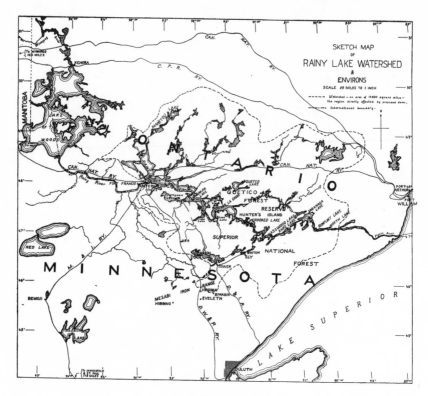

Rainy Lake watershed

I

To the End of the Earth

[1]

Out of the Vast Unknown

Near the end of his life, Ernest Carl Oberholtzer wrote of his childhood in the booming river town of Davenport, Iowa, that "what probably impressed me more than anything else were the long rafts of logs that came down the Mississippi . . . to be sawed at Davenport and Rock Island—out of the vast unknown North!"[1]

This was late in the nineteenth century, and those logs stretching northward on the shining water were tremendous lengths of virgin Minnesota pine, three and four feet thick at the base. Their source, "the vast unknown North," was a mystery to the young Oberholtzer, but would not remain so. Indeed, the child who gazed longingly northward there beside the springtime swelling of the river would in time become, for many, the embodiment of that source and its mystery.

There is expansiveness in the image of those great rafts of logs that stirred the imagination of the young Oberholtzer, and if in truth there is an innate image that underlies a life, guiding its direction and choices, Ernest Oberholtzer's was surely an expansive image, one which contained as well an ample measure of the stuff of the epic hero. For half a century his home would be a tiny Rainy Lake island on the boundary between Minnesota and Ontario, but, nearing his end, he would write that he had lived "on a vast wide open stage."[2] And indeed he had. Complex and enigmatic, Ober, as he was called, somehow managed to be deeply rooted in the wilderness of Quetico-Superior while at the same time being a citizen of the whole wide world.

The Ojibwe would one day name Ober "Atisokan," meaning "legend" or "teller-of-legends" or stories, and Ober was indeed such a teller. His childhood in Davenport was wonderfully rich, and it is surely the true storyteller's selective hindsight that led him to choose those "long rafts of logs" that metaphorically suggested so much of what was to come in his life as *the* childhood image that impressed him beyond all else. Though he would be forever unable to directly capitalize on his instinct for story—for legend—that instinct, both consciously and unconsciously, through word and deed, with great surety wove his life into the pattern of legend.

In time Oberholtzer would journey northward beyond the source of the Mississippi to the even purer waters of a wilderness that would prove healing to him. Among the countless journeys of his life, there would be two great ones, the first literal, the second metaphorical, and much imbued with the qualities of the first. That first began in 1912, when, with his aging Ojibwe mentor and companion Billy Magee, he embarked on an "impossible" canoe voyage into the "vast unknown" that would bring him to the source of himself. Paddles flashing in the strange light of the Canadian barrens, Ober and Billy pressed northward on an exploratory journey into one of the last unmapped regions on the North American continent. This journey was to be the great purification ritual of Ober's youthful life. Returned to civilization and the surface of himself, he was prepared then for the journey that was to dominate much of the remainder of his long life. This, the journey of struggle to preserve the Quetico-Superior wilderness, would begin with a nine-year face-off with the last of the great lumber barons, Edward Wellington Backus, whose intention was to build a series of dams and turn the Minnesota-Ontario boundary waters into a huge storage basin for industrial power. Had Backus succeeded with his plan, Voyageurs National Park, Quetico Provincial Park, and America's most popular wilderness, the Boundary Waters Canoe Area Wilderness, would never have come into being.

According to Charles Skrief, a long-time student of the life of Ernest Oberholtzer, the struggle between Ober and Backus was the most consequential event in Ober's public life. It was at the core of his great contribution to those who love the wilderness. Had Ober not taken on the Backus challenge, he and his life, no matter how fascinating, would have been known only to the lucky few who were close to him. Because he rose to the challenge, however, he became the very symbol of the effort to preserve the Quetico-Superior wilderness.[3]

It is remarkable that Ober, small in stature and financially limited, should prove so able to stand up to the physically imposing and politically powerful Backus, said to be worth $100 million as their struggle began. Much of the source of Ober's strength of will and character can be discovered in the story of his Davenport childhood. Fate, however, would place him in position to be of use. "My life," he would write, has "been more accidental than planned."[4]

The struggle with Backus was much at the source of Ober's one-time fame, but his contribution went well beyond a successful effort to block the Backus dams. As president of the Quetico-Superior Council, he would be for decades the overarching visionary, figurehead, voice, and central activist of a seemingly unending struggle for preservation in the region. There were of course hundreds of others making significant and necessary contributions, but Ober, it seems, was the personification of the preservationist effort during its first twenty years. And he would continue to be its hard-working ambassador and, eventually, grand old man for yet another twenty. In addition, even in this new century, concepts Ober developed for the Quetico-Superior program continue to be of use in wilderness planning.

There were then two great journeys or stories in Ober's life, but he cannot be contained, even metaphorically, within only two stories. One might think for a time that "you have him," but always and ever another Ober emerges. His complexity has intrigued and baffled many an astute observer. In an *Oberholtzer Foundation Newsletter* published in 1994, seventeen years after Ober's death, newsletter editor and poet Edith Rylander wondered about the many facets of the man she discovered upon first visiting Ober's Rainy Lake home on Mallard Island:

> I still remember the blur of impressions I gathered on my first few days on the island. I looked at the sheer physical beauty of the place, and there was the man who had seen this beauty and preserved it. I looked at the many island buildings and saw another Ober, the man who had so carefully sited these dwellings, designed and directed the building of them.
>
> I remember poet-musician Bill Holm leading us on a brief tour of the astounding book holdings in the various island houses, and got some measure of Ober the bibliophile, Ober the patron of the arts. Later, hearing Bill play both of the island pianos, I was introduced to Ober the musician, the man who took his second-best violin along on extended canoe trips.
>
> Ray Anderson (and all the photos on the cabin walls) introduced me to Ober the photographer. Ted Hall's reminiscences introduced me to the personal Ober, the charming eccentric, the magnificent companion. Ted also introduced me to Ober's long and ecologically significant feud with Edward Wellington Backus, and to Ober as lobbyist for the wilderness. Through research in the collections on the island, I have come to know and admire Ober the environmentalist, the lifetime president of the Quetico-Superior Council, one of eight original founders of the Wilderness Society and this organization's honorary vice president when he died at age 93.
>
> Then I listened to Allen Snowball talk about Ober from a Native American perspective. Here was yet another Oberholtzer, friend and respectful student of aboriginal lifeways and spiritual practices, the man of spiritual power [who it seems took the medicine path himself].
>
> Who was this guy? Why did he live the way he did? Does any of it matter? Clearly it matters to me and to the many others for whom The Mallard has become a spiritual retreat and place of solace.[5]

Rylander is not alone in her wonder over the "many Obers." Almost all who are introduced to the complexities of the man the Ojibwe named Legend ask the same questions as she.

Ernest Carl Oberholtzer was born of the marriage of Henry Reist Oberholtzer and Rosa Carl on February 6, 1884. For some reason Rosa's father, Ernest Samuel Carl, was in Washington, D. C., on that day, and he received a telegram announcing his grandson's birth: "Mrs. Carl says it is a ten pound boy. Rosa doing well as could be expected."[6] That large baby boy would grow up to be a small, agile, and compact man with brown hair, which would whiten early, and blue eyes, the light in which would often be commented on. He would grow up to be a man of quick intelligence, warmth, humor, and kindness, a man, according to Ober's long-time friend Marnee Monahan, "with a magnetism you can't describe."[7] And this magnetism would draw a complex community of people to gather around him for his presence and to support his goals: Indians and fisherfolk, carpenters and wealthy businessmen, members of the cultural, scientific, and political elite.

The family of Ober's father, Henry Oberholtzer, came from German Switzerland. On emigrating to the United States, they settled in Pennsylvania, among those known as Pennsylvania Dutch. They then resettled in Council Bluffs, Iowa. Henry later attended a business college in Davenport where he met Rosa, and they were married on December 28, 1882. Ernest was their first child. Their second, Frank, was born October 30, 1885. The marriage, however, was not a happy one, and on October 18, 1890, Rosa filed for divorce on the grounds of desertion. The allegation having proven true, the divorce was granted the following month. For the

Brothers Frank and Ernest Oberholtzer

Oberholtzers, however, the tragedy of that season was not yet over. In February, their son Frank, now five, died of inflammation of the brain, apparently caused by a severe fall. Rosa had returned to the Carl family home of her childhood. Now, deeply depressed, the young mother clung to and bonded powerfully with her remaining son, seven-year-old Ernest.[8]

Whatever the return to her childhood home meant for Rosa, it was first-rate luck for her son. The Carl home was an exceptional one—prosperous, loving, and disciplined—and it is next to unthinkable that Ober would have become what he did if he had been brought up in the home of the green and struggling young businessman, Henry Oberholtzer. Almost certainly his father would have provided lesser guidance and insisted on something more practical than the expansive and heroic vision for his life that was allowed young Ernest in the Carl home.

Ober's grandparents were an exceptional pair. His grandmother, Sarah Marckley Carl, born on a small plantation near Alexandria, Virginia, was of Scotch and English ancestry. In the early 1850s, her family moved to Davenport where her father carried on a small housing business. Ober's grandfather, Ernest Carl, was born in Germany, but there was a twist to his ancestry. In a letter written shortly after Ober's death, a distant cousin pointed out that the Carl family was in fact French and had escaped to Germany just ahead of the falling guillotine:

> the Carl family, of which my father and Ernest's mother were descendants were of French origin, nobility, in fact, who escaped into Germany during the French Revolution. Ernest had some noted ancestors. The French family name was Charles, but in Germany took the name of Carl.[9]

A great deal had been lost from Rosa's life, but young Ernest remained, now the central focus of her attention. Though not physically affectionate, Rosa was kind and gentle and a woman of considerable power. Photos of her, heavy and stolid-appearing in her later years, have caused some to breathe, "the Great Mother." And this woman of power now lavished all her attention on the one fledgling left in her nest, creating psychologically what has been termed a "boy god," one so honored and emotionally nourished by the mother that he grows up without the usual sense of limitation and self-doubt. Young Ernest would have no inferiority complex to be gotten over. Instead, however, he would suffer from a self-imposed burden of high expectations. The "boy god" is often of course subject to dangerous ego-expansion, but highly developed self-awareness and a lifelong lack of financial means would ever hold Ober in check.

While telling of Ober's inability to compromise on preservation issues, Ober's long-time friend and the archivist of his thousands of photographs, Ray Anderson, stated sardonically that Ober was a spoiled brat.

Though Anderson's statement can apply to only a small portion of the spectrum of Ober's personality—his fairness, generosity, and personal discipline are well known—one can get the point. In childhood young Ernest was unquestionably a cherished and fully nourished lad.

Ober's strong early bond with Rosa was never to be broken. He would call her "Mam," others would often call her "Mrs. Ober," and she would follow her son to Harvard, to Europe, and to Rainy Lake. Nevertheless, one must not think of Ober as a mama's boy. He went his own way, making the decisions for himself and often for Rosa. On unconscious levels, however, Rosa's influence was great, and when she died Ober had a death mask made of her face, with several smaller copies, to be kept close around him for the remainder of his days. Children are often subliminally called to live out the unlived life of their parents, and there are those who believe that Ober's unyielding bond with Rosa was unhealthy for him, that his identity with her was so intense that it did not allow free and natural expression of his libido and was therefore at the source of a lifetime of sexual repression and ambivalence.

"My mother was always firm with me," Ober would write, "even critical if she thought it necessary. She believed in some physical punishment, administered quickly, but never enough to prejudice me, even when I thought it unjust. My grandfather struck me only once and then under severe provocation, when I called him a foul name that I had heard for the first time on a street corner. They all expected me to do my part always, expressing approval at most, rather than ever praise. My grandfather told me early never to be proud, to be truthful and honest, since without these there was no basis for the good life. He surely exemplified these truths, and when he died suddenly at fifty-eight, left behind him untold numbers of admiring friends."[10]

The large and gracious Carl home stood on the corner of Sixth and Perry, on the first rise of ground that overlooked to the east the thriving, river-front-level downtown district of Davenport. At the time of Ober's childhood, Davenport was an ambitious city of some 30,000 that manufactured tin cans and plows, brooms and freight cars, macaroni, crackers, and cigars. The young Ober was excited by that world and felt connected to it. Early on, he attended the "old stone school," only a block from his home at Seventh and Perry, and the Unitarian church but four blocks away at Tenth and Perry.

Though Ober talked and wrote little about Unitarianism, it is clear that the church's liberal and well-defined values, which include respect for the interconnected web of life, early on permeated his consciousness. In addition, the religious pluralism embraced by Unitarianism would have grounded him generally in the spiritual, while opening his mind to the value in all religious traditions, preparing him for acceptance of what he later found in Native American religion. At the same time, his Unitarianism may have been at the source of what seems to have been a gentle but continuing distrust of institutional religion and traditional Christianity, especially when the missionary zeal of these negatively influenced the culture and religion of native peoples.

One Unitarian in particular, the Reverend Arthur Judy, worked a strong influence on Ober. In 1891, when Ober was seven and had just moved into the Carl home, Judy started the Outing Club, a Unitarian organization that guided local youth into constructive outdoor activity. The focus of this club seems to have been on games such as tennis, but one would guess there would have also been activities such as canoeing and camping that would have introduced the bright and enthusiastic young Ernest to the world of nature. Ober would never forget the importance of Arthur Judy in his early life, and in his will he would leave the Unitarian Church of Davenport $200 in his memory.

Grandfather Carl was certainly the most important adult male in Ober's early life, and Ober would ever speak of him with something like reverence. He considered him to be a man of the highest character, and the elder Carl's story took on mythic proportions for young Ernest. "[Grandfather Carl] was born in Saxe-Coburg, Germany," Ober would later write, "and came to New York at the age of fifteen. He had had an ex-

Ober's gracious childhood home in Davenport, Iowa

cellent education and speedily learned to speak fluent idiomatic English without accent."[11] It is not clear how Carl came to meet and marry Sarah Marckley, but "soon after his marriage at the age of twenty, he took a steamer from New York to Panama on his way to the gold rush in California. On the way, he met a Mr. Lovejoy of Boston, U.S. Consul at Callao, Peru, who persuaded him to take a job at the consulate. Soon afterwards my grandfather was promoted to Vice Consul and continued there for two years, until his health broke. In that time he had prospered, since sea captains of the time were men of little education and all took their accounts to him. Fees of this sort were then permitted to the Vice Consul. My mother had been born in his absence, and Sarah refused to join him in Peru. There was nothing for him to do but to return to [Sarah's home in] Davenport, where the opportunities for a man with a little money appeared alluring.

"Whatever merits I gained in my upbringing," continued Ober, "must have been due to my mother and my maternal grandparents. My grandfather on his return from Peru started a small grain company, which prospered at first but soon ran into a panic (there was no hedging in those days). My grandfather, already well known, put up everything he had, including his home, at auction to pay his debts. My grandmother, all unsuspecting, was sitting on her porch, when the man came to tack up the for sale sign. She attempted in vain to drive him off. Poor 'Grinnie' knocked the sign down as fast as the man could put it up.

"Two days later they were sitting on the same porch considering what to do, these 22-year-olds, when a hack drove up and out stepped four men in silk hats (customary then for notables). They'd come to pay their respects to a man who would pledge everything he had to pay his debts. More than that, they offered him the tellership of the leading bank in Davenport, the Citizens National. They were all directors of the bank. One of them was New England–born Frank Griggs, whose room at Hollis 6 I occupied at Harvard more than 50 years later."[12]

Ernest Oberholtzer was a complicated individual, and it is a trifle difficult to reconcile the wilderness preservationist he was to become with his enthusiasm for and pride in the "notables" and community builders who were a significant presence throughout his youth. In mid-life, Ober made an extensive series of detail notes for a work of autobiographical fiction he intended to write about his childhood. The young central character, Willie, is Ober. Though later in life Ober would despair over the moral laxity and environmental indifference of "founders" and "empire builders," these notes show that, in memory, he continued to hold the Davenport "notables" of his childhood in the highest esteem, especially his grandfather's employer, the leading Davenport banker, Frank Griggs:

Mr. Griggs [cherished] in secret his days at Harvard and [held] fast to all the old ideals of honor.

The men of the card club were the founders of new banks, new industries, new learned institutions, new universities. Great homes scattered in all parts of the city. Remarkable tolerance of opinion. The men stood for honesty, efficiency, helpfulness, cheerfulness, good fellowship.[13]

Ober's life in the Carl home and his Mississippi River town was overflowing "with special interests of many sorts, especially out of doors, *except sports*—birds, plants, animals...."[14] The emphasized "except sports" is interesting. Clearly rough and tumble were not to Ober's liking. Though tough and incredibly unrelenting in pursuit of his chosen goals, throughout life he would be thought of as a kind and gentle man, indeed a gentleman, and as he had little taste for competitive sports in his youth, he would later have little taste for the harsh confrontations in which his preservationist positions often placed him. This is by no means to say that Ober was without physical ability. Beyond becoming an exceptional canoeist with all the related wilderness skills, he would be in fact something of a playful showman. In the journal he kept during his 1912 canoe voyage, he noted that on the shore of Hudson's Bay he was able to impress two Inuit boys: "I amused them with some of my old juvenile tricks, such as high kicking, walking on my folded knees, and climbing over a stick, none of which either of them could do."[15] According to Ted Hall, a former correspondent and New York deputy bureau chief for Time-Life, for whom Ober was a mentor in his youth and a friend throughout his adult years, Ober maintained his great agility and flexibility well into old age and was able to do something most often associated with advanced yogis—to sit down and lace both feet behind his neck.[16]

Ober would grow to only five feet six inches in height, and, in his youth at least, he was greatly bothered by his lack of size. It seems that it was not so much that he suffered from a small man's complex as that his size did not jibe with his sense of self. He seldom took his limitations lying down, and, according to Hall, "As a young man, he desperately tried to get taller, to stretch himself. He constantly was reading about ways people could get taller, like hanging from a tree limb for fifteen minutes."[17] He apparently even researched a stretching machine "guaranteed" to contribute inches to one's height. However hard he tried, though, he was unable to add those inches, and, in compensation, as an adult he would strive to be larger than life.

Young Ernest found good guidance in his home and from figures such as Frank Griggs and Arthur Judy, but there was another individual, one who lived much closer to the earth, who would have at least as significant an influence on his life as his other, more civilized mentors. The man was gravedigger Tom Burke, and it may be that Ober—who would sometimes call himself Indian—discovered something in Burke that he would later find in Native American people. Ober met Burke shortly after moving to the Carl household.

"An activity that began soon after my brother's death," he wrote, "when I began to read voraciously, was to accompany my mother in a horse and buggy to the rarely beautiful and wild cemetery where my brother is buried. There I found a real pal of the first order in an Irish grave-digger who knew human nature better than anybody I ever knew. He could remember humorously all the characters of Cooper, Scott, and Dickens in great detail, and had never had any schooling. We called him by his last name—Burke. He was the only one my mother would let me go with at that early age, exploring the wild Duck Creek and unused pasture lands adjacent to the cemetery. This was a real fairyland for me—nothing sad about it, especially with such a companion."[18]

As part of his 1967 series of columns in the *Minneapolis Tribune,* "Nature's Caretakers," Jim Kimball wrote that, "Listening to the little old man known as Ober tell the story of his life, I learned that an illiterate gravedigger in Davenport, who 75 years ago had taken Ober for walks along a creek, may have done much to save the Quetico-Superior wilderness."[19]

It has been argued that there are always two factors present in the childhood of significant environmentalists: first, they develop a strong early love bond with nature, and, second, an admired adult mediates this relationship and teaches respect for the natural world. For Ober that adult was the gravedigger Burke, an uneducated yet literary man who knew the book of nature and opened it for the boy's eager eyes.

Kimball wrote that Burke took Ober for walks along Duck Creek, which, despite the surrounding cornfields, seemed a wonderful wilderness to eight-year-old Ernest. Their imaginations attuned to the excitement of this exploration, they turned it to myth. "They waded out to a little island, and because Burke was sure the boy was the first to ever set foot on it, he named it Ernest's Island."[20] In addition, then, to mediating nature for young Ernest, Burke was whetting his appetite for exploration as well.

In the detail notes for the fictional work Ober planned to write about his childhood in Davenport, both the gravedigger Burke and young Willie's (Ober's) love bond with nature are much in evidence:

Willie's delight in nature, when out with Burke. The feel of the moss, the hollow of the tree, the smooth-worn swimming hole, the swirling water, the gravel banks at the glen. The world shut out by corn fields. Potter's clay—a wonderful discovery. Discovering Ernest's Glen. [At this point, Ober forgot that the character was Willie.]

Conversation between Burke and Willie. Burke laughs about the boy's seriousness and adult intuition. Burke a fascinating character because first he shared the boy's enthusiasms; second, because he knew and loved nature; and third because he opened a whole world of stimulating adventure through his contact with death and the dead. Seemed in touch both with nature and the supernatural.

The Irish superstitions in Burke. His humanity, his kindness. His disregard of money. A kind of wisdom and philosophy all his own. A philosophy of unpossessive worldliness. New values. No ambitions. No egotisms. An amused observer and sympathetic friend was Burke.

Burke always kept his hat on, because he was bald. Once "made love" to Mam when he was drunk. ["Mam" is Ober's mother; it's clear that this wasn't meant literally.] Otherwise, always kept away from the lot during a spree. He said he remembered two things about Mam particularly—her look from the top of the hill the first time she visited the cemetery and her attack on Charley Perry when he stood on the grave and hammered with a great sledge hammer.[21]

Ober seems to enjoy Burke's perhaps crude interest in and appreciation of his mother, her early attractiveness, and her fiery response to what she felt was a desecration of her son's grave. Ober remembers himself, as Willie, with pride and warm appreciation, surely a sign of a happy childhood:

Willie a boy of energy and imagination. No other boy shared his association with Burke. What a delight Willie was to Burke—a bright, kind-hearted, enthusiastic, admiring boy. What man would not have been made better?

Planting the flag on the crest of Ernest's Glen. What hand or storm, not guessing its significance, removed it?[22]

As he grew older, Ober began to make excursions into the countryside by himself: "After I got a bike, my interests in summer took me many miles into the country over macadam roads deep in Iowa dust, which was all right so long as I returned before dark. I delivered my newspapers that way too when weather permitted and sang out my wares as loudly as anyone; it was a big help later, when my work called on me to speak at meetings of all sizes. During the Spanish-American War, I sold as many as 400 Chicago newspapers at one and a half cents profit each on Sunday mornings, making me quite a magnate."[23]

Throughout his life, Ober would be a caretaker, often mentor, even healer of the sensitive, distressed, and gifted, and he was enlisted very early for this role. He was asked to go into business with the troubled daughter of Frank Griggs: "I was in the poultry business with a woman almost my mother's age," he wrote, "who had been despaired of in a mental institution, but had been advised to cooperate with some vigorous young person. She was the gifted daughter of F. H. Griggs, president of the First National Bank of Davenport where my grandfather worked. They had a large city lot, an incubator in their well-ventilated basement, and an outdoor brooder. We used to send the chicks to the Griggs farm, when they were old enough. The partnership proved very beneficial. Bessie Griggs improved rapidly enough to have a 'coming-out party' for our first hatching. She eventually married Arthur M. Judy, Pastor of the Unitarian Church, who had just refused to accept the presidency of Antioch College. Judy was a Harvard man and had quite an influence on me."[24]

Ober took naturally to the role of caretaker and keeper. Highly sensitive to need of any kind, his care-taking role would eventually broaden to include troubled wilderness regions that he sometimes personified. In an address prepared for the Quetico-Superior Council of which he would be president for more than forty years, he wrote: "If we had a beautiful and talented daughter, we would not condemn her to ashes and drudgery. We would give her godspeed to sing her way into the hearts of mankind. All that is proposed for the border lakes is that we work *with* nature, not against."[25]

Though he was successful in his early poultry business and he loved the bicycle, it should not be assumed that Ober was handy with tools and technology. In truth, his technical ineptitude, perhaps largely self-chosen, would be a continuing source of humor among his friends. Boat motors, tape recorders, and typewriters would often prove a struggle for him, and he would never own or even learn to drive an automobile. There was at least one "tool," however, with which he became proficient: at the age of eleven, he began a lifelong study of the violin and its classical repertoire. He took this discipline seriously, and though he would never become a professional musician, he would often say that, if worse came to worse, he could always earn a living with the violin. Financially, worse would often come to worse for Ober, but the violin would never be the answer to his need.

In part at least, Ober's introduction to the violin had to do once again with the healing of a young woman; this time it was Rosa, his own mother. In her youth, she had studied music under a Professor Cramer and become a proficient pianist, but with the death of her second son and the breakup of her marriage, she gave up her music and sank into depression: "When I was 11, my grandfather gave me a three-quarter size fiddle and charged my mother to see that I practiced an hour a day (a hard prescription for the first year).... Part of the strategy was to restore her interest. This finally succeeded and continued throughout her life, and in fact became a major interest. She even had a piano at Rainy Lake, when she finally decided to join me there."[26]

Indeed, through each summer on the island, Rosa prepared for a concert she would deliver on her return to Davenport in the fall. According to Ted Hall, Ober found only two habitués of his Mallard Island home to be satisfactory accompanists when he played the violin. One was Rosa, the other the New York writer and music teacher, Katherine "Kit" Bakeless.

Though some who were admittedly not enthusiasts of classical music did not like Ober's "scratchy" playing as he practiced, others thought him quite good. Bob Hilke, a long-time friend of Ober's and the recent owner and captain of the Voyageurs National Park tour boat, played the violin in his youth, often with Ober. In the deep silence and cold of Rainy Lake winter nights, they listened to sonatas and played duets. In an interview, Hilke said, "I rate Ober as a good violinist. He had good intonation, a lot of technique."[27] In another interview, Kit Bakeless, who wrote biographies of important musicians and was a musician and piano teacher herself, spoke even more highly of Ober's musical ability:

> Ober could play the violin very, very well. When he was at Harvard, he studied with the concertmaster of the Boston Symphony, so he must have been well prepared before that. His mother must have seen to that. And the things he could play—I couldn't understand how he could manage his fingers when he was doing such rough work, grasping paddles and such. When I studied in Baltimore, my teacher said, "Don't hold anything hard. Don't iron. Don't ride a bicycle." But look at Ober. And oh, he played well! I remember he worked hard on the Brahms A Major sonata. We got that going quite well. And then he had a piece—a Spanish symphony, by whom?—I forget, but it had a terrific cadenza and he sailed right through it. It was great.[28]

Whatever his level, and it seems to have been relatively high, Ober would never cease to play and be inspired by great music, often in most difficult circumstances.

In the fall of 1899, Ober's beloved Grandfather Carl died. His death had enormous impact on this sensitive family. It is common for a spouse to die shortly after his or her partner—and Sarah did—but one has to wonder as well about the impact of Ernest Carl's death on young Ober, who would later write: "The large and hospitable home in Davenport had to be given up after my grandfather died in October, 1899, and my grandmother died the following spring, while I was ill with a long siege of rheumatic fever."[29]

Even as he mourned his grandparents, the seventeen-year-old Oberholtzer lay bedridden for three months. When the disease subsided, he was left with a heart condition that would haunt him for decades. For the remainder of his youth, doctors would tell him he was unlikely to survive the year. It would be hard to overestimate the impact of such an illness on the life of a young man, and in his fiftieth anniversary report to his Harvard classmates, Ober would write: "Probably a severe bout with rheumatic fever at 17 made more difference than anything else, for it put a premium on health throughout college and for long afterwards."[30] Beyond the need to survive in health, the decade and more during which he felt himself at the edge of the infinite certainly opened spiritual dimensions far beyond the normal in the sensitive young Oberholtzer. And certainly life itself, moment by moment, and the detail of the natural world took on special luster for him. As with so many others who were to become caretakers, preservers, and healers, fate asked that he first find a way to heal himself. When he did, his discovery of the healing power inherent in wilderness living became one of his most important gifts to the world.

Despite the richness and happiness of his childhood, there was much now for which Ober would have to compensate in adult life through personal growth and achievement. To his lack of a father and his lack of size and of success in competitive sports was added a heart condition that promised to greatly limit the length and content of his future.

The empathetic young Oberholtzer, who would one day, according to the best available evidence, enter the Grand Medicine Society (the *Midéwi-*

Ernest, Rosa, and the beloved Grandfather Carl

win) of the Ojibwe, sensed early on that he might have a capacity for healing: "My experience with Bessie Griggs and similar lesser contacts with other cases encouraged me to think I might have some fitness for what is now called 'psychiatry.'"[31] This hope was destroyed, however, by his heart condition. Medical opinion held that a professional career as demanding as psychiatry was out of the question. His care taking, preserving, and healing would have to take place on a different stage.

Before the death of his grandfather, Oberholtzer's childhood in Davenport had been idyllic, culturally rich and close to nature. Books had been an important part of his early years, as they would continue to be. Even when he had no time to read, which was often, a surrounding abundance of good books was necessary to his sense of well-being. "I've had periods in my life," said Ober in the oral history interviews, "when I read a great deal. When I was a boy, I read before I went to school. I was reading fairy tales when I was a little bit of a kid, and all through grade school I was a great reader. When I got into high school, though, I read very little. I got involved then in different kinds of activities, including poker. And the violin became quite an important activity for me."

The often rapturous notes for his never-to-be-written childhood story—one of many such "starts"—contain abundant proof of the fullness of Ober's early years. They reveal as well that the adult consciousness that made those notes is ripe with loving appreciation for the detail of the world. Interestingly, that consciousness explored the seeds within its early self that would in time blossom into the mind of an adult storyteller of power who would be called Atisokan:

> The stories I used to tell the Davis children. Pictures I gave them for being struck by lightning; after every flash, I decided who had been struck.[32]
>
> Make the boy hero of the story an incomparable liar, full of sudden inspirations, improvisations. Spontaneous liar. Never premeditated. He starts something, that suggests more, and before he knows it, he has told a whole romance.

Ober remembered too a shelf of books from his childhood that nourished his early consciousness:

> The old bookcase and the books it contained—St. Elmo, Family Physician (Dr. Gunn's), Shakespeare, Goldsmith's Animated Nature, Code of Iowa, Classics in English (Pliny, Plato, etc), Germans of Iowa, Miss Fearing's Poems, Burns's Poems, Ernest Linwood, Dora Deane, Maud Miller, Japanese hand-painted pictures ...

He remembered as well the great river and the stories of it that fired his imagination:

Listening to the Mississippi at night. Speeding south. Turning over in its bed. Whipping a branch that hangs into the flood. No longer the clear stream it had been in the days of the explorers. Channel cats. The roustabout's story of the channel cat. His strange fascination for the boys. But he passes on and they never see him again. Whispers of Paul Bunyan. His yarns a mixture of Bunyan and Negro dialect. Ranged the whole Mississippi.

Then, poetic flashes describing first awareness of the sometimes-painful complexities of life:

Summer seasons of opera. The actresses that Willie fell in love with.

The joy of the first consciousness of the change of seasons. No taint of knowledge of the end of life.

The story ending just where Willie is beginning to have a new consciousness—a strange delight in the violin, a gloomy interest in religion and the meaning of the world, a youth's confidence in his power to become what he will, and reflection upon his own actions. Belief in the justice and goodness of the world; automatic balance of conduct. Repugnance at the thought of hell.

And finally, remembered details of the garden:

Hops ripe in autumn and hanging in clusters from the arbor. Pansies, verbena, sweet Elysium, sweet peas, petunia, fever fews, forget-me-not ...

Oberholtzer would not forget the Eden that his early years had been to him, and the richness of those memories would resonate within all the adventures and works of his adult life.

[2]

The Harvard Years

Influenced by banker Frank Griggs and Unitarian minister Arthur Judy, Oberholtzer chose Harvard as his college and entered there in the fall of 1903. There was enough money in the Carl estate to support this choice. Since his heart condition made studying for a career seem dangerous, even pointless, Ober was liberated to follow his abundant enthusiasms. He went to Harvard "to discover the possibilities," and he studied under some of the great minds of the era, including philosopher George Santayana, psychologist William James, and landscape architect Frederick Law Olmsted, famous for his design of New York City's Central Park. He would also study under and establish a lifelong friendship with an idiosyncratic and famous English professor named Charles Copeland, whom he called "Copey." While at Harvard, the young Oberholtzer also made lifelong friends of two fellow students who were to become famous: poet and fiction writer Conrad Aiken and historian Samuel Eliot Morison.

In the oral history interviews, Ober remembered his Harvard years with loving detail. In them, too, he recalled how difficult his final year of high school had been: "I'd contracted a desperate case of rheumatic fever, and had to drop out of school. I fell half a year behind my class and had to go into another. It was then that I began to prepare for the special examinations for entrance into Harvard. I took up Greek because it counted for a lot. You could learn as much Greek in six months as you could of certain other things, and you got more points for it. So I did do that, and that's the way I got into Harvard."[1]

Ober's early fluency in German, which would one day allow him to briefly become vice consul at Hannover, Germany, also aided his efforts to gain entrance to Harvard: "I had taken German all the while I was growing up in Davenport. Half of the people there are German, you know, so it was always on the schedule. My grandfather wanted me to speak German, but I never liked it. When I took my examinations, I was sure I'd flunked it, but I got a good mark. I've thought that perhaps they never read the exam. Perhaps they read my German name and said, 'Well, we don't need to read that.' So that was fine. Everything went swimmingly well."

Nevertheless, the entrance exam did not go smoothly for Ober. Undoubtedly, his sickness hindered him, and he was one of those who, inspired by love for a subject, found easy success, but without such love often failed entirely. "The things I didn't care about I flunked." And he in fact "flunked" geometry, chemistry, and history. "You would think I would have been very much absorbed by history, but, strange to say, I never was, except the history of exploration. Political history was just the most tiresome thing in the world for me, so I flunked history. I went to Harvard, then, with those three 'conditions.'"

Upon arrival at Harvard, Ober's enthusiasms led to his carrying heavy credit loads: "The usual was four courses, but you were permitted to take as many as you could handle, and I carried five or six every year that I was there. They weren't limiting you then the way they do now. You didn't have to specialize or major in some one subject. I think that was good for me, except that I never learned a trade. I never learned anything that I could earn a living with. But I found out more about myself and what my interests were, you see. I took everything that seemed extra good—fine philosophy courses under the wonderful philosophers they had there, including Santayana and James. I had a wonderful geology course under a man named [Nathaniel] Shaler. My senior year I took a course in philosophy that was given by four different professors, each in his own turn. It had James. It had [Hugo] Munsterberg, a psychologist who had introduced many new ideas in his field. It had [Josiah] Royce. I took this, even though I was taking another course in Greek philosophy under Santayana the same year, which was, of course, marvelous."

Ober still had to face his three "conditions" in history, chemistry, and geometry, subjects he disliked. He was supposed to make them up "and take follow-up examinations on them later. I had to take a history course that was huge and very disagreeable. It was world history. They had the class divided into sections. There was a little man that you'd meet with. When he saw that I wasn't applying myself, he made himself just as disagreeable as he could. If I'd had a man like Sam Morison [soon to become Ober's friend], it would have been totally different. But this course was a horribly cut-and-dried thing, and so I did only enough studying to pass it, in order to get rid of that condition. It was the same with chemistry. In all the other things, I easily got good marks because I was interested in them. After a while, they decided I was all right, that I was capable of going on in Harvard, and they never asked me to take geometry."

Ernest Oberholtzer's personality was extremely complex, and it is sometimes hard to reconcile the cultured and fun-loving young student with the future wilderness figure and preservationist of such discipline and endurance. However, he would, throughout his life, express great capacity for enjoyment, and at Harvard, freed to follow his enthusiasms, it seems that this bright, sensitive, and alive young man with delicate health enjoyed himself immensely: "I got up early and did my studying. I never studied at night. I don't know if it was so necessary as they thought. I led my social life at night, before I went to bed. I went to the theater or a concert, something like that. But I didn't study at night. Ever since I'd had rheumatic fever, this had been my regime, to get up early and study. Anyhow, I got through college with remarkably little study. With the courses I enjoyed, I didn't call it study when I read the books for these. The 'poorer' courses, well, I'd just stick with them enough so I could get through without too much disgrace."

Music continued to be of great importance to Ober. A college friend, remembering Ober's enthusiasm for music, later penned a letter of introduction for him, hoping it would help him land a position as a music critic. He wrote that, "during his course at Harvard, [Ober] played in the college orchestra, took several courses in the department of music, and attended for over two years all the concerts of any consequence that were given in Boston."[2] And, as has already been mentioned, during his Harvard years, Ober studied the violin under Willy Hess, the concertmaster of the Boston Symphony.

It is not certain where Ober lived during his first three years at Harvard. It is known, however, that in order to be near her son and to enjoy the cultural refinements of the Boston area, his mother kept an apartment in Cambridge during much of this time. Almost certainly the two lived together when she was there. In not considering Rosa's presence an intrusion, Ober was clearly different from most young men. His recent illness and continuing health problems, coupled with the sudden loss of both grandparents, would surely have had something to do with his welcoming Rosa's presence in Cambridge. The two were now largely alone together in the world. It should be understood as well that Rosa did not smother or particularly try to control Ober. Letters she wrote and the testimony of many who knew her make it clear that Rosa was a shrewd, sophisticated, and humorous woman, kind to the point of selflessness, and she placed few limits on her son's behavior. As he would often say, she would offer her opinions, sometimes objections, but if his mind were set, she would invariably support his decisions.

Ober during the Harvard years

In addition, she seems to have allowed and perhaps even empowered his imaginative and impractical dreams for the future, dreams that a strong and controlling father would very likely have deflated, at great cost to Ober's later life. In any case, during the Harvard years, Rosa was *the* woman in Ober's life, as she would continue to be until the time of her death.

As to Ober's living quarters during his senior year at Harvard, he explained that each year he "tried to get enrolled in one of the old revolutionary dormitories that had been built in 'The Yard,' as they called the campus there. Those rooms were assigned by drawings, and I'd never been fortunate enough to get one. Then, in my senior year, I got up early one day, and passing the dormitory, I noticed in the window a sign that read: 'Hollis 6 for rent.' I went right in and said:

"'Is that true?'

"'Yes.'

"'Is it all right for me to sign up for it?'

"'Why, certainly, yes, you can sign right away.'"

As he described his new lodgings, Ober's lifelong aesthetic appreciation for living spaces is apparent: "It was just one square room with two closets, one of which held coal. The room had a washstand and windows out onto Harvard Square. The toilets were down the hall, and there was a showerbath in the entry for the four rooms on that floor. There were two dormer windows that looked out on Harvard Square and a window seat. Oh, it was very nice and old."

Ober's description of the floor of Hollis 6 reveals another facet of his mercurial character—Ober the clown, the trickster, who found joy in a bit of foolery: "The floor was wavy. Not too wavy, but still it was a little unsteady. It wasn't a good place to walk when you were tipsy. I never got that tipsy while I was there, though I pretended I was sometimes. I got a lot of fun out of that."

It was at Hollis that Ober discovered the budding historian Samuel Eliot Morison: "He was living on the same floor as I was, the second floor. He had a front room looking right out on the yard. I don't remember how we met, but it wasn't very long, of course, before I knew him. He was a shy lad. Oh, very shy. Not what you'd, at that time, have called a good mixer, but he was extremely scholarly.

"Often I would go out to a concert or something in the evening, and when I came back, I could always be absolutely sure that Sam's light would be burning and that he was in there studying—anytime. I never knew him to be doing anything else, you see.

"Sam would say, 'Come in,' and he'd look at me with a kind of half-smile and say, 'How do you do, Ernest? Well, what have you been doing this evening?'

"I'd start to tell him, get in a couple of sentences, and Sam would say, 'Well, I think now perhaps you'd better go to your room.'

"Well, I'd never had that happen before—with anybody—to be so promptly told, 'I think you'd better leave now and go to bed.' We'd had our conversation. Two sentences. Well, I sort of felt licked every time he did that, but I went on with him and didn't resent it. I never resented it. Instead, I did quite a bit of thinking about him, and I thought, well, isn't it really strange that he can be that way. I admired him for it. I really admired him very much. More and more as I got to know him."

Ober himself was by no means the great scholar that Morison was, but one could nevertheless argue that he gained as much from his years at Harvard as did Morison. The intellectual sophistication and depth of insight he acquired there were resonant through all his later life and works.

Morison was of a type—shy and talented "sensitives"—to whom Ober felt drawn, and though Ober was by no means to become Sam's "keeper," there was another within the Morison family who was much in need of Ober's exceptional interest in and capacity for giving such help:

"I discovered that Sam was a grand-nephew of Harvard's President Eliot, and that his mother had one of these old mansions on Beacon Hill near the capitol. After I had known him a while, he invited me home with him for Sunday dinner, and Sam's mother invited me to become the tutor and caretaker of her retarded son [Bradford]. I was paid a very, very good salary for those days: one dollar an hour—nobody got one dollar an hour—and my meals while I was at their house."

To this point Ober had been supported by family money. Though the Carls had been reasonably well-to-do, they had not been wealthy, and this new income from caring for Bradford Morison was very welcome. Ober scheduled his classes for the afternoon and would arrive at the Morisons' by nine o'clock in the morning. "I would generally take the boy out walking for the morning. Sometimes we would go way out to a distant point on the streetcar and then walk in. Sometimes we'd go to the bank for his mother, downtown, take care of something for her, maybe cash a check, come back and then go out walking. Weekdays I would be with the boy from nine in the morning till about a quarter of one. I'd have lunch there and go right back to Harvard.

"On Sundays I remained until the middle of the afternoon. We'd go to church and we'd have a nice dinner. Then I was free to go home. On Sundays, [Bradford] always said grace, stood up while he said it. It was the most affecting thing you ever heard in your life. This boy, in this monotonous, monotonous voice. To hear that boy say grace in his very simple way, you see, without inflection, it was almost like a priest chanting. Then he'd sit down, and he'd never say anything throughout the meal. But he'd eat the same as everybody else. When he'd turn his head, he'd always turn it rather fast, as if he were trying to see if there was something going wrong. Otherwise there was nothing peculiar about him, unless you looked directly into his eyes, and then you saw there was something wrong all right."

The Harvard years were not, of course, all work and study and culture. Throughout life, Ober cherished adventures with friends that he could turn into story. He was grateful to have "had that little episode together" with a comrade. Often the story Ober would tell displayed self-deprecating humor while at the same time making a point of his personal resourcefulness. One such story is of a time when Morison invited him "to a home they had in New Hampshire, near Mount Monadnock. He had a horse there, a favorite horse, and he would ride out bravely like a man of the knighthood about to spear something. He'd go right over a stone wall like nothing. There were stone walls everywhere around there, you see. His horse knew just how to take them. He jumped over them without any trouble, and Sam said to me:

"'Now, Ernest, you do it. You do that with this horse.'

"'Oh, I don't think I'd better try that.'

"'Why, sure, all you've got to do is press your heels into his sides just before you get there, and he'll go right over.'

"Well, I must have pressed too lightly. The horse got up to the wall and just went over with his front feet. And there he was with the stone wall touching him underneath, you see. Impaled on the wall. The horse panicked a little bit. Not too much though.

"Sam came running up, all out of patience, and said, 'Now, look what you've done!'

"'Well,' I said, 'you were warned. I don't think there's anybody to blame but yourself.'

"I told him that very frankly. And he said, 'I'd like to know what we're going to do.'

"'Well,' I said, 'I think I know what we can do, all right. We'll take this wall down.'

"It was loose rock, you see. So, I had the wall down to about half its height, and then the horse pulled his legs back over. He got across without damage except for a small cut in the fetlock of one foot. You should have seen that horse go for Mount Monadnock. Across fields and over walls. And these two young men trying to catch up with him. We finally did, and Sam rode him home. I walked. So we had that little episode together."

It was during his Harvard years that Ober made his first trip to that vast region of interconnected lakes to which, twenty-two years later, he would securely fix the name Quetico-Superior. This was the north country of which he had dreamed as a child gazing out over the great rafts of logs on the Mississippi River. The trip would again prove an adventure, far more significant to his life than that with Morison's horse, and he would often turn it into story. It was story that once again provided ample opportunity for self-deprecating humor and occasional cautious self-congratulation. In the summer of 1906, between his senior year and graduate study, determined to live as fully as possible despite his heart condition, Ober embarked on a train for the lively wilderness outpost and mining town of Ely, Minnesota, near the Ontario border. He arrived there innocent of the fact that he was to be the original architect of a program that would be instrumental in the region's becoming America's most popular wilderness area.

On the surface, Ober's first wilderness trip was less satisfying than might be imagined. Late in life he would talk thoughtfully of Native American alcoholism and the effects of other "white poisons," and it is clear he felt most of the blame for these problems did not lie with the native people. Nevertheless, the twenty-two-year-old greenhorn's Ojibwe guides did not make his first canoe voyage an easy one. As would often be his practice, Ober kept a journal of his baptismal trip into the boundary waters. Its contents reveal hints of grim humor over his predicament, but also excitement and a deep appreciation for the world he was discovering. His plan was to paddle from Ely through the interconnected lakes in a westerly direction, on to the little town of Tower. Less than one day out, his first guide, Joe, got drunk, and Ober had to paddle back to Ely alone and pay someone to return for the man. His second guide, Duncan Cameron, was likeable, but a drinker as well:

August 10, Friday: Weather fine. Paid $1.85 insurance. Wrote Mam [Rosa] again. Duncan was sober but bought quart bottle at [the lakeside community of] Winton. Left Winton at 10 A.M. Reached Pipestone Falls about one o'clock and had lunch. I ran the first rapids above alone. Not advisable. Pipestone Falls beautiful on account of rocks. Dunc kept drinking and showed effects plainly after lunch. After leaving last camp on Basswood, Dunc became uncertain where Blackfish Bay is. Camped at what we supposed to be an island opposite Little American Point. Heart bothered me after I lay down. Very unpleasant night. Dunc drunk. Drank whole quart of whiskey before morning. Not quarrelsome. No sleep for me. Dunc made me tea. Surroundings of our camp pretty. Lake wide, bold bluffs covered with trees. Island about five acres in extent. Dunc has no maps and doesn't know where to go. Dunc told story about boat capsizing and beans swelling, split bag and showed location of wreck.[3]

August 11, Saturday: Fine sunrise. Sun shone into tent. After starting, I felt better. Dunc was gradually sobering, but was not sure of his way. He worked well all day and did most of the portaging. Found Basswood River at last where we portaged twice, waded the rapids three times and shot them once. About noon reached very bad place and by following my advice got into a bad fix: "God damn it! if we do, swim or drown."

It is interesting that Ober felt competent to give advice to Duncan on how they might shoot a rapids, and his guide's seemingly angry response to the possibility of their capsizing was no doubt justified.

On August 12, Ober and Duncan entered Lac la Croix and could not find the portage out. Despite their predicament, Ober was sensitive to the beauty of this lake. He noted two fine waterfalls:

> ... especially the lower one which really had three parts. . . . Shores heavily wooded. A number of islands. Irving Island has beautiful crag 50 feet high. Pink, green, gray, brown lichens. . . . The scenery this day was the most beautiful of all. Much real pine forest on Lac la Croix.

On the thirteenth, the pair continued lost. They paddled thirty miles and ended up where they had started. On the following morning, Ober woke "resolved to return home as quickly as possible now that we could do nothing but return." They paddled back to Ely in a single day. This is the first indication of the strange contradiction between Ober's heart condition and his tremendous endurance as a canoeist:

> Made the entire distance from about two miles below the entrance to [Lac la Croix] to Winton by seven in the evening. Made seven portages, waded with the canoe through three rapids, paddled up two very swift places and covered a distance in all, according to Dunc, of over 50 miles.

Throughout his life, Ober would be as interested in native lore and story as in the wilderness, and in his journal he described an Indian grave they passed that day and related a tragic story told to him by Duncan. Like that of the capsized boat and the swelling beans, it is a story of the sort that, throughout his life, Ober would commit to memory and find joy in telling. It is clear as well that Ober collected such stories hoping that they would one day prove useful to his literary ambitions:

> ... Also saw grave of Indian. It was boarded over and protected by a table structure at the head of which is a flag-staff and a white flag. The flag could be seen waving at a considerable distance. Broken dishes, several tools, a feather daubed in green paint and some small (tobacco?) boxes. At the side of the grave was a pile of carefully cut hard wood which was covered with tar paper and birch bark to keep off the rain. Heavy wind from the southwest troubled us on Basswood Lake. Dunc told about squaw who got lost from her sucking baby and returned to find it dead. She carried [a dummy papoose] for years and would not allow anyone to go near it.

Back in Ely, Ober's magnetism and charm, already famous among those who knew him, worked its magic on the local people. As would be the case during most of his travels, he had brought along his second-best violin:

> Played violin all evening at Mr. Cowen's house. During the day met Mr. Sture, cashier of the Bank of Ely. Everybody sorry that I could not complete the trip.... Mr. Sture offered me a position in the bank and asked me to write when through college. Dunc wanted to try trip again some year.

In the end, despite his tragicomic baptism in the chill purity of the boundary waters, Ober fell in love with the region through which he and Duncan had wandered lost. In the spring of 1909, he would return with a vengeance, and, it is said, he would one day know the region better than anyone alive.

Ober received his bachelor of arts degree in 1907. The following year he devoted to graduate study in landscape architecture under Frederick Law Olmsted. His studies with Olmsted, thought to be the leading landscape architect of his time, proved of great practical importance. Not that anything Ober learned was ever to be of much help in his efforts to make a living, but the general principles of harmoniously integrated land usage that he learned in graduate school were to serve him well, whether in the evolution of his Mallard Island home on Rainy Lake or in the development of a plan for the preservation of a vast wilderness.

Under Olmsted, Ober grasped the balanced, multiple-use concept in which utilitarian, recreational, aesthetic, and ecosystem values are given equal weight in planning. Perhaps the single most important concept he carried with him from graduate study into his future was that of zoning, which was to become the key principle in his multi-layered Quetico-Superior program.

In telling of his studies in landscape architecture, Ober repeated the fact that he had pursued his studies with no practical purpose in mind: "As I've said, my main reason for going to college was that I might become more familiar with the possibilities, so that I'd be better able to judge what I might like to do. That was my sole idea. It wasn't to get proficiency in some one thing. But, then, in my senior year, I took a preliminary course under Frederick Olmsted, who was the great landscape architect of the time, and there I happened to just hit it right. I made out very well and got the top mark in my landscape project. I did my project on a lake—a freshwater pond, they called it—that supplied the water for Cambridge. It stood out all by itself in an area that was in a way barren, but it had certain trees and grasses. It was wild, just as wild as could be. My project was, as a landscape architect, to recommend the finest possible treatment for this pond. My chosen remedy was not simply a wilderness remedy."

This final statement is significant. In later years, many, especially his environmental enemies, would think of Ober as an unrelenting purist in relation to wilderness issues. In fact, he knew all too well it would be impossible to maintain as pure wilderness the huge region he envisioned protected by his Quetico-Superior program, and as in his college paper, he took pains to develop a substantial multiple-use approach to the region under review. As for that fateful college paper, he said, "I tried to show what they should do to provide the necessary protection for the pond as well as what would be necessary for both practical utilization and enjoyment, while at the same time maintaining or even increasing the height of its wilderness charm.

"This paper brought me quite a lot of attention. The men at the head of the landscape architecture program strongly urged me to go into their profession. I gave it serious consideration because it had so many things in it that appealed to me: the outdoors, parks and forests, planning so that we could experience to the utmost nature in its wild state, for beauty and inspiration.

"The two top men in that program, Olmsted and Pray, invited me to go on in the course and to be an assistant the next year. I was to be paid three hundred dollars. Well, three hundred dollars in those days seemed like some help, but, as I've told you, for caring for Bradford I was paid a very, very good salary for those days. Oh, that employment was very helpful, and I continued with it rather than take the assistantship. Besides, it was better than marking papers, and I also got my exercise.

"But I did go on in landscape architecture the next year. I went over to the Morisons every morning at nine and stayed till twelve, had lunch, and returned to Harvard. This left me only my afternoon and evening to carry out the landscape architecture schedule, which was very heavy. And that first year was devoted almost entirely to architecture. Architectural drawing was dreadful for me, that formal drawing with all those tools. You almost always had to work with an architect in this kind of planning, except for the wilderness planning, which was the thing, even then, that appealed to me. All the other boys in that course were just perfect at drawing, but my drawings were all smeared up and—oh, they just broke my heart. I didn't have enough time, either. I had never done any studying at night before, but I had to do it now to get through.

"On the other hand, there was a required course in free-hand drawing. I think I could have acquired a certain facility there. The course was held in the Fogg Art Museum. They had many beautiful paintings there, and the instructor was a sensitive wonderful fellow. If I could have had a man like that for some time, he might have done an awful lot with me, because I did manage to draw, and enjoyed it. That was the thing, as long as I was enjoying it, you see.

"But the rest of it was architecture, pure and simple, and we had a man who was the worst bore I have ever known in all my life. He had a great reputation as an architect. Before you got through with him, you'd look at a building and it would be all cornices. He'd talk about cornices and their relationship to the whole building until all I could see was cornices. And then I had to do these mechanical drawings, at night, very fine drawings, and my eyes became very troubled by this. I had to wear glasses, magnifying glasses, not because I was deficient, but my eyes just didn't focus well enough to do this work. It was only when I got up here in the wilderness that I was able to take them off again.

"Well, I finally got through the year with a good enough mark. I suppose I got a 'B.' But I didn't go on. I haven't any doubt that I'd have had some wonderful experiences if I had. I might have loved a lot of it later, planning national parks and all sorts of things. And I would have been out of doors a good deal. But I've never had any regrets in all my life about anything I've given up."

Oberholtzer was clearly ready to move on into the unrestricted adventures of his early adult life. To do so he also had to turn down a wonderful, expense-free opportunity to continue his education, this time in France, but again he said no:

"The Morisons wanted me to go to Europe with them, to Paris, where Sam was going to go into the Sorbonne. Mrs. Morison wanted me to go to the Sorbonne afternoons, but continue to care for Bradford in the mornings. I was to have all expenses and a thousand dollars a year. That was very good, you know. But I turned it down, much as I liked these people. Our relations had just been marvelous. Mrs. Morison was a delightful woman. Everything was just fine, except that I had this feeling.... I couldn't move this boy. I tried and tried and tried, but there was no fundamental change. He learned to comb his hair, and he learned to sit down at the right time and stand up at the right time, but that was all. And so I said: 'No, I need my liberty now, too.'"

[3]

Travel with Conrad Aiken

"After my year of landscape architecture," Ober explained in the oral history interviews, "when I cared for Sam Morison's brother, I went over to Europe with Conrad Aiken." Aiken, who was to become a famous writer and poet, fascinated Ober, whose descriptive analysis of his young friend, "by all odds the most sensitive man I have ever known," reveals something of Ober's own sensitivity and insight. Older than Aiken, Ober assumed the role that had become so natural for him: he became a caretaker for the young poet-to-be while they were together at Harvard, providing him with a "certain protection against the clash of the world around him."

Ober met Aiken through a college classmate named Harold Tillinghast, whose father was Aiken's guardian. The Tillinghasts became acquainted with Rosa as well: "We used to invite back and forth for dinner Sundays, and we always enjoyed this very quiet family. There I met, one Sunday, a cousin of Harold's named Conrad Aiken. He was a very handsome, shy youth of perhaps, at that time, fifteen years. It turned out that he was the son of Mrs. Tillinghast's brother, who'd had a very tragic end, and Mr. Tillinghast had been appointed Conrad's guardian.

"Conrad always maintained high records in scholarship—that sort of attainment—but not as an athlete. He was tall, with a great shock of light hair, very blue eyes, a pale face, and was very shy, *extremely* shy. But his wasn't the kind of shyness that comes from fear. You realized right away that it was a shyness of self-confidence. He knew he had ability, and he wasn't overawed by anything. It was just a natural retreat into himself before the multitude.

"Well, from the moment I saw Conrad I was attracted to him, and we became very good friends. I'd seen him quite a number of times before my final year at Harvard, and then he entered Harvard himself, as a freshman, and began coming to visit me. It was nice to be able to provide him a certain protection against the clash of the world around him. That is, when there were situations where he was, perhaps, not embarrassed, but ill at ease among some of these cruder people whom you're bound to know, you see, like me. Conrad, by all odds, was the most sensitive man I have ever known in my life, and when I say sensitive, I don't mean that he took umbrage, but that he was sensitive in his responses, as if he heard and saw and felt everything differently from an ordinary being. He had that marvelous quality."

The Tillinghasts had told Ober the core story of Aiken's youth, and certainly Ober's own childhood loss of his father and brother must have resonated in him as he retold it: "It seems that Conrad's father had trained in medicine," said Ober, "with the idea of doing research work. He was evidently the same type of man that Conrad was, extremely shy and withdrawn. He fell in love after he had completed his medical course and married before he had been able to go ahead and do the sort of distinguished research he would like to have done. He located in Savannah, Georgia, close to the Atlantic. There he had three children, Conrad being the oldest. It was painful, evidently, for him, as for Conrad, just to meet people. In Conrad, you could almost see a sort of— Well, I never saw his father, but you could see in Conrad something that moved across his eyes, like a blind, to prevent damage from this, maybe, over-buoyancy [of the surrounding world].

"One morning this extremely sensitive twelve-year-old boy woke to hear two gun shots. He dashed into his parents' bedroom, and there on the bed were his mother and father dying. His father had shot his mother and then himself, and there they were, lying in their own blood."

Aiken later said to Ober, "Ernest, on that day a great poet was destroyed." Nevertheless, Aiken did become a significant poet, but Ober agreed that his greatness was limited by his tragedy: "Well, he wasn't just talking. To have a thing like that happen to *that* boy. It would be a terrible shock to anybody at that age, but to a boy organized as he was—The incident didn't *prevent* his writing poetry, but I think his work is very restricted, remote from most people's experience and understanding. It may appear greater and greater as time goes on, for that very reason, you see. But it doesn't have a large audience. He's never been able to make any money on it. Of course, that wouldn't prove it great. He wouldn't let anybody steer him in the direction of any kind of cheap success, and he's perfectly satisfied with what he's done."

Ober had somehow managed to become a member of the board of the Harvard literary magazine, the *Advocate*, to which Aiken began contributing when he entered college, and he too was nominated for membership on its board. "This was going to be a great trial for Conrad. I'd gone through the initiation, and it was a trial even for me. Some of the boys on this board have become very distinguished. One of them was Van Wyck Brooks [who later became a famous and respected literary critic and prolific author]. Another was Max Perkins [one of America's most important editors with Charles Scribner's Sons].

"I had gone through the initiation, which was rather trying. Oh, they weren't rough. They asked you to do things: 'Imitate such and such.' Or: 'What do you consider to be the three main values in life?' Things like that. If you could be funny about it, they'd have a lot of fun, you see. Well, certainly their questions aided you in that direction. When I went in, oh, I was just quaking, but I came through with flying colors. I don't know how. My gift of gab came in handy, and they seemed to be much amused by some of my replies. And so I was in a position to help poor Conrad when it came to his initiation. He was just speechless at the thought of it. I put in a word here and there to prompt him, and he got through without fainting, and he was very grateful to me for that. I continued to protect him, and he produced these very sensitive things that we used in our columns. He was forever after me to write. Oh, he wanted me to write. But I was taking six courses every year...."

Avoidance would continue to be Ober's typical response to a writing opportunity. According to all who knew him, he was a truly exceptional communicator, and throughout his life he would write and write well. There would be an endless flow of letters, often delightful; a number of adventure stories written for boys' magazines in hope of earning badly needed income; and finally many articles in support of wilderness preservation. But, when it came to writing that might distinguish him as a literary figure or to the writing of that book which would have placed him on the shelf that holds so many of America's other prominent environmental figures, something rose in Ober and blocked him, despite the fact that his journals bristle with self-recrimination for not writing such a book.

Wanderlust was to be a dominant theme in Oberholtzer's life. His spirit would ever seek new adventure, and, finished with college and back in Davenport, Iowa, he discovered an inexpensive opportunity to travel to the British Isles: "I found that I could buy a ticket from Davenport to Liverpool," he explained, "coach ticket to Quebec, a cabin in third class, steerage, from Quebec to Liverpool on the *Empress of Ireland,* a lovely boat, and the right to a ticket to London, if I wanted, for $42.50. This included all of your food on the steamer. So I got in touch with Conrad, and we decided to go over there. This had high appeal for him. He was going to take his bike. I didn't have one, so would rent or buy one in Liverpool."

With Aiken, Ober was about to embark on his first step in "breaking loose" from the scheduled and orderly world of his academic life at Harvard. This step would also distance him even further from normal career expectations. "I met Conrad in Quebec," he said, "and we climbed up onto the Plains of Abraham and looked down at our steamer waiting for us. We went aboard and found that we had just the nicest cabin, spick and span as it could be. We had supper on board that night, and the menu was excellent, except that the ice cream wouldn't melt. The tables were clean, and the patrons were mostly very nice, old-time people. The passengers in third class with us were immigrants who'd come to America within the last three years or so, who'd prospered and were returning to their homelands for the first time, due to this wonderful deal during this period of recession. They were going back for the first time to Sweden, Norway, Denmark. . . . There were Jewish rabbis, and there was a very fine Swedish minister from Minneapolis."

Throughout life Ober would say that, if worse came to worse, he could always somehow make a living with his violin, and just in case worse came to worse, he had packed it for this trip: "I had my fiddle along," he said, "which I thought I could use if we ran out of money. We had very little money, and I thought that I might play to earn enough money to get along. I was ready to play on street corners or any place else. It would be an adventure, you see. The people saw us get on with the fiddle, and these foreigners were terribly curious to hear me play, but I kept postponing it.

"Conrad never encouraged it or discouraged it. He didn't seem particularly interested. Conrad of course was always deeply immersed in thought. It was a psychological field. I think it was closely akin to what in some cases becomes insanity. Underneath it all, there was always in Conrad Aiken a strange undercurrent of—not animosity—but of almost annoyance. It was there when you could get down to it. Of course, I never saw this very much, but I did get to see this during our long trip. It came partly as a result of my penetrating this sanctity of self that he was deeply immersed in. And anything that pulled him out of that, the mere petty things of life like picking up his spoon, counted for a whole lot and set him on edge."

Perhaps not many had had the will and insight necessary to penetrate the psychic shield with which Aiken protected himself from the world. Ober undoubtedly did, however, and it may be that Aiken was sometimes more annoyed by this than even Ober has mentioned. At the same time, it should be understood that during a strenuous and extended trip such as Ober and Aiken had embarked upon a certain amount of friction will inevitably arise between even the happiest of companions.

"It was beautiful weather," said Ober, "just beautiful. We could be on deck and see the people up above on the first- and second-class bridges. They'd be looking down at us, and we'd be walking around in the sun, lounging and reading. It was very comfortable indeed. But they were after me to play. So finally one day—a lovely day with no wind—the pressure was so great that I thought I'd better have it over. I came out and put up my stand. I didn't play anything from memory. I spread out my music and began playing. I guess I played three-quarters of an hour or longer. I could see people up on the bridge. I was a curiosity. They were wondering what kind of immigrant this was.

"When I finished, the Swedish minister walked up—I'd had very nice contact with him—and he bowed and presented me with a hat full of coins.

"'Why,' I said, 'I'm not going to accept that. I wasn't playing for money.'

"'Oh,' he said, 'you can't give this back. We don't know who gave these coins. People up there gave some, the rabbis gave some. There's no way we can give these coins back.'

"I was independent, you know, and wasn't going to accept that. I hadn't been playing for money. I decided to find out what this hat-full was worth. It was in many currencies, you see. I didn't know about these things. I gave the money to the purser and let him determine how much was there. Well, I think there was something like sixteen dollars, in spite of the hard times. So, there were two deck boys, as we called them. One was eighty—poor old fellow. He earned his food and very little else. The other was a boy about fourteen—that difference between the two. They took care of the decks, cleaned them, put the chairs away, that kind of thing. They got their food, and I don't know what, if any, money extra. Anyway, the sum was added up and divided between these two 'extremes in age,' and you never saw two people so grateful in all your life. You would have thought I had bestowed a fortune on them. They couldn't do enough for me."

Ober's journal of that day reveals that time had somewhat inflated the generosity of his audience:

> *July 12, 1908:* Played on deck Sunday morning till people grew tired. Swedish man collected coins in a hat. Divided the sum ($3.47 in English, U.S. and Canadian coin) between deck-boys. One deck "boy" was (90?).[1]

Throughout the concert, Aiken seemed to be lost in his "psychological field." But, more than forty years later, when he published his tangled stream-of-consciousness autobiography, *Ushant,* Ober was to find that the incident had impressed that remarkable consciousness. His moment of musical grace and generosity emerged in the book in which Aiken speaks of himself in the third person and "Ober" has become "Ebo":

> "... all the countless other ships he had sailed in, forever pointing a hopeful bow in a new direction: towards Liverpool tonight, as on the first of all occasions from Quebec, with ... Ebo playing his fiddle on the steerage deck: towards foaming Ushant...."[2]

"So, we got across the ocean," said Ober. "Conrad had his bicycle from home. I negotiated to buy one"

July 18: Conrad [sick] stayed in bed till 2 P.M. while I spent my time examining bicycles. Finally purchased a Mead Roadster on Paradise Street for P5.11S....

"It was an English bike," said Ober, "a three-gear arrangement, so that you could change the number of times the wheel went around, you see. If you were going up a hill, it would go around oftener, but it wouldn't be so hard pedaling. That was good for me, because I had been in the hospital quite a bit with this little heart defect I had left over from rheumatic fever. I couldn't allow myself to get winded. I didn't feel I could ride the way Conrad could. As far as health was concerned, his was just immaculate—never had anything wrong with him. I *looked* stronger, but I did have quite a bit of trouble with this condition, so I was glad that I didn't have to pump as hard uphill. It was pretty hilly where we went. Conrad was slender and could pedal like everything, up and down the hills. And we rode great distances."

Ober is rhapsodic about the kindness of the English toward the "two young fellows that they were" and rhapsodic as well about the English Lake District:

"We decided we'd hit first for the English Lake District. The first night, going out of Liverpool, we came to a little crossroads place and it was time to stop. I realized then that I would have to make all the arrangements, that when it came to arranging for the night, Conrad was speechless. It would have been better for him, maybe, if he had been forced to do some of that. We had a very small sum of money between us, so, when we came to a crossroads place, I would ask:

"'Is there a place to stay around here?'

"'Yes, you go up to the Hesketh Arms.'

"They called those little inns 'arms,' you see. We would ask there, and they were astonished when we told what we wanted to pay:

"I'd say, 'Can we get bed, breakfast, and supper for the two of us here for two and six?' Well, two and six in those days was sixty-two-and-a-half cents. For bed, breakfast, and supper.

"'Oh, yes, you come in.'

"Nice looking place, and they'd have the stairway going up under homemade hams that hung over your head. Well, we got along beautifully that way. In each new place I'd have to go and ask the same thing:

"'Have you got bed, breakfast and supper for two and six?'

"At noon we would stop and buy something we saw advertised everywhere in Britain, Hovis bread, which was a small loaf of very hard, beautifully baked bread. It was a wonderful whole wheat bread, very solid and crusty. Just marvelous. We'd start at the southeast corner and eat right through to the northwest. Once in a while when we felt flush, we'd buy a piece of ham with it. Only rarely did we exceed the two and six.

"So we went ahead, up and down these roads, generally pretty good roads, macadam roads, some of them much smoother than others. Some were rough. And it was amazing how well the people treated us. We never found anything but kindness everywhere we went in England. I think England's the most courteous country in the world. I don't think there's any other like it, with such natural courtesy. They like people and they like to be friendly. You hear the opposite. Well, that may be true among the upper class. I didn't run into that. I didn't see any snobbery.

"Once in a while I would ask for a room, and they'd say, 'No, we don't have those accommodations, but we'll send a boy, or a girl, out into the neighborhood where I know there's a woman who'll be glad to take you in.'

"And the woman would take us in. They gave us meals that they couldn't possibly serve for that price, but they liked to please us. Some of those women where we stayed were elderly. They liked the two young fellows that we were, and they went to a lot of trouble for us.

"We got into the Lake District, and that was, of course, just the most heavenly place. It was very beautiful, and we lingered there. This region appealed to Conrad especially because, of course, he knew all those poets connected to the region, Shelley and Keats and the others, all by heart. Then there were the very beautiful lakes. Just how they could have such beauty and not spoil it in any way, as we do, is a wonder. The buildings didn't intrude. Nothing did. There was nothing wrong. It was just as natural and beautiful as if it had been set down there from heaven.

"We got to Windermere—one of the larger towns—where they had a hotel called the Sun Hotel that was quite imposing. It seemed impossible that we could be put up there, but we went and they had no guests. The woman in charge was a motherly woman, a widow, who had two sons of her own. We made our offer.

"'Well,' she said, 'oh, come in, come in.'

"She gave us a beautiful room. We were so taken with it that we stayed there a whole week, walking in all directions around these beautiful lakes. And Conrad read, of course. All the time he was reading, every moment he got, when he wasn't on his bike. And when he was reading, he'd forget everything else. He didn't know anything else was going on in the world.

"Our landlady would send her son up into the hills, and he'd shoot grouse or other game birds, and she'd serve us that for dinner. Oh, we were living high and paying very little."

The experience of the young pair was imbued with the presence (and their knowledge) of the writers and poets of the places they traveled through. They were now in Wordsworth country:

July 26:... Modest tombstones. On that of Wordsworth's brother is inscribed the beautiful epitaph, "silent poet." ... As we came down toward Ambleside at about 8:30 P.M., we were surprised by hundreds of hopping, darting rabbits in the high ferns and on the meadows. Birds flying out ahead of us, startled by our approach. Heavy rams lying down for the night....

July 27:... Rose late and started alone for Comston via Bowness.... Had lunch at farmhouse on the hill to Comston. (Paid 1/3). Sat for two hours reading Wordsworth's preface to the Lyrical Ballads and some of the poems. Splendid large fire-place covering nearly the whole of one wall. Hand-hewn beams across the ceiling....

Ober and Aiken finally did leave Windermere and the Sun Hotel and pedaled north to Scotland:

August 3: After an hour's rest following lunch, we rode into Carlisle, the famous border city, where we met droves of sheep in the street and where we were viewed with curiosity.... We entered the cathedral in time to hear the organ and part of a service.... It is an imposing structure on a slight eminence and surrounded by accessory buildings such as the parsonage. Some of these structures are very old, their arches standing partly buried in the soil. The church itself has a lovely acoustical property which carries and purifies the chants and organ chords.... When we asked a question in Carlisle, the whole population seemed to run to our assistance....

Throughout his adult life—as a canoeist and, on this trip, a bicyclist—Ober, in defiance of his heart condition, pushed his endurance to the limit. Given what is now known about the heart, this may be one reason he would live into deep old age. Such was not, however, the prevailing medical wisdom of the time. Nevertheless, the pair pedaled forty and fifty miles a day through the ups and downs of the Scottish countryside, and at times Ober did pay a price for this extreme exertion:

August 13: A perfect day without a cloud in the sky. Not being well, I spent my time lying in the heather, reading, writing, and walking to Cally Bridge. Watched the sunset from my heather bed.

August 14: Still troubled by heart pains. Remained quiet all day, repeating my practices of [yesterday]. In much doubt what to do for the remainder of the trip....

August 15: Clear again. I felt some better.... I crossed the brook and climbed the hill in the afternoon. On my way back, I slipped and fell in the water....

The pair had bicycled, said Ober, "all through the lake district of Scotland. We pedaled into the Grampian Mountains, and we climbed them. We climbed the highest mountain in the British Isles, up into the clouds. Hardly any people lived up in that region, just scattered little settlements.

We slept out two nights in the heather. It was cold. Luckily it didn't rain. And we could hear the capercailzie in the morning, barking. These were large [grouse] that lived up there in the heather. They knew we were sleeping below them, and there was the greatest clatter just at sunrise."

Sleeping out in the heather, Ober was exhilarated by the abundance and tameness of the wildlife that surrounded him. His journal entry for August 19 might have come from the pen of St. Francis:

> ... A grouse pecked at my ear, a deer sniffed at my feet, and a rabbit, leaping upon my breast, stamped his foot over my heart. ...

What that final message might have meant to the sometimes mystical Oberholtzer, whose heart was expected to soon fail, one can only guess, but one thing was certain: that heart was set on exploring the wilds of Scotland. On the other hand, Aiken, who had to return to Harvard for fall classes, wanted to turn south again, back toward Oxford and the world of English culture:

"'Ober,' he said, 'I think we should go back now.'

"I was set on going on to the islands on the west coast," said Ober, "to the Hebrides, the Isle of Skye particularly. Of course, I am always more interested in the wild places. I thought Conrad had been planning to go, too. But he was going back to college. I didn't have to go back to college. I was unlimited, perfectly free, if I could exist. Conrad wanted to go down and see Oxford before he left. Well, that would have been a terrific ride, and he could pedal much faster than I. It was hard for me to pedal that fast, so I said:

"'Oh, no, Conrad, let's go on.'

"'No,' he said, 'I think, Ernest, we ought to go back. I want to get back. I have to take a steamer, you know. I have to be in college this fall. I want to go down to Oxford first and then go back, and I'd like you to come down with me.'

"During the previous two days, Conrad had hardly spoken to me. There didn't seem to be any ill feeling, but you just couldn't penetrate him. He'd been reading, reading, reading, and writing poetry. He wrote every day. He was writing poetry all the time. On any scrap of paper that came to hand. He got into one of those periods of silence for several days, never answered me at all. So I thought, well, it'll be a good thing for him to go back alone, a good experience for him. I began to wonder if it was the best thing to continue to make all the arrangements for him. He'd have to deal with these practical problems throughout his life. I thought about the situation a great deal. Anyway, I began to think, why should I stop now, why not keep on? We wouldn't be together very much longer anyway. Finally, I said, 'Well, now, Conrad, I think I should go on up north. You've got this other idea. Much as I regret it, I think you and I ought to go different ways here.'

"It was a hard decision for me to make, because I was very fond of Conrad. I parted with him with very great regrets. It's something that has always bothered me. In the morning, I paid the bill and bought sandwiches done up in a little package for him. I went out and tied the sandwiches on his handlebars and said:

"'Well, Conrad, good-by.'

"He got on his bike and never looked at me and rode away and never looked back. I heard, when I got back to the Sun Hotel, that Conrad had pedaled that day from our parting point all the way back to the Sun Hotel—over one hundred miles in one day—because he didn't want to have to make arrangements for himself with strangers. The landlady said:

"'I felt so sorry for that friend of yours. He was here and he shut himself away in his room three or four days before he left, and he never said a word.'

"Of course, I wouldn't have missed that Scottish part. And I was through college and my year of graduate work. I stayed in Liverpool that winter until Christmas time, and then went back, steerage, alone, with four hundred Finlanders, in a terrific storm. That was 1908."

It may be that Aiken was not so silent and passive in parting as Ober described. In *Ushant* he wrote of that "parting with dear Ebo in the middle of Scotland, at Persey Bridge, after the quarrel (ah, that fantastic quarrel). . . ."[3] It may be too that this parting marked the end of at least the close friendship between the two. After Ober's return home, Aiken's aunt, Mrs. Tillinghast, sent him a letter in which she wrote: "I don't think Conrad will ever forgive you for that."

Ober wasn't so sure of this: "Once in a while, I've sent a card to Conrad, and I'd get a card back. No letters. I never expected letters from him, but the cards were always friendly and nice, just the same as ever. And that's all I'll tell you."

Oberholtzer's relationship with Conrad Aiken was yet another expression of the "keeper" in him, but it was overridden by his passion for adventure in wild country. In a decision similar to his choice to discontinue caring for Bradford Morison, Ober had again selected his freedom over continued care taking. He had chosen instead the freedom to explore wild country, and, with only occasional breaks, his exploration of the wild would continue now for years. His immersion in the wilderness would prove to be a healing experience that would underlie and support a greater caretaking responsibility that would be unrelenting through the second half of his life, a commitment from which he would also yearn to be free.

[4]

The Three-Thousand-Mile Summer

Throughout his life Oberholtzer spontaneously practiced what is now called networking. Though an unlikely interest for a man so identified with the wilderness, it would prove an extremely useful skill for the future leader of a wilderness movement. The processes of establishing and maintaining connections were as natural as breathing for Ober: he made friends because he liked people, and once the bond had been established, people seemed to want to do what they could for him. On his return from England, he was therefore quickly able to find a job as the interim managing editor of the *Rock Island Union* in Rock Island, Illinois, just across the river from Davenport. "It was a good job," Ober recalled. "The pay wasn't high, but it gave me a lot of experience in a short time. I knew the publisher [S. W. Searle], and he persuaded me to fill in for an editor who had taken ill."

During that winter, Ober's own health once again failed, and his doctor told him he likely had but a year to live.[1] One can only wonder if he would have survived had he continued in that division from self which is usually necessary in building a career. Ober, however, made no such choice. Nor did he give in to his doctor's prediction. Instead, he went with the energizing and healing flow of his enthusiasms, and in late spring of 1909 he entered the Quetico-Superior region with the exuberance of a stream just released from winter's ice. One outcome, as Ober told it, was that his health "improved with every stroke of the paddle."[2]

Nineteen-nine is an important year in Ober's story. This was the year that the government of Ontario set aside a million acres in the Quetico Provincial Forest Reserve. And a few weeks later, as a reciprocal act, Teddy Roosevelt established the Superior National Forest, setting aside another million acres on the U.S. side in Minnesota. It was in 1909, too, that the United States and Great Britain (negotiating for Canada) established the International Joint Commission to study and advise on matters relating to boundary waters between the two countries. In the coming decades, the commission's rulings would prove deeply important to Ober's dream of protecting the border wilderness. Nineteen-nine was also the year in which the industrialist and last of the great lumber barons, Edward Wellington Backus, who was to become Ober's archenemy, was nearing completion of his large hydroelectric dam at the outlet of Rainy Lake. This dam would power his Minnesota and Ontario Paper Company, the parent company of his industrial empire. It was the first in a planned series of dams, a project that, if completed, would turn the boundary waters into a great storage basin for waterpower. Finally, it was during the open water season of 1909 that Ernest Oberholtzer paddled his way into a position of prominence in the Quetico-Superior region: "I spent the entire summer of 1909 in the Rainy Lake district," said Ober, "traveling continuously by canoe. With local Indians as paddling partners and guides, I am supposed to have paddled some 3,000 miles that summer. That was the beginning of my knowledge of the region. In that one summer, I attempted to traverse all the main canoe routes in the Rainy Lake watershed [of 14,500 square miles]. It was a colossal job, and it was the first time I'd ever traveled widely by canoe."

The young man who would one day accept the leadership of the struggle against Edward Backus's intended dams arrived in the frontier town of Koochiching, now International Falls. He came by way of a railroad that Backus had recently built, which, like his dam, was another key to his growing financial empire. Ober was now twenty-five, and he had no idea how he was going to make his living. A bookseller in Davenport who had always been interested in his "wild ideas" had suggested that he might be able to sell travel notes to the railroad, which turned out to be excellent advice. The publicity agent for the Canadian Northern, Arthur Hawkes, soon to become an important figure in Ober's life, responded enthusiastically.

Ober had written Hawkes with his proposal: "It was wonderful," he recalled, "how receptive this man was. 'I don't want a job on the railroad,' I said. 'All I want is an assurance that at the end of the summer you will be willing to consider purchasing my notes if you find them of value. And that maybe you will permit me to plan a pamphlet describing the area canoe routes which you could use to promote summer travel.'"

Hawkes sent Ober a railroad pass, and they met in Winnipeg. Ober was terrifically impressed by this man who was to become something of a mentor to him. According to Ober, the builders of the Canadian Northern had handpicked Hawkes to be their publicity agent. They had found him in England, where, at the age of nineteen, he was working as the London correspondent for the *Manchester Guardian*. "Just think of that," said Ober, "and he'd never had college or anything. He was a brilliant fellow. A great big man weighing about two hundred and twenty-five pounds, and well disposed toward everybody."

In "The International Forest," an article Ober would write later that year, he described Hawkes as the "magician" who, working behind the scenes, had been able to quietly bring about the simultaneous Quetico Reserve and Superior National Forest set-asides.[3] However fully Hawkes can be credited with that wonderful outcome, it is clear that, without the aid of Hawkes and the railroad, Ober would have found it impossible to complete his "colossal job" of canoeing the entire Rainy Lake watershed in a single open-water season. Hawkes gave Ober a special railroad pass—Winnipeg to Port Arthur—for himself, one companion, and his canoe and outfit, good for the entire season. The men who worked the trains were soon caught up in Ober's high-spirited enthusiasm: "The instructions were that wherever I wanted to get off—it didn't have to be a town, it could be a creek or anything else—the train would stop for me, even in the middle of the night. The men on the trains were so delighted to please. They'd do almost anything. They'd unload me on the siding, and you might not even have been able to see the creek on which I was to start off in the morning. We'd be there alone in the ditch.

"That's how we were able to get around so well that summer. We'd go to a certain point and then make a great circuit out by canoe, then catch the train again at another point and return to civilization. Mine Centre was one of my main centers of operation. There was another fine railroad man there named MacBeth, a one-armed man. He was really into the spirit of what I was doing."

Here as throughout his life, Ober's bright enthusiasm and magnetic charm were drawing in others to support his wild venture, allowing him to accomplish things he never could have on his own. He would ever recall these helpers with warmth and gratitude.

"I also had the privilege of using the telegraph," he continued. "The railroad owned the telegraph and I could send messages from any point along their road. They kept in touch with me, but they didn't supply any money. I was on my own. I could do exactly as I pleased. I kept voluminous notes, and at the end of the summer, the railroad bought them. It wasn't a large sum, but it took care of my expenses. And they bought my pamphlet which described the canoe routes of the region over all the different portions of the watershed, giving distances and the time it would take a well-qualified person to travel over them. The lengths of portages were described in chains [a surveyor's unit of measurement equaling 66 feet]. The pamphlet also described which side of the stream the portages were on and what their character was. It described the lakes and timber, the fish and game, and any Indian works that were around."

In his 1967 *Minneapolis Tribune* interview series, "Nature's Caretakers," Jim Kimball wrote that Ober "sold his notes and photographs to the Promotional Director for the Canadian National Railroad for $400. 'It wasn't much money,' said Ober, 'but I was having a wonderful time and, in a way, it was like being with Burke [the Irish gravedigger] when I was a little kid.'"[4]

It is more than likely that Ober's 1909 traveling companions and mentors knew the book of nature even better than had Burke, and, unlike

Ober's guides of three summers before, these men knew where they were going. In a lecture written in England in 1912, Ober said that he traveled with six different guides that summer, and "they were the pick of the land for experience and knowledge of wilderness ways."[5] Ober believed that two of these native guides were truly exceptional men. In his description of these two, Ober the storyteller, the maker of myth and legend, comes to the fore. The first was Pat Cyr, sixty-nine years old at the time, a brother-in-law of Louis Riel, who had led the Red River Rebellion against the Canadian government in 1869:

"Pat was of French-Indian extraction, about one-quarter French and the rest Indian. He was a high-grade man whom everybody knew. He was tall and very strong—so strong and so healthy that, as he was growing up in his native land out in the Red River valley, near Winnipeg, Fort Garry, he actually had the idea—he said so and I could well believe it—that he would never grow old and feeble, that he would never die. He had unlimited strength and never knew what illness was. He told me many wonderful anecdotes about things he'd done in his youth that described his remarkable resources. He was the only man to tell me he had seen a Windigo [a supernatural creature that feeds on humans]. According to his story, he was actually pursued by a Windigo for a good many hours before he escaped."

Ober was fascinated by Cyr, and as they traveled together, wrote down much of what he told him. Ober accepted his stories with his usual whole-hearted enthusiasm, not questioning their more extreme claims. It may be, in fact, that Ober was as enthusiastic about myth as reality, and that he well intuited the ways in which the one permeates the other:

> Pat could portage 700 lbs. His father, a Frenchman, lived to be 96 and his mother, a half breed from Sault Ste. Marie, lived to be 112.... [Pat] is one of 18 children, some of them twins.
>
> Pat always wanted to work for best man and when he heard people praise another man, he resolved to do better. Came to be known as best oarsman and best packer.
>
> At portages Pat would seize his pack strap beside oar, grab his pack, put on another, run along side of boat, jump ashore and travel at a trot to keep first place. A 500 lb. pack was like a small stone to him. When Pat [was hired to work] for 3 months at Fort Frances he had no idea of marriage—afraid of it and believed made in heaven. Indian agent Pithers and Hudson['s] Bay clerk were both after Pat's future wife. In fun he asked and in fun she answered, giving him the rings of Pithers and clerk. She has never given him an angry word. Expert needle woman, some of her work to England for exhibit.[6]

During the long struggle to preserve the wilderness of Quetico-Superior, Ober was thought to know the region better than anyone alive.

In the same 1909 notes in which he told of Pat Cyr, his early passion to acquire this knowledge is apparent in entry after entry, as is the fact that his interest in the region went far beyond the knowledge of waterways and portages. His holistic nature sought to understand the human story within the region and its complex interconnectedness with the natural world:

> Government forest has nothing to do with preservation of game or scenery. It is a business proposition. [Government] will not interfere with interests of private owners who happen to be inside.
>
> 15,000,000,000 feet of pine estimated to remain in district. Fire rangers: 2 on Quetico Lake, 5 on Pickerel Lake, 4 on Saganagons Lake, and 3 on Basswood Lake.
>
> Pat says stumpage from the Canadian Government now costs $7.00 a thousand; used to cost $3.00. It will sell out at an average of $21.00 a thousand in Fort Frances, more farther west, and company's scaler must be approved by government and the government appoints one of its own. All timber must be cut, the company paying for what it leaves.
>
> Story of ghost in shack at head of Eye Lake, where we camped the night of Aug. 11. Pat's superstitious fear of having the door open. Upper and lower bunks, lamp, old stove, bottles, blankets. Owner dead. Uncanny noises.
>
> In Lower Manitou the Indians were afraid of the mascallonge [*sic*]— some of which they reported to be as long as whales.
>
> Small lakes usually more beautiful than large ones because proportions between height of shores and expanse of water are better.
>
> There are some painted rocks on Manitou Lake and Loon River as well as on Clearwater and Trout Lakes. The Loon River rock looks like a rooster and is called by the Indians *Oh-pa-say-gon*. Indians usually leave tobacco at these places. Most of the Indians are now dead.
>
> Mrs. Fuller told of man whose son had been stricken with typhoid having to be carried on father's shoulders 20 miles to a doctor. A storm arose and father wrapped boy in tar paper which he tore from inside of a deserted cabin. Boy recovered. He carried son slung across his shoulders like a pack sack.[7]

The 1909 notes also brim with Ober's scribbled early efforts to learn the Ojibwe language:

Annie moosh = dog
goochi moosh = go away dog
mache moosh = bad dog
mache manitou = devil
Namakan = sturgeon....[8]

It is in these notes as well that first mention is made of the man who was to become Ober's most important wilderness mentor and traveling companion, Billy Magee:

Tay-tah-pa-sway-wi-tong. . . . Name of Indian at Mine Centre who told us about Quetico Reserve. He had been with surveying parties and seemed well informed. Said half of the lakes, even big ones, were not on the map. His home is on Seine River.[9]

And in the oral history interviews, Ober expanded on this first meeting with Billy: "Above all that summer, I met Billy Magee whose Indian name was Tay-tah-pa-sway-wi-tong. His English name, his 'store name,' up at Mine Centre was Billy Magee. You're not supposed to say the Indian name to an Indian. It's not courteous. It's a spiritual thing, you see. The name has been given, generally through a dream. Or maybe it was given to you by your mother or another relative at the time you were born, transmitted by spirits. Such a thing is sacred, and it's bad business to reveal it. It's all right for somebody else to tell you, but not for you to ask the one who bears the name and who is supposed to treat it with sanctity."

Ober held a deep lifelong respect for this very quiet Ojibwe man, Billy Magee. "I believe," he would later write, "that he talked more to me than he had ever in his life before."[10] The bond between the two, between a somewhat reluctant representative of modern white consciousness and a dark-skinned man of the wilderness, echoes others in the mythology of the American frontier. Indeed, there seems a desire among many who told and still tell stories of Ober and Billy to inflate their relationship to mythic levels. Ober himself often resorted to hyperbole when telling of Billy.

"Of all the Indians I have known in my life," he said, "with the single exception of his older sister, Billy was the most wonderful. He didn't speak

Ober's guide, mentor, and long-time traveling companion
Billy Magee, or Tay-tah-pa-sway-wi-tong

fluent English, but you could still get along with him without knowing much Ojibwe. I was learning phrases when I was out with these people, but I hadn't studied it.

"We went into Quetico Provincial Forest Reserve, as it was called then. There were one million acres in the reserve. [In Canada the word] 'reserve' meant that resources would be preserved for the future. In case there should ever be an emergency need. In the case of Quetico, this was because it held such superb timber. Very rich timber, the finest, most wonderful timber ever seen in the north. There was nothing like it anywhere else. They were the largest pines I have ever seen, almost solid white and Norway pine—miles and miles and miles of it. Very, very old and solid and fine.

"Later, after a burn in the Quetico, they authorized logging and then it was called a park. Little fires just gave an excuse for logging. The lumber company people could ask, 'Well, don't you want to salvage this burned timber?'

"'Oh, yes, the government would say, we want to salvage that.'

"'Well, you can't expect us to go in there and spend all that money on dams and cabins and such unless we have a whole'—I think the word for it was 'berth'—'a whole berth of timber.'

"There may have been twenty or thirty acres burned in there, or at most a hundred, but the rest would be virgin pine, rich picking, and once they got in...."

Once they got in, as Ober would come to know so well, the intention of the lumber companies was to take it all.

A shoreline scene in the Quetico

Ober had six weeks in the Quetico with Billy that summer. He had hired him because Pat Cyr had been unable to continue. Although Cyr had once been a man of great power and resource, Ober explained, "that was when Pat Cyr was young. When I was with him, he was sixty-nine and not suitable for any long travel. He gave up on one of my trips because he didn't want to take the risks."

In fact, as described in Ober's journal entry for August 19, Cyr had fallen and injured himself:

> When I awoke, I found Pat unable to walk. Something had to be done quickly. So I paddled him to the bridge, cached my outfit, and flagged the west-bound train at 7:40. Pat advised me to get Tay-tah-pa-sway-wi-tong, and I [decided I] would do that as go on my trip alone.... On inquiry everyone spoke highly of Billy Magee.... Maclaren, the foreman [of the lumber camp where Billy worked] and I paddled to the camp in the fall of a bad wind. The Indian consented readily to go with me at $2.00 per day....[11]

Further along in the entry, it is clear that Ober's memory of the men who had guided him out of Ely in 1906 had not dimmed:

> It was midnight when I returned to the station to shiver, till the train came. Billy was asleep on one of the benches and to my great content, perfectly sober.
>
> *August 20:* Train came after four o'clock during all of which time I was too chilly to lie down on the bench. At half past five, Billy and I were put off at Steep Rock ready for a two and one half mile [carry] to Jack Fish Creek. After breakfast we paddled about three miles up the creek, which is in a muskeg and full of logs, to Jack Fish Lake, a small grassy pond with no good timber. Billy paddled straight for the next creek where we had endless trouble with fallen trees and where we made two fairly rough portages of half a mile each. The last took us to a nice lake of no name, where we had lunch....

This same entry provides examples of the kind of information Ober was gathering for the railroad and his travel booklet:

> Passed from Helen Lake to *Kah-wok-wi-a-ga-mak* Lake (Owl Lake) without difficulty except from fallen trees in the creek. This lake is pretty and has some good Norway [pine] on the east shore. The next portage goes over the divide at a beautiful hill on the south side of the lake. Then comes a short paddle across a little lake and up a narrow creek to a six chain portage on the west shore. The paddle from there is uninteresting till one reaches the entrance of the next lake, where the rock on the west shore forms a long slanting wall topped with conifers. The lake itself is one of the most interesting I have seen, especially in the evening light. It has real distinction, due partly to the variety of wood and rock composition and partly to the splendid pines that far out-top the trees nearer the water's edge....

Ober and Billy struggled through many a portage together that summer of 1909. Indeed, in the coming years, portages were to become a major part of Ober's life, and in an article he would later write, "Portage Philosophy," he provided a panoramic picture of portages he had known: "For years I was on the move—by canoe in summer, by snow-shoe in winter. Portaging was a daily occupation. There were all sorts and conditions of portages—long woodland trails, short pull-outs, precipitous hill-sides, bottomless swamps, some portages that led to lands of heart's desire and others that ended nowhere, only to be retraced. Between lakes and streams, wherever the course was obstructed, canoe and contents, including at times a three months' stock of provisions, had to be packed on our backs to the nearest navigable water. Even in winter, when traveling with dogs, there were times, in deep, loose snow, when dogs and all had to be carried across the trails between the wind-packed surfaces of frozen lakes."[12] And in a script for a lecture to be given in England in 1911, he wrote, "At times [portaging] is almost beyond endurance, but it is remarkable how soon you get used to it and how even a pygmy like myself can take his load."[13]

In the oral history interviews, Ober explained that at the outset of their travels together he gave Billy this directive: "'Now, Billy, I want to see everything. I don't care how hard it is.' And we went into places through which I could never have found my way. Billy said he could *feel* the trail under his feet. Where it once had been, you see. These were not voyageur trails, but old Indian trails. Billy took me up into that area by the route he used in the autumn as he traveled into his trapping grounds. His family had trapped there when he was a child. He had grown up there, and nobody knew the reserve as he did. I always carried maps, but I didn't have to depend on them when I was with Billy. Still, I would refer to them, try to check them against the places we went. The good maps in those days were geological maps, on a scale of about four miles to an inch, but they only showed the main routes. They hadn't yet been able to survey the tributaries, and of course the whole country was loaded with tributaries. There were lakes and streams everywhere.

"But the main routes were shown, and we would follow those. And when we passed anything that looked intriguing, I'd ask Billy: 'Well, couldn't we go up in there? How long would this route take? What's this like?'

"Billy was very indulgent with me. He was willing to show me anything, if he thought it was worth my while. It was very rare that we let a portage stand in the way of what we wanted to see. And I saw that Billy was extremely intelligent, well informed, industrious, and willing to do almost anything to please."

On August 22, paddling on Quetico Lake, Ober and Billy discovered an exceptional example of the region's ancient rock paintings:

The whole west shore above the inlet, particularly from the inlet to the foot of the big island above, consists of fine, high cliffs with deep ledges and battlements. At about half way, in a deep protected niche of the rock with concave top, is the best preserved Indian painting I have seen. There is an obscene dancing figure of a man with his hands over his head, the head of a bull moose with wide spreading antlers. Several other animal figures. Some magic crosses and a number of indistinct images, the whole constituting a very elaborate picture.

On the twenty-fourth, the pair arrived at an Ojibwe village on Lac la Croix. Ober was clearly fascinated by what he saw, but, as would often be the case in his youth, frustrated in his efforts to gain information from and photograph the inhabitants of the village:

> ... Dogs whining and howling and swimming across the river. Birchbark canoes passing each other at the inlet. ... Indian village of cedar houses, wigwams and ... *wini-guy goo* wigwams, that is, bark wigwams. ... I went ashore to get a picture, but the boy ran and the squaw told me to go away. The other squaws laughed. Strange voices of the women. Cedar strips drying for baskets. Bearskin on a rack, bear paws cooking. A few old men, patriarchal forms, ... "Tattered Ensigns" of a departed host. We landed again at the chief's house hoping to get information and his influence for pictures. He was a gentle-looking small man of about sixty. ... I gave them tobacco, but they told us nothing. Wanted $5 for permission to take pictures. Old man said he had killed all the caribou. We left in disgust. ...

It was during this summer of 1909 that Ober first discovered his passion for photographing moose. He saw them on almost a daily basis, and these primordial-seeming creatures excited him:

Lone Ojibwe man in birchbark canoe

August 29: ... Just as we were entering a grassy pond near the first portage, we came upon a young cow moose which we surprised as she was swimming across. Paddled around her till I had taken four pictures and then we let her go ashore for the last one of my roll. She began to look cross at last. ...

By September 10, the moose were entering the rut:

... in a minute a cow ran down the shore and into the marsh. Immediately two very large bulls came out of the thicket about 50 yards from me. They were about 10 years old and both out of velvet. They walked stiff legged and very slowly. Hesitating whether to attack each other. Now and then their antlers would touch with a metallic sound and then they would stand motionless for several moments with heads lowered. Slowly they followed the trail of the cow until they disappeared. They would growl but did not fight as I had hoped. ...

It is easy to forget that whites had been traveling through the Quetico long before Ober's arrival. In his journal, for instance, he noted that fifteen years earlier Billy had guided timber estimators in the region for eleven months, and on September 9 the pair came upon a remnant of a much earlier era, "the foundation pits for the five houses of the Hudson['s] Bay Post" which the Indians had called "*Ca-o-cau-si-kak*" (Pickerel) Lake Post," over which a "red flag with the Hudson['s] Bay letters in white used to fly from a staff fifty feet high." And on September 20, Billy showed Ober "a large pine which had been hewn away and curiously inscribed. He says an old Indian long dead told him that these marks were put on by a white man over 100 years and maybe 200 years ago to show that this was the American boundary."

In the oral history interviews, even in distant memory, Ober's terrific enthusiasm for the two wilderness areas that had so recently been set aside shines through: "There were about a million acres designated on each side of the border. Carlos Avery, the most famous game commissioner in Minnesota history, traveled that same summer in Superior National Forest and wrote an article for a magazine called *Recreation.* And I, having traveled at the same time in Quetico, wrote a similar article [also for *Recreation*]. They appeared within about a month of each other the following winter or spring. These were the first articles to be published about these newly established areas.

"After threading about for so long in the Quetico, we came back along the international boundary, and I was so impressed by the whole region that I wrote another article in which I strongly urged there be some action to make this officially an international area. I sold that to *National*

Geographic, but they never published it. They used to buy with the idea of having things ready in case something came up. They have never published it to this day.

"But that was the way I became so very well acquainted with the Indian, Billy Magee. Our trip together was wholly harmonious, and he seemed to enjoy it as much as I did."

Despite such statements to the contrary, Ober noted in his journal that by mid-September Billy had had enough of their harsh regime of paddling and portaging. They parted on September 22 in International Falls:

> I took him to supper at the hotel and afterwards crossed the river with him. At the barber shop in Fort Frances I bade him good-bye and at last he seemed agreeable again. That was the last I saw of Tay-tah-pa-sway-wi-tong.

The two, of course, had many portages yet to cross together, and Ober himself had not yet finished his 1909 odyssey. Undoubtedly inspired by the fact that he had the health and fitness to do so—instead of having been lowered into his grave as his doctor had predicted—Ober continued on until ice and cold forced him to shore: "That year I traveled from May until after the freeze-up," he said. "The last thing I did, when you couldn't travel the lakes any more, was to go down the Rainy River alone. I did the first big rapids down there all alone. I think they're called Manitou. I asked somebody up above about them, and he said:

"'Oh, it's all right, the Indians go down them all the time.'

"Well, it was really very much worse than I thought it would be. And

Thought to be the first ranger to work in the
Quetico Provincial Forest Reserve

of course it was the beginning of winter and severely cold, so if you upset, you'd never have gotten out. You'd have been gone. I got down them all right, but I *didn't* go down the Big Sioux Rapids. By that time it was so fearfully cold that you just couldn't stay out there. I really suffered. So, then, one night—I'd gotten as far as Barwick on the Canadian side—I carried my canoe up to the railroad station."

Ober's 3,000-mile summer had come to an end.

The wilderness waterways the young Oberholtzer traversed in the summer of 1909 had nourished and healed him. In that single season of open water, he moved from tenderfoot status to descriptive translator of the entire region, a giant step in the life of a growing legend. He had come a long way, as Arthur Hawkes would write, in his effort "to master the territory."[14] His booklet describing the canoe routes remained in use for twenty years, until the effects of logging and other encroachments had changed the character of the waterways. In his unpublished *National Geographic* article, he urged that "there be some action taken to make this an officially protected international area." His vision for the region, then, had already emerged in his mind.

[5]

Photographing Moose with Billy Magee

As the border lakes froze, Oberholtzer returned to Davenport where, through family connections, he found a job for the winter in a Chicago brokerage firm. Later investment correspondence makes it seem likely that the firm he worked for was that of Hurlburd, Warren & Chandler. He was now, however, hooked on the canoe country wilderness, and shortly after spring ice had blackened, then dissolved, under a sun that had once again leaned near to the north country, he returned to the border lakes. Hoping to turn his enthusiasm and growing expertise into a way to make a living, his intention was now to photograph and write about wildlife, especially moose, an animal that excited his sense of the primal.

It was Ober's belief, as he reminisced late in life, that his early photographic study of moose was, to that point in time, the best that had yet been done. In truth, this was largely because his were among the very first daylight photos of moose ever taken. One cannot of course compare wildlife photography of 1910 with that of today. Ober's success with moose was not due to his skill with the camera—his lack of technical aptitude has already been mentioned—but to his intense perseverance and the fact that Billy Magee could take him to where moose were abundant. Together they worked out a way to approach these towering and powerful creatures in daylight.

Traveling on the Chicago, Burlington, and Quincy Railroad, Ober left Davenport on May 22, 1910, with sixty-eight dollars in his pocket. In the Twin Cities on the twenty-third, he spent the morning buying $16.75 worth of camera supplies and testing light filters in a park. The following day he was in International Falls–Fort Frances, where he picked up a letter from Louis Hamel, postmaster and trader at Mine Centre, Ontario: "Billy [Magee] was camped at mouth of Big Turtle River." Ober carried his canoe down to the railroad depot and was in Mine Centre at 3:30 that afternoon. It may be that his excitement at returning to the wilderness had overwhelmed him, for he had forgotten his paddles, exposure meter, and baker oven and had to wire his friend Jack Holland in Fort Frances to send them by the next train. In Mine Centre, trader Hamel told Ober that Billy had complained that the previous summer Ober had "overworked him and fed him too little."[1]

In the oral history interviews, Ober recalled the opening days of this expedition with Billy in great detail. It was late May and Halley's comet was visible across the evening sky:

"I came up here in the spring and went out for the purpose of studying and photographing moose. And Billy said he knew the very place and he did and he took me up Big Turtle River. That was the most wonderful habitat for moose in the entire area and maybe—I don't know—in the entire world. You couldn't go out for a day without seeing moose just everywhere. You could go weeks and not see another human being, but moose you were absolutely sure to see. We were gone a little over two weeks."

> *May 26:* ... Left Mine Centre at half past ten as soon as train arrived with missing equipment.... Had lunch at the first portage, where two young Indians were tussling with a load of [moose] meat for the Martin Lake [lumber] camp.... Cut grasses floating on the water, a sign of moose, like tokens Columbus found before he sighted land....

"It was a nice enough day when we started," said Ober, "but by the time we [arrived at our base camp on] what's now called Eltrude Lake—it was Big Turtle then—it was snowing. And there was a freezing wind. Oh, it just got to be a tempest. We found a thoroughly sheltered place and put up our tents. There were poplar woods all around us, good sized poplar, ten inches to two feet in diameter. Billy made a huge roaring fire in our clearing, right in this dense poplar woods. He took these poplars and cut them, oh, eight feet long, and made the fire right in the center of them. When it gets really going, that green poplar, the whole underside of it is covered with white ash, and through it you see the embers glowing, working up farther and farther until they emerge on the upper side. Then you put on more. We had such a fire that, even though it was raining and snowing, with this awful wind, it was pretty comfortable in there."

Ober's immediate impressions of this scene were recorded in his journal:

> *May 29:* ... Here, shut in by bushes and trees with the wind seething overhead ... I am as cozy as beside my own hearth-side. I can watch the gray wood ash flecks whirl on the breezes and the glowing pictures under the four great logs while I write. Check, what, an Indian comes to visit. He wears a sombrero like the jolly fellows in Rip Van Winckle [*sic*], and he has long black locks neatly chopped round the cheeks. Also has necktie, heavy watch chain and a Norfolk reefer. Intelligent, pleasant face.... Upper lip always raised, exposing a row of perfectly formed yellow teeth. He is polite, too, for he just said 'May-gnetch' when I gave him a stick of gum. As soon as he came, I said in Indian, "It is a big wind," and now I am looking through my vocabulary in vain for some other appropriate phrase. There is nothing; so I examine the visitor again, while he is not looking. He wears moccasins wet on the bottoms. Thick lips. Wrinkles. He is entirely at ease. He and Billy recline on the other side, talking together in low tones. Both are whittling.

Ober appreciated the great ease of the two men across the fire from him. At that point in life he was willful and driven, but, perhaps unaware, he was learning from the image of relaxed patience across the fire from him, and one day he too would be known for his patience. Some might disagree with this—Ober's personality was many-faceted—but in an interview, "Buck" Johnson, who remembered Ober as an elder, said that, as far as Ober was concerned, "Wherever he was was where he was supposed to be."[2]

It was important to Ober that he be a gracious host to his visitor:

I proposed that we should have tea, and I knew by Billy's radiant face I had scored.... The other two Indians soon arrived and the three stayed all afternoon. I practiced all my Indian on them.

One of the Ojibwe turned out to be Billy's brother-in-law, Jack Pot. He was "one of the most famous Indians in this region. He was older than Billy, a great big handsome fellow and pretty vain. Billy was so modest, but Jack Pot was boastful. He was married to Billy's younger sister. He'd already been married several times before. He was the kind that was likely to have several wives. Most of the big Indians at that time did."

Jack Pot told stories in Ojibwe that Ober could not yet understand, but "I could tell what was happening by his actions," continued Ober. "He was acting it all out. I saw a fellow sitting on a log, and a bear came along in front of the man. He was so scared he fell back over the log. Nearly scared him to death. Thought the bear was still coming, so he kept rolling backwards till he ran into a tree. When he had regained his senses, there was no bear there. Then he discovered he had hurt himself against the tree. And the group laughed and laughed about it. Of course, as Jack Pot told it, I can imagine it *was* extremely funny."

At seven o'clock I had to order tea for them again. They laughed at the sausage skin. Soon afterwards, though the wind was still strong, they embarked in their birch-bark canoes. I went to bed at 9 o'clock.

The next morning the sun came out, and the temperature soared to seventy degrees. "That afternoon," said Ober, "the flies were buzzing all around us. It was a rare day, remarkable. And all the snow disappeared. The wind went down, and we went out and immediately began seeing moose. O, gee, moose everywhere. It was the most wonderful thing. There were Indians around, and they lived on moose, and these moose were hardly scared of us. Well, the Indians didn't slaughter for the fun of it. They only killed what they needed. But there were white fellows that went in from Mine Centre all the time—not yet as far as we went—who killed deer right in the summer, for their heads. As soon as the heads were in any kind of shape in late summer, they'd be after them. They'd sell them to outside organizations, especially on the U.S. side. They'd get big prices, and they just slaughtered right and left. Of course, that was after we were there. The same fellows were shooting for meat all the time, too, and selling it at Mine Centre. Or shipping it to the fort.

"Well, Billy and I had those two weeks together there with the moose, and that was very wonderful. I came back vastly elated because, oh, I'd had this wonderful opportunity, not only to photograph, but to study their habits. Very little was known about moose in those days. People had hunted them, but they didn't know anything about them. People thought they always fed on lily pads. Those moose weren't eating lily pads at all. It was wild rice they were eating while I was there. When they had wild rice, they took that in preference to anything else. Not the grain. It was the green shoots [that at this time were emerging from the bottoms]. They're very succulent, and the moose had them hanging from their jaws, chewing away like a cow."

Ober was indeed as excited by the opportunity to study the habits of moose as by the photographs he was taking, and a year later, while living in Europe, he would publish "On the Habits of Moose" in the June 1911 *Proceedings of the Zoological Society of London*. In warm weather, the moose stayed in or near the water a good part of the day. "Partly to get rid of flies," said Ober. "They go in right up to their necks, and then they put their heads under. They get a little relief that way. The flies are worse for the bulls. Their antlers are forming during the summer, and they're just full of blood. The flies can get this blood very easily. The velvet will be just a mass of flies. The poor moose, chewing all the while, will put his head under and keep it there as long as he possibly can. Then he'll pull up his head, and you'll see the long shoots hanging from his jaws."

According to Ober, up until this time almost all of the photographs of moose had been taken at night, using flashlights with trip wires so the animals would trigger their own photographs. Ober's daylight success came because he photographed from his canoe. "We had the most wonderful luck you ever saw in your life," he said, "so many moose and so near. You wouldn't think it possible. Again and again, we were within twenty-five feet of an animal, and they didn't seem very much bothered by us. We followed a very careful strategy. When they first saw us, we froze. We just sat absolutely still. We didn't move. Well, they were feeding and didn't like to be interrupted, and they'd put their heads down at last, about to go under for more rice. Then they'd look up quick, to take one last look. Then they'd put their heads under and maybe keep their ears up—listening for any movement. Well, we'd still stay frozen. Until they'd gone through all of that two or three times, and were reassured. You'd be surprised, some walked toward us."

In an unpublished narrative essay titled "In Domestic Circles," Ober illustrated more fully how he and Billy camouflaged themselves: "What a puzzling monstrosity we must have been. The front of the green canoe held a bower of poplar branches, through which on an improvised stand stared my huge black camera and behind that, in gray shirt and green slouch hat, I myself. In the stern, only his head and shoulders showing above the gunwale, sat Billy. Such a conglomeration, moving and yet without animation."[3]

In the August 1915 issue of *American Photography*, Ober published an article titled "Photographing Wild Moose" in which he offered much of his thinking on the subject:

> If you want the suspense of a detective story, . . . the tense employment of your every muscle, together with sudden turns of fortune—all these in one pastime—go hunt the moose with a camera. It is not new; a number of people have tried it; but its fascination deserves to be shared by a larger part of the world, especially by that growing company of fit and spirited men who have had to forsake the gun. . . .
>
> I do not care for photography at long range with the inordinately long-focus or the telephoto lenses, partly because the results are doubtful . . . but principally because you lose the crowning value of it all—the intimate point of view. I do not care a rap for pictures except as they bring me into touch

Close-up of young bull in water

with the idiosyncrasies of the animal and in turn reveal them to the less fortunate nature-lover at home. One way of getting close, of course, is to steal
up at night and to operate with flashlight; but even this, enjoyable as are its
sensations, I should reject, because it allows no observation and portrays
every animal in the one unnatural state of being startled.

For myself, I prefer a lens of about seven inches' focal length and the
largest possible aperture, a stout camera with no worrisome attachments
to limit my freedom, a steady canoe man to do the steering . . . and then to
photograph by daylight, when your own ingenuity is pitted against all the
faculties of the moose and when your own eyes can enliven and supplement
the testimony of the camera. . . . It is man against moose, with the odds
about even and in any case no harm done. Moreover, I doubt if there is a
creature in the world, however wild, which man may not approach almost
within touch *by long practice and thorough knowledge of its habits. . . .*

The principal thing to remember is that the moose, like most wild animals, is a creature delicately organized—a hulky, lumbering beast, but none
the less full of nerves. He hears better and scents better than man; and, if
you want to make his acquaintance, you must take jolly good care that you
never jar his sensibilities. Haste, sudden movements, the odor of your body
thrust into his nostrils by a capricious breeze and, above all, the sound of
the human voice (that uncanny, demoniacal chant, wonderful beyond anything else in the world) will break the spell as if it had been an air bubble. . . .

I remember particularly a yearling bull—a winsome little fellow that held
his ground knee-deep in the river after all his companions had walked away
in stiff-legged skepticism. We let him feed a while, till he seemed perfectly
calm. Then, inch by inch, scarcely moving, Billy propelled the canoe forward, while I knelt in the bow, camera in hand. The sun was fiercely hot;
there was only a breath of breeze. The little bull several times raised his
head to gaze at us wonderingly; and each time Billy stopped paddling. Thus,
during the moments when the moose's head was submerged, we advanced
till we were only twenty feet away. The bull edged off a foot or so, turned his
back, suddenly faced round again, whined ever so slightly like a dog and at
last, after a moment's reflection, dipped his head under water. I was itching
to take his picture, but I noticed something remarkable. Instead of im-
mersing his head completely, as is the custom of the moose when feeding,
he left half his long ears protruding. He was *listening*; and I was afraid that,
if I clicked the shutter, he would scamper away. When he raised his head
again, however, I decided to chance it. I clicked. He flinched, moved away a
step again and then resumed his feeding. He seemed completely reassured,
for I noticed now that even the tips of his ears were under water. We were
still gliding nearer. I took another picture, a third, one after another. At last,
lo and behold, the little fellow got down on his knees on the river bottom,
and for a second or so his body was wholly lost to sight. His head came up
first, with ears pricked. He shook it and the ears flapped drolly against his

cheeks. When he rose, he looked at us inquiringly, almost mischievously, with his languid brown eyes. His shaggy winter coat was still clinging in patches to his hind quarters. . . . To my great surprise he calmly stepped toward us and sniffed with his long snout; and I could have touched him with the paddle. But Billy, always cautious and respectful toward a moose, backed the canoe a few strokes. Thus for fifteen minutes we played with this strange neighbor. . . . In all, I made eighteen exposures, quietly changing the roll of film twice; and it was only at last when I spoke—that wicked human voice!—that the trusting little bull took to the woods. . . .

A full-grown bull moose is taller than a horse and, when hard pressed, is undoubtedly a fierce, ruthless fighter. On the whole, however, the sport of photography is less dangerous than exacting. Out of some five hundred moose which I have tried to approach, not one has ever attacked me; though perhaps if I had used a gun, there might have been a different tale to tell. . . .[4]

Ober used a large and heavy 3A Graphlex camera. According to his photographer friend Ray Anderson, it was about the size and weight of a six-pack. Belying his well-known technical ineptitude, Ober carried a portable developing box with him on this and other photographing trips: "Every day," he explained, "I developed the pictures I'd taken. I didn't print them. All I wanted was the negative. I'd string them up from the canoe, and they'd be drying as we traveled along. But I remember that I had trouble two days after the snowstorm because the surface of the water was so warm I couldn't use it for developing. Seventy-two is about as warm as you can have it. Then the emulsion gets soft. So we couldn't develop until just before dusk, when the water would rapidly cool."

On June 9, the pair saw their record number of moose. Ober described this experience of abundance in his journal:

Fair day. Rose at half past six. Billy said he had seen five moose in the far bay. . . . Found five moose in [what they had come to call] Bull Bend—at least four of them bulls. Took pictures of all of them. . . . Stayed in camp till half past four on account of Billy's illness. . . . [Then in] fifteen minutes we saw nine moose on the creek and took pictures of 8 of them. . . . Sun hot, blue flies buzzing. We were able to get near the animals. Enormous bulls. Saw a cow with teats and a bell. After we took her picture, we heard her call her calf. Belching, snorting sound. Some of the moose cough. In two hours and a half we saw 25 moose. On the river just below the creek they were coming out in troops at seven o'clock. From every direction they came peering through the bushes. Different colors—some nearly black, some brown and black, some brown with buff under parts. Light spot near the vent. Sometimes they walk with heads under water. Total count for the day of 6½ hours paddling—44 moose. . . .

A moose cow with calves is extremely shy and protective, and Ober had found it impossible to photograph such a group. The next day, however, his luck changed:

> *June 10:* Another warm fair day with slight wind. Rose at half past five and developed a roll of film. Left camp at about half past eight.... In Bull Bend there were ten moose and we heard another in the bush. Among them was a cow with twin calves—the best find of my life—and the wind was favorable. We advanced very slowly, never expecting to come anywhere near the calves. One by one the bulls moved away without showing alarm. Only one was left, and the calves were sucking. Presently the cow turned round, waded into the water, and began feeding. We drew nearer, inch by inch, the innocent little calves looking at us without surprise. They stood leaning against each other. Little calves still blinking with the novelty of life. Perhaps 10 days old. At last, we were only ten feet away from all of them. I took one picture after another—ten in all. The cow at last climbed ashore and stood at bay with her children.... All that frightened her was my attempt to change the roll of film....

Ober worried that their benign presence around the moose would lead them to become overly tame, and his essay "In Domestic Circles," largely based on the above-described scene with cow and calves, ends with the following sad statement: "It was hard to leave such agreeable acquaintances and harder still to imagine what a shock their confidence may have once the meat hunter arrives. For even the babes are sometimes sacrificed."[5]

"The best find of my life": a cow with her calves

Their morning success with the cow and calves was not the end of that day's excitement for Ober and Billy. That afternoon they had an interesting encounter with a bull:

> After [the noon meal], the water being too warm (75 degrees) to develop pictures, Billy proposed that we chase a bull swimming in the farthest bay. He kept sinking [and rising] in the water till we were 20 feet away, when he slowly turned. In the deep water it was an easy matter to head him off, though he kept dodging us very cleverly by a quick turn. I took three pictures and then let him go ashore. He had a bell about a foot long....

At this point, that intimacy which Ober sought with his moose subjects may have reached its zenith:

> About 100 of his flies clung to my back all the way to camp and the only way I could get rid of them was to smoke them off.

In his efforts to please and gain the friendship of his wilderness mentor, Ober relinquished more and more control to Billy, who was after all almost twice Ober's age and far more experienced. Despite the fact that Ober was paying him, Billy had had enough of the young man's unrelenting drive, and he began to decide when and whether they would go out to photograph. The tension between them can be seen as cultural: white anxiety over the passage of time has long been a source of humor to native people, and conversely whites have often spoken derisively of "Indian time":

> All afternoon we stayed in camp, drinking tea. I also took a swim. Five o'clock came and still Billy showed no inclination to go. I suppose I am a moose hog. I ought to be in the seventh heaven over the pictures of the calves this morning, but here I am grieving over the loss of the finest afternoon of all for moose. It has been hot and still, and the flies are plentiful. Yet it is not half past eight in the evening and Billy instead of suggesting a paddle up the creek is calmly cooking beans. Worse yet the water is so warm that I can't develop the calf negatives. All I can do is go to bed, hoping for better results tomorrow. We paddled four hours today and saw 28 moose altogether. Might easily have seen 60 or 75 if we had made an effort.

Despite this written complaint, Ober knew full well that Billy had provided him with the photographic opportunity of a lifetime. They had managed roughly 260 moose sightings during their two-week excursion: "[Having developed my film,] I knew the negatives," said Ober, "and I was just overjoyed as we went back to Mine Centre. I had, unquestionably, the best photographs of moose that, to that time, had ever been taken. Because I'd had such wonderful chances to see them. Of course, I had this man who knew more about moose than anybody else—Billy Magee."

June 12: Got up at half past four. Fair morning. We embarked [for Mine Centre] at seven with the negatives suspended from poles in the canoe.... Found draft for $100 waiting at post office. Hamel cashed it at once and I paid Billy $36 for wages, $5 for present. To bed at 10:30. Hotel full of drunken rowdies.

Before parting, Ober had asked Billy to help him approach and photograph bear, just as they had with moose. Billy was wisely afraid of bears, but he agreed to meet Ober and go out with him again at ten the following morning.

It was a Saturday, and in the oral history Ober told of the "drunken rowdies" in the hotel and that night's lumberjack revelry. He also described a system in which the employer of these men got back their week's wages: "There was a small lumber mill down there on the lake just above Mine Centre which was owned by a doctor from [Fort Frances]. His was a wonderful arrangement. He paid off his men on Saturday afternoon, and they'd all be planning to go to the Fort for a good time. But the train from the east didn't come until twelve o'clock at night. They'd sit waiting in the little hotel there, and in a half hour they'd be just roaring drunk. Oh, their checks went fast. One after another they would treat with all the money they had. Then another would treat. Pretty soon they'd all be lying on the hotel floor.

"When the train came at midnight, none of them could get up to get onto the train. They'd sleep there on the floor and snore most of Sunday. Monday morning they'd be ready to work, absolutely broke. And, you see,

Young bull in velvet swimming

the hotel was owned by this same doctor they worked for, so it was a very profitable venture for him. He got all their wages back. They didn't even eat over the weekend. He got all their work through the week for the cost of the liquor they drank on Saturday night. And that was the way it always went."

Trying to sleep in a room above the revelry, Ober never got a wink: "The noise, oh, was like [being in a] cattle train. The grunts and roars and growls and singing. And, oh, the terrible tramping sound down there."

It turned out that the lumberjacks were not the only ones celebrating that night: "As I walked toward the shack Billy had slept in," said Ober, "I saw him coming toward me, staggering all over the path.

"'Billy, you're not in any condition to go out with me this morning as you agreed.'

"'Oh, ho, ho. Yes, guess little bit drunk. Ah, ha, ha, ha.'"

Ober admitted that he lacked patience at the time: "I was just at the age where every minute seems important. Not like now where it seems I've got a thousand years to do something. Then, I couldn't waste an hour, had to be right off again." Ober told Billy that he was going back to Fort Frances to get someone else to help him find bear. A half-century later, he enjoyed repeating Billy's response:

"'Guess no cry. I'm not very sorry about it. You see, you damn fool.'

"So I hopped the train," said Ober, "and went down to the Fort. I didn't want to leave, for Billy was the one fellow I wanted above all else, but I couldn't wait for him to sober up. I was mad because I'd paid him, paid him extra, you see, and I thought he ought to have been more decent about it. It was a terrible disappointment."

As is often the case with such a break in plans, something new and unexpected opened up for Ober. Back in Fort Frances, he found waiting for him a telegram that he would not have received if he and Billy had paddled out after bear.

"And this," he recalled, "changed my whole life."

[6]

Travel and Work in Europe

The telegram awaiting Oberholtzer in Fort Frances had been sent by Harry French, a young man who had been Ober's best friend as they were growing up in Davenport, Iowa: "He'd just graduated from Harvard Law School with high honors," said Ober, "and as a reward, his father, who was a very well-to-do man, had given him a three-months trip to Europe with one friend. Harry had chosen me to accompany him.

"Well, if I hadn't gone back looking for another man— It shows how things are affected by just chance. All my life I've seen it, again and again. If Billy hadn't got drunk, I wouldn't have gone to Europe. I wouldn't have been American vice consul to Germany. My life might have been changed a lot. I hesitated, of course. In the first place, I was all set to do these other things [in the wilderness] which were my whole life. Oh, I was just so enthusiastic to do these things. On the other hand, Harry and I knew each other so well, and I knew his father was perfectly able to afford this. But it was a big thing to accept from anybody."

Ober did agree to accompany French, and he plunged into this new adventure with characteristic zeal. Harry French would in time become a very successful lawyer and a lifelong supporter of Ober's aspirations, but at that point he was yet another of the extremely shy young men for whom Ober felt he must act as caretaker:

"I knew that, for Harry, it meant everything that I go with him. He was not the sort of fellow who could go and look after himself. He was very timid about making arrangements, and I was supposed to be bold. Nobody seemed to think I was bashful. I don't know why. I thought I was quite bashful. Anyway, as long as I'd missed the other thing with Billy, I decided to go. I met Harry just as the steamer was ready to leave from New York. We went up the gangplank together and had a very lovely passage."

It was to be one of those rite-of-passage trips to the continent for well-to-do young men. With French, money seemed no object, and they were free to go wherever and do whatever they liked:

"Harry had no idea where we were going. I could have had almost anything I wanted. He was certainly considerate." The two talked about going to Iceland, a choice of Ober's, but, in this case, Harry did say no. A woman of title, a Miss Favaire who had lived for forty years in Davenport, had recently returned to her family estate in Hungary and had cabled them an invitation. They would go there. But first there were London and Paris. In London, the interests of the young travelers were mainly cultural:

> *July 13:* ... we saw "The Arcadians" at the Shaftesbury Theatre. Pretty scenery and chorus; insipid jokes.[1]
>
> *July 16:* Harry was my guest at the Covent Garden where we heard "Madame Butterfly." Destinn was without charm or illusion, Rostowsky as Pinkerton was mediocre; and in fact the only one I cared for was Sammarco. The end is swift and pathetic ...

Correspondence during this period in Ober's life suggests that he was flirting with the idea of becoming a music or drama critic, and, given the authority with which he would ever comment on performances such as those he and Harry were now enjoying, it seems likely that he had considerable potential for such a career. Had Ober become a critic, one wonders if he might not also have become something of an aesthete. Likely, however, the intense rigor with which he approached life would have saved him from the negative implications of the word. In any case, two years later, wandering lost on the Canadian Barrens with Billy Magee, the world of the Shaftesbury Theatre and Covent Garden must have seemed incredibly remote.

In his European trip journal, however, the critic continued strong in Ober, even in response to services at Westminster Abbey:

> *July 17:* ... This service consisted almost entirely of standing, while the choir chanted or sang. The congregation never participated, the church was crowded, the organist raced ahead of his choir, and the dean seemed an old hypocrite. It was a most disappointing and exhausting experience.

Ober and Harry traveled to Oxford by train: "Fifty miles or so through beautiful countryside," said Ober. "Coming back, we were in one of those compartments that go across the car, and there was an old man in our compartment with us. We were passing through one village after another, and they were just bowered in trees and flowers. There were tiled and thatched roofs. Oh, it was beautiful.

"'Now, Harry,' I said, 'we ought to walk. I'd give anything to be in these villages. We don't see enough this way, sitting in the train. We saw Oxford, but we don't see anything here, and every one of these villages is a gem.'

"'Well, we've seen Oxford,' Harry said.

"'I know, but that isn't like going through the country and seeing and meeting the people.' We were about halfway in, I guess. 'If you'll get out with me and walk from here, I'll get you a drink at the first inn that we come to.' Harry just looked scornful. 'In fact,' I said, 'if you'll get out, Harry, I'll buy you a drink at every inn we come to, all the way to London.'

"'You fool,' he said.

"And so we just sat there, not saying much until we got into Padding-ton Station in London. Then the old man who'd been sitting by us, never winking or blinking an eyelash through all of our conversation, got up, and as the door opened and we were going out, he looked at me and said:

"'What I wouldn't have given to be your friend!'

"Harry and I knew right away what he meant, you see, and that gave us a good laugh. And he laughed, too. Harry thought I was constantly try-ing to get him into physical activity he didn't want. He never wanted to lift a hand unnecessarily. So he got out of that walk to London."

The two young travelers moved on to Paris, where they stayed at the Grand Hotel and where they connected with a friend named Henry Miller, not, of course, the famous American who was to write of riotous living in Paris in the 1930s. Nevertheless, this Henry Miller helped to acquaint Ober and Harry with the nightlife of that joyous city:

> *July 22:* . . . All of us went out together in search of impossible adventures. We even visited the neighborhood of the _____ , but no one seemed to think the fun would be worth the price of admission. . . .

"I'm not going to tell all about our time in Paris," said Ober in the oral history interviews, "but we did everything we were supposed to do there, without being nicely behaved American kids. We saw most of the sights and spent a full night at all the big cafés and night places in Paris, each in proper order. The first was the Café de Paris, where you couldn't get in un-til twelve o'clock at night. We stayed about an hour and a half until they'd got most of our money. They didn't ask what you wanted to drink. As soon as you came, they'd bring champagne. That was expected. And two very wonderful-looking girls would sit down at the table with you, and, oh, they were so very nicely mannered. They were dressed entirely in black with big picture hats on the side of their heads. I sat under the slanting roof of one. The waiter brought us the champagne and asked these two girls:

"'What would you like?'

"'*Peche cardinal.*'

"I didn't know what those were, but two of the most measly looking peaches you could imagine were brought in and one was put before each girl. She would sip her champagne, then pick up a peach and take a little tiny bite and put it down again. They could fill that bite with plaster, I guess, and serve it to them again with the next customers. These girls got a rake-off, of course, and the peaches cost two dollars and a half apiece on our bill. For peaches you could have bought for two cents apiece over here.

"After the girls had flirted with us for awhile, they stood up and said how delighted they were to have met us American gentlemen. I said to one of them:

"'May I have a dance?'

"'Oh, no,' she said, 'you can't dance on this floor because it's forbidden without dress clothing.'

"We hadn't known that before we went, so we couldn't dance. They got up, and we watched them go over to another table with some other men who had just come in. I had never before drank all champagne all night like that. I'd had it before, of course, but it's the only time I ever drank it all night. Well, not all night. By four o'clock we were in places down in Pigalle that were about the last step off. There you were asked what you wanted and nobody bought champagne. But there were a lot of girls. Not quite as nice-looking. They were more mature. Some had begun to look even elderly. Harry and I got separated in one of these places. Of course Harry didn't know at all how to perform in such a situation. I don't mean to say I did, but I wasn't as completely unresponsive as he was.

"I saw him sitting on a sofa about fifty feet from me on the other side of the room. There were two girls with him, both very mature, sitting one on each side, with their arms around his neck. Of course, he couldn't say very much, because he found it hard to get his wind. It was kind of warm, too. Harry would take a drink every once in a while, for consolation. Of course, he'd seen that the two girls also had something to drink. Well, he sat just bolt upright. By and by, he managed to get disentangled. I saw him standing and thought he was coming over to me, but then I saw him walk out the door. I wondered where he was going, so I walked out into the hall and saw him going into the ladies' toilet. He didn't know he'd got in there until he was inside. Well, he came out and said:

"'Ernest, why didn't you tell me?'

"'Well, I didn't have any time to tell you, Harry. And I hadn't had a chance to look things over yet. I'm kind of careful where *I* go, you know.'

"I teased him ever after about that. 'Harry,' I'd say, 'was a real Parisian. He felt as comfortable in the ladies' toilet as in the gentlemen's. It didn't make a bit of difference to him which he went into.'"

Harry had rented a room for each of them at the Grand Hotel, and Ober lay in bed throughout the next day, his heart racing from the effects of his long night of drinking: "I felt very strange," said Ober. "I didn't know just why, but I had a tremendously high pulse. Oh, it was just awful. I got into bed intending to sleep, but from that moment till six o'clock the next evening I didn't sleep a wink. I thought I was going to die. I think it was very dangerous. I really think it was awfully dangerous for me. I wasn't sick at the stomach or anything. I might have been better off if I had been. But I had this pulse that was just throbbing. Oh, I could hardly breathe.

"Sometime in the afternoon, there was a knock at the door, and there stood Harry French. He said: 'Ernest, aren't you going to get up?'

"'Why, no, I-I-I'm sorry,' I said, 'I can't go out with you tonight. I'm sick.'

"'Oh!' he said, 'you've got to get up, you know. I've got Ali Kuli Khan coming with tonight.'

"This was a friend he'd met at Harvard who was later to become the Persian minister to Washington. Harry'd invited him to the French comic theater, *Comédie Française.* And for dinner first.

"'Harry,' I said, 'you go and do anything you want tonight, but I can't leave. I can't go out with you. I'm really sick, and I can't go to the dinner.'

"Harry seemed to be all right with this for a time. He came back a couple times to see how I was getting along. Well, it was time for him to be getting ready. I don't think he'd done anything yet, except wait for me to get better. Then he came back about five and said:

"'Now, Ernest, you've got to go. I can't go there with Ali Kuli Khan and entertain him and everything all alone. You'll have to come with.'

"He was so insistent that finally I got up and got dressed. I've never felt worse in my life. I was just in a daze. When I sat at the table, I could see this man opposite me who looked all swollen and really big. I couldn't eat or drink any of the stuff prepared for me. At the *Comédie Française,* I never understood a word. I saw people up there going through these strange gesticulations, and I heard their voices, but I didn't understand a word."

From Paris, Ober and Harry traveled to Vienna and then to Hungary, where they enjoyed several weeks of fantastic hospitality from the titled Miss Favaire who had formerly lived in Davenport. They returned by way of Switzerland and Germany, arriving in England in mid-September. As they traveled, Ober continued to maintain a heavy correspondence, much of which had to do with his writing career and the sale of his moose pictures. A post card sent to his mother revealed that he had "received a letter from Mr. Hawkes asking what I will take to work for the Canadian Northern Railway—work similar to what I did before. Do not mention it to anyone." Then, mysteriously, "Do not send articles anywhere else and, if anyone mentions Mr. _____'s article, pretend to consider it a good joke. Everyone is making fun of me."[2] The article in question is unknown, but Ober was soon to receive a letter from Hawkes that offers the likely reason for his embarrassment.

Beyond testing his interest in working for the railroad, Arthur Hawkes also urged Ober to stay in England and write about the North American wilderness for English publications. Having been a journalist in England,

Hawkes had connections there, and he sent Ober letters of introduction to editors of newspapers and magazines. With Harry's approval, Ober did choose to stay on in England, and so once again he did not return to America with his traveling companion. Harry sailed on September 17. On the nineteenth, Ober rented a room from a Mrs. Leesons at 23 Great Russell Street in London.

In the oral history, Ober described Hawkes's motivation for encouraging him to stay: "[Mr. Hawkes] thought the more publicity the region and the railroad got over there. . . . Well, I didn't have to say anything about the railroad, but anything about the game animals, the hunting and the fishing in the region would prove helpful to them, you see. He urged me to stay in England all winter, and I finally did, with the consent of my traveling friend, Harry French."

In the following months, Ober wrote many pages of undated notes about the people and life in England. It is certain that he hoped somehow to use this material in his writing. His notes also contain page after page of well-organized information about English newspapers, periodicals, and editors likely to be interested in his work. At one point, Ober jotted down admiring anecdotes about Arthur Hawkes's achievements as a writer in England. It is clear that Hawkes had become a mentor for the fatherless young Oberholtzer, now seeking to find his way in the wilderness world of the unconnected free-lance writer. On October 7, Ober received a $25 loan from Hawkes in the mail, and in a later letter from Hawkes there appears what seems to have been the explanation as to why Ober was being laughed at by "everyone." Pre–World War I tensions had been growing, and during his wilderness travel in 1909, gleaning every bit of information he could about the Rainy Lake watershed and having as well a German name, someone had decided he was a German spy. It seems he had actually spent a night in jail:

My Dear Oberholtzer:-
. . . I have seen the [Kenora] constable's report about you, & have given the Department a letter saying that I know that everything you have told him, as he reports, is true of my own knowledge; & that there is no man for whose absolute reliability I have a higher regard than I have for yours. The constable quite frankly says he did not see how you could be a German spy, camping in lonely places, but a German name makes an official look twice these days, & he has only done his duty, first in letting you go, & then in reporting what he has done.

In case anybody else should be curious you may of course make every possible use of this letter; & if you should meet any friend of mine this will be an intimation to him that any kindness he does you will be regarded as having been done to me. . . .[3]

Ober chose not to use Hawkes's letters of introduction: "I didn't tell Arthur Hawkes that," he said, "but I never did. I always had a feeling that I'd be taking advantage of the other man, and that it would be better to go it on my own. But I'd go to publishers, mostly not those he'd suggested. They'd be having a forest fire out here, and that would give me a chance. I could say, 'I was there a year ago. I know where that place is, and I know what this means. Would you be interested in something about it?'

"The English had this very fine magazine called *The Field*. It's been around for ages. It was very high-class and scientific and beautifully done. I think they got it out weekly. They were very receptive to small things I might do. I did quite a number of things for them.

"This was 1910. I stayed right in London. I was living upstairs, over a hairdresser's place, near the British Museum. I did whatever I could to earn some money. I went to a lecture bureau. I don't know how I ever had the courage to do that. It was called Christie and was the best lecture bureau the British had. I showed the man my photographs. I had lantern slides, black and white, and I told him quite a bit about them. And he said:

"'Why, yes, I'm sure we would have had engagements for you if you'd come earlier, but all our lectures are filled up now. But, Mr. Oberholtzer, there *will* be vacancies. You hold yourself ready, and whenever there is a vacancy, we'll call on you.'"

Ober managed to find one lecture opportunity on his own. On November 14, 1910, he gave a presentation, illustrated with lantern slides, called "The Top of the Continent," in which he told of the Rainy Lake watershed and his experiences there. The advertisement for the event listed the lecturer as Ernest C. Oberholtzer, M.A. One must wonder whether necessity had led Ober to claim the degree he had not completed in order to be accepted as a lecturer or if "M.A." was an adornment given him gratis by the promoters of the program.[4]

Once again in the service of his career vision Ober was able to overcome his technical ineptitude: "In the course of the winter, I bought a second-hand enlarging machine. I had never enlarged anything in my life, but, in my single room, I put the paper up on the wall at night. I made huge enlargements of my moose things—at least sixteen by twenty—and somehow the London Zoological Society got word of them, and they wanted to see them. I went there, and they asked me if I could make them a whole set. I must have made twenty-five, anyway, of those enlargements for them. Then they asked me to give a talk on the subject of moose. But not for pay. It was supposed to be an honor to get invited. And I said, yes, I would do that, but before I could I was taken ill."

Ober was frequently troubled by minor illnesses that winter, but he still managed to spend a great deal of time in the British Museum library, studying the Canadian Barren Lands in preparation for an expedition about which he was dreaming. He was also studying everything available on the subject of moose: "I had a stall, and I could get everything I wanted. I had everything that you could possibly find on moose, and you'd be surprised at the stuff that had been printed. Just nonsense. Since I couldn't give a talk, I wrote a paper and sent it to them. In it I quoted a lot of what I'd been reading, you see. I had pictures, and I offered the conclusions I'd arrived at. [The London Zoological Society] had somebody read the paper for me, and they published it in their proceedings. Well, of course, that was quite a boost for me, because they were the top in that sort of thing."

In this paper Ober quoted a letter he had received from Mine Centre trader Louis Hamel. Billy Magee had told Hamel that a group of some twenty of Ober's "moose friends" had broken through the ice that winter and drowned. Ober theorized that, though the moose might have been sensitive to such danger in relationship to their individual weight, this awareness had not extended to their collective weight.

Ober was asked to do a substitute program for the Christie Lecture Bureau that winter. He was to fill in for the top man of the day on the English lecture circuit, the explorer Sven Hedin. Ober had begun to model himself after men such as Hedin, was beginning to create such a persona, and the opportunity to "be Hedin" for a night may have made a significant impress on his psyche. It seems, though, that he was not yet ready to fill Hedin's shoes. He was unwell and ill prepared. As Ober tells it, it is a sad, hilarious tale:

"I hadn't been feeling very well, and the thought came to me, 'I haven't been getting enough exercise.' So I took a train way out from London and walked thirty miles back. I got home about seven in the evening. My landlady said:

"'There's a telegram awaiting you.'

"It was from Mr. Christie of the lecture bureau. 'Mr. Oberholtzer,' he said, 'we find that we're in quite an emergency for our lecture in Liverpool tomorrow night.'

"I was to fill in for Sven Hedin. He was *the* man in that day. He'd recently been to Tibet, you see. The first man of that era to do so. His reputation was tremendous. But he was ill, and so they were asking me to fill in for *Sven Hedin*, the top man in the lecture series.

"I was all tired out. I had thought, now, tonight, I'm going to be able to sleep. I got in all dusty and tired and suddenly I was asked to lecture the next night in place of Hedin in the largest hall in Liverpool. My first impulse was to call Christie with my excuses. But he had said, 'Don't fail us now.' He thought he was offering me a great opportunity, you see.

"Here I was faced with the necessity of leaving at six the next morning for Liverpool. And I was tired. I thought, 'well, I've got to sit down right away and make an outline.' But, between my tiredness and my frustration, I couldn't do a thing. About eleven, I thought to myself, 'this is non-sense—you *must* sleep. That's the main thing—sleep. Haven't you talked a lot about your subject in the past? Can't you get up there and *just talk*?' Of course, I didn't really know what my mother's old aunt [Grace Park-hurst] knew when she said I had the gift of gab. I didn't realize that I had this gift.

"I went to bed and couldn't sleep a wink. At five o'clock, my landlady came in with two watering cans, one with hot water and one with cold, and a tin tub. I got up, bathed, snatched some food, got on the train. I thought, 'Now, just take it easy, relax, sit back, shut your eyes, and think about this.' But, oh, I was completely distraught, and there was an old Englishman sitting beside me.

"'Young man,' he asked, 'you're an American, aren't you?'

"'Yes.'

"'Well, what part of America do you come from?'

"'Iowa.' 'Don't get into this,' I thought.

"'Well, how do you happen to be over here?'

"He went on and on. Finally, when there was a little interval, I got up and walked out in the aisle and leaned against a partition. He came right out and leaned against the partition with me.

"I got to Liverpool at seven that night, and the lecture was to start soon after eight. I went to a hotel, dressed, but didn't take any food. I didn't feel good. I had a headache. I went to the hall and the most agree-able man met me and shook my hand.

"'I'm really so sorry that this should have happened to you,' I said. 'I haven't felt up to doing this at all. I'm not feeling well, and I have had no chance—'

"'We realize that fully, Mr. Oberholtzer, and your audience will also. You will have the most accommodating audience you ever could hope for. You won't need to worry about that. You've got your lantern slides, haven't you?'

"'Yes. Would you get me a pointer please? Would you put that in there?'

"'Yes, I'll take care of that, and here's your check—$60.'

"Well, that was a lot of money for me in those days. I don't know how much Sven Hedin would have gotten, but $60, I would have thought that was enough for even him.

"The time for the lecture arrived, and I went into this lighted hall—a vast place—St. George's Hall. I hadn't dreamed it would be so big. I thought, well, this is probably just a scientific society, and they will want to know brand new things that nobody else knows. This isn't just for entertainment. But I found out later it was a lecture course *for* entertainment.

"I had splendid photos, and if I'd had any sense as well, I'd have put them right on. I could have talked without any trouble then. I'd have been in the dark—not conspicuous—and with the pictures, I could have gone on endlessly. They would all have had a good time.

"But instead I felt I had to give them some new information about the region. I had to talk big. So, pretty soon—I thought I had a loud voice that carried—somebody said:

"'Louder, please. Louder, please.'

"And there was no response. The audience was as quiet as a hidden mouse. There was a clock for me to watch. The time just dragged. Oh, it was terrible. Twenty minutes seemed like twelve hours.

"Finally, I asked for my lantern slides. They put them on, and then I couldn't find the pointer. It was right behind me, but I didn't see it until I was leaving.

"I showed them these very lovely pictures of the moose and Indians and the scenery. Up till then there'd been no response anywhere. I think they all felt sorry for me. But then I told them the 'Legend of the Black Sturgeon' that Billy Magee had told me in broken English that first summer, when he had made such a great impression on me, and I got a very good hand, and that was the finale."

The "Black Sturgeon" seems to have been Ober's favorite among legends he was told by the Ojibwe. It is a strange tale, which Ober liked to tell in the broken English in which Billy had told it to him. In it, the fishermen in a camp of some fifty white wigwams have tremendous luck one day catching black sturgeon. They are cleaned and hung on poles to dry, and the men and women of the camp feast and dance that night. One young woman, however, did not join the revelry. She sat on a hill behind the camp, hour by hour brushing her flowing black hair. When in the morning she returned to the wigwams, she found that everyone in the camp had died in their sleep. She hurriedly paddled back to the main encampment and returned three days later with ten men to find neither bodies nor drying sturgeon. Instead, there were squiggle marks through the sand that led into the water, showing that all the Indians had been transformed into black sturgeon. As Ober told it, from that time on Indians of the region considered black sturgeon to be poison and never ate them.

Even the telling of this legend, however, seems not to have salvaged Ober's program: "When I came out into the anteroom," he said, "there was no one to meet me, and no wonder. The man had made his escape. But, when I opened the door, there stood a young friend of mine whom I'd met two years before in Liverpool, right after my bicycle trip up into Scotland with Conrad Aiken. There he was, this friend, a Rhodes scholar, becoming a doctor, an intern in a big hospital, shaking hands with me.

"'How in the world did you know?' I asked.

"'Well,' he said, 'I saw it in the paper this morning.'

"'Nortje,' I said, 'I'm sick. I've got a temperature—I know I have.'

"'Well, I was just going to take you out to eat.'

"'I haven't had anything to eat all day, but I don't feel like it.'

"'Oh, yes, you come out and eat, and I'll take you up to your room and take your temperature.'

"Well, when he got me up there I had a temperature of 102.5, so of course I didn't feel so good. I stayed there a couple of days and then he said, 'I fixed you up and now you and I are going on a bike trip over into Wales, before you go back to London.' So I took a five-day bike trip with him. It was very nice indeed. And that was the last time I saw him."

Later that winter, after numerous minor health problems, Ober became seriously ill. Although there was fear that he might have rheumatic fever again, he did not and soon recovered. Upon his recovery, he found himself in need of money to pay medical bills. It was then that he got a letter from Hannover, Germany: "It was from the American consul there," he said, "inviting me to become American vice consul at Hannover. A friend of mine had been over there and met the consul, and the previous vice consul had taken ill and left. My friend told him, 'I think I know just the fellow.'"

Though he had another long-term plan—an expedition into the Barren Grounds of Canada—financial necessity forced Ober to accept this new opportunity. Beyond the fact that he was generally well educated, his knowledge of the German language was surely the reason he was offered the position. Ober would ever be proud of having held this post, but it is unlikely his duties went much beyond detail work in the consulate office, surely not very appealing to the young adventurer. In addition, the emotional tenor of the Germany he discovered upon his arrival proved repulsive to him:

"That was just before the First World War," he said, "so I saw the preparations. I saw the Germans when they were under great pressure and so terribly tense. It was very disagreeable. I didn't like it at all. Everything was regulated, you see. You could hardly open your mouth without getting into trouble. This was in 1911, and they nearly went to war while I was there, over the Algeciras Conference, you see. Britain and France and Spain were dividing up Africa, and Germany wanted a slice."

Ober described the marching German troops with evident distaste: "They didn't look like human beings. They were covered with dust from the old Macadam roads and were marching along like automatons. They'd come some incredible distance, carrying heavy stuff in hot weather. Well, none of that influenced me very much." Ober's response to the soldiers was typical of the young wilderness figure who shunned killing animals, even for food, and who in fifteen years would be working to designate the Quetico-Superior region as an international peace memorial in honor of those who had died in World War I.

"It was eight months before I was relieved and could leave Germany," he said.

At this point, once again following in the wake of her adventurous son, Rosa arrived from America. She too, however, had a heart condition that was to plague her later years: "My mother came over to meet me and take the boat home with me, but on arriving in England she was taken ill and couldn't leave for home. She was very ill. The doctor said she would have to go to southern England for the entire winter.

"'I'll find the right place,' I said, 'if I have to walk every foot of the shore of southern England.'

"We went to the end of the southwestern railway, and we discovered a place right away [Kingswear Lodge in Kingswear, South Devon]—just wonderful—where we stayed all winter."

During his forced stay in England, Ober continued to plan what was to be the greatest expedition of his life, a canoe journey into an unmapped region west of Hudson Bay. "I had done a great deal of study in the British Museum library," he said. "I looked up everything there was on the Barren Lands. I was full of this idea of going to the Barren Lands."

Ober had discovered an area—600 miles north and south by 400 east and west—that no white had penetrated since the Samuel Hearne expedition of 1770. "The authorities were in agreement," he said. "If you want to go to a place where the information you bring back will really be valuable, this is the place to go."

Ober was deeply influenced by the exploration and writing of Dr. J. B. Tyrrell, whom he described as the dean of Canadian geologists and explorers. In 1893 and 1894, Tyrrell had headed two expeditions into areas near the unmapped region and had written that a "magnificent field for exploration remained" in that far northern country. Ober would later write that, "These words and Tyrrell's own never-to-be-forgotten report on his exploration of the Kazan River, the vast herds of Barren Ground caribou encountered, and his discovery of a hitherto unknown band of inland Eskimos, living entirely by their own stone-age economy, had fired my imagination. I had been in fruitful correspondence with [Tyrrell] and had had bestowed upon me by him an Eskimo vocabulary of some 200 words."[5]

When it became clear that his mother's health would allow them to return home in the spring, Ober wrote a letter to Louis Hamel, the trader in Mine Centre, Ontario, who bought furs from Billy Magee: "I asked him to have a talk with Billy," said Ober, "to tell him that I wanted to canoe north into the Barren Lands for an entire summer. To tell him that I didn't want to feel that we had to get back at any specific time, that we would be gone at least all summer, that we could only hope to get back before winter, that we'd be going into the wildest country I'd been able to discover in Canada, and that this would be the hardest thing that Billy would ever do in all his life. And Billy had worked like everything, had carried the big packs for the Hudson's Bay Company. But this would be by far the hardest thing he'd ever done in his life. I wanted him to go with me. If he couldn't go, then I wasn't going to go. And I was awaiting his answer.

"In due time—before I left England—I got his reply. Billy couldn't write, but Louis Hamel wrote me and said he'd explained it all to Billy and that Billy had replied: 'Guess ready go end earth.'"

[7]

To the End of the Earth

In his reply to Oberholtzer's request that he accompany him on a canoe journey into a region west of Hudson Bay, as yet unexplored by whites, Billy Magee expressed a willingness to go to the outer reaches of his endurance. There were surely times on the Barren Grounds when this forest Indian knew he was fulfilling his promise. Canadian authority on exploration R. H. Cockburn has written that Oberholtzer and Magee, "in the summer and fall of 1912, carried out one of the most commendable canoe voyages in history."[1] One must smile at the understatement in his choice of the word "commendable."

The vast unmapped territory into which Ober and Billy were heading, explored by only one other white (Samuel Hearne in 1770), presented an immense challenge. Yet, unlike almost all other such expeditions, they, with brief exceptions, traveled without the help or guidance of native people. Ober fully intended to hire a guide but was unable to find the satisfactory person, and he and Billy continued, sometimes with great difficulty, to make their way alone. In the end, he took great satisfaction in the fact that they had managed to do so.

Ober would later write, "Our destination was uncertain but in the direction of the magnetic pole."[2] His "object in going north . . . was not to make any record journey, nor particularly to do any exploring, but only to study the natives and the wildlife of those parts."[3] Though always carefully modest about his intentions, Ober in his letters makes apparent that he hoped, through this journey into unknown territory, to establish a niche for himself as a wilderness figure and explorer from which he might begin to earn a living as a writer and lecturer.

In 1912, Ober was twenty-eight, five feet six inches in height, and weighed less than 140 pounds. As the story is told by those who knew him, medical opinion held that he would never return from this journey. Billy was about fifty and twenty pounds heavier than Ober. In his short sketch of the trip, wilderness authority Calvin Rutstrum, ignoring Ober's heart condition, wrote that together the two men were an ideal combination of age and experience. He pointed out, too, that due to Ober's reluctance to kill animals, he and Billy did not plan, for the most part, to live off the land. They therefore had to carry far more food which, when fully loaded at the start, necessitated five round trips at each portage, and their loads

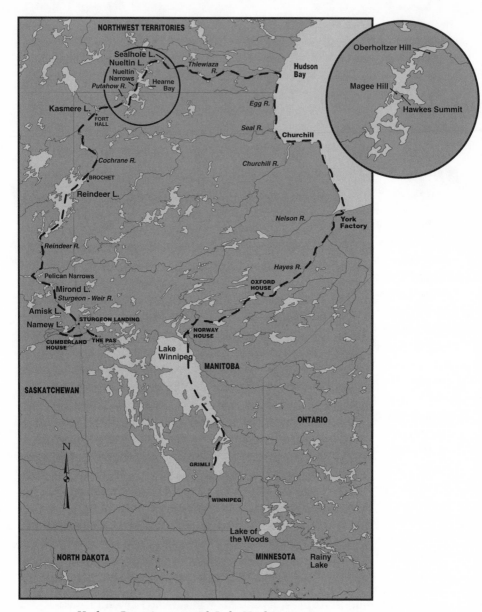

Hudson Bay trip map with Lake Nueltin insert

averaged 125 pounds apiece. "One cannot even imagine the labor entailed in five trips over portages without knowing about the Little Lakes Country... [where] portages become a job of clawing over precipitous eskers, and virtually sliding down their steep slopes on the other side."[4]

This was to prove the most significant outward adventure of Ober's life, and memory of it would haunt him until the end of his days. At the advanced age of seventy-six, surely hoping even then to tell the entire story, he completed three rough, single-spaced pages of an account of the trip: "Since last seeing Billy," he began, "I had served temporarily as American Vice-Consul at Hannover, Germany, saving my meager earnings for this very purpose. I crossed the sea in a one-class steamer to Boston just after the Titanic disaster, and after visiting my home in Davenport, Iowa, finally reached Fort Frances, Ontario, the middle of June, 1912."[5]

Rosa accompanied her son on the train as far as St. Paul: "Such a trip as this," he explained in the oral history interviews, "was the last thing she would ever have wanted me to do. She was all alone. But she never did anything but cooperate when she thought I was set on something, you see. And she gave me the dollar-and-a-half watch and the dollar-and-a-half compass with which I made a map of absolutely new country, four hundred miles long, all on a scale three miles to the inch. We had no instruments other than that. I wouldn't have known how to use them, and they'd have been too expensive and heavy to carry."

In his three-page account of the expedition's beginning, Ober wrote that he met Billy in Fort Frances, Ontario, and Billy was "much plumper than when I saw him last, but still fit at the age of 50.... He was wearing a tan shirt and, of all innovations, a blue tie! When we shook hands, an observer might have thought that we had never met before. Billy was as hesitant and unsmiling as ever. Both of us, I'm sure, had in mind the morning of our last parting. We had just had a glorious two weeks photographing moose.

"'Did you think you'd never see me again, Billy?' I asked.

"'Yes,' he replied, 'guess neber see 'gain.'"[6]

Ober had already bought what he believed to be the best possible canoe for their expedition. Its canvas-covered wooden structure was of a kind that Billy had liked before, and Ober expected him to be overjoyed, but Billy shook his head:

"'No good.'

"'No good! Why, what do you mean? I thought you liked canvas canoes.'

"'Somebody make it new canoe—Canada canoe—canvas canoe just same, only bigger, stronger. I show you.'

"We went together to the hardware store to see.... They were just new on the market—a product of New Brunswick. One look was all that was needed. Here was a canoe for rugged use—deep, wide, strong, exquisite lines and craftsmanship—such a canoe as I had never seen before. Of course, it was heavier, about 105 pounds as I recall; but for our purpose, on the big and stormy waters of the north and with months of supplies to carry, it was the ultimate answer. I reserved it at once and put my own on sale and have never made a wiser decision. I can't conceive of our ever having made our trip without this true and sturdy friend. We came to love it like a comrade."[7]

In Winnipeg, Ober took Billy with him when he bought supplies, "partly to show him the sights and partly to consult his taste. We bought 700 pounds of food, principally the three staples of the north, flour, pork and tea; but also such luxuries as evaporated potatoes, raisins, cornmeal, oatmeal, cocoa, sugar, beans, rice, and dried fruit."[8] Billy would do much of the cooking on their journey, and Ober said of his bannock, the unleavened griddlecake that was a staple of the far north, that it "served a dual purpose. You could sit on the big circular loaf in great comfort and without apparent harm to it."[9]

On June 25, the pair arrived at Le Pas, Manitoba, at the end of the railway. In the careful journal he kept throughout the journey, Ober wrote:

> ... Arrived at Le Pas soon after three and had our truck carted over a dreadful road to the river front.... We camp for the night and have as visitors the watchman, the Indian preacher... and the [Hudson's Bay Company agent]. Warned against thieves.... Pessimistic predictions of the inhabitants about [the outcome of] our trip....[10]

Such predictions were to be the never-ending refrain from those they met along the way. Still, Ober decided he would wait until they reached Cumberland House, Hudson's Bay post, before hiring a guide, not imagining that doing so would prove difficult. In their rugged new eighteen-foot Chestnut Guide Special canoe, the pair began their paddle up the Saskatchewan. For the first 500 miles, all river-paddling would be against the current. They were in the latitude of late-night sun, and as they continued north the land would become increasingly parklike, with large trees and less and less underbrush, till in time they would leave the trees behind.

On their first day out, Ober wrote that they "make good distance and camp at nine o'clock on a very muddy shore. Billy dips up muddy water with the bucket attached to a long stick. Go to bed at a quarter past ten." On the second day, they "passed what seemed to be a Hudson['s] Bay [Company] dog ranch. Shaggy dogs of all descriptions barked and howled at us. They looked well." These were sled dogs being held till their period of usefulness in winter. On June 30, their fifth day out and a hundred miles upstream, now in Saskatchewan, Ober and Billy arrived at Cumberland House. This post had been established in 1773 by the only explorer to have preceded Ober into Nueltin Lake country, Samuel Hearne.

R. H. Cockburn, the one person to have written extensively about the Oberholtzer-Magee journey, indeed the lone authority on it, notes that "Oberholtzer was hosted handsomely by one of the most interesting and winning HBC personalities of the period, post manager H. M. S. Cotter."[11] It seems that Cotter was the one individual Ober and Billy met along the way who believed the two might succeed in their bold plan, and he would later write comforting letters to Rosa after she had begun to fear for her son's life.

Ober failed to enlist a guide at Cumberland House, and it was becoming apparent that finding one would not be so easy as he had imagined:

> *June 30:* ... Prices are very high on account of the railroad [being constructed].... All men want $2.00 to $3.00 a day and pay for the return trip.... I decide to go as far as Pelican Narrows alone....

On the following day, they started northward again. On the next, stormy weather forced them to sit tight in their camp, the first of many weatherbound days they would experience in the coming months. On July 5, Ober and Billy were once again on the water:

> ... We begin paddling up rapids at once and meet about eight during the day. Very exhausting work—first wading, then poling, then paddling at full speed. Sometimes we had to carry part of the packs over a portage. Trails all good; abundant flowers and berries. Many ducks. Yellow water lilies; scarlet tiger lilies....

When rivers widened into lakes, it must have seemed a welcome relief from their incessant battle against the current, but the lakes, too, could become a challenge:

> *July 7:* ... At half past eight we venture round the first point and, finally, after a long cold wait in a bay where the wind allowed no landing, paddle in the worst waves I have ever known round the next point. It gave me new confidence in the canoe. I prayed for our deliverance.

In 1912, these waterways were the thoroughfares of native populations and the operations of the Hudson's Bay Company; and during the first stage of the journey Ober and Billy fell in with travelers on almost a daily basis. On the evening of July 11, they entered Pelican Lake, and as they were setting up camp the silence of the lake was broken as a large craft, propelled by oars like the Greek argosies of old, appeared before them. This was a York boat, one of those that did the heavy hauling for the Hudson's Bay Company:

> "...we heard a loud, ominous swish repeated at regular intervals; and there, rapidly approaching, appeared a York boat. It was full of half-breeds. They landed in the bay beyond our canoe; one man jumped over the prow; two oars were tied together as a gangway; and down came the whole crew—some twenty men and a squaw with two children.... One old fellow, who Billy thought was a Sioux and who had told a funny story about squaws, was squatted in front of the fire with a bent pan in his lap and kept beating it in two-fourth? rhythm and wailing a queer, wild monotonous dance. When I went over to see him, he was wrapped in a blanket, his head bobbing time and his face drawn with lines of pleasure that stood out black in the firelight. Billy says this song is called the "Squaw-tent".... The last thing I heard at night was a low sort of chanting like a prayer."

On the following morning the York boat "moved out upon the calm lake. Her great oars washing like the slow beat of a funeral drum, she was magnificent. We heard the rub of her oars for half an hour afterwards."

Later that day, July 12, Ober and Billy arrived at the Hudson's Bay post at Pelican Narrows. Ober's first thought was to find a guide, and he went round at once through wigwams and log shacks and innumerable dogs to the Hudson's Bay store where he met the clerk, Mr. Thwaites. After discussing the situation with Thwaites and the post's Catholic priest, it was decided that Ober should attempt to hire an Indian named John Neenin, but Neenin drove too hard a bargain:

York boat with crewmembers and passengers

He wanted to travel with his family to the south end of Reindeer Lake, then in my canoe to Du Brochet and back in a birch-bark canoe which I should buy. He also wanted $2.00 a day paid in advance and food for his family.... That night in the tent I decided to go alone in spite of everybody's warnings.

The following day Mr. Thwaites made two sail-boards for Ober and had a sail sewn from eight yards of cotton drilling. This new equipment would, in time, prove important to Ober and Billy. As they were leaving Pelican Narrows in the rain, they received what was surely a warning that the two were now in urgent need of a guide. Paddlers in a canoe that had started before them "shouted back something unintelligible and pointed to Neenin who was standing on the shore."

July 18: ... Another wearisome day. Billy paddles poorly and I feel very stiff and sore. The Steep Hill portage which we reached at ten o'clock in the morning was only about 6 chains long. Billy cut himself another piece of balsam tree. [It would seem that Billy had become constipated.] ... In a heavy rain we cooked oatmeal for dinner. After a wait of several hours we paddled on into an endless river.

Ober carried with him a copy of the report of J. B. Tyrrell's explorations that had influenced him so deeply. It included a sketch map made by Tyrrell that would now begin to prove useful. On July 19, the pair entered Reindeer Lake. In the oral history interviews, Ober explained that Reindeer was "a very large lake, over a hundred miles long. We had no modern map, but there was a sketch map Tyrrell had published in the report on his trip. As I recall, it was about twenty miles to the inch. It was a beautiful lake with very clear water."

July 20: ... It was hard to tell where we were but the signs of old camp fires were reassuring. We had supper out among the islands off Priest Point; and then, though I had felt dead sick of paddling, we went on another hour. I think we had come nearly 40 miles. At last, Billy's balsam tea had done its work. He was like a young man all day and never have I seen him better.

The canoe route up Reindeer Lake is in fact 170 miles long, and it would take Ober and Billy nine days to reach its northern end. Unguided, the pair threaded their way uncertainly through its labyrinth of islands, long bays, headlands, and points. They were often lost. On July 23, assuming they were close to Du Brochet, the Hudson's Bay post at the lake's north end, Ober "shaved. Put on my green tie, and took my pipe: all ready for *Der Brocket.*" In fact the pair would search for four more days before finding Du Brochet. On July 27, now some 500 miles from Le Pas, Ober and Billy finally did arrive at the little settlement at the north end of the lake.

R. H. Cockburn writes that Du Brochet had once been important as a post where various bands of Chipewyans provided the Hudson's Bay posts and their York boat crews with pemmican made from caribou meat. That era was now past, however, "and for the next thirty-five years Brochet, drowsing in its isolation, would remain one of the least changed posts in all the North."[12]

Ober immediately went in search of a guide: "Allan Nunn, the assistant factor, introduced me to Andrew Flett, a half-breed, and a red-head named Roland, with whom he was playing pool. They listened in astonishment to my plans. Then all of them, together with the Indian named Alphonse Chipwayan, and several others, carried my outfit up into the kitchen." Chipwayan had recently taken a priest named Father Surgetill to Churchill by dog team and returned by canoe up the Little Seal River. He looked like a good man, and Ober tried to hire him but was once again unsuccessful: "Alphonse . . . decided on account of his wife not to go." Having been shown the nearby entrance of the Cochrane River, Ober and Billy left Du Brochet alone "at nearly six o'clock on a beautiful clear evening." They were soon to enter unmapped territory, and the next morning they were reminded that the open-water season could be a very short one:

> *August 1:* . . . All the river was hung in vapor and the woods covered with frost. The water in the bean pot and Billy's wet socks had frozen solid. He had had an uncomfortable, cold night. We warmed what cocoa was left from the night before and then with gloves on paddled an hour and a half up the river. At one shallow place, I got out and waded, to Billy's great astonishment, who forgot that it was only the wet shore and not the water that was cold. . . .

They were now entering the land of caribou and the wolves that shadowed them, culling the herds of their weakness. For more than a month, they would meet with them daily:

> *August 6:* . . . On the way back I heard Billy whistle and soon he was pointing out to me three large bucks with fine antlers which seemed to me to be still in the velvet. The biggest old fellow had a gray shaggy neck. A number of does and fawns also appeared, but soon the foremost buck stopped feeding as if to listen; and then, wheeling round, led them all up the hill at a gallop, the three bucks circling shoulder to shoulder like circus horses. It was a fine sight and a fine sound. . . .

In the journal entry for August 7, an almost slapstick description depicts the excitement Ober and Billy felt at being among the great herds. Ober's desire to document the trip with photographs is also apparent:

> . . . I ran over the hill barefoot between innumerable caribou bones to the look-out. One picture I snapped from below and just as I came back we saw some fifty large bucks, which I had first spied way up on the opposite

beach. . . . Billy ran with me over the hill to the [Chipewyan] hut and when the deer [caribou] got wind of us and started down the shore for our camp, he drove them back in a whirlwind stampede of swaying antlers and thudding hoofs. Back at the point again, where Billy was shouting and waving his arms and running full tilt, the deer hesitated, wheeling round, stood a moment helpless, and then plunged one upon the other into the water. Billy said some of them nearly ran into him. . . .

Day following day, the physical demands on the two were intense. Billy often took the lead in their struggles, but by no means always:

. . . Half a mile below we saw a crooked rapid which we were afraid to run in the dusk. So I began to wade among the sharp hidden rocks, while Billy limped along the shore barefoot, sometimes holding the rope, sometimes helplessly watching me. Again and again the canoe nearly went smash on the countless rocks and as many times I went in the cold water nearly to my waist. I had to keep feeling my way with the paddle. . . .

The unspoiled world they were passing through was as beautiful as it was demanding:

. . . A balmy southwest wind had been blowing us along . . . and the last quarter moon had just come up red. Billy made a fire and gave me some hot cocoa water for I was a little wet and cold. There were no trees or poles that we could see, so we made our bed on the dry sand using the tent for a cover. The sky was full of stars. At the first darkness, while the sky was still luminous, it seemed as if the trees were all reflected by starlight; then came a time just before moonrise when the shores appeared as black masses only,

Caribou in motion

without detail. Now and then the aurora flared green across the sky and sent great reflected streamers across the water. . . .

August 8 found Oberholtzer studying what maps he had and, undoubtedly, trying to imagine those large blank areas they did not cover. The time had come to decide the route he would take to Hudson Bay. His options were to go straight north along a known but longer route to Lake Ennadai and then down to Chesterfield Inlet, or to turn in an easterly direction, following the Thlewiaza River, which, according to word of mouth native descriptions, flowed both into and out of Nueltin Lake. They could, Ober hoped, paddle north through Nueltin Lake, then follow the re-emergent Thlewiaza down to Hudson Bay. This second route was through the unexplored region that had drawn Ober from the beginning, and he chose to take it. He would soon begin the demanding discipline of mapping their route with the aid of watch and compass, distances established by the estimated speed of their paddling. In the midst of their uncertainty about entering the unknown, it must have seemed welcome that, on the Thlewiaza, their travel would be, for the first time, with the current.

On Theitaga Lake, nearing the Thlewiaza, they found themselves "in sight of an Indian encampment" that was populated only by women and children, "the most intelligent of them," wrote Ober, "[was] a thin keen-eyed boy of about twelve, who pointed out the mouth of the river and who, like the old squaws, indicated his inability to understand by exclaiming and putting his fingers into his ears." Ober first shook hands with two elder women, both of whom sat down for a photograph. One of the old Indian women "with a hideous twisted face and exposed teeth charged upon me with a stick as if to break the camera, but as everyone laughed, I did not move."

That evening they entered the swift-flowing Thlewiaza and encountered a stench of rotting caribou. Ober does not reveal whether they had been slaughtered by Chipewyan, which would seem likely, or had died from drowning: "We counted 25 in the first 15 minutes of paddling and from there on saw them all the way down to the point on both sides, sometimes whole, sometimes only the blue decaying meat, nearly always the white antlers." An Indian named Null-get Josay joined them in their evening camp. "He had one of the long, shallow kyack[*sic*]-like canoes used for deer hunting with a skin in the middle for a seat, a long bloody-headed spear, and a single and a double paddle. We gave him some supper, matches, and a smoke; for which he seemed grateful." Ober and Billy would visit Josay's camp the following morning and then not see another human being for thirty-four days.

In the journal entry for August 9, Ober provided a brief written sketch of Billy as master canoeist:

> ... Perhaps a mile below the first rapid, there is a second of the torrential variety which the Indians may shoot but which was out of the question with loaded canoe. The water seemed deep except at the very end. We went down as far as we dared then started to carry everything six or eight chains across the very unsteady boulders. Suddenly to my wonderment, I beheld [Billy] crouched in the middle of the canoe, swinging his paddle from side to side and bobbing up and down on the flood of the rapid. He made a sudden turn and came in quietly in the eddy, great beads of sweat on his forehead....
>
> *August 10:* ... we gave chase to five young black geese that had waddled over the rocks into the bush. One of them—a beautiful large bird with black head, wings, and tail, and gray throat and breast—Billy caught [by hand] and I photographed. I protested against killing him and Billy in a sudden change of purpose let him go....
>
> *August 12:* ... Once more, too, I was assailed by the intrepid screeching little gulls which seem to take umbrage at my white hat. I had to use the paddle to keep them off.... It now began to rain again and we were both very cold....
>
> *August 15:* ... As we came through the narrows expecting to find a river beyond, we were both surprised to see a large bay to the west. We kept north past a rocky point, where the lake again turns east and many of the hills are barren. I began to think we had reached Nueltin Lake....

They had indeed entered the vast inland sea of Nueltin, which, according to Ober, was properly pronounced Nu*the*ltin, meaning "sleeping island lake" in Chipewyan. The lake was to be a labyrinth that, as they sought its exit, would test to the limit Ober and Billy's endurance and resourcefulness. Nueltin was unknown to white travelers. Ober only knew, from the vague descriptions that had been passed along to him, that the Thlewiaza River flowed out of the lake and down to Hudson Bay, but where in this 120-mile expanse of headlands, bays, and islands—complicated as the nighttime field of stars—did the river exit?

> *August 16:* ... We soon found that the lake extended eastward as well as north; and, to make sure not to miss the river, we went almost straight east for an hour and a half.... After dinner we paddled again east and slightly north, constantly surprised by the size of the lake or the bay (we did not know which) before us...."

Nueltin expands into broad, island-studded reaches, then contracts briefly into narrow passages, only to expand vastly outward again, over and over, five times in all. At each narrowing, the uncertain paddlers must have held hope that they had at last discovered the entrance to the Thlewiaza

River, their channel of escape down to Hudson Bay.[13] Over and over they were disappointed:

> ...After a two hour paddle against a light east wind (altogether perfect weather), we arrived at a stony narrows where the lake seemed to end. After I had climbed a barren hill for a view, we found an opening on the south side.... Contrary to expectation, this barren entrance leads to a wider stretch....

Fascinated by the increasingly treeless world they had entered, Ober explored the lake's islands and shores, but, on August 17, he re-read Tyrrell's sometimes harrowing report and was pierced by anxiety: "I was sorry I had not traveled all day. I began to realize what an expense it would mean to me to arrive at Churchill much after September 1st, and made preparation for a very early start in the morning."

But now it was not simply a matter of pushing on in haste. Where within this vast maze through which they paddled was their exit, the Thlewiaza? Assuming—but with no certainty—that their channel of escape to Hudson Bay would be on the lake's east shore, they followed its myriad indentations with great care. They simply must not miss the river. Or had they already? Surely they felt very small, these lonely travelers, as under a vast sky, through an almost treeless landscape, they continued their search—one week, then two. Each stroke of the paddle must have been laden with uncertainty.

> *August 18:* ... Where high bare pinkish hills appear in the north we had to turn farther west; and, when I climbed up on a barren little island at five o'clock to look, I was surprised at the view. Everywhere blue avenues of water between irregular little islands....
>
> *August 20:* ... We went ashore on a stony island, where there was a deep landing and Billy moored the canoe while I put up the tent. Then, while we sat round the fire waiting for the rain, we both came to the conclusion that perhaps we were going back down the lake where we had come from by a different route....

Physical exhaustion, the vast emptiness through which they traveled in isolation, and fear for their survival surely led to strange mental states, and now and again a hallucinatory quality crept into Ober's journal entries. Though finding firewood had become difficult, somewhere in the distance a forest fire was blazing: "When we were traveling in the smoke, we might have been approaching a Pittsburgh or an Edinburgh, so like steeples or smoke stacks did the few indistinct trees appear."

Rain forced them to spend a day in camp. Both were emotionally and physically exhausted. Ober, the storyteller, "tried in vain to think of a story" that would lighten the hour. "Billy who had slept all morning lay by the fire all afternoon but in the evening succeeded in making two bannocks."

On August 21, the anxious pair arrived at an island esker, some twenty miles long and 660 feet high, an eminence nearly a thousand miles north of Winnipeg that, through the years, would grow increasingly symbolic in the minds of Ober and of those who know his story. Ober was uncertain now that they would ever make it back, and so, at the very top of the esker, a height future explorers were sure to climb, he left a note in a can, secured in a cairn of rocks. The note was for his mother and for the world.

> ... We began to climb [the height] at five o'clock and were well repaid. The contour for miles around looked like a great relief map. Far on the east, north, and west were high hills or ridges. Long narrow bays extend south. The islands everywhere resemble the lake in shape, narrow necks connecting larger bodies, sort of figure eights. ... At sunset on a rock at the very top I left a can, in which was a page out of my ... book. It gave the date and condition of our supplies and said that we had named the hill "Hawkes Summit" in honor of Mr. Arthur Hawkes. ...

Named for Ober's friend, mentor, and perhaps father figure, "Hawkes Summit" is now found on modern maps.

In his article on the journey, R. H. Cockburn vividly imagines what the searching pair must now look and feel like. In the long evenings, they would sit by the fire with aching bodies and sun-blackened faces. Their eyes would burn in the shifting smoke. Their fingernails would be "cracked and black, their hair foul and tangled." Their heavy clothing would be "reeking of woodsmoke and holed by cinders." Cockburn imagines Ober, "driven by ambition, curiosity, and the logical imperatives of mapping," writing in his journal, "his features stern in the jumping firelight."[14]

August 28 proved an eventful day for the searching paddlers:

> ... The sun came out hot for a few minutes, and we went on down into the bay to investigate. We heard a very big fish flop right behind the canoe and Billy said it must be some new kind he did not know. Not even a sturgeon would jump behind the canoe. The next minute he was calling for the gun. Right behind us was a black head, which kept following us about. It was a seal. I had hard work to persuade Billy not to shoot him. ...

This seal, strangely so far inland, can be thought of as a creature of welcome, for, after two weeks of unrelenting anxious searching, the pair now found their exit:

> ... Somehow we had the feeling that we were near the river. The ridges looked as if they were on the brink; all the land to the east seemed lower. Yet there was no large opening. Finally, as we were approaching the most

northerly of the several small indentures, I noticed that the [underwater] weeds were all pointing the same way. Then I got out on the point and saw that the water did extend half a mile farther at least and there the next moment, having passed through a very narrow but deep channel, we noticed a slight current, which became stronger at the next narrows and brought us to the head of a rapid....

They had discovered the entrance to the Thlewiaza, their channel of escape to Hudson Bay! Ironically, it was at this moment of triumph that they suffered what Ober described as their "first real mishap." As they entered the rapids, their canoe became wedged between rocks:

...The water flooded in over the packs, even while I was hurling them ashore; and the good things that were being lost in each flashed across my mind—all my pictures, my camera, the notebooks, the cask of tea, the hardtack in the jumbo pack, and finally (when all else was ashore) the beans. I was sure they had gone, but no, there they were on shore....

When they finally took stock, Ober and Billy found that they had lost one spoon and their rifle. Ober dove into the icy water in search of the rifle and was "whirled ten yards down stream" by the fierce current. Though there is some confusion in the accounts, it would seem that they had lost not a .22, as noted by Cockburn, but a 30–30. They still had a revolver, but for all the good their firearms did them on the journey, they may as well have left them behind.

As the effort to find the exit from Nueltin had been the most emotionally draining stretch of the journey, the trip down the Thlewiaza proved the most physically demanding. Buffeted by harsh winds that were often cold and filled with rain, Ober and Billy found the descent of the river terribly grueling. The almost treeless landscape was littered with a great glacial rubble of rocks, some the size of boxcars. The riverbed too was filled with rocks, creating rapids that demanded they constantly wade and line and portage, and portaging through such rubble was cruel and dangerous to feet and ankles. They woke to ice, but when the weather warmed during the day, black flies emerged and their exposed skin became a mass of bleeding bites.

A gale wind filled with rain kept them weatherbound for two days. Ober crouched by the fire. A little snow bird, he wrote, was his only company: "He hopped all round me almost within reach, now dozing for a minute or so under shelter of the pans, then humped up close to the fire and even hopping on to the burning stick." On September 1, the weather lifted and they continued on down the harsh rocky bed of the Thlewiaza.

September 2: . . . The walking in the portage was the worst I have ever known—one mile and a quarter across huge boulders with only here and there a slight filling of moss. We took the canoe part way down a channel at the back, but long before we could get across, night fell. . . . There was not a stick of wood in sight, our feet were soaking from the bushes, the only level place of moss was drenched with rain and the evening threatened other showers. . . .

Fearing they would not make it through to salt water, they rose ever earlier in the morning:

September 3: . . . I got up at half past three. . . . For half an hour after dinner we went darting down the broadened current of the river simmering with rocks. Then, on Billy's advice, I got out for a survey of the channel. I wanted badly to try running the rest of the way, especially as I could see several miles of shallow water; but, when we crossed the river for another survey, Billy's word settled it. He said, "A fish [much less a canoe] couldn't go through that channel."

Once again, for two and a half days, they were held weatherbound in camp. It was perhaps here that Ober's anxiety over their situation reached its zenith:

September 5: . . . The east wind became stronger with a few drops of rain. While waiting in the tent, I read again Mr. Tyrrell's report and realize how serious our position is beginning to look. Bad weather is undoubtedly near and we have no notion how far we are from Churchill. Probably the worst of

Billy portaging through rubble that was cruel to feet and ankles

the Barren Lands to come and we are travelling hardly more than five miles a day and both of us rheumatic. . . .

As ever, when the opportunity presented itself, Billy escaped into healing sleep. Ober read from Robert Louis Stevenson's "Walking Tours" and other essays. Luckily, they had found a stand of tamaracks in which to pitch their tent:

> . . . No sooner had we gone to bed than the gale increased; I was sure the tent would soon tear or blow down. So I got up again in the dark and chopped down a large tamarack for a shelter. I had to call Billy to help me drag it in front of the tent. Then I ran down to do what I could to secure the canoe. . . .
>
> *September 6:* The wind continued all night and at daybreak drove a fine rain before it. Had to turn in the rubber blanket to keep off the wet, slapping sides of the tent. I had a restless night and Billy says I talked in my sleep. After breakfast at about nine o'clock, we went back into the tent, where I looked over all my maps and papers. The prospects for reaching home or even Churchill before winter look very dark, but I am resolved to make a desperate try.

On September 8 the weather allowed them to once again resume their "desperate try." They rose at three in the morning and found much better going: "For three hours we paddled and sailed to the tune of five or six miles an hour." The river widened into a lake that extended "almost straight southeast with apparently no shoals and no islands. The shores in contrast to those of the river above, are rounded and smooth affording fine pasture to the deer. We saw many bands. . . . An easy day and perhaps 25 miles covered."

> *September 10:* Up at three o'clock. . . . All day we [felt the tension of] looking out for rocks and some of the rapids took our utmost vigilance. At the foot of one long stretch which had become worse and worse, we had to make a little portage of about three chains. Here I had to carry the canoe alone over some very rough rocks; I was barefoot and angry.

Assuming Ober's weight loss due to the rigor of the journey and the canoe's gain due to soaking and patching, it must by now have been equal to his body weight. As to Ober's anger, it is amazing that, given the pressure of their days, so little suggestion of animosity appears in his journal. Still, there would surely have been many bitter moments between the two during the months of their trial of endurance. It should be remembered as well that Ober had hired Billy for this trip, and, as "boss," he would surely at times have made demands that created unease between them.

That night, triggered by strain and anxiety, Ober's unconscious once again erupted in his sleep:

September 11: In spite of our good campground I had a restless night and Billy said I made dreadful noises in my sleep.... [The river was now] so broad that in the still places we often had trouble to know where to go....

On September 12, Ober and Billy finally arrived at Hudson Bay. As a seal had greeted them at the entrance to the Thlewiaza, in a bit of synchronistic magic an Inuit angel awaited them at its mouth:

... The river quickly broadened to a mile or more and we soon saw with fresh hope a great opening before us. Low, stony shores and islands—with grasses all yellow and brown. Soon after I had tasted the water, Billy saw two queer curling columns shifting against the gray eastern sky. If not smoke, he said, he had never seen anything like them before. Then, while we were marveling at the phenomenon, I saw something black moving on the water and presently there was a boat coming toward us. I saw at once that it was an eskimo in his kyack [*sic*]. Swinging his double paddle slowly from side to side and with two little red flannel streamers on each end of his boat, he came up beside us, and extending his paddle for me to take hold of, shook hands. Then with easy strokes he led the way over to his camp on the north shore.... The Eskimo said his name was [Bight].... [He] waded into the water in his seal skin boots, carried the packs, and brought us wood and his sail to cover the canoe. I gave him in turn tobacco, a knife, a pipe, tea, and sugar. We arranged as well as we could with our few words that he should take me to Churchill in his sail boat....

Ober and Billy had arrived at Hudson Bay near Eskimo Point, 125 miles north of Churchill. The exhausted voyagers had traveled a thousand miles

The Inuit, Bight, awaited them in his kayak

and had a return trip of a thousand miles yet before them, one fraught with suffering and danger, but they would never again feel so alone, so at the mercy of the fates. "All our troubles now seemed over," wrote Ober in his journal for that night, "and I thought ourselves truly blessed."

[8]

A Race Against Winter

Oberholtzer was greatly moved by Bight's friendliness, generosity, and life-spirit: "Before he even attended to his own family, [Bight] made us a wigwam of his sail and carried over his stove for our warmth. This courtesy I quickly refused."[1] Later in life Ober would say that he found the Inuit to be the most hospitable, the brightest, and the smartest people he had ever met.[2] Though Bight visited Ober several times about the money he would earn for transporting the travelers to Churchill, he immediately passed along Ober's presents to his children, "knives, needles, and all. The baby chewed the tobacco and the ten year old boy with the pipe in his mouth took on a shrewd, wizened appearance."

Billy, who apparently was seldom comfortable with the native people of the far north, "lay at the side of the wigwam shivering in his blanket." He was deeply rooted in and identified with the Rainy Lake watershed and was unprepared for the world they had entered. It seems that, within the immense emptiness of the treeless barrens, his sense of reality grew shaky. He found healing and escape through sleep.

On September 14, with a white wolf running along the shore behind them, the party started for Churchill. The Hudson Bay shore was a vast, flat expanse, and the tidewaters were extremely shallow.

> ... All we could see was the gray sky streaked with light along the horizon, water, and rocks. Again and again we scraped bottom, but [Bight] was predicting Churchill in three days when at nine o'clock we ran aground.... [Bight] and Billy got out up to their knees, but the rocks were springing up all around us and all [Bight] could do was to prop his boat.... All of them were smiling in spite of adversity.

His boat grounded, Bight generously made preparations to paddle ashore where he and his family would spend the night. Ober was surprised to find that he and Billy were to be left alone aboard the whaleboat:

> Against my protests he put his necessary outfit and his whole family into the canoe and pushed off with the rough sea. His wife and little children were almost crying from fright as they bent over to avoid the projecting oars to which the canoe had been tied. I watched them out of sight in the dusk and prayed for their safety.

At a quarter past six the following morning, "with one reef in the sail and with a clear sunshine we got away in the billowy green water. All was easy and happy." Bight deposited his family at an Inuit camp near Egg Island and enlisted his brother Ahmat to help them on the rest of the journey. At the camp, Ober bargained for sealskin boots for Billy, getting them in exchange for a package of 30–30 cartridges for which they no longer had use. In his journal entry, Ober noted that Eskimo life was laborious. He saw an "old woman go over for a big load of sticks, which she carried on her back, hobbling along with two sticks [used as canes]." Ober's photograph of this woman is perhaps the most admired of all his photographic work. Despite the rigors of Inuit life, as they continued down the coast "there was great merriment and the good humor was infectious."

Due to bad weather, the mixed group of sailors was held ashore for two days on the trip down to Churchill. On September 18, as they waited for the weather to lift, Bight's propped-up whaleboat tipped and filled with water. With the help of the Inuit, Ober struggled frantically to rescue his equipment:

> The film sack was floating on top; I untied it as soon as I got in the canoe and there to my great delight and thanks to the care I had taken to pack it in a food sack the films were not touched. All else in the sack was soaked.... The men sorted the bad from the good packages of tea and kept the bad [which would still be a luxury to the Inuit if used quickly]; rubbed the numerous needles with duck fat; and put the tobacco before the fire to dry.... We all went to bed early, [Bight] holding matches for me to see until I got wrapped in my blanket.

On September 19, they finally reached Churchill. In his journal entry for the day, Ober certainly understated his relief and pleasure upon arriving at this distant outpost of civilization: "Just at dusk, we sighted land and, half an hour later, in the wildest confusion, we dropped anchor among the breakers at the west side of a bay...." Constable Rose of the Royal Canadian Mounted Police "got out of bed, made supper, and gave us a royal welcome. I talked to the men till nearly midnight, sitting in the kitchen by the warm fire."

Ober and Billy may not have made it through to Churchill had not Bight been waiting for them at the far point of their journey. It is sad, therefore, to read that Mr. R. J. C. Handford of "the Company" took an interest in keeping Eskimo wages low:

> He did not believe in spoiling the men. From his house we went over with the Eskimos to the store. Thirty skins [about ten dollars] were doled out to [Bight] but he was not satisfied and had to be given forty. To Ahmat I gave

*"The ten year old boy with the pipe in his mouth
took on a shrewd, wizened appearance"*

Bight's sons, Ootoopulyak and Ohrutyuk, with Billy sleeping under canoe

Inuit women and girls

Ootoopulyak beside meat-drying rack

Old Inuit woman "hobbling along with two sticks"

ten skins and to each some presents of candy and tobacco and ample provisions for the return trip.... Afterwards talked at Handford's house till ten o'clock.... Slept on a couch between a pair of new H. B. blankets.

Now in a race to stay ahead of the sub-Arctic winter, Ober and Billy left Churchill on September 22, carrying just enough food to sustain them on their 300-mile trip south to York Factory. There is a nightmarish quality to their long paddle down the shore, and more than fifty years later Ober's emotions were still intense as, in the oral history interviews, he told of their struggle to reach York Factory: "These shores have such a gradual slope that [in order to be in enough water to float the canoe] you may end up anywhere from two to twelve miles out during low tides. Traveling at a speed of 3¾ miles an hour, possibly four under very favorable conditions, you might have to spend a couple of hours just traveling away from shore."

They had to time their departure perfectly or become grounded: "We couldn't risk being stranded out there in a storm. That would have been an extremely dangerous situation. I thought about this constantly. It was my responsibility. Billy had never done anything like this before. He had to trust me. I kept track of this situation with my cheap watch."

On September 23 and 24, they were held ashore by heavy winds. On the twenty-fifth, they were able to continue:

Sky still overcast. Light breezes. Launched the canoe on rising tide at half past seven and paddled till half past five in the evening without going ashore. A calm sea and intermittent breezes, veering toward evening to the northeast.... We paddled hard and every bone in my body ached. It was warm enough paddling but, if we stopped to eat, we were quickly chilled....

September 27: Listened for some time to the occasional flurries of snow against the canoe. Got up at five o'clock. Very light north breeze, but the sea was rough. The tide came in in huge breakers, making it impossible to launch the canoe. This was a great disappointment.... Got to bed early, but could not sleep for the mice. Had to get up again and again. The tide roared like a lion.

September 28: The morning felt warmer. Billy who had slept in lazy oblivion during all the trouble with the mice, found two holes in his new sealskin boot. Launched the canoe on the breakers at eight o'clock and paddled on a heavy sea.... We came to a long point where the waves were spouting over the reefs, for a mile out, like volcanoes. We hardly dared go outside and the beach looked too rough for a landing. At last, after a big wave went down my neck, we paddled straight for shore and were thrown high up on the sand beach.... Toward evening the wind went round to the southwest; once more I thought of traveling all night, if the tide should come in mildly. Billy evidently dreaded the idea.... Only the courage was lacking to face the same difficulties as in the morning at night and to make Billy face them.

The following day they paddled until well after dark:

September 29: ... All day the sun shone and at evening went down in a rich sunset. A clear mass of color, toning from wine at the horizon to old gold above. ... There was no wind after dark, but the tide came in over the reefs ... leaped like white fire and with the sound of a sky-rocket. It was almost terrifying in the dark. Then the night was misty and we could only guess where the shore was by sounding with our paddles and listening to the surf. I had all I could do to restrain myself from trying to land too soon. The night turned cold and stung my bare hands. ...

Ober and Billy had paddled for thirteen-and-one-half hours. And the next day, sheathed in ice, wild hay piled round their feet and legs for warmth, they paddled for fourteen hours:

September 30: ... At ten o'clock we were off once more on the rising tide. Billy predicting rain and a big wind. The wind was northeast and we hoisted the sail at once. ... We both had a queer, bewildered feeling: the low tide had left us beyond sight of any definite shore.

They paddled on into the night:

We were able to follow the shore quite easily in the reflected moonlight. ... Hour after hour we paddled on wearily but strenuously in the chill wind. ... With all my resolution, I held off from shore till I thought the tide must have turned. It should then have been midnight. ... We had paddled 14 hours or more without stop and had come between 40 and 50 miles. Billy said in the morning when the sail was skipping us along: "Go some now. Not just same yesterday at all."

It seems that a man named Hegen had an established camp somewhere along the shore that Ober did not want to miss:

October 1: ... The fear that we might pass Mr. Hegen's camp in the dark decided me to wait till night to start. This would give us a good rest. ... Had our supper after sunset and then Billy went back to bed while I waited beside the fire for high tide. ...

In the oral history interviews, Oberholtzer described the night that followed in great detail: "There was a lot of dry wild hay just at that time, and you could use this to get your fire started. But the driftwood gave off vapors that were very hard on your eyes, very pungent. Oh, it smarted. This was because of the salt, you see. I had gathered a lot of wild hay for the canoe, to put around our feet, because they got so cold. I had that ready and our packs loaded."

Ober's journal entry expanded on that lonely and demanding moment:

… It was a clear starlit night with a light and not cold southeast wind. I felt very tired and would have given most anything to go comfortably to bed instead of paddling all night on the bay; but I was thinking of home. At eleven, when I had cooked soup and tea, I waked Billy, who got up glum and very reluctant. …

Ober gave Billy some hot soup. "He was very grateful for that," said Ober. "Then he carried the canoe out. The tide wasn't quite to its full height, but somebody had to stand there with the canoe.

"'You stay here,' said Billy.

"He went back. You couldn't see any moon, but there was some light. I stood there holding the canoe so it wouldn't get away as the tide came in. Then Billy came back with an enormous load. It rose way up in the air. He put this load in the canoe and went back. Well, it must have taken three such loads. We loaded everything, packed in the straw and got in and began paddling, straight out into the night.

… We had got off just before high tide and now the wind seemed to be changing. Billy asked in a bewildered sort of way how the compass pointed. … The grayness of the sea and heavens sent a strange gloomy ache through the body. … I seemed to be moving in a nightmare. …

"My feet were in the hay, but they were soon awfully cold, just painfully cold. I was wearing everything warm that I could put on. I just didn't know what to do with myself. I began counting endlessly, without any meaning. I didn't want to count, but I had to count. I'd go: 1, 2, 3, 4, 5, 6, 7, 8, 9, 10, and I'd think to myself, 'you damned fool,' and I'd go 1, 2, 3, 4, 5, 6, 7, 8, 9, 10, 12, 14, 16, 18, 20. … It was just involuntary.

"I didn't feel like making any effort at all, but we paddled hard. We always paddled hard, all the way, every day. We paddled just up to our utmost. I don't mean we used a racing stroke, not like that, but just the fastest we could go with good energetic paddling. And we went on and on and on."

Ober resisted looking at his watch for fear he would be disappointed. "I didn't want to waste matches either. I kept resisting. Then I saw something moving, almost whirling, in the sky, far off to the southeast. I finally said to Billy:

"'Can it be that it's really getting to be morning?'

"Well, he didn't answer, and we continued on for some distance, paddling with all our might. Then, to my amazement, I saw what must be a mirage, off to our left. There were certainly trees. 'No,' I thought, 'there couldn't be trees out there, way out in Hudson Bay. What can you be imagining?' I'd better watch myself, I thought. I didn't mention it. And Billy didn't say anything. Of course, he must have seen it too."

Following the shore, the paddlers had entered the wide mouth of the Nelson River. The trees were on the far shore of the river. They had made better time than Ober had imagined possible, and by traveling through the night had done exactly what he had hoped to avoid: missed Mr. Hegen's camp in the dark. Ober hardly dared believe they had come so far. "But I was soon convinced," he continued, "that we were at the Nelson. Its mouth was probably five miles across. I didn't want to go right straight across. A wind might come up."

For fear he might yet be wrong, Ober did not voice his excitement to Billy: "I was afraid I'd disappoint him. But then I reached down, put my fingers in the water, and dripped it into my mouth.

"'Are you asleep?' Billy asked.

"'No, I'm not asleep, Billy.' It was *fresh* water! 'Taste the water,' I said.

"So he takes his paddle and drips water into his mouth.

"'Billy, do you know what that water is you just drank? That's *Tchi-ma-og'-ane*' River.'

"Water from the Seine River. So, he knew that it had come from his home. He knew instantly what that meant. He knew that it connected with his home."

The pair took the chance and paddled straight across the wide mouth of the Nelson, then continued down the shore. Almost immediately they came upon a great wooden structure: "It was maybe twenty-five feet across at the base. And built up perhaps thirty feet high—something like that—with cross-pieces. I should have known that this structure marked the entrance to the Hayes River, but it was so close to the Nelson that I could have hardly believed it. Apparently they're only about two miles apart there. So we went on past the mouth of the Hayes [and York Factory, which was a bit upriver] without realizing it was there."

The Hayes River was to provide their escape inland from Hudson Bay on their return journey home. A bit farther down the shore, they landed, and for the first time in weeks there were trees with which to tie up their tent. Exhausted, Ober sank into a deep sleep. He was awakened sometime later by voices. A young Cree Indian from York Factory, hunting polar bears along the shore, had come upon them. In broken English, he explained that they had overshot York Factory by about seven miles. On questioning him, Ober found that, the tide being out, he could walk back along the shore, then use the young man's canoe to cross over the Hayes to York Factory. The young Cree and Billy would paddle Ober's canoe and outfit over when the tide allowed.

Without bothering to eat, carrying their pistol and a bit of chocolate, Ober hiked the seven miles back but was unable to find the Indian's canoe. "Finally," he explained, "I could see York Factory. It looked about a mile away. It was on a high bank, with a building that looked like an exposition building—all whitewashed. And there were several others. Oh, it looked enormous. I could see that there was a stairway going up from the water."

Ober came to a haystack opposite the settlement. A cold wind was blowing, and he was exhausted, "I felt, oh, very bum. I had terrible thoughts like, well, wouldn't it be something if, after having gone through this incredible trip, having traveled all summer, I were to die here at this place, tonight, so close to an outpost. Dismal thoughts, you see. They were with me, and I couldn't get rid of them. Evidently I was low in some way, in my physique, though it came back up like everything afterward."

He fired the pistol several times, but there was no response. "I was kind of surprised. I wasn't, though, when I got over there. It turned out to be three miles away instead of one. The second or third time I fired, I saw some men come out, little miniature men in the distance come out on the level, go down the stairs and get into a sailboat. They put up the sail and started right over. I thought, oh, well, they did hear me then. They see me; they're coming to get me. Well, of course, they never saw or heard me at all.

"Then, at dusk, I looked down the river, straining my eyes, and I saw a canoe. I took a big bunch of wild hay, lit it with a match, and waved it. The second I did this, I saw the canoe turn and come in my direction, straight toward me. When it came up, poor Billy was in the greatest state of perturbation you could imagine. The poor man! He was overjoyed to find that he wasn't going to be left there, stranded, all alone in that desolate country. He was always afraid of that, and he couldn't get me into the canoe quick enough. They made me kneel in the middle, and they went right on paddling. I spoke to the Indian:

"'Where do I go to find somebody?'

"'You go up that stairway and knock at the first door.'

"I went up and knocked, and a man came to the door, most hospitable, and said: 'How do you do. We're so glad to see you.'

"'I've just come from the north,' I said. 'I've just come down from Churchill and a long way before that.'

"'Come right in,' he said. 'We've had engineers arrive just this afternoon, to survey for a harbor on the Nelson River, and we're having tea. You're just in time. Come right in.'"

... [The post manager George] Ray was ... as much bewildered when I handed him the letters from Churchill as I was by all the strange faces. Soon I was eating fried trout and tea and cakes and butter and all sorts of delicacies. Then I got Billy in a tent with some Indians, changed my clothes, and spent the evening telling the company in the billiard room about my trip. I had a kind and appreciative audience.

"I explained that I planned to start out again the next morning," continued Ober. "The Hudson's Bay man said:

"'Yes, but you can't go this late.'

"'Oh, I have to go. I have to get back.'

"'Yes,' he said, 'you have to go, but you can't help it if you're blocked. It's too late to go such a long distance south.' He told me how many hundreds of miles still lay before us.

"'Don't tell me that,' I said, 'because I'm going to go anyway. I know you have the authority to hold me, but I'm sure you wouldn't use it.'

"'There's only one condition under which I'll consent to let you go,' he said, 'and that is that you must make an arrangement to go with the Indians who just came down.' There were six Indians in two canoes. 'You make that arrangement.'"

Somewhat bitterly, Ober came to terms with the group of Swampy Crees who were heading back upriver:

> *October 4:* Nothing would do, according to all the men at the fort, but that I must go back to Oxford House with the same Indians that had brought down the last party. The leader of the Indians said I might get drowned on the rapids and all the white men as usual were sure I would get lost. Much as I disliked tying myself to the Indians, I had to dicker with them till they agreed to take some of my packs and to see me safely over the rapids for $2.00 apiece....

Their journey would once again be against the current, up the swift Hayes toward Lake Winnipeg. The Swampy Crees were sitting on the bank of the river the following morning, waiting:

"'We no like see white man drown,' the old fellow said.

"'Well, that's very good of you,' I said. 'We've traveled all summer through some very hard, rough places, where we paddled with all our might, and I think we will make it up this river, too.'

"'No,' he said, 'you can't go. You can't track. It takes three men to track.'"

When the current is too strong or the river is otherwise too unmanageable for paddlers to make headway against it, experienced canoeists often resort to lining or tracking. One paddler must stay in the canoe to guide it, while the others pull it along with a rope from the banks. As Ober and Billy soon learned, there must be at least two men on the rope for the system to work.

"Two men get out on the line," said Ober, "pulling for miles and miles, high up on the shores. The shores were very high. Billy finally said:

"'Maybe guess make 'um portage.'

"That meant: 'I think we may find a way.' And so we started out. I took the stern, to steer, so the canoe wouldn't run into the shore. Billy went ahead, pulling. With two men pulling, they both pull, but the man in the back lifts the line off sticks and bushes, all kinds of things that it gets entangled with. But one man alone— Oh, it's a terrific job.

"Billy tried it, and he soon had to admit it was too much for him. Well, of course, he was fifty years old, fifty-one, maybe. So I said:

"'I'll try it.'

"I found that with my tendency toward short breath, I couldn't do it either. I played out completely in less than no time. I knew this would be very bad, a serious thing for me to try to do. We held another conference, and Billy says:

"'Maybe try 'um a *An-ga-si-mo'n.*'

"That was the sail. We put it up. We had a straight wind from the north, and we followed the shore just as close as we could. The shores were steep and it was deep, and we sailed so close that we could almost touch them, utilizing every little jut out into the river, taking advantage of that little break in the current.

"With the sail up, to our surprise, we saw we were going along very well indeed. We paddled hard, and that night we continued to paddle on to an island about two miles beyond the party of Indians. This had an instantaneous effect on them: they couldn't do enough for us from that time on. In the morning, they brought us moose meat they had cached along the shore. They were very friendly, and they stayed close to us from then on.

"These Indians were really of great help to us at the point where we struck the real rapids. The rest of the lower portion of the Hayes didn't contain rapids. It was just swift water. It was relentlessly swift. We went at least one hundred fifty miles upriver before we came to these rapids. It was relentless, just going hard all the time without a break. And by this time there was lots of snow. The Indians told us:

"'Tomorrow lots of rapids. Make 'um portage.'

"They had expected to help us with our portaging, but our provisions were low, and the weight of what we were portaging was as low as it ever got. And we were stronger than we had been at any time during the whole trip."

> *October 10:* . . . Indians helped me a little on the portages, but we were usually ready first. Made eight portages and paddled a number of miles in the afternoon above the last on a lake-like piece of river with few swift places. . . . Had to break ice to land or embark at most of the portages.

"These rapids were all just the same. There'd be a widening in the river with a cluster of islands causing the river to turn wild. Maybe as many as fifteen islands clustered, and it became very difficult to know which channel to follow. If we hadn't been able to follow the Indians, we might have wasted a lot of time finding the right channel. Maybe we could have gotten up others, but they surely chose those that were easiest."

On October 13, with the rapids behind them, the travelers arrived at Oxford House, the post near which the Indians lived. "They went in ahead of us," said Ober. "I finally entered, shook hands with the factor [Raymond Bayer], bought a few things, and then I said: 'Now, these men have been very good to us. They gave us moose meat. Here's my Hudson's Bay letter, and you can see that I have only a little money left. So I can't do very much for these men, but I do want to do something.'

"'They told me they don't want anything,' the factor said. 'The old fellow says, in all his years he's never seen anyone paddle up the Hayes River before, two men in a canoe.'

"Well, I gave them some small sum [$2.50 apiece]. Oh, they were very nice. They gave us a fine sendoff."

> ... As soon as Johnie [the old Indian leader] had told Billy how to go down the lake the 34 mile stretch to the river, I started off again, hoping to reach Norway House [at the top of Lake Winnipeg] on the 17th....

Johnie had given his directions in Cree, and since Billy did not understand them, the pair spent almost two days trying to find their way out of Oxford Lake. In the excitement of moving ever-nearer to journey's-end and civilization, Ober was impatient and vexed with Billy for not having understood Johnie's directions and those of other Indians they encountered.

> *October 15:* ... Heard gun shots across the lake, but I thought it was no use crossing if Billy could not understand. After lunch, paddled way back to the opening on the south side and soon found an old shack answering the description given by the Cree guide at Oxford. Still, it was a long paddle to the southwest before we found the mouth of the river.... At noon, Billy had refused to eat, probably because I had scolded him about not paddling....

It would appear that Billy's refusal to eat and to paddle was in response to Ober's irritation with him. In the oral history telling, in which Ober makes no mention of his apparently unjust anger, it is clear that Billy's not paddling was a more significant matter than suggested by the journal entry: "Suddenly the next morning, to my surprise, Billy wasn't paddling. He was steering perfectly, but he wasn't paddling. I made no remark. After traveling with him for so many months, I didn't want the slightest thing to interrupt our fine relationship. But he continued not to paddle. I thought, 'you've got to ask him about this,' so I said:

"'Billy, don't you feel well?'

"'Oh, yes, I feel all right.'

"'Are you hungry?'

"'No, not hungry.'

"'Is there anything wrong?'

"'No, nothing wrong.'

"But he didn't change. He'd take a stroke with no effort in it and just turn his paddle, you see. This went on until evening, and oh, my, I was troubled. I didn't want us to be held up now, maybe indefinitely."

The next day Billy again did not paddle. Ober had had all he could take. "I just turned right around in the canoe and faced him. I looked right at him and said:

"'Now, Billy, I asked you yesterday if you were sick, and you said, "No." Hungry? And you said, "No." Anything wrong? "No," you said, "nothing wrong." Now, for two days you've been sitting back there, and you haven't been paddling at all. You've been steering. Nobody can steer the way you do. Perfect. Nobody can paddle the way you do, if you want to. But I've got to get home, and I want you to understand that, if there's nothing wrong with you, *you've got to paddle. Now do you understand that?'*

"I looked right at him and saw a strange look move across his face. Oh, the most quizzical expression. You couldn't tell what was happening inside that man. He continued to look at me. He didn't hesitate to look at me. Billy opened and shut his mouth a few times, as if he was about to say something, but nothing came out. Then, finally, he spoke:

"'Last springtime, ask Louis Hamel, guess better go on long trip? Him say: "Guess pretty hard trip. Awful hard trip, Billy." Guess pretty good man.'

"Nothing more. He didn't say, 'Guess pretty good man' again. Well, I knew what he meant. He knew how to say it in the shortest way. He didn't need to argue with me at all. I turned right around and began paddling, and he started to paddle so that the canoe went from side to side, just swaying. Oh, I knew he was good and mad. By and by, he settled down, and then he just paddled as he always had, just beautifully."

Though the context here is hazy, it would seem that Billy felt he had been mistreated. Perhaps Ober's frustration, even anger, over Billy's inability to understand directions in Cree had triggered the situation. If indeed Ober had scolded him for this, he surely was unjust in doing so, and Billy made it clear to him that he had had a "pretty good man" at the other end of his canoe for the past several months. Having in this objective manner made his point, Billy allowed his anger to subside. Anyone who has made an extended canoe voyage with another will fully understand how anger can build, and it is indeed wonderful, given the demands and duration of their trip, that Ober and Billy had gotten along so well as they had.

It seems that Billy then felt guilt for what he had done in making his point: "That night," said Ober, "he just couldn't be nice enough to me. When I had tea, he poured the cup and handed it to me. Then he began to talk about things I had asked him about three months before and he'd never answered. He'd had to think them over all that time, you see, to be sure that they were absolutely correct. Then he had to have the right occasion, and he evidently thought the time had come to respond to me. And so it was very nice."

In his article, R. H. Cockburn, quoting from Ober's journal for October 19, described what he recognized as a transitional moment for Ober and Billy, now nearing Lake Winnipeg: "... as they were ghosting past an Indian settlement, 'an old fellow chopping wood' called out to them to stop. 'He shook hands and spoke fair English. Talked of working for surveyors and of long trips and waterfalls and seemed to be wandering in his mind.' As, leaning into their strokes, they left this gaunt, murmuring figure behind, they withdrew also from that vast, timeless wilderness which was to haunt them for the rest of their lives."[3]

But one significant adventure remained for Ober and Billy. They arrived at Norway House at the north end of Lake Winnipeg too late to catch the last southbound steamer of the season: "When we got to where we were to meet the steamboat, we found it had left two days before our arrival. The last boat. Two hundred sixty miles left to go down Lake Winnipeg [to Gimli, with its railroad spur by which they would return to civilization]. At the beginning of winter. And these northwest gales! They were blowing all the time. And the only way to go was down the east shore, because to cross over to the west, we'd have miles and miles and miles before we had any protection. The only thing for us to do was to go down the east shore. Which was all covered with ice, all the rocks—everything—so when you wanted to get off the lake, it made it very hard."

The trip down the lake was to take eighteen days. They were held snow- and wind-bound for six.

October 20: In the night I felt a wet snow on the edge of my blanket. It was still snowing when we got up at about sunrise. Billy made a fire among some balsam trees, where the ground was dry. The wind was northeast and paddling in the driving snow was far from comfortable. We went on a short way and then made a long stop for lunch under some balsams. Another half hour's paddle and we camped for the night. . . . Still snowing hard. I took my notes while Billy cooked.

They were finally on water for which Ober had good maps, and place names now appear in the journal:

October 21: . . . We put across straight for Montreal Point, where we had lunch at three o'clock. I felt very cold and worn out. The wet snow seemed to go straight through my boots. Paddled till sunset on a billowy lake and camped a few miles above Spider Island. Billy cut boughs and started a fire, while I carried the packs and brought wood. He dried me some straw for my boots, made baking powder biscuits and oatmeal, and left the canoe for me while he slept beside the fire. It was a lovely frosty night; a three-quarter moon had appeared high in the east before sunset and gradually mellowed with a clear soft light. The water seemed the color of oil as it rolled up on the steep sand beach. Our fire was among trees bowed with snow.

At this point, though he does not tell what is wrong, Ober seems to suffer his most serious health lapse of the journey. Perhaps luckily, the pair would be weather-bound for four days: "The wind was—Oh, it was just howling," said Ober. "We couldn't go at all. We were still sleeping under our canoe, facing away from the wind. We'd build this long fire right out in front of us, burning, oh, maybe half the length of the canoe. Facing this fire, we were very comfortable.

October 22: ... Sat in front of the fire for two hours after dark, listening to the roar of the waves and watching the fleecy clouds scurry round the moon up above the swaying tree tops.... Now and then [Billy] got up to peer with a lighted stick into the baker [oven. He] reminded me of some stealthy wood spirit stealing out from behind trees and retreating again into the gloom. He sat on his feet, all his body relaxed and his face as inscrutable as a sphinx. Over at the side, the black pot suspended from a crooked stick shone like ebony.

October 23: ... Wind still south and breakers just the same.... Gimli seemed a long way off. I began to feel better, though, for my rest. While we were getting under the canoe for bed, I told Billy the sort of man I had wanted for my trip. [Billy] said, No, he was not that sort. He was too old.

Ober and Billy taking a rest

October 24: . . . The wind had got more into the west and was very strong. . . . After breakfast . . . I sat a while trying to think up stories and then took a long walk along the sands to the point near Spider Island. . . .

The beach sands revealed the dangers of traveling the stormy waters of this reef-ridden lake:

Within one mile I saw three sail booms and a heavy mast 20 feet long. There were also a number of large old boats and a lot of timbers riveted together. . . .

October 25: . . . I still felt unfit for hard paddling and was not altogether sorry that the wind was still blowing.

On October 26, the weather and Ober's health allowed them to start out again. They paddled until ten o'clock that night, under a full moon. On the twenty-seventh they were once again weather-bound. "[We] watched and listened," said Ober. "If we heard the wind go down at two o'clock in the morning, we packed right away and started. Maybe we could paddle till five before the wind came up, or seven. Once in a while we'd have a day we could travel all day."

October 30: . . . Billy said the only medicine man he ever knew that could really stop the wind was "Wah-booso-suh-wee-aha," but he had been dead five years and his bones were five hundred miles away.

October 31: . . . The water froze in my coat and gloves as fast as it sprayed. . . .

November 1: . . . We left at eight o'clock, rounded the point safely and after three hours and a half of churning stopped for dinner in the mouth of the little river beyond Catfish Point. The front of the canoe and my clothes were covered with ice. The little river was frozen solid. . . .

Ober and Billy paddled all through that night:

At two o'clock, having paddled a long way round the shore of the bay, always in sight of Black Bear Island light house, we had a meal on a rocky point probably near the mouth of the Bloodvein River. . . . Camped at five o'clock on a quiet bay of one of the islands. . . .

Ober had come to accept that he would never fully penetrate Billy's mind, but he came closer to doing so at this time than at any other. Perhaps the deepening snow and the sense that they were now paddling ever closer to home brought on the storytelling mood:

November 2: . . . Round the fire in the dark Billy began chanting a portion of the *Ati soh kahn* in a soft musical voice. It was the episode of the two old women that bumped their heads and died in trying to see a moose swim the lake. Then he told me how the old men used to tell the story to the children snowy nights and how it was passed on from generation to generation till now the children have lost their interest. The hero of the story is Nanna-bow-shoo, who first told it. . . .

As they continued on through the wintry waves of Lake Winnipeg, Billy's softly chanted legend would surely have continued to sound in Ober's mind.

November 3: . . . Paddled on till half past two [in the morning]. . . . Cold and confusing in the dark. Sky soon overcast. No moon. Tried to land in bays, which were full of floating ice. . . .

November 4: . . . Started off at ten o'clock in a gentle wind, crossed to the south side of Punk Island, bought fish from a young Islander and got caught in a snowstorm near Gull Harbor Light House. Hard paddle in the cold wind. Had a fine lunch on the gravel beach below the light house. . . .

Again they paddled deep into the night. Their senses now attuned by many months of life in the wilderness, it must have seemed strange to paddle on water over which drifted the pungent smells of civilization:

For three hours more or until one o'clock we continued down the coast in a quiet sea. Could smell barnyards and sooty chimneys and smithees all the way. . . .

November 5: American election day. A light snow in the night. Waked by pleasant sound of dogs barking, cows lowing, and chickens crowing in a clearing behind our grove. Weather warmer and lake calm. At half past nine in clear sunlight we started again. Fishermen putting out in their boats all along the shore. A light variable wind. Reached point near Gimli at half past one o'clock and Billy cooked lunch while I walked into town to send a telegram. Dr. Dunn, the druggist, telephoned my message in the railway station and I told him about my trip. . . .

In the early afternoon of November 5, 1912, Ober and Billy had arrived at the little Icelandic settlement of Gimli. Their great canoe journey had ended.

Ober had told the druggist about his experience, but a bit later he felt the need to protect his story:

Dr. Dunn was asking me more about my trip, but, having learned that he was the correspondent of the Winnipeg Free Press, I had to close down on him.

One wonders if Ober made a mistake in doing so. It is difficult for an individual to convince the world that he or she has done something wonderful, and as would become apparent, Ober might have more wisely allowed Dr. Dunn to celebrate his story in the Winnipeg paper as fully as possible. This preliminary publicity may have led to an enthusiastic acceptance of Ober's complete version of the story.

"We stayed overnight in Gimli," said Ober, "and each of us got haircuts. I took Billy to one barber, and said: 'Give him the best haircut you can.'

"I went to the other. When I came back, I looked into the lobby and saw a man sitting toward the back. I walked toward him, but it didn't appear to be Billy. So I went around to the clerk.

"'Have you seen that Indian who was with me?'

"'Oh, yes, he's in there, in the lobby.'

"'No, he isn't in there now. I just looked. There's just the one man.'

"'Well, that's him.'

"I walked back into that rather dismally lighted place, looking at this man intently, and he was looking at me, scrutinizing. It was Billy, and he had ears for the first time all summer. He had had hair down to his shoulders, you see, and the barber had given him a modern cut, way up the side of his head. We hadn't recognized each other."

The two weathered men with fresh haircuts who faced each other wonderingly that night, in a dimly lit hotel lobby in Gimli, Manitoba, had completed "one of the most commendable canoe voyages in history." They had risen to enormous challenges, and both would be forever haunted and empowered by the months they had spent together in the wilderness.

"This true and sturdy friend"

For those who knew Ober and Billy, their immense journey would in time take on mythic proportions, and it may be that, for Billy at least, the journey was experienced mythically, within a mythic imagination peopled by those archetypal powers of nature with which they had day by day struggled. Ober would never find financial profit in what he had accomplished. The journey, however, established him as a wilderness figure of significance, both in the outer world and, in a psychological sense, within himself.

A journey is imbued with a mythic sense. It is symbolic of a life and of long and difficult stretches within a life. For Ober, "the Hudson Bay trip" would surely serve as an underlying myth, promising in the end a good outcome for another, far longer and equally challenging journey: the journey of struggle to preserve the Quetico-Superior wilderness.

The final pages of Ober's trip journal tell of his transition back into the civilized world:

> Learned to my amazement of the Bulgarian Victories in Turkey and of the Roosevelt exploits. Telegram from home. A warm bath before bed.
>
> *November 7:* Slept at the Fort Frances Hotel from three till eight in the morning. Then called for my suitcase at Holland's, changed my clothes, found a letter at International Falls from Mom, and returned to Holland's for dinner. Listened an hour to pieces on the Victrola. With the aid of the interpreter, found Billy at the hotel at four o'clock, and paid him $84.35 in cash (I had advanced $10.00 at Winnipeg) and a check for $200. This was $2.00 a day for 144 days, railway fare twice and return to Mine Centre, and board and bed at Fort Frances. He said he would deposit $150 in the bank. Then he took my pots and Eskimo boots and shook hands....
>
> *November 8:* Registered at the Ryan Hotel, St. Paul. Wired Associated Press and received negative reply about my story....

How could anyone have communicated in compelling fashion the essence of such a journey in a telegram?

> *November 9:* Arrived Davenport half past six in the morning. Mom at the station, looking very well. Dinner that night at French's.

There with his mother in the warmth of the French's luxurious dining room, light glinting from silver and fine crystal, Ober's story must have gone on far into the night, and his weather-burned face and the light in his eyes must surely have told their own tale to the listeners seated there.

[9]

In Search of Atisokan

Emotionally freighted with the immensity of the Hudson Bay trip, Ober spent much of 1913 in Davenport working out its implications for his life. The shift back to everyday civilized living cannot have been easy. Even as he reveled in his safe return, his body soaking up rest and nourishment, the rhythms of the paddle and the simple yet vital elements of the life he and Billy had shared must have continued in him. Sleeping and awake, primal scenes, vast images of rock and sky and water, must have continued to swirl through his mind.

In Churchill on Hudson Bay, a letter from Arthur Hawkes had awaited Ober. It contained an editorial Hawkes had written about him shortly after his departure into the wilderness. In it Hawkes reveals profound admiration for the young Oberholtzer. He begins by voicing his concern over the trip and the many risks Ober and Billy would be taking. He then makes much of the fact that Ober has inspired the devotion of Billy, an Ojibwe man twice his age: "It is worth much to know a young fellow like Oberholtzer.... When a boyish fellow like Oberholtzer can command such service ... he has a rare and winsome strength in him." Hawkes then tells of the summer he first met Ober "and saw the transparent character that has won the devotion of Billy Magee." He concludes with the following:

> The spirit of the Vikings, the adventurers—who cleared the way for you and me—is not dead. It doth not even sleep. It oberholtzes ... and it sends a wave of admiration and solicitude through the heart of one. Here's to Oberholtzer, and his safe return.[1]

In a letter to Hawkes posted a week after that safe return, Ober wrote, "Thank you very, very much for ... the enthusiastic editorial about a man bearing my name."[2] The two exchanged several warm letters in the following months. Ober also wrote the Canadian geologist J. B. Tyrrell, whose reports had done so much to inspire him to undertake the expedition, and Tyrrell too responded with enthusiasm: "I heartily congratulate you on having made a good adventurous journey which will add materially to our knowledge of that portion of Northern Canada.... I shall hope to see a splendid account ... in one of the good magazines very soon."[3]

Ober then wrote the Reverend J. Lofthouse, bishop of Keewatin in Kenora, Ontario, who had traveled the shores of Hudson Bay as a missionary. He hoped the bishop could help him pinpoint exactly where he and Billy had arrived on Hudson Bay. This was the one part of his sketch map of the unexplored region that troubled Ober. In their letters the two could not come to an agreement as to where exactly the Thlewiaza entered Hudson Bay, but modern maps reveal that Ober's assessment was the more accurate.

Ober had already written J. E. Chalifeur, the chief geographer of the Canadian Department of the Interior in Ottawa, describing his sketch map: "...no pains were spared to secure the greatest possible accuracy under these circumstances. I had the watch and compass before me constantly in the canoe and made the sketch from point to point as we went along, allowing for wind and current in the rate of travel."[4] After receiving the map, Chalifeur responded with interest, but he either could not or would not pay for the use of it. In a letter written December 29, 1913, Ober, close to anger, refused use-rights to the map unless remunerated, adding, "I am under the necessity of making these expeditions pay for themselves."[5]

That final comment expressed more of Ober's hope than his reality. The need to earn money to support the lifestyle he was imagining preyed on his mind. On March 13, 1913, he answered a letter from a fellow Harvard graduate who had written with enthusiasm about Ober's adventures: "My life since graduation may sound interesting, but so far there has been no money in it."[6] The "so far" makes clear that he still hoped his wilderness lifestyle and rapidly expanding knowledge would one day pay off financially. In truth, he would forever make decisions that would make his life interesting rather than lucrative.

In the letter sent to Churchill, Hawkes wondered if Ober had taken steps to get the story into the newspapers on his return. "The Associated Press should be glad of a first class exclusive news story, and of course when you get back to the wire you must not give anything away until you know where you are at."[7] As described earlier, following the advice of his distant mentor Ober had wired the Associated Press from St. Paul, only to be immediately refused. Other publications did show interest, however, including a London-based periodical called *Empire*. In a letter to Hawkes, Ober stated with confidence that he was "writing up a long narrative of the trip and feel sure I can get it published—only the returns are in doubt. I have some fine material." As ever, Ober found it far easier to lecture than to write, and he tells Hawkes that on "the 28th I am to try another lecture [on the trip] here in Davenport."[8]

Though a conflicted desire to do so haunted him into old age, Ober would never publish or even complete a written account of the Hudson Bay trip. Over the years, whenever he did try to write of it he was overwhelmed with emotion. One is reminded of Meriwether Lewis's inability to write of his great wilderness adventure. As with Lewis, Ober's careful journal of the trip may in itself be the significant book he hoped would one day tell his tale.

As an immediate boost to Ober's hazily imagined "wilderness career," it must be concluded that the journey amounted to very little. On the other hand, what Ober valued most was experience—exciting, empowering experience—and from this point of view the trip was an enormous success, a feat akin, say, to climbing Mount Everest with limited technical support. Having accomplished such a thing, having so touched the absolute in one's self, one is changed. And it should again be pointed out that, in both an inner and outer sense, the trip established Ober's authority as a wilderness figure. Neither he nor others who would learn of the trip would doubt this authority, and it would give him an edge when, in the halls of political power, he negotiated to preserve the wilderness with which he had become identified. The experience of his journey with Billy would resonate in Ober to the end of his days, lending him confidence in the face of challenge after challenge.

After his return, Ober was no longer the young fellow who had come out of Harvard with such entrepreneurial drive. He had been deepened and quieted by his great journey, and increasingly his correspondence reveals a self-defeating tone of disgust over the need to "establish some sort of record or do stunts" to succeed in writing for magazines. This is not to say that he ever gave up his ambition to write. Indeed, he never ceased writing, and he lectured frequently and well, but he was conflicted over the value of the kind of writing that might have popularized him. He wondered if such writing was not simply egotistical indulgence.

Ober's hope was that he could somehow find a way to support himself by doing careful studies of wildlife and native people of the north, especially the people. He was powerfully drawn to the native people he had known, and he believed there was much to learn from them. In a personal sense, he seems to have believed that such study would lead him toward greater freedom and authenticity. While in Davenport, therefore, he decided that his next life move would be to once again paddle north and live with indigenous people for long periods of time. He would immerse himself in their culture and collect and write about their lore and legends. He was not formally trained for such work, but he hoped and believed that personal study, intuitive insight, and continuing rich experience would combine to make his work fruitful. He believed it important that he would not be working in a university setting but would instead be on the scene in remote native villages for long periods of time. This would be his advantage. His hope was that, if his work had value, he would be granted enough financial support to continue.

Characteristically, Ober went to leading figures for help. He wrote the famous anthropologist, Franz Boas of Columbia University, telling him, "I have in mind to devote five years or more to living and traveling alone with natives."[9] Ober wanted to know the value of what he might collect and to get information about scientific methods of studying native culture. In the oral history interviews, commenting on his exchanges with Boas, Ober explained that he did not know "how he may have been in actual life, but he was very forbidding, and he didn't encourage me in any way to go ahead without my at first spending about three years with him studying phonetics.

"But Goddard at Harvard—he was the man there when I first went north—was very encouraging. I was trying to find out if some institution might not enable me to do this work, you see. They wouldn't have had to pay me very much, but I wanted to be able to live up here. My handicap was that I had no *official* training, and they didn't think I could do it. But I had one thing that the rest of them didn't, and that was very rich material, very rich."

No one has ever described Ernest Oberholtzer as a shrewdly practical man, and he greatly underestimated professional resistance to an amateur's receiving such support on the strength of a few, even brilliant letters. Unable to find institutional funding for his new dream, Ober then did what by this point one might expect: he went ahead on his own. More than anything else, it was the experience he craved, and maybe, in the end, something could be made of it. In late June of 1914, he arrived again in the border town of Fort Frances, Ontario, on Rainy Lake. Though both his plans and his finances were at best skimpy, he was prepared to paddle north again.

At five-year intervals, Ober's Harvard class of 1907 privately published reports on its members. Most people have individuals or groups, often parents, to whom they look for affirmation about the course of their lives. For Ober, lacking family other than his mother, his Harvard classmates were one such group, and his reports to them were rich and lively, among the best in the collection. In the Fifteenth Anniversary Report, published in 1922, he wrote with more certainty than communicated by his journals that, "In Spring of 1914, I returned to Rainy Lake with the intention of going through to Hudson Bay once again, this time by way of Trout Lake and the Severn River."[10] And late in life, his Fifty-fifth Annual Report, written when Ober was seventy-eight, explained that, "If I had been able, I would have located at the isolated post of Fort Churchill on Hudson Bay, for the next five years at least, studying the wildlife and the native tribes—Crees, Chippewayans, and Eskimo."[11]

Before leaving Davenport, Ober had received a letter from Mine Cen-

tre trader Louis Hamel telling him that Billy Magee was visiting somewhere on the U.S. side, but, on passing a Fort Frances hardware store,
Ober looked in to see his old traveling companion. Ober was surprised
and, it seems, dismayed by the news that Billy had married since they had
parted. "His excuse," wrote Ober in his journal, "was that his stepfather
had died and he was lonely."[12] But, yes, Billy *would* be interested in a two-
or three-month trip north with him.

Billy's canoe, that of the Hudson Bay trip which Ober had given him,
was being stored at Fort Frances. It was in rough shape, and Ober, digging
into his limited financial reserve, had it repaired that very day. They were
to leave the following morning, but Billy did not appear. Perhaps he had
got to thinking about their last trip and how lucky they had been to make
it back alive. It was pow-wow season, and traditional dancing and celebrating may have seemed a more pleasant alternative to a newly married
man in his early fifties. In Ober's Fifteenth Anniversary Report to his Harvard classmates, he wrote that Billy's wife had "put her foot down on any
project of more than a few hundred miles,"[13] and this may well be the
truth of it. Ober's friendship with Billy continued to be one of the most
important relationships of his life, but from this point on, Billy would often prove elusive.

Ober waited five days for Billy before giving up on him. He had drawn
on quite limited resources to repair the canoe, but, as it was Billy's, he decided against taking it. Instead, he bought a new, lesser one for $42.50 and
began paddling northward alone. In 1909, Ober had mapped the region of
interconnected lakes and streams he was now paddling through, and
much of it, even its people, were familiar to him. Nevertheless, he had
some difficulty finding his way, and paddling alone is far harder than
with a partner. Still, he had acquired great skill with the paddle, and,
though small, he had the strength and endurance to push steadily on. He
passed an Indian camp at Bear Pass, and on July 14 he arrived at Gold
Rock, a failing mining town. As usual, he had his violin along, and the per-
former in him now enjoyed the opportunity to provide music for the local people:

> At eight o'clock paddled across to Martin's Store where I had been invited
> to play the fiddle. Had to repair the tail piece first with a piece of hay wire.
> Mrs. Martin played the piano accompaniments.

At Gold Rock, Ober paid two dollars to have his canoe and equipment
hauled over a long wagon portage by a careful Danish farmer who wa-
tered his horses at each opportunity. Paddling again, nearing the tiny settlement of Wabigoon, Ober was almost capsized by a large passenger boat
that served the region. A handsome Indian caught his canoe deftly with

a boat hook, and Ober was given free passage to Wabigoon, where letters from home awaited him.

Ober found Wabigoon to be an attractive settlement, set well above the lake of the same name. At least one of its more substantial homes reminded Ober of an English inn. He camped on nearby Powder Island and began making friends with local people. Like many, even educated people of that era, Dr. White, the pharmacist from whom Ober bought medication, found it hard to understand why anyone should be interested in Indian culture. What, he wondered, could be Ober's "purpose in studying the Indians"? However, Dr. White liked Ober and gave him a tour of the islands in his sailboat. Then there were the Pidgeons, a couple in the currently lucrative business of live-trapping breeding stock for fur farms. Ober noted in his journal that "all of their red fox and many of their mink and fisher had only three legs," undoubtedly because they had been caught in leg-hold steel traps.

The Pidgeons took Ober cruising about the lake in their motor launch, the husband piloting, the wife caring for the engine. Ober was enamored of the pair, especially Mrs. Pidgeon, who painted and played musical instruments. They were unabashed poachers and told of a time when game wardens arrived at their home:

> Mrs. P. had hidden a shoulder of venison in the oatmeal bag. In the barn a kitten was playing with part of the deer heart. She stepped on it. Held out the kitten to the officers to admire and slipped the heart up between her legs. This shows her resource. She is wary, observing, versatile. Knows how to get around Indians and understands animals. If they are to be believed, they are making money and having a good time to boot.

Ober thought the Pidgeons would be good source material for stories, but he seems never to have written about them. He also got to know Guzlick, the Indian who had fished his canoe onto the Wabigoon passenger boat. Guzlick had good English and was educating his children at Kenora. He gave Ober the Indian name "Man of the North," and when he heard Ober's plans to live with and study Indians in remote villages, he offered to join him at two dollars per day. Ober, however, had reservations:

> *July 18:* . . . He probably has good qualities, only he strikes me as too white and talkative. Becomes a boor by his insistent praise of himself. . . .
> *July 20:* . . . I am completely at sea about going north. I have no money and know I might not go. Yet Guzlick (Day) is anxious to start.
> *July 21:* . . . I went to town half intending to wire Harry French for money, but my pride rebelled.

After anguishing over the situation, Ober gave Guzlick ten dollars to cover his hotel bill and told him they would not be going. In his journal, he listed three reasons:

1) Poor news from the markets. [Apparently Ober had received a small in-heritance from his grandparents.]
2) Lack of money.
3) The need of writing immediately.

Ober concluded this entry with, "The thing now is to act immediately on my resolution to write."

On July 25, Ober paddled on to Dryden, a somewhat larger town situated on the railroad. He had been told there would be camps of Ojibwe berry pickers on nearby islands, and he hoped to learn from them while he worked on short stories for boys' magazines. He had been told about some of the Ojibwe people he might meet. One was an ancient woman named Joemie who had "never smoked or taken a drink of whisky. Reported to be 200."

Ober located Joemie's camp that very evening. It was a friendly group of women, children, and dogs. He was to "return in the eve for Atisokan [legends], but [was] too long in finding a camp." He pitched his tent down the island from Joemie's group, and the following morning "heard footsteps of berrypickers around me several times, but only saw one of them—a boy who came to my tent, but hurried away." When he later went over to their camp, Ober found that men had arrived and the women were now more reserved:

July 26: ... Two men were present. ... [The] younger one of some white blood who went into his tent and let his young [woman] fondle him in plain view. This was a modern tent, containing pillows, a suit case, a small trunk and a phonograph. ...

[The young woman] was the most beautiful [Indian woman] I have ever seen—dark, Roman nose, raven eyes full of spirit and a frank open manner. ... By and by she began telling a wonderful story, full of gestures and life—something about a canoe. Her eyes sparkled, she laughed, and her hands were busy portraying her meaning. The man too took part in word and gesture and the others laughed or threw in an occasional comment. When she had finished, I said, "Is that part of the Atisohkan?" "No, I was talking about the movies at Dryden." The man said they did not know the Atisohkan. ... On my way back I had a rather hopeless feeling about the possibilities of making friends with the Indians.

Ober was far too aware not to be laughing at himself, at least in part, at this point. In the journal, he rebounds from his depression, writing:

Barriers between whites and redmen. Good essay. "Visit to an Indian Camp." Or a story about a high-minded young man who idolizes a beautiful young Indian girl and then finds his mistake. She cannot understand his ideals.

Ober had been raised in the tradition of the Victorian gentleman, and though, like most people, fascinated by sexuality throughout his life, he would never be comfortable with open sensual expression. As previously suggested, it seems as well that his sexuality was confused and never openly expressed. He soon became friends with a number of Indian men and boys:

July 30: [Lands's] boy Phillip, aged 13, is . . . keen. When the girl hit him in the balls with a stick, he said, "Look out, you will kill all my kids."

July 31: . . . The boys had their shirts strapped on as bathing suits and I wore a bandage.

August 18: Paddled to town in the afternoon, stopping on the way to watch the boys swim in the bay. There were 15 of them in at once—all youngsters.

Ober continued to think about the attractive young Ojibwe woman:

August 2: . . . I found at the camp the same girl who had talked to me in English the Sunday before and who was then making love to a man in the tent. She is pretty and speaks good English with a pretty foreign accent. Does beautiful bead work.

Another young woman found him attractive, and was aggressive about it:

August 16: . . . As I left [Sohgum's] youngest daughter, seated on the bank, boldly shouted some unclean insinuations about sleeping in my tent, etc. She is decidedly forward and unattractive, in spite of her big legs, which she probably prides herself on.

In all of his writing, one searches in vain for any hint that Ober ever succumbed to such an advance.

This summer of 1914 marked the beginning of World War I in Europe, and Ober, given his recent extended stay and embassy work there, was both troubled and excited by the news. He could get the Canadian papers in Dryden, and night after night he stayed awake past midnight, reading accounts by candlelight in his tent. On August 8, "After some hesitation I sent the following night message ($1.00)—"

Secretary of State
Washington D.C.

Have honor to offer my services at Washington, abroad, or preferably in Canada during present emergency, if useful in any capacity to State Department. Experience Vice Consul Hanover Germany, 1911. Record and references on file in Washington. Residence, Davenport, Iowa. Present address, Dryden, Ontario, Canada. Could report immediately.

Ernest C. Oberholtzer

In the August 15 journal entry, he noted: "Received acknowledgement, by mail, of telegraph to Secretary of State." No mention was made of its content, but the United States was several years away from active involvement in the war, and it is clear that he received no call. On the eighteenth, however, he received a mailing from his mother containing his old passport, which would identify him in case he was again "arrested as a spy." As described earlier, in the summer of 1909 Ober had been under such suspicion and briefly arrested. Given attitudes of the time, this young man with the German name, fluent in the German tongue, who asked so many questions and may have talked of his work as vice consul to Hannover was ever in danger of being considered a spy. Increasingly during his stay in the Dryden area, he was accosted and insulted by men and women aflame with anti-German sentiment.

In Ober's Fifteenth Annual Report to his Harvard classmates, he wrote that, "In 1914 at the village of Wabigoon in Ontario, my work among the Indians was so incomprehensible to the few white settlers of the region and my name appeared so wicked, that I was detained for a few hours as a German spy. When it was found that I neither intended to blow up a Canadian bridge or to take a census of Indian men available as soldiers, I was finally given a delightful note from a Government official, urging me to go on with my work, but for my own safety's sake to change my wicked name."[14]

At his island camp, Ober was now writing stories intended for *Youth's Companion* and studying the Ojibwe tongue. He was less than certain, however, that his language study had value:

July 30: ... The Indians here speak a lingo—perhaps a conglomerate of several dialects—so that perhaps I [am] wasting my time trying to learn it. Lands says every reserve has its own dialect....

Ober found the Ojibwe response to his efforts to learn their language interesting:

August 9: Amusing and somewhat disconcerting how the Indians [respond to] a man who is trying to learn the language. If he happens to say a word correctly, they laugh in a surprised, indulgent way.... No offense. They are pleased and [are expressing] their wonder.

Apparently the members of the Ojibwe community had begun to appreciate Ober's interest in their language and culture, and his relationship with them grew warmer. On August 23, he joined in a big dance, which he describes with exquisite detail in his journal:

... In the afternoon, while I was in the shack, Alec's uncle came and announced that a lot of Indians and "girls" were coming for a dance. Ed (True

Carpenter?) had brought his fiddle. I put on a clean shirt, a tie, and my green hat for the occasion. The day was getting colder, so that I had to wear my woolen over shirt.

Such a dance—Drops of Brandy, Breakdown, Scotch Reel, Sets and a Virginia Reel (called Ginger Ale), which I taught them. The wooden platform over by the shack was soon in ruin owing to the hilarious breakdown of a few of the men notably Alec's brother. This fellow is a really handsome Indian—tall, spare, well-proportioned, and with a nonchalant manner. He enjoys life, like one for whom life is easy and good. He was the mirth of the crowd, bringing down the house by some of his variations. The girls are all slovenly dancers—without rhythm or zest. One very pretty girl from the far island, Sohgum's daughter was dressed with diamond (?) ornaments, rose-colored hair ribbons, big combs, and half tan shoes. She is a minx with sly eyes and a shifting resentful mouth. Even the girl who had brought me the blue berries joined in. She was the best dancer of all. All the time Ed played the fiddle and rattled his feet like a jumping jack.

I tried teaching them the Virginia Reel out in the grass. No doubt their naming it Ginger Ale was a sly dig at my objection to whiskey. They are prone to laugh at silly things and to ape white men. Ed looked like an old man, when he tried to dance. He is stiff and worn-out and shows plainly that he is not well. Rather a sad expression at times. . . . I left them at half past six, hoping to catch a fish.

Ober had begun writing in earnest. Near his island camp, he discovered and cleaned an old shack furnished with a table and chair. In it he could write more comfortably, especially in bad weather. He had always loved to tell stories and as an assistant Boy Scout leader in Davenport during the past year had held the young scouts spellbound. He thought therefore that he might earn money by selling short stories in the boys' adventure genre. This writing moved rapidly forward:

> *August 18:* I finished the "I'm Madt" story and tried to start another. . . .
> *August 19:* Finished story of sick Indian on Hudson Bay. . . .

On September 21, Ober paddled to Dryden and sent off ten short stories to *Youth's Companion.* For his stories in the boys' adventure genre, Ober used the pen name Ernest Carliowa, a nod to his beloved grandfather, his home, and the richness of his childhood. He had worked hard at polishing these stories, perhaps overly hard, for the most frequent editorial criticism of them was that they seemed strained and artificial, that they did not have a "tone of reality and naturalness."[15]

On September 24, Ober gave "Fly [a dog that had been abandoned on his island] a full meal of liver and bread," then pointed his canoe southward toward the United States. He spent the night in Wabigoon with the Pidgeons. Having slept on the ground throughout the summer, it is not surprising that his final journal entry for that date was: "Delightful, soft bed."

On October 6, back at Fort Frances, Ober spent his "last 5 cents for ferry boat" to cross the Rainy River to International Falls, where he was forced to survive for several days without money. He had considered wintering north of Wabigoon in an abandoned house of the Minnehaha Mining and Smelting Company, but at Fort Frances he heard that a family named Ogaard had a new cabin on Rainy Lake a mile above Ranier and might like a "sitter" for the winter. And indeed they would. Ober paddled to the Ogaard cabin, where he found they had left delicacies for him to eat as well as dishes and utensils. His local address was now Ranier, Minnesota, as it would continue to be for most of the next half-century.

Throughout the summer, Ober had occasionally received checks from his home in Davenport. Whether this was his own, possibly inherited money or Rosa's is uncertain. In any case, in his journal entry for October 20 he was able to write, "I am again a Lord of money." On November 5, however, he received bad news: "Word that *Youth's Companion* had returned all stories...." And then on November 11: "I write Harry [French] and borrow $100."

Ober had previously published in *Youth's Companion,* and one of the rejected stories would eventually appear in *Boys Magazine,* but it was clear that such writing was not to be an easy means of support. Time would tell that success in the genre of boys' adventure writing would require a developmental effort that Ober was not prepared to make. In part at least, the problem was that he probably approached these stories, not seriously, but as "potboilers" with which to support his life in the wilderness, hence the criticism of artificiality. If, on the other hand, he had brought his full depth and complexity, his authenticity, to them, it is unlikely they would have remained suitable for the boys' adventure market.

Throughout the winter, Ober continued his cultural work with nearby Ojibwe, and by the spring of 1915 he had collected a considerable amount of material. His principal informant was Pierrish Jourdain of Fort Frances, a man of French and Indian descent nearing 100 years of age. A Davenport friend had connected Ober with Dr. Truman Michelson of the Department of Ethnology in Washington, D.C., and Michelson requested Ojibwe stories from him. On May 8, 1915, Ober sent him two of them. In his cover letter,

Pierrish Jourdain,
Ober's principal source of
Ojibwe legend and lore, 1915

he explained an apparent delay, telling Michaelson that Rainy Lake had been open in the middle and he had to carefully choose his times in crossing over to Fort Frances.[16] Dr. Michelson's response was appreciative. He had read the two stories with interest, especially "the Nanabojo [*sic*] story... as it was the one I could most easily control, namely, by use of Jones' Ojibwa texts.... The most valuable part of your work is the accenting of the Ojibwa words which Jones ordinarily does not do...."[17]

Michelson's letter becomes technical, and Ober's reply is, if anything, even more so:

> I am glad to have the suggestions in your letter of May 22. The phrase "mi ima kaye win eji nimit" and the preceding two puzzled me; and I see now that my final solution was incorrect. If there is any error in the text, it is more likely in the word "wabamak" than "nimit" for the words were carefully reread. I shall have to report to you later on this point.... I think you are right about "wabamaat Nanabojoon." No "w" was sounded between the two "a"s but the same difficulty has appeared elsewhere and seems to be solved by your suggestion....[18]

In reading these exchanges, it is apparent that Ober had been an adept student, that he had a wonderfully sensitive ear to language, and that, at least on the page, he was becoming fluent in Ojibwe. At the same time, as professional interest seemed focused on details of language rather than on mythic content, one begins to wonder whether the young Oberholtzer, whose imagination was forever casting about for new adventure, would continue with this work for the long haul, especially since there seemed no ready way to derive an income from it. In truth, though his dream of living with native people and studying their lifeways would never leave him, his collecting would not develop much beyond what he had achieved by 1915. Once again, however rich and valuable the experience for Ober himself—such study grounded him ever more fully in his adopted place and its story—it had come to naught in terms of his effort to establish himself in a sustaining career.

[10]

Rainy Lake Living

By 1915, Oberholtzer had established himself more or less permanently on Rainy Lake, a 330-square-mile expanse of clear water with some 3,000 forested islands on the Minnesota-Ontario border. In the early years, Ober camped on various islands during the summer and lived in a beached houseboat on the mainland in the winter. His mailing address was Ranier, a village near the southwest corner of the lake, three miles east of the much larger town of International Falls. As he was often on the move enjoying and studying the region, it could be argued that Ober's home had become the entire 14,500 square miles of the Rainy Lake watershed.

Nineteen-sixteen was a year of transition for Ober. In March, still focused on collecting Ojibwe legends, he made a physically demanding trip to the Red Gut Indian Reserve on the far north end of Rainy Lake, which he reached by cutting cross-country. A warm sun had caused the snow to melt during the day; then the thermometer plunged. In his journal for the trip, Ober wrote that while pulling a toboggan through deep snow he froze his right foot:

> *March 12:* . . . It was now very cold and still. Moonlight. I went ahead carefully on the edge of the river which was broken in many places. From the mouth [of the river] the wigwam is less than a mile away from the point of the first island. I cut off my snowshoes and began chopping wood at once, for my feet were like rocks. Pat [Ober's Ojibwe companion] kindled the fire and put the packs inside but offered no other assistance. He was too anxious to sleep. We soon had a warm fire but I had great trouble getting my moccasins off. My whole right foot, heel and toes were suspiciously white. I used snow in a pan and kept putting it on for three hours without getting much of the white out. Then at midnight I began to think perhaps the whiteness was due only to [callused] skin. So, dead tired, I went to bed. Immediately, however, the pain in my foot gave proof of freezing. I spent a very disagreeable night and rose at 8 in the morning with a badly swollen, inflamed foot. The dogs, of course, were too tired to haul me and there was nothing for it but to tramp 22 miles or more to Red Gut.[1]

Despite Pat's indifference to Ober's frozen foot, the journal of this trip reveals a growing respect for Ober among the Ojibwe. This may have been partly due to Billy's telling of the Hudson Bay trip—surely this story had been told and discussed many times—but it is clear too that Ober's generosity, his growing knowledge of the Ojibwe language, and his continuing and sincere interest in Ojibwe culture all played a significant part. It is in this journal that the name the Ojibwe gave Ober is first revealed:

> *March 29:* At noon one of the little boys led me round to a delightful fishing scene. We walked an eighth of a mile round the point on the right. There nestled a multi-colored colony of blanket wigwams, each sheltering a fisherman. The poles can be driven into the snow and the blankets arranged according to the wind. Today the wind was from the north-east and the sky heavily overcast. Without exception the women objected to photographs. One, old Hard-Ground's wife, was exceptionally picturesque. She had caught a considerable number of fish and sat on her bough dais in perfect well-being. Her head was bound in a red handkerchief. Her large round figure looked healthy and comfortable. She laughed heartily and told how the children said: "There comes Atisokan. . . ."[2]

Atisokan, meaning "legend" or "teller-of-legends." The name was given Ober because of his unrelenting interest in those important Ojibwe tales. When after several days of hard travel Ober caught up with Billy on his trap line, Billy's first words to him were:

"*B'jou',* Atisokan."

In the oral history interviews, Ober explained that the demands of the trip to Red Gut led to the return of his heart condition: "Due to overconfidence on one of the severe winter trips, I came under doctor's care again and was in danger of having to leave the region for good. I had evidently overestimated what I could do. I had two occasions when I blacked out: once when I was crossing the street in International Falls, and once when I was trying to start an outboard motor. Anyway, I was allowed to stay, under strict restrictions as to what I could do, and all that summer I lived on an island with my mother."

Rosa had first visited Rainy Lake the summer before, in 1915. Her intention was to drag Ober away from this "northern nonsense, now he's so well again."[3] Ober, however, remained the authority in their relationship—at least outwardly—and, as it turned out, Rosa herself found a home in the north country. According to Ober, her first two days on the lake put her to the test:

"I'd rented a cabin on the Canadian side from Dr. Dunsmore of Minneapolis, a very generous summer resident, who took great throngs of people up to his place and entertained them during the summer." The Ogaards, whose cabin Ober had "sat" the winter before, offered him the use of an old boat with one of the "earliest outboard motors, which were never very reliable. When my mother arrived on the train—there was a day train then to Ranier—we started out that same afternoon for our cabin.

"It was kind of amusing. It was a nice summer day, but blowing very hard from the south and very warm. It was seven miles over to the cabin, directly out into the open lake. We hadn't got very far—maybe two miles—when the motor stopped. The boat was heavy and clumsy and couldn't be rowed back. We drifted with the wind. And soon there were signs of a storm—thunder and occasional lightning as evening approached. Finally, we were able to land on a little island, and we made up our minds to stay there for the night. My mother wearing her white dress.

"Well, I was pretty well prepared for the situation. I put up a little tent, and I assured Mother that she'd be all right. This was hard for her to believe. She'd never spent a night outdoors before. She sat bolt upright all night in the tent as lightning flashed in all directions. And she was imagining every moment that the tent, at least, was about to burn up, if she didn't. Or both of us. She was mostly concerned about me. She didn't want to lose me. She'd always been devoted to me, but never an affectionate mother. But I knew that she thought I was worth preserving."

The following morning, with the help of a friendly man who lived on a nearby island, they were able to make it across to Dr. Dunsmore's: "By now," said Ober, "it was mid-morning, and my mother [feeling bedraggled] begged plaintively:

"'Now, when you go up to Dr. Dunsmore's, if he's there, don't mention that I'm along.'

Ober and Rosa in camp

"I went up and asked for the key. Dr. Dunsmore was a very gallant man. His wife had been dead for quite a number of years, and he always had all these girlfriends up there—women of various ages. Usually there was one special one he devoted himself to during a summer."

Dr. Dunsmore did somehow manage to discover that Rosa was along:

"'Well,' he said, 'I must go down and see your mother.'

"That was just his nature. So he went down, carrying about half a crate of muskmelon under one arm. He presented this to my mother with his compliments and said how happy he was that we were going to be his neighbors. Then he said:

"'But you must come up now. My daughter is here with one of her friends.'

"'Oh, Doctor,' my mother said, 'that's so kind of you, but I'd like to get installed over at the cabin first. Then we'll see you at the first opportunity.'"

Despite protestations, the disheveled Rosa was led by the arm to dinner at the doctor's. "The other two women were in immaculate white, you see, and they looked very charming indeed." After dinner, Rosa was again unable to escape:

"'Now, we're going out in our cruiser,' the doctor said, '*The Explorer*, this afternoon, Mrs. Oberholtzer. We're going to the northern part of the lake, which is the most beautiful.'"

Rosa was "propelled into the boat" and given the tour. "She was very much relieved at the end of the day when we were able to go over to our own island."

On arriving at their cabin, Ober had an experience expressive of the mystical side of his nature: "Then something happened that was very strange indeed. I don't know how I happened to be in such a psychic state that something so appalling.... I went in through the kitchen first, opened the door, and walked into the living room. And there appeared to be a corpse—that was the impression I received as I walked through the doorway—of someone laid out and covered with a sheet. It was an instantaneous impression. Then I realized that, of course, it was impossible. A minister, Faries, and his wife had lost their only child while living in this cabin. They had a four-year-old child who drowned. They had packed all their things in this room. That's how I got the impression."

This sudden vision was so strong that Ober feared his mother might see it: "I snatched the sheet away, and it was gone before she could see."

With the return of his heart condition, Ober was, comparatively speaking, laid up during the summer of 1916. Nevertheless, the one-time student of landscape architecture supervised the building of a summer

home for an old family friend from Davenport whom he had guided on a
canoe trip into the Quetico the previous summer: "The friend was Major
Horace Roberts," said Ober, "and the island was named Atsokan." Using a
variant spelling, Roberts had given his island Ober's Ojibwe name. "My
mother and I camped out on the island during all of the summer, and we
cooked out of doors, something she had never done before."

In 1916, the United States and Canada were edging ever closer to involvement in World War I, and once again Ober felt it necessary to ask
Arthur Hawkes to write a letter, to be used while traveling in Canada, that
would identify him as a patriotic U.S. citizen. Ober was truly interested in
the international situation, but, given the strength of his pacifism, it was
lucky for him that he was never able to pass a military physical exam. In
a letter written to William Hapgood, soon to become his business partner, Ober's intensity of feeling about the oncoming war is apparent:

> ... It is hopeless, it seems to me, to reiterate those perfectly easy platitudes
> as to the origin of the war or to hold any individuals or set of men responsi-
> ble. There is a larger and, I think, truer way of looking at it, which holds
> every one of us responsible. It is the world as constituted at the time the war
> broke out, our colossal ignorance and selfishness, that is to blame. You
> know how it strikes me? I feel as if men everywhere, spiritually oppressed
> by the uncomprehended evils of society, have mistaken their enemies and
> hurled themselves against the only tangible units, other nations; in other
> words, that all men, though they know it not, are fighting for the same goal.
> And the only actual result of it all, if even that shall come, will be to flood
> men's consciousness with light and show that the problems are internal,
> problems of government, of organization, of ideals.... If we believe in war
> and killing as a means to an end and an end that we believe in, then all right;
> if not, why not some great act, that shows our conviction in peace and the
> ways of negotiation. Agreement, not dictation, is the goal....[4]

Ober's suggestion of "some great act, that shows our conviction in
peace" was to become a continuing theme for him, and in a decade he
would be advocating one such great act: that the wilderness of Quetico-
Superior be set aside as a peace memorial dedicated to the war dead of
Canada and the United States.

By mid-1916 it seems to have become clear to Ober that his work with
the Ojibwe would never support him financially. This was underlined for
him by the return of his heart condition. Synchronistically, it was then
that, on Atsokan Island, he met William Hapgood, to whom his letter on
the war had been addressed. Hapgood was a fellow Harvard graduate and
a member of a wealthy and influential eastern family. It has been written
that he and his brother Norman, the editor of *Collier's Weekly,* were able
to converse through extended periods of time using only quotes from

Shakespeare.⁵ Almost immediately William Hapgood enlisted the bright and charismatic young Oberholtzer to manage (and eventually become his partner in) a project to develop Deer Island on Rainy Lake for agriculture and tourism. For Ober, who lived in at least intermittent anxiety over his lack of gainful employment, the Deer Island project seemed a blessed opportunity, and he threw himself into his work on the 375-acre island with his usual intensity:

"This was a large operation that I'd been given scot-free permission to plan," said Ober. "Of course I kept Mr. Hapgood informed." Ober planned to divide the island into zones, similar to his later approach to the entire Rainy Lake watershed. "We decided we would take the interior of the island and gradually clear it where it had good soil and carry on a farm operation there. And also raise sheep. We were going to keep the outside of the island wild, with summer cabins along the shores. Mr. Hapgood purchased a large boat, and we built a store. Whatever we couldn't furnish at the store, I'd simply mark down, and the first time I went to town I'd bring it back out."

Ober and Rosa were supposed to have a farmer working with them, but this was often not the case. Luckily, Ober's health had once again stabilized. They raised chickens as well as sheep: "We had an incubator and we raised chickens in large numbers. It became my duty to execute all the chickens, which I didn't enjoy very much, but I did it. I'd pick them clean and we'd sell them [in International Falls]. We sold eggs, too, at a high price. We got $1.00 a dozen during the First World War. We also sold lambs. My mother was called in every once in a while to help with farm operations, though she'd never been a farmer. She played the piano instead. But she always willingly took part, if there was no sign of suffering on the part of the victims."

One farm operation that Rosa wanted no part of was "docking sheep's tails," said Ober. "They all had to be docked, you see, and we had no help at the farm. One morning I told my mother:

"'We've got a little job I'd like you to help me with.'

"'What is it?'

"'We've got to dock the lambs. Otherwise they'll get flyblown. Very dangerous.'

"'Ernest, I can't do it.'

"'Well, there's just nobody around. We can't get a soul to help, and I have to do this right now. I can't wait.'"

Finally, Rosa agreed. "But, oh, my, she didn't like this idea at all. I'd catch the lamb and put it in her arms, and she'd turn her head away as sharply as she could, and I'd burn the tail off. It's the approved way. You heat the iron to just the right temperature, and off comes the tail. The little lamb jumps, but then it goes right over to its mother and starts nursing, you see. And my mother had to endure this, one lamb after another, over a hundred times. It was just as if you'd burned *her*. She got burned over a hundred times. When we were done, she said:

"'Never again. Never again, Ernest. Don't ever ask me to help dock sheep again.'"

On another occasion, Ober needed Rosa's help barging sheep to town: "'Now, somebody will have to be in the barge,' I said to my mother.

"As a tranquilizer, you see. So they wouldn't all jump overboard. If one jumped over, they all would. [The gunwales] weren't very high, and it would have been a terrible thing to have all those sheep in the lake. So there she was, my mother. And the motor wasn't running right."

Motors often did not run right for Ober. It was a "four-cylinder motor, in a big boat," he said, "with about two hundred feet of rope connected to the barge behind. The boat would stop every once in a while, and I'd have to kneel down to work on the engine. I finally got it going on about three cylinders, thinking I was lucky to have managed this. I was just congratulating myself on the fact that I had it all going, when I turned around, and *the barge was gone!* I didn't know where it had gone. I didn't know. I was all alone. Working on the engine, I had drifted north with a south wind, you see, toward Canada, out among the islands. My mother was out there alone somewhere with all those sheep. She was somewhere on the other

Rosa with sheep

side of the islands—just where I didn't know. After a little exploring, I got around to the north side of the islands, and there I saw my mother standing at the front of the barge, waving at me."

Ober and Hapgood hoped to expand their operation beyond Deer Island to another owned by the province of Ontario. An indication of Hapgood's clout was that the acting secretary of the U.S. Department of Agriculture agreed to write a letter on their behalf to the minister of Lands, Forests, and Mines in Ottawa. Containing a smelly sort of patriotism, it reveals much about the tenor of the time:

> Two American citizens, Mr. William P. Hapgood, of Indianapolis, Indiana, and Mr. E. C. Oberholtzer, of Davenport, Iowa, have started a sheep raising project on some little islands on the American side of Rainy Lake, where Mr. Hapgood has had a summer camp for some years. They have gone into the sheep raising business largely from patriotic motives, with a view to increasing the food production of the country in war time. . . .
>
> They find that their small islands are hardly large enough for the development of the project they have in mind, and are anxious to lease some lands on Sand Point Island which they understand is the property of the Dominion government. Their object is not primarily profit, but a patriotic one. Of course they hope to make both ends meet and come out at the end of the year with a small profit, but whether the profit is small or large is to them a matter of strictly secondary consideration.
>
> These gentlemen are both American citizens, born in this country and born of parents who were born in this country. Mr. Oberholtzer comes from Swiss stock, though from his name you might suppose he was of German ancestry. Mr. Hapgood comes from one of the best known and most public-spirited American families. . . .[6]

With the old-boy network working for them, Ober and Hapgood were allowed to buy Sand Point Island—desirable property because of its fine beach—but they were never to develop it. Another letter of this same period, from Ober to his Uncle Henry in Iowa, reveals how fully he was consumed by his new work:

> I was of course delighted to receive your kind and appreciative note about the little article I wrote for the Duluth paper about Rainy Lake. . . . I really do not have any time for that sort of thing nowadays, nor of course do I ever do any of the old traveling with Indians. It is all farming and developing land on a 375 acre island. We've had a very busy summer, though not nearly such hard physical work as for the last two years. . . .
>
> My mother has been here with me since April—in fact she has only been to town twice in that time. [The letter was written in October.] In spite of the fact that she is never very well, she raised over 600 incubator chicks,

geese, and turkeys. . . . She will return to Davenport, I think, as soon as cold weather comes.

It has been a very good summer here for crops—no frost on the island till the night of Sept. 29th and then a very light one. We raised over 400 dozen ears of sweet corn on half an acre of land. . . .[7]

Ober continually tried to find farm workers so he could concentrate on management: "One spring we hired a family to help with the farm, and the week they arrived [one of the children grew very ill]. It had become difficult to cross the ice, and I had to make the expedition into town. I brought the doctor out over the ice at the end of a rope, [pulling a sled]. It was Doctor Mary Ghostley. She's a famous person in the north. A very, very fine woman. She brought all the diphtheria antitoxin they had. The father had told me he'd lost another child the same way and that it had taken on the same peculiar color this one had developed. Well, the child *did* have diphtheria, and the doctor used all the antitoxin she had on all the members of the family.

"'I'm almost certain the baby is going to die,' she said.

"And the baby did die a few hours later. Dr. Ghostley told me I would have to go into town and get permission from the coroner to bury the baby. We went in again that night, and I didn't get back out until the following afternoon. In the meantime, I'd got a Swedish worker we had with us to dig the grave. I had to be the preacher and perform the ceremonies. The next morning the parents sent word over to our living quarters that they thought they were getting diphtheria. I didn't think it could have developed that soon. I looked into their throats and couldn't see a thing wrong, but they were panic-stricken.

"It had frozen hard that night, and I knew if we were going to get them across, we had to do it right away or not at all. The family was so frightened they couldn't walk. All they could do was get onto the sled. It had iron runners and the snow was entirely gone from the ice, so I was able to pull them the two miles to the nearest habitation where I could phone Dr. Ghostley."

Ober then pulled the family to the mainland where they were placed in a smallpox "pest house" for observation. As it turned out, he had been right, and the family was soon determined to be well.

In a recent interview, Ober's long-time friend, photographer Ray Anderson, stated that "people have said that after her husband died [Dr. Mary Ghostley] would have married Ober in a minute. I don't know if it was true or not, but I know he had a lot of respect for her, and she was up here on the island. There are pictures of her on it. And Ober told a story: He said he'd always wanted to witness an operation. So, she made arrangements for him to come and see an appendectomy. It was in the winter, and he had to walk across the ice to get to town. Anyway, he walked into the surgery—It was warm and he'd come in from the cold and there was a certain amount of ether in the air. And he passed out immediately."[8]

Others agree that Ober could have found a partner in Mary Ghostley. One old friend of Ober's, Marnee Monahan, remembered Dr. Ghostley as an admirer of Ober, but, she said, "Ober had a way of running away."[9]

There has been and continues to be considerable unresolved conjecture as to Ober's sexual orientation. At this point in the story, he is a young man of great charm, now in his mid-30s, who seems not yet to have established a romantic relationship of any kind. Many believe he was a repressed homosexual. Others think he was simply sexually repressed or even asexual. The early death of his brother Frank and abandonment by his father surely burned deeply into Ober's psyche, as well as that of his mother, and Marnee and others believe that Rosa somehow stood between Ober and love relationships with women. They believe that, due to her simultaneous loss of a son and husband, she had taken a desperate psychological grip on her surviving son, a grip from which he was never to be free.

Rosa had followed Ober to Harvard, to Europe, and now to Rainy Lake, but, strangely, this continuing bond between mother and son was maintained without physical contact. In his telling of the story of their first, storm-filled night together on Rainy Lake, Ober pointed out that Rosa was never an affectionate mother. He went on to say, "I don't think she ever kissed me in her life, unless it was when I was a baby and can't now remember it. She had a certain reserve, and this was more or less peculiar to our family. Quite different from some distant relatives who kissed at every possible moment. When they came to visit us, there would be quite a kissing match at their arrival, and I would run up into the attic to avoid it." Indeed, Ober would eventually build for himself in his Big House on Mallard Island a secret attic hideout—equipped with bed, bookshelves, and a writing table—which he apparently sometimes used for just such emergencies.

According to Marnee Monahan, Ober carried what he called "a certain reserve ... peculiar to our family" with him into old age. It was an aura that surrounded him that one did not pass through. Despite an otherwise fine warmth, a marvelous sense of humor and an exceptional "magnetism you can't describe," he was not to be touched.[10] Others have pointed out, however, that this prohibition against physical touch seems not to have applied to boys and young men, which surely supports the argument that he was a repressed homosexual.

A great aunt of Ober's in Davenport, Grace Parkhurst, with whom Ober was very close, longed for him to marry and believed she had found the ideal mate for him. In a letter written after Rosa's death, she pleaded:

Oh, Ernest, putting all jokes aside why can't you see Camilla with our eyes. She is pretty, good, sweet, faithful, industrious, a perfect woman, and loves you.... She would be as devoted to you as your own dear mother was.[11]

After Rosa's death, Ober would in fact begin a relationship—a deep and loving friendship—with a woman named Frances Andrews that was to last until her death more than thirty years later. By all accounts, however, their tie was a platonic one, and Ober was careful that it be seen as such.

In 1920, Oberholtzer and Hapgood made the decision to incorporate the Deer Island project. At this time, perhaps to gain both financial and legal support, they took on a third partner, an International Falls attorney named John Brown. The articles of incorporation show that the capital stock of Deer Island, Incorporated, was to be $50,000, divided into 500 shares, with a par value of $100 each. The peak allowable indebtedness of the corporation was to be $20,000. An annual stockholder's meeting was to be held on the Monday following the twentieth of July of each year. William P. Hapgood was the first vice-president and secretary, Ernest C. Oberholtzer the first president and treasurer. On December 31, 1920, the assets of Deer Island, Inc., amounted to $22,465.15. Its liabilities were $30,909.61.[12]

The thirty-six-year-old president of Deer Island, Inc., Ernest Carl Oberholtzer, must have felt that questions as to his career had been finally resolved. To boost tourist rentals of shoreline cottages, he ran advertisements in large-circulation magazines, including *The New Republic* and *The Atlantic Monthly*. Everything seemed to be flowing along nicely. Then, in 1921, Hapgood's Indiana business, the Columbia Conserve Canning Company, suffered reverses. One hearsay story has it that a son who was a political radical organized the company's labor force, thereby triggering his father's financial difficulties. Whatever the reason, Hapgood began to withdraw his support for the Deer Island project. Then he began to liquidate its assets as well.

Ober, whose contribution had been his and his mother's unrelenting work, was now left holding a rather empty bag. Exchanges of letters in 1922 show that the final settlement of affairs with Hapgood was a bitter experience for the now not-so-young Oberholtzer. In settlement, he was offered either $5,000 in cash to be paid only after all other corporate debts had been paid or Sand Point Island, an attractive property with a fine beach on the Canadian side of the lake.

It seems that, in lieu of salary, Ober had already been promised three of the four Review Islands, a cluster a half-mile south of the Canadian border, locally called the Japanese Islands because of their narrow shape. One of these was the Mallard, an acre and a half island near Deer Island on which Ober and Rosa had been living. Their shelter had consisted of a pair of old houseboats. The first of these, the Wannigan, had been a floating kitchen for lumberjacks of the log booms and then a floating casino, crossing borders as need be to stay ahead of the law. The other, Cedar Bark, had for a time, it is said, been a brothel, perhaps a floating one, serving the jacks of the booms a different fare from that which they had enjoyed on the kitchen boat.

The deed for the Mallard was mailed to Ober on March 9, 1922. Part of the deal was that, should Ober in the future decide to sell the island, Hapgood would have the option to buy it at current value plus cost of improvements. Ober would therefore lose any inflationary increase in the value of the island. This detail stuck in his craw, but it perhaps kept him from selling out during the depression when he was often financially desperate. In a letter, the third Deer Island partner, attorney John Brown, advised Ober on his settlement with Hapgood:

> ... I have looked over the excerpts of correspondence which you sent me some time ago and I am of the opinion that if you brought suit against him for an accounting that you could very likely establish a right to a share of the Deer Island property or at least secure adequate compensation for the work you put in there during the last few years. I think the court would undoubtedly view the enterprise as a joint adventure between you and Mr. Hapgood, you putting in your work and time and Hapgood the money. But litigation is always attended with a good deal of inconvenience and loss of time and particularly in a case of this kind would not be at all pleasant. By taking the Sand Point property you are probably taking a loss at this time but I feel confident that in the course of a few years you will more than make up that loss by the increased value of the property. ... [13]

Following Brown's advice, Ober accepted Sand Point, the property they had bought from the government of Ontario. Ober would own this island for more than fifty years, and though it held the finest beach on Rainy Lake, he refused to develop it and kept it open to public picnicking, swimming, and camping. In 1975, less than two years before Ober's death, the "227 acres of golden beaches, forest and granite ledges on the south shore of Sand Point Island" was signed over to the Province of Ontario "in consideration of a sum of money between $35,000 and $40,000."[14] Ontario has continued to use the island in a public-spirited manner in accordance with Ober's wishes.

The Deer Island venture was Ober's final serious effort to build a career—likely one in which he would have succeeded had not his partner failed him—before his leadership role in the Quetico-Superior struggle would emerge. It is ever the case that, when one is losing, one is also learning, and in the Oberholtzer files there appears a torn scrap of paper containing the following:

> *What I've Learned from My Experiences with the Hapgoods*
> Always to question the authority of opinions. Never be overawed.
> Be self reliant. Trust my own convictions and more inclusive views.
> Develop your own individuality. Insist on your rights. Speak your mind and demand your own.
> Avoid the pitfalls of impulsive good-nature. Do not be an easy mark. Keep in mind and emphasize your personal purposes....[15]

In his Fifteenth Anniversary Report to his Harvard classmates, written in 1922, Ober offers a lively description of the Deer Island project that contains but little bitterness:

> We investigated the raising of deer, goats, and fur-bearing animals and the culture of wild rice and blue-berries, but finally settled upon sheep raising.... The activities speedily developed into a ten-ring circus—land-clearing, the moving of cord-wood ten miles to town on barges, a store, gardening, sheep and poultry, construction of farm buildings, docks, piers, and cottages, a marine railway for hauling out and repairing boats, and lastly a summer resort. Though I was not able to pass any of the tests for the army, this was in fact a five year orgy of physical activity, with no books, magazines, or music and practically no contact with the outside world. It was the life of a day laborer among the half breeds, Indians, and outlaws of the north woods; and as a result at the present time I have nothing to show for my activity except larger muscles, improved health, and a certain fluency in northern profanity....[16]

In this report to his classmates, Ober revealed that during the Deer Island project he had turned down two jobs that his work kept him from considering: In 1918, he was offered the position of scout executive at Davenport, Iowa. And then, "In the Spring of 1921, I was offered tentatively a position on the faculty of Antioch under the new plan of education just inaugurated; but this letter had to wait three months for a reply, because it was the season of the Spring break-up on Rainy Lake and in addition I was in the middle of an epidemic of diphtheria and smallpox without help on Deer Island."[17]

After the break-up of Deer Island, Inc., Ober was uncertain as to whether he would even stay in the north country. He had always been drawn to urban high culture, if not to other aspects of urban life, and in 1922 he spent time in Chicago, apparently managing a securities account for his mother for which he received $1,800. The Internal Revenue Service questioned his expenses, and in his letter of response, he explained:

> The salary paid me by Mrs. Oberholtzer was for the management of a securities account with Messrs. Hulburd, Warren, and Chandler, 208 S. La Salle St., Chicago. This account was conducted largely on borrowed funds. Owing to its hazardous nature and the rapid fluctuation of values, I was obliged to make two trips to Chicago and to spend a total of 16 weeks there in 1922....[18]

Rosa's federal tax return for 1922 shows that she made a profit of $8,458.23 from the sale of securities that year, suggesting that Ober had done good work for her during his stay in Chicago. It was while in Chicago that Ober wrote his Fifteenth Anniversary Report to his Harvard classmates. In it he described his re-immersion in urban culture, and his uncertainty as to his future is apparent:

> By means of books, the movies and white friends I have been adapting myself to the changes of the past ten years—to "jazz," Bolshevism, and psychoanalysis; but the adaptation has not yet been complete enough to convince anyone that I am worthy of a job. My plans therefore are somewhat indefinite and running pretty close to the breadline. I am in doubt whether to keep on trying to regain the estate of a white man or to take the short and easy road of the aborigines. The chances are that I'll be back on Rainy Lake again this summer, sitting in smoky wigwams and recording ancient tales in Ojibway.[19]

Ober did return to Rainy Lake. His Deer Island career had dissolved, but, in compensation, a new freedom opened before him, and, as can be seen in the following list, his multitudinous enthusiasms once again rose to the surface:

> *Program for Summer,* 1923
>   Narrative of Trip to Nutheltin.
>   Adventure book for Boys.
>   Short stories: Crusade of Children for Peace. Marysport Subject. Boy's
>   Adventure. Nature articles.
>   Indian Study: Language. Customs. Atisokan.
>   Violin. Memorize. Play with piano.
>   Note-books.
>   Photoplay study.
>   Photoplay writing: Children's Crusade. Northern story.
>   Swimming. Nature study. Investigation of islands. Visits to Indians.[20]

In the three years after Deer Island, Inc., folded, Ober went through a confused scattering of efforts to make a living. In the above to-do list, he included a daunting number of writing projects, none of which were brought to fruition. Near the end of the list is the fragment, "Investigation of islands." The tourist side of the Deer Island enterprise had made Ober aware of the value of island properties for those who wanted summer retreats. With the advice and a promise of financial backing from Harry French, the childhood friend and now successful Davenport lawyer with whom he had traveled to Europe, Ober began to explore possibilities in area real estate. He thought he could manage business of this sort without too much damage to his "real interests." Though he wrote flocks of letters and otherwise spent considerable time exploring possibilities, there is no indication that Ober ever earned a dime in these early efforts to buy and sell Rainy Lake real estate.

In 1923 and 1924, Ober was twice forced to borrow $1,000 from Harry French who, it seemed, would do almost anything to help his struggling friend. One is reminded here of Arthur Hawkes's editorial description of Ober's capacity to inspire devotion, noting that "It is worth much to know a young fellow like Oberholtzer." A letter from French dated January 30, 1924, displays the tone of his generosity:

> I note you state you have written me relative to an additional loan. I have not yet received this letter and accordingly do not know the amount you desire. Any amount which you would be likely to ask would be entirely convenient to me. If you are in a hurry, I suggest you draw on me at the First National Bank, Davenport....[21]

And in a letter posted a day later:

> I have at hand your letter of January 27th and in reply thereto I take pleasure in enclosing remittance for $1,000. I called on your mother yesterday evening and was glad to find her well and cheerful....[22]

In the summer and fall of 1924, a wealthy Chicago industrialist, Bror Dahlberg, formerly of International Falls, was building a large and impressive lodge to be called Red Crest on nearby Jackfish Island. Dahlberg was in Chicago, and, knowing that Ober had supervised construction of Major Horace Roberts' summer home on Atsokan Island in 1916, Dahlberg now hired Ober in an effort to minimize costs and control the drunkenness of his builders. In a letter to Ober that preceded their arrangement, Dahlberg complained bitterly of Emil Johnson, a master carpenter who would prove central to the development of Ober's own Mallard Island buildings and over whom Ober seemed to have considerable influence:

> From the reports I get he has done no work whatever and not only did he do no work but he was plain drunk all of the time.... As a matter of fact, not only has he been almost perpetually drunk himself, but he got his men into

that condition also, so that not only has he accomplished nothing for me but he so conducted himself that none of his helpers or men did any efficient work.[23]

Under Ober's supervision, the construction of Red Crest did move forward to completion with efficiency. The terms of his agreement with Dahlberg are not known, but on September 20 Ober received a check from him for $877.21.

It may be that Ober's greatest achievement during this time of flux was the early development of his own tiny home island, the Mallard, and with it a natural, yet culturally rich and elegant lifestyle. During the Deer Island project and again at Red Crest, Ober had discovered the carpenter Emil Johnson who, when sober, was considered a genius with wood. It is said that whatever Ober could imagine, Emil could build. And the cost of his labor "was right." As late as 1940, Emil was charging Ober—who usually paid above scale—forty cents an hour. Lucile Kane, who conducted most of the oral history interviews with Ober, wrote of the island's evolution: "With the aid of local craftsman Emil Johnson, [Ober] began constructing a series of buildings that utilized native materials and conformed to the natural landscape. Given names like ['Japanese House,'] 'Cedarbark House,' 'The Bird House,' and 'Old Man River House' these

Japanese House, built as a study for Ober in the early 1920s

marvels of native architecture served as home for Oberholtzer, his mother, and their many guests."[24]

Journal entries for a 1924 trip to the Red Gut Reserve in Ontario suggest that Ober was now interested in authentic, high-quality Indian crafts, perhaps for resale to his "many guests," the often prosperous friends who had begun to arrive for visits on the Mallard. In addition, some of these visitors paid rent for extended summer stays. For such friends, Ober had a number of brochures printed called "Canoe Trips Arranged By Oberholtzer" in which he listed lakes, streams, portages, and campsites. This factual material was interspersed with anecdotes and bits of local color.

Indeed, as Lucile Kane described it, the Oberholtzer mystique and his island lifestyle had caught fire in the imaginations of many: "Summer brought a steady stream of visitors to the Mallard. Oberholtzer entertained his guests with canoe trips, violin concerts, and his gift for storytelling. He often arranged for his friends' sons and other boys to stay at the Mallard and accompany him on canoe trips."[25] One of the boys with whom Ober would paddle was his long-time friend Ted Hall, who has often attested to the excellence of Ober as a mentor. Hall also recalled that Ober was by nature a caretaker:

> Ober had a way of making a camp so congenial you never had the feeling you were roughing it. He had a way of facing the fly of the tent just so or

Dramatic events were encouraged.
Ober second from left; Rosa fifth from left.

finding little places to cook, so that suddenly you felt this little outdoor apartment had been designed particularly for you.[26]

Surely, much of Ober's solicitousness had been learned from Rosa. After her death, he would write of her self-sacrificing nature that, "Though weak and crippled for years, she continued to administer without murmur to the sound and able-bodied, even though it meant the denial of much that she held dearest."[27] It is Ober's contention that Rosa, whose health was seldom good, managed to maintain high spirits even while regularly cooking for ten or fifteen guests in the kitchen boat. In an interview, one of these guests, Katherine "Kit" Bakeless—that woman who, along with Rosa, Ober thought a worthy accompanist to his violin-playing—attested that Rosa was indeed a good and happy cook with sparkling black eyes. Kit found Rosa, like Ober, to be a fine storyteller. Photographs of Rosa show her to have had a rather forbidding appearance, and Kit could not deny this: "Well, she frowned. She had a tick, that kind of thing, but, oh, she was jolly. She was very jolly."[28]

Kit Bakeless and her husband, John, were New York writers, and John would one day dedicate his biography of Daniel Boone to Ober. In her interview, Kit told of their first arrival at Ranier: "There was Ober meeting us at the train, dapper little Ober. He was shorter than I. [He had] wonderful blue eyes from gazing off over lakes. Do you remember his eyelashes? His eyelashes would make a girl swoon."[29]

Ober's charm was clearly exceptional, and dozens of friends doted on him. Though he lived with anxiety over his lack of a clear-cut role in life and his inability to earn a good income, the young man who had once troubled Billy Magee with his incessant drive was now also able to become lost in imagination and creative play, in story and music and the beauty of place. This ability to lose himself in the moment may have worked against his ability to earn, but it had much to do with the personal magnetism that drew others to him.

One frequent guest at the Mallard during these years, a favorite of Ober's whose wit and *joie de vivre* perhaps equaled his own, was a young New York lawyer named Sewell Tyng. He and John Bakeless had been at Williams College and then Harvard together, and he was the one who had introduced John and Kit to Ober. Tyng was a member of "the Deer Island gang" and was married to Ruth Hapgood, the daughter of Norman Hapgood, the editor of *Collier's Magazine*. Sometimes innocent, sometimes devious, Tyng was a large, nerdish-appearing man with thick glasses who experienced wide fluctuations in weight. His energy was immense and his genius considerable. He was an eastern blueblood, his mother a mem-

ber of the Biltmore family, her second husband a Vanderbilt. In World
War I, Tyng served with the Red Cross ambulance group in France, then
as a second lieutenant in the Air Force. At the Paris Peace Conference, he
was Herbert Hoover's private secretary. According to Ober, Tyng was as
comfortable with woodsmen and Indians as with the financial and cultural elite, and under Ober's tutelage he too bonded with the waterways
and portages of Quetico-Superior.

Ober and Tyng inspired each other, and when they came together, life
grew more abundant. In a 1924 letter in which Ober responded to Tyng's
request that he share a canoe trip with him and Ruth, the flood of joyous
affection between the two is apparent:

> Sure, 'tis strange to have a friend in Wall Street; that magic world seems so
> out of the ken of a humble woodsman. In truth, it could not be credited
> except for your picture of the bronco canoe, recalling unmistakenly our
> Sewell of so many exploits, the restless explorer, him of the prodigious land-
> clearing and of the Seven League Boots, who wandered "lonely as a cloud"
> one moon-lit evening over the whole terrain of the Jackfish hinterland. You
> are fast becoming for those of us, who still survive a sort of legendary char-
> acter, the Paul Bunyan of this region....
>
> A number of happenings are giving us hope. The sun shines brilliantly
> every day and, though water still freezes every night, summer is gaining.
> The narrow places between islands the last few days have again become
> azure blue water. The big lake will soon follow. Spring birds are return-
> ing—cautiously—and singing lustily every time the north wind abates. Two
> days after Easter my mother returned and took up her abode in that same
> paper-shelled cedar[bark] boat where I languished and shivered all the live-
> long winter. And now, before I'm fully thawed, I'm invited to go exploring
> with Paul Bunyan and his wife, northward bound....
>
> So this is all. We are looking forward eagerly to your return. If I cannot
> join you in rediscovering the north, maybe I'll be able at least to go as far as
> the first portage; and in any case I'm ready to load you down with misinfor-
> mation about portages, camp sites, and mythical lakes. It would be alto-
> gether too simple for you and Ruth without misdirection of the kind in
> which I love to specialize....[30]

The friendship between Ober and Tyng was, however, to go far beyond
high jinks and enjoyment of the wilderness. With exceptional energy, intelligence, legal acuity, and an array of important contacts, Tyng would
become a central support figure for Ober through the first two decades of
the soon-to-emerge struggle to preserve a wilderness. From the point of
view of conservationists, Tyng was to prove himself a man of great heart,
ready to generously give his all to preserve the natural integrity of the border lakes region.

Ober had been allowed exceptional freedom to work out his youthful enthusiasms. During the time of life when most are taken over by the demands of establishing career and family, the ongoing necessities of child-rearing, Ober continued to self-actualize. He had been allowed to be, as Nietzsche described it, a wheel rolling out from its own center. That is, he had been allowed to become more and more fully his authentic self. His secure and protected early childhood in comfortable circumstances, his adventurous spirit and richly eclectic education, his health problems, his empowering mother, and perhaps even his repressed and sublimated sexuality, all allowed him freedom from the usual developmental limitations. Instead, he deepened and individuated. Though he was never to become a biological parent, he would become a cultural parent of significance, a great teacher, a mentor to many exceptional young men. In this way, he would pay for the many gifts he had been given.

From the psychological point of view, Oberholtzer had gone through a tremendous developmental effort that seemed to have led nowhere. At the age of forty, he had yet to create a public persona that reflected his many facets. He had no clearly understandable role. Nevertheless, he was admired, and no one could deny his great discipline and capacity for self-denial when expressed through his chosen interests. This was true even of the Deer Island business venture, the failure of which, as has been noted, cannot be blamed on him. It must be mentioned here as well that the Deer Island project provided Ober a great deal of practical experience in the everyday world of the Rainy Lake watershed, experience that would soon prove useful.

Here at the end of the story of Oberholtzer's youth, a story so absolutely fundamental to the contributions of his middle and later years, it is interesting to note that had he succeeded in establishing his career as a writer or as president of Deer Island, Inc., he would not have been free to give his life to the wilderness movement with which he was soon to engage. The myriad streams of his life, so many of which seemed to have run dry, had prepared him exquisitely for his soon-to-emerge true calling.

II

Quetico-Superior:
The Program

[11]

A Mission of Transcendent Importance

Oberholtzer once wrote: "Man was made for broad scenes and tall shadows. He craves a noble background. Cramp him, and he revolves in an ever narrowing circle, until finally he doubts his own destiny. The song goes out of his heart."[1] In the mid-1920s, the forces of civilization, embodied in one powerful individual, became a threat to the "noble background" Ober had chosen for his life.

By this time, Ober's bountiful enthusiasms and abilities had led to a fascinatingly holistic lifestyle—integrated with nature and yet cultural and congenial—in which scores of people were privileged to participate. Theoretically, he could have chosen to protect and cultivate this private life, perhaps even have found a way to earn an acceptable living while doing so. It is seldom, however, that someone blessed with exceptional capacities is allowed a life of private enjoyment. Somewhere around midlife such a person is awakened to responsibility for something larger than him- or herself. He or she awakens to the realization that one is not isolate, but deeply interconnected with the larger whole. One aspect of Buddhist thinking has it that the laws of life keep one from coming to rest in private bliss, that one must eventually take on the bodhisattva role and work mightily to "save" the world. It may be that, when one wakes to the call, opportunities to do such work are always close at hand. In any case, Ernest Oberholtzer found it so.

In 1924, the year in which Ober turned forty, conservationists began to hear whispers of a threat to the lakes and streams of the Rainy Lake watershed. By the following year, they had come to know of a plan to turn much of the watershed into a hydroelectric power basin through the construction of a series of seven new dams. The size of the area to be affected was 14,500 square miles—an area larger than Massachusetts, Connecticut, and Rhode Island combined—and it contained within it the Superior National Forest and the areas that were to become Voyageurs National Park, Quetico Provincial park, and the Boundary Waters Canoe Area Wilderness. The mastermind of the plan that would have drowned these areas was lumber baron and industrialist Edward Wellington Backus. A figure of great power and prestige, Backus had yet to fail, in any significant way, when it came to wresting what he wanted from the wilderness. In Backus, Ober had found an opponent well able to take his measure.

Though in later life Ober sometimes talked and wrote as if he were one of the first whites to enter the Quetico-Superior region, more than two centuries of white activity had preceded him there. From the beginning, the vast majority of those of European descent to enter the region were not subsistence oriented, but extractive in their intentions. They sought furs and minerals and lumber. They sought material wealth.

In the 1890s, Billy Magee, perhaps unknowing of the inevitable result, had guided timber cruisers into the Rainy Lake watershed. By the 1920s, much of the region's great virgin forest of white and Norway pine had been cut. The early lumber industry was a brawling, often lawless enterprise, and many lumber barons of the time gained immense tracts of land through fraudulent homestead claims. Edward Backus was something of a late-comer to the region, but he played its harsh and often questionable games with ruthless mastery.

In the years just preceding the threat of Backus's proposed dams, another struggle had begun, triggering public debate as to the best human use of the area. This controversy had to do with the building of roads into and through the wilderness. The lumber industry wanted roads to reach desirable stands of timber, and the U.S. Forest Service felt it needed roads to patrol Superior National Forest and protect it from fire. Real estate developers wanted roads opened to pristine lakes; county governments wanted new landowners and dwellings on these lakes to add to their tax rolls; and the local tourist industry wanted roads that would allow visitors to enter the region comfortably in that recent invention Ober would never learn to operate, the automobile. Even as the pressure for more and more roads grew, the border lakes region was becoming popular as the most wonderful canoe country on the planet. Spearheaded by the Izaak Walton League of America, those who favored traveling silently by water fought the building of new roads.

Ober played no part in this struggle to limit the building of roads, but surely he absorbed much of the story of this early preservationist effort. In that his lone year of graduate study at Harvard had been in landscape architecture, it is interesting to note that three of the most important early visionaries in the effort to preserve the wilderness character of the region—Frank Waugh, Arthur Carhart, and Paul Riis—were also landscape architects. These three either worked for or otherwise advised the U.S. Forest Service on how best to manage federal lands, and they were in agreement that wilderness canoe travel was the best possible use for the boundary lakes. In the past the Forest Service had assumed its central role to be the support of the lumber industry, but it had begun to see that wilderness recreation might also prove an important use of its lands, and under the influence of the three landscape architects, the service began to limit its plans for new roads.

The Forest Service did not, however, cut road-building plans enough to satisfy the Izaak Walton League. It was at this point that service employee Aldo Leopold, one of the great environmental minds of the twentieth century, indeed, of any century, worked out a compromise with Seth Gordon, conservation director of the Izaak Walton League. Leopold convinced Gordon that the Forest Service plan, which included some roads and a smaller wilderness area than the Waltonians wanted, was nevertheless far better than long-term stalemate, during which much could go wrong. Their agreed-upon plan, with its balance between commercial and recreational activities, had something in common with and was surely at least an indirect source for the one Ernest Oberholtzer would later develop for the area.[2]

The Izaak Walton League was satisfied with the Leopold-Gordon compromise, and in 1924 conservationists breathed easier. But for only one year. In the oral history interviews, Ober described the emerging threat posed by the Backus plan: "In early 1925, rumors began to emerge of a new industrial project, fostered by the great timber user of Minnesota, E. W. Backus. He lived in Minneapolis, but way back in 1909 he had constructed a dam across the Rainy River. Then, in 1925, it was suddenly rumored that the great industrialist who had constructed the dam and established a large paper mill at International Falls had envisioned and was working toward a much more ambitious program. It would involve not just Rainy Lake, but the whole watershed. This meant the whole area drained by the Rainy River, spreading like a great fan out into Ontario and northeastern Minnesota. It included thousands of lakes of every possible kind, all connected by waterways, so that one could put in a canoe at any point [and reach any other] within the watershed. About two-thirds of the overall area was located on the Ontario side."

In a series of articles written for *American Forests and Forest Life*, Ober more fully explained the Backus threat to the boundary lakes: "So completely successful had [Backus's] man-made operations proved that . . . the author of [so much] local prosperity [then thought it acceptable to unfold] a project for the final development of the entire watershed. Initially, his plans contemplated the construction, not at private but at government expense, of a series of dams controlling all the remaining border lakes and converting them into four main storage basins."[3]

The dams would impound water in these basins "at new heights, varying from five to eighty-two feet above the natural levels. . . . To aid [in this] development and assure a fair share of the power [for] the United States, the Ontario outlets of some of the main lakes like Saganaga and Lac la Croix were to be blocked and their waters diverted ... [south] to the International boundary. There they could be stored in years of plenty and drawn upon in the intervening lean years. Assurance was likewise given that in due time the same perfect control would be extended to all the [area's] tributaries both in Ontario and Minnesota."[4]

Ober argued that Backus's "modest proposals" would "strike a death blow to the distinctive appeal of the region. To say nothing of ... inevitable extreme fluctuations, the [proposed] new maximum levels would spell the ruin of all the visible features of the lakes and streams controlled by dams. ... All these lakes are dotted with islands and have shorelines as intricate as any jig-saw puzzle. The tragedy is that on all these shores, in the margin between the old water level and the new, the vegetation will be killed; and all the natural features will be obliterated."[5]

Even early on Ober wondered about Backus's motives: "The promise [that these dams would provide] more power and more industry was not altogether convincing. ... The engineering figures submitted, though they indicated a considerable increase in the already large potential power of the Winnipeg River far away in Canada, showed only a 700 hp addition on the boundary at International Falls and Fort Frances. Students of the project began to wonder whether power after all was the chief consideration or whether the explanation lay in [Backus's gaining] monopoly control of the remaining timber supplies or in the suggestion, lightly stressed, that the two governments [as part of the overall project] institute international condemnation proceedings to clear up the legal muddle in which [Backus's Minnesota and Ontario Paper Company] finds itself as the result long ago of appropriating shore rights never paid for."[6]

These shore rights had been "appropriated" through flooding, and the Backus plan would have these private holdings condemned and their owners compensated for their loss by the two governments. "These last expenses, to be included in the costs to the governments, are estimated at many millions of dollars."[7]

Numerous landowners, including Ober himself, had long suffered from flooding caused by Backus's original dam, which controlled the water levels of Rainy Lake. As far back as 1917, in a cry for help, Ober had written the secretary of war in Washington:

> Under acts of congress authorizing the construction of the dam across Rainy River at International Falls, owned and operated by the Minnesota and Ontario Power Company, I believe that the Secretary of War and the Chief of Engineers have certain authority in the regulation of lake levels in the public interests.

Pending an investigation by the International Joint Commission, there seems to be a tacit understanding that the power company shall be permitted, though on whose authority is not known, to maintain a maximum level in Rainy Lake at what is called Bench Mark 497. Residents on Rainy Lake have long tolerated the idea of this maximum, though it considerably exceeds any natural high water level and though it results in the power company occupying [flooding] private property year in and year out without any compensation.

However, the attitude of the company has been to maintain the maximum level, whenever weather conditions permitted, regardless of risk from flood. In 1916, either, as it seemed to us, intentionally [to maintain peak power at the mill] or through poor judgment, the company held back the waters until they became entirely unmanageable and reached a level of nearly 501. Great property damage was caused at that time but no damages were paid.

At present . . . when the lake is normally dropping rapidly, the company has been able to maintain close to the maximum all winter. Those of us most familiar with conditions in the watershed, knowing that the swamps and all tributaries were full last autumn and that we have had a winter of abnormal snowfall, believe that, unless the lake is lowered many feet before the spring break-up, we shall have a far more disastrous flood than in 1916—one involving not only great property damage but even loss of human life. We do not believe that the power company is qualified to judge what is in the public interest and that therefore your Department should act immediately to do everything possible to avoid what threatens to be a serious disaster.[8]

As had so often been the case when confronting Backus through official channels, Ober's letter was passed on, then lost in the bureaucratic shuffle. This was a battle Backus felt he could not afford to lose. So much depended, or so he believed, on his power dam, and he wanted to build seven more of them initially, and then again more, a hoped-for total of sixteen. But damage caused by high water due to his dams proved a point of vulnerability for Backus that, in the coming years, Ober and his conservationist allies would exploit early and often.

Edward Wellington Backus, sometimes facetiously called "King Ed," was a farm boy from Featherstone Prairie near Red Wing in southern Minnesota. He was born in 1860 and entered the University of Minnesota in 1878 where, in good late nineteenth-century tradition, he supported himself with various part-time jobs, including delivering newspapers. In 1880, not quite finished with college—a rare failure which troubled him throughout life—he entered a small Minneapolis lumber firm as a $9-a-week bookkeeper. By 1885, he owned this firm outright. And by 1891 the Backus mills were sawing 70 million board feet of lumber annually. Through the depression of 1893, Backus kept his lumberjacks working for "meals, socks and tobacco. ... His teamsters said that they returned to camp so late at night that they met themselves going out in the morning."[9] This was still the era of the empire builder, and in those early years Backus's flamboyant and magnetic personality, his expression of certainty and authority, were all his creditors needed to maintain confidence in him.

In August of 1893, a twenty-block fire in Minneapolis consumed Backus's two mills, but, with a $400,000 insurance settlement, he resumed the building of his enterprises with ever-increasing zeal. In 1899, he strengthened his growing empire by joining with William Brooks—soon to become a Minnesota state senator—to form the Backus-Brooks Company, of which Backus would be far the dominant partner.

Backus only regretted that "the good cheap things in Minnesota timber had all been picked up" before his time.[10] Then he "peered over the continental divide and there looked into an empire where the rivers flowed north."[11] Here were great forests of spruce and white and Norway pine. The story was often told in lumbering circles—indeed, it became a central myth in Backus's life—of how, in the winter of 1898, he and his head timber cruiser trudged 200 miles on snowshoes from Brainerd to the Rainy River on the Canadian border. The Winnipeg stagecoach then picked them up and carried them to the Fort Frances Hudson's Bay post where they arrived "at 1:30 on a February morning with the thermometer registering forty degrees below zero. It being a clear moonlight night, and hearing the water roar over the [Koochiching] Falls, Mr. Backus decided to inspect this waterpower before taking to his blankets, and upon doing so decided then and there to purchase [this great flow of power]."[12]

The beauty of the moonlit falls had moved Backus less than the 35,000 horsepower he estimated to be contained in their roar. It is said that the flow over these falls at the outlet of the Rainy Lake watershed was greater and more dependable than that of the Mississippi that powered the great mills of Minneapolis. In a bold move, Backus sold out in Minneapolis and started building his huge power dam and the first of several forest-product plants at the site of that wonderful waterfall, thereby ending its existence. At this time, too, he built a pair of water-storage dams on either side of an island in the outlet from Namakan Lake into Rainy Lake.

Backus then organized the building of a railroad to his new center of operations, an investment that another empire builder, James J. Hill, said would never pay for itself. But pay it did. In 1908, Backus incorporated the Minnesota and Ontario Power Company—later to be called the Minnesota and Ontario Paper Company—and there followed in the coming two decades a bewildering array of substantial subsidiaries, almost all relating to the production of lumber, paper, and other forest products on both sides of the border. Most of these were within 200 miles of the home plant at the Rainy River dam. In 1917, Backus ran twenty-three logging camps that employed 4,000 workers, and he controlled the timber rights over immense reaches of Minnesota and southern Ontario. He referred to a 40,000-square-mile area of prime timber as "my back yard." In good part, he "owned" the region's forests, controlled its water, employed its people, and set its prices. By the mid-1920s, mills operating day and night, Backus paper manufacturing operations had become second largest in total production in the entire world.[13] By 1929, a printed arm-length of Backus enterprises was estimated to be worth $100 million.

Backus was a great admirer of Napoleon, considering that warrior to be a model for his business conduct. Stories of Backus's cold-heartedness are legion. In one telling, he cheated a widow with ten children out of her means of livelihood. And it has been written that a provincial commission once came close to charging him with murder.[14] Nevertheless, his success was meteoric, and much of it depended on waterpower. To maintain that power at its peak, Backus did not hesitate to flood lake cabins and the low-lying lands of recent homesteaders. He had great financial and political leverage, and though constantly in court, seldom lost. He was a power in both the Minnesota and U.S. Republican parties, and sometimes spoke of a little black book that contained the record of his heavy contributions to politicians on both sides of the aisle.[15]

Despite his capacity for ruthlessness, within his own set and as a businessman Backus could be an undammed river of charm. He was a handsome and imposing man, standing six feet in height and weighing 200 pounds. His appearance was thought to be senatorial, and he often wore striped trousers and dark coats. An International Falls journalist wrote that, "Mr. Backus was a man of splendid physique, and it was truthfully said of him that he had the 'head of a statesman and the shoulders of a gladiator.' His beaming eyes denoted his keen intellect, and his retentive memory caused all with whom he came in contact to marvel. Of command-

Edward
Wellington
Backus

ing appearance, he was a man of note whether in village circles or in the financial centers of the east."[16]

Backus provided fabulous entertainment in support of his business. In the fashion of the Roaring Twenties, he "catered parties on his Rainy Lake island . . . [which] featured imported fresh clams and seaweed, whisky smuggled from Ontario during prohibition, a hired brass band, and Indians in traditional dress. . . ."[17] He sometimes spent thousands of dollars on special party trains: The Backus-Brooks Special included "Pullman sleepers, dining cars and railway official business cars." One such seven-day "Outing Party," given in September of 1927 for railway officials and Backus's newsprint customers, began on Monday afternoon with a visit to the Backus home on Lake of the Isles in Minneapolis. The party then traveled north by rail to inspect Backus plants and enjoy golfing, guided fishing, and celebratory meals in "Backus communities." On Thursday and Friday nights they slept in large tents on a Lake of the Woods beach near Kenora, after enjoying a barbecue and sturgeon dinner. Members of the party then moved on to Winnipeg where they were provided with the private clubhouse section of the Winnipeg Jockey Club at the races. They then joined a private garden party "attended by the principal dignitaries and business and professional men of Winnipeg. Music . . . furnished by the famous Princess Pat Band."[18]

It is remarkable that, in the emerging struggle over the fate of so huge an area, its two principal figures, Backus and Oberholtzer, embodying opposing visions of humanity's role in relation to the natural world, should, during the summer, occupy neighboring islands on Rainy Lake. The elaborate Backus family summer home, equipped with a large houseboat on which Mrs. Backus often entertained, was but a fifteen-minute canoe-paddle across the shining waters from Ober's Mallard Island with its recycled houseboats and cabins, which many have found somehow finer than the Backus retreat. Both men had the manners of Victorian gentlemen, and local legend has it that once a year these two, alternating between their separate islands, set aside their struggle and had a polite cup of tea together. Given the differences in their physical stature and their relative wealth, it is notable that R. Newell Searle should once have described their conflict as "A Clash of Giants."[19]

The Backus threat proved to be, in many ways, Ober's life chance. Or better, his second-half-of-life chance. Up to this point, psychologically and spiritually, he had gone through a great developmental effort that remained largely unrealized in the outer world. The pressure created by the emerging threat would now bring him into meaningful focus and crystallize a public persona through which he could release what he had become into the culture of his time. The Backus threat provided him with a mission of transcendent importance, one for which the complex threads of his past had thoroughly prepared him. It would even, in a limping sort of way, become his means of material support.

Once he was engaged in the battle to preserve the Quetico-Superior wilderness from "the most ambitious project for hydroelectric development ever launched in America,"[20] Ober's convictions, his early experience, and the forces of his time would hold him to that stage on which a new national idea about the use and value of wilderness was struggling to be born. His life no longer belonged to himself alone, but to the collective as well. He would never fully accept his fate—a source of difficulty if not tragedy in most people—and some part of him would ever hold to a dream of a more personal life of immersion in nature, culture, and Indian lifeways. From this point on, however, heavy responsibilities would limit his connection to that dream and sometimes even take the song from his heart. Whether he fully accepted it or not, his fate had now found him.

[12]

The Rainy Lake Reference

Oberholtzer's public defense of the Quetico-Superior wilderness began on September 28, 1925. The occasion was a three-day hearing held by the International Joint Commission on the future of the Rainy Lake watershed. The question to be addressed was: should the region's lakes and streams become a storage basin for industrial waterpower? More specifically, should the planned Backus dams be allowed and, if so, what would the building of them entail?

The International Joint Commission was playing a critical role in the complex drama that the struggle for the future of the region's waterways had become. Created by a treaty negotiated between the United States and Great Britain (for Canada) in 1909, its purpose was to evaluate, arbitrate, and settle disputes arising along the shared boundary waters of the United States and Canada. As the drama played out, Backus increasingly saw the IJC—if it would rule in his favor—as the key to his plans for industrial expansion in and control of the region.

Earlier, in 1912, the IJC had initiated the Lake of the Woods reference in an effort to decide whether the water levels of that huge lake should be controlled and, if so, at what levels. Since the waters of the Rainy Lake watershed flowed out of Rainy Lake, over the Backus dam, then down the Rainy River westward into Lake of the Woods, issues relating to Lake of the Woods were closely connected with those of the Rainy Lake watershed. In 1917, after five years of study, the IJC concluded that the waters of Lake of the Woods should be held two feet above their natural level. Low-lying lands that would be flooded at this new level would be condemned and the landholders compensated for their losses by the two governments. The owner of the lake's control dams (soon to be Backus) would therefore be freed from further responsibility in the matter.

However, upstream, in the Rainy Lake watershed, things were very different. The two governments had not as yet interceded, and Backus's dams at the outlets of Rainy and Namakan Lakes had been creating floods off and on for years, often doing significant damage to both private and public property. The situation was a legal nightmare for Backus. Through exertion of political leverage, he had managed to stave off most of the consequences, but, in 1915, the Minnesota Supreme Court determined that he was indeed liable for damages. The case in point, however, was then quickly settled out of court, and Backus's political influence and a continuing rumor that the IJC was soon to rule on the matter kept the State of Minnesota from pressing suit. The suggestion that the two federal governments would pay off the plaintiffs was somehow kept in the air.

In its Lake of the Woods ruling, the IJC had suggested that, since maintaining Lake of the Woods at the new higher level would draw down waterpower from the Backus industries above—never mind that he would gain that power in his industries on Lake of the Woods—consideration should be given to creating more waterpower for the International Falls–Fort Frances industries. This, the commission wrote, would be accomplished by raising water levels further east in the Rainy Lake watershed. The commission argued that the two governments should acquire flowage rights of at least five feet above high water levels throughout the watershed. This was a page out of Backus's own dream book, and surely he had cultivated commission members to produce just these suggestions. Were they to become a reality, his flood-related legal problems would be solved, and at government expense. In addition, since he owned or controlled all the feasible dam sites in the watershed, he would also have monopoly control of the region's waterpower and most of its timber.

In the years following the IJC's 1917 ruling, Backus fought hard for the recommendations that so neatly supported his ambitions. The U.S. government backed his goals; Canada, however, was reluctant to commit to them. Finally, in September of 1925, the IJC's Rainy Lake reference to study and decide on the matter was initiated at the hearing held in the Koochiching County courthouse in International Falls. Had there been no serious opposition to the Backus plan at this hearing, it is likely that the IJC would have supported it as a matter of course. Backus had "massaged" the IJC for years, and he was, after all, the region's main employer, its most powerful and influential individual.[1]

In the oral history interviews, Ober explained that conservationists welcomed the hearing since it had been difficult to obtain the basic facts of the Backus plan. Local people were mostly worried about the possibility of increased flooding. "The outsiders, on the other hand," said Ober, "were concerned about the preservation of the very remarkable—in fact unique—wilderness character of the entire watershed. There were men like myself who had traveled year after year in and out of these waterways who knew that this was one of the great [wilderness] areas of the world.

"Well, at the hearing, Mr. Backus appeared as a proponent of his program, which he outlined, apparently with some reluctance, and only as a result of questioning. It seemed that he envisaged the use of all the timber and water resources of the Rainy Lake watershed, on both sides of the border, so far as there was anything left. The timber resources were not emphasized, but it seemed apparent that the man who controlled all the waterways would control all the timber.

"Mr. Backus very frankly said that he thought he should be allowed to raise Rainy Lake another five feet beyond the point to which he had already raised it. There were a lot of questions as to just how much that was. Some felt it had been raised five feet already. Generally, of course, the power people said it hadn't been raised anything like that. Old-timers thought it had been raised a good deal more.

"There had been one especially serious flood that had done terrific damage in 1912. As soon as the dam established between International Falls and Fort Frances had had time to fill the basin, we had this tremendous flood. It caused huge damage. The people assembled at the hearing carried the memory of that flood with them. In many cases, the water had risen over their personal property. An entire group of homesteaders on the Minnesota side, for instance, who had laboriously proved up on their lands on Black Bay, had been drowned out. The water had been raised right into the windows of their houses. They had located there because the low-lying land around Black Bay was arable.

"Beyond Rainy Lake, the additional dams that had already been established at the outlet of Namakan Lake, which flows into Rainy Lake, were to be raised still higher. Those dams, built with the final approval of the War Department on the U.S. side, which generally oversaw things of that sort, had raised the water ten to fifteen feet above the natural level, and they caused a great deal of destruction around the shores.

"Beyond Rainy and Namakan, as you went along the boundary, every large lake was to be raised, generally from twelve to eighteen feet. This included Lac la Croix and Basswood and Saganaga at the other end of the Quetico. Then Mr. Backus said frankly that, in order to make the thing perfectly logical, he would eventually have to do the same with the large tributaries in both countries, in order to make the project feasible and practical.

"The Backus plan also included shutting off the Namakan River, through which all the waters east of Lac la Croix passed down from the Canadian side into Namakan Lake. He wanted to do this because the boundary wasn't a continuous line, as many people thought. There were several places at which the boundary went north of Hunter's Island, and this hadn't been fully understood at the time of the drawing of the final boundary by the two countries, under the Webster-Ashburton Treaty. Though the treaty had been fully approved by the two governments, Mr. Backus evidently sought to rectify the situation by moving the rivers forming the boundary down to the accepted boundary.

"This plan would particularly affect the Namakan, not a long river—only about twenty-five miles long—but a very large one with many big drops, beautiful waterfalls and rapids. Well, Mr. Backus proposed to shut this outlet from Lac la Croix off completely and send that water down to Little Vermillion Lake on the boundary, which was on a separate chain. At this point his plans included a dam seventy-two feet high. This, of course, was a startling proposal. Anybody who knew the region understood that a dam seventy-two feet high was bound to flood a vast area—wooded and beautiful and natural—and substitute for it a huge masonry dam.

"Mr. Backus was asked how his project was to be paid for, and he explained very logically that he expected the two governments to pay for it, but he would pay his share for benefits to his power sites. He said too that he had already spent some $50,000 investigating the program. The inference gathered by most of the people present was that the governments might end up owing Mr. Backus a considerable amount.

"Mr. Backus seemed very pleased and affable at the start, very agreeable, but the questions finally annoyed him. There was a widow who had lost the resort she had put all of her money into. Her land survey showed she owned certain land, but her house stood in the water, and she seemed to feel that the company was in some way responsible. And there were a good many others in similar situations. Some of the little conflicts that arose between Mr. Backus and the people who testified led to warmer and warmer responses from Mr. Backus. He finally was quite indignant, and said—I think the testimony will bear this out—that it seemed to him very strange that these people should have come into this country after he had built his mill and expect to locate wherever they pleased without coming to his office and consulting him.

"I was there as a man who had spent a large part of his life investigating and traveling all over the region. I also spoke for a group that had been set up in Fort Frances because they were alarmed at the possible effect of the project on their resources and the future of their town.

"At the hearing, I think there was only one person other than Mr. Backus who spoke in favor of his program. There were probably two hundred who didn't seem to like it. On the basis of the hearing, which lasted several days, alarmed groups began looking around for effective ways of dealing with the situation. Mr. Backus had been so wholly successful whenever he had undertaken to get something from [either of the two] governments, that the prospects for stopping his program—even if it was a bad program—seemed very poor."

By this time Ober likely knew the Rainy Lake watershed as well as anyone alive, and few could have understood the threat so fully as he did.

When it came to legal and political maneuvers, however, his swashbuckling young lawyer friend Sewell Tyng was far ahead of him. A junior partner in a prestigious New York law firm—Larkin, Rathbone and Perry—and former secretary to Herbert Hoover, he understood how the world of men like Backus worked. He knew that a body such as the International Joint Commission could not be influenced by unorganized opposition.

In late summer of 1925, while vacationing on the Mallard, Tyng became aware of the Backus threat and the impending ijc hearing. He was popular in the region, and he urged leaders of Ober's home village of Ranier to take action against Backus. Then, in a letter to Ober dated September 19, he described his plans for an anti-Backus campaign. The letter suggested that he hoped to enlist his former boss Herbert Hoover in the effort, but that the time to do so would not be right until the hearing was over and the Backus position had become clear. Tyng mentioned as well that he had been in touch with the Arrowhead Association of Duluth, the most powerful commercial organization in northeast Minnesota, and they had urged him to bring his friend, the popular author Rex Beach, to the region to gain publicity for it. Tyng found this suggestion somewhat humorous, and he doubted that the Arrowhead people had the stomach for a fight with Backus. He then gave instructions for Ober to follow: "[At] the hearing it is particularly important . . . to get the names of all the people and interests who appear . . . and also copies of their briefs and also get a copy of the stenographic minutes which will probably be taken of the hearing. The latter will probably be expensive, but I believe it will be worth it." Finally, Tyng asked Ober to arrange for him to buy a small piece of property on Rainy Lake so that he would have personal standing in the imminent fight.[2]

Three weeks later Tyng wrote again, thanking Ober for the "interesting account of the proceedings at the Falls." He then plunged into a description of one of the most important ideas in the early history of the emerging movement:

> It occurs to me that from our point of view it might be well to file a statement or brief with the Commission after a careful examination of the record, analyzing the various arguments advanced and supplementing or emphasizing them where desirable. I think that to arouse interest in the situation it very desirable to have some compact statement of the case which can be distributed where it would do the most good. In talking the matter over with various people I have felt the lack of any printed paper which I could hand out and say "Here, here it all is, see for yourself."[3]

From supporters of his cause, Ober raised the money necessary to buy the bulky transcript of the hearing. Documents of the period put the cost of the transcript at $478. "It was a large hearing," said Ober, "and the transcript amounted to a whole book when finally printed. I was to furnish what I knew of the geography and character of the region, which, of course, I was only too eager to do."

With the transcript as source material, Tyng wrote a legal brief in reply to the Backus plan. Ober provided the above-mentioned content, approved of its arguments, and gave it its final polish. It was then filed with the IJC. Though too legalistic to have the popular appeal Tyng had hoped for, the brief was substantial in its arguments against the Backus plan. Ober sent it to his friend Harold Ickes, a Chicago lawyer and soon to be U.S. secretary of the interior. Ickes's son Raymond had spent the preceding summer on the Mallard, and in his letter of response on the brief, Ickes thanked Ober for the fact that, "Raymond has done better work in school than he has ever done before. . . . I think he has gained steadily in self reliance and initiative." As for the brief, "It is a very carefully prepared and well done piece of work. It makes out a strong case indeed and I don't see how it could be improved upon."[4]

Ober described the brief's immediate impact on the IJC: "There was a very noticeable change in the attitude of the Joint Commission. They were for the first time given the impression that the Backus program might run into very serious resistance. Up until this filing, they might have felt that it was a more or less routine matter, and it shouldn't be bothered with too much. Now, it seemed to us, they were more responsive. I think I might have felt the same had I been on the Joint Commission. As Mr. Tyng characterized it, before the filing, we were a lot of farmers with pitchforks against a man with a Gatling gun."

For more than a year, Ober worked with the conservation group across the border in Fort Frances, but he was then to discover he had a group of supporters in the Twin Cities as well: "The people in the fort were doing as much as they could, and we, as individuals, continued to be very active in the matter. But we didn't have any funds. Then one day [in early summer of 1927] I went to town in the boat for supplies, and I found a letter there from a man I'd never heard of before named Hubachek. It was a very appealing letter, very beautifully done, telling me that Mr. Hubachek represented a group of young business and professional men who were alarmed about Mr. Backus's project. They had learned of my interests, my many years of living in the region, and of my attitude toward the whole situation, and they wondered whether it would be possible for us to cooperate in some way. The letter asked that I go down and meet with this group one evening soon to discuss possibilities. If I'd come, they would pay my expenses.

"I was puzzled by this. I had never heard the name of this lawyer before. I had been warned that, if I was going to oppose something as large and important as this, I might expect a whole lot of surprise moves on the part of my opponents that I wouldn't at first understand. I could easily be trapped in some position that would leave me feeling very sorry.

"When I got back to the island, I read the letter over several times, then told my mother about it. 'I wouldn't answer it,' she said, 'I think it came from the other camp, and you'd better stay away from it.'

"'Oh, I don't think so,' I said. 'I think I ought to answer it. They might be of some help.'

"I answered saying that I'd be glad to go down and meet with this group of young business and professional men. A date was set, and I went down. I found they met only at night, cautiously, in the basement of an architect named Mr. Tussler. They were very cautious. They told me promptly—I don't know whether or not this was exaggerated—that they were all just getting started in their careers and that it was possible for a man as powerful as Mr. Backus to damage every single one of them. Mr. Hubachek was a junior partner in his father's firm, and it appeared that this firm could be greatly harmed. So they had to be very cautious not to show their hand. I was given every courtesy, and we had a long evening of very thorough conversation. I answered all their questions to the best of my knowledge."

The Twin Cities group, which had originally been organized by Wilbur Tussler, Welles Eastman, and John Reynolds, proved to be both idealistic and extremely capable. In all, they were a group of some twenty conservationists of whom three proved to be, like Ober, tenacious almost beyond belief. These three—Frank Hubachek, Charles Kelly, and Fred Winston— were young lawyers who would stand by Ober and the Quetico-Superior struggle for more than forty years. According to Ober, throughout the decades, the four were in touch on almost a daily basis.

The three young lawyers were a remarkable trio. On canoe trips during his youth, Hubachek had developed a deep and undying love for the boundary waters. He attended the University of Minnesota and Harvard law schools. During World War I, he volunteered for the French ambulance service and was awarded the croix de guerre. He then became a pilot in the U.S. Navy. He was a blunt man who battled for his convictions, once raging that those who despoiled the boundary waters were "sons-of-bitches, each and every one, and I intend to do what I know to be right."[5] Still, he was a realist, and sometimes, in later years, his bluntness would turn to ire against Ober for his unwillingness to compromise. Throughout his life, Hubachek would be personally generous to the movement, with both time and money. He would also prove an effective fundraiser and an exceptionally cagey strategist with significant clout in the Republican Party.

Charles Kelly, who worked and would become a partner in the Hubachek law firm, was a meticulous man who through the years would provide Ober day-to-day detail support. He had been raised on a Wisconsin dairy farm, and when Ober first met him in the mid-1920s, he had just graduated from the University of Minnesota law school. Though less blunt and flamboyant than Hubachek and never a wilderness canoeist, Kelly was also deeply committed to the preservationist movement, and he would eventually serve for decades as the chair of the President's Quetico-Superior Committee. During his conservation travels, Ober would often stay at Kelly's home and his relationship with the family was a close one. Kelly's son, also Charles, explained that, his father having been gone when he was born, Ober was the one who brought him home from the hospital.

Many years later, in a 1965 letter, Ober described Charles Kelly to Orville Freeman, the new United States secretary of agriculture:

> May I add a word about Charlie Kelly? He has worked quietly but with great earnestness, distinction, modesty, and not least without reward. He it is above all that has guided the President's Quetico-Superior Committee through these many later years, when large appropriations for land purchase were needed, the airspace reservation was secured, and firm connections made with the Province of Ontario.[6]

The third of the young lawyers whose support for preservation of the border lakes wilderness would never wane was Fred Winston, a tall and elegant, deeply respected man of liberal values from a wealthy family. The Winstons before him were engineers who had built the Great Northern Railroad and many of the government buildings in Mexico City. Fred worked as a public defender in Minneapolis, representing those who could not afford legal help. Like many young intellectuals of the period, he was attracted to communism and the Russian experiment and would one day travel to Russia to study it close-up. In support of Ober in the Quetico-Superior cause, he worked silently in the background, stepping into the light only when necessary. When the budget ran low, he often supported the project with his own or his family's money, especially that of his mother. A man of Gandhiesque qualities, he gave himself to what he believed to be the greater good, always thought the best of his opponents, and was fearless in the midst of the angry confrontations that were to prove unsettling to the gentle Oberholtzer.

"The group," said Ober, "assured me that they could and would give great help to those of us who were working against the Backus plan. They could raise funds that would allow us to distribute information, but they had to be absolutely sure that this information was correct. They asked if I would, on the basis of the hearing testimony and what we'd written in the legal brief, prepare for them an analysis of the Backus project, as outlined by Mr. Backus, so far as we understood it at that time. They wanted information definitely paginated, so that one could quickly turn to any point of the testimony."

Clearly, this group saw Ober as the authority, not only on the region, but on the Backus plan as well. And indeed, through work on the brief and the writing of this requested analysis, Ober did rapidly gain intellectual control over the complexities of the emerging situation, its threats, and, perhaps most importantly, its opportunities. He claimed as much in the oral history interviews: "I was pretty thoroughly informed by then. I had the testimony and went over it, and prepared the analysis. It must have been about 5,000 words long, pretty long, but it pinpointed every important question and Mr. Backus's reply to that question. He was definitely on record for certain things."

The conservationists now had the concise explanatory document that Sewell Tyng had longed for. "I dubbed the analysis 'Conservation or Confiscation,'" said Ober, "and I brought it down, and we read it all at another night meeting, maybe a month after our first. Not a word was changed in it. Not enough about the situation was known over the state as a whole, and the Minneapolis group intended to circulate quite a number of copies."

Ober and his newfound allies had been drawn together by their mutual love of the boundary waters and their anger over the intentions of Edward Backus. The Twin Cities group was made up of quite exceptional men, and Ober could and did take considerable satisfaction in his leadership role among them. In addition, he had begun to establish friendships that would prove among the most rewarding of his friendship-filled life.

The Program

Ober recalled that, before circulating the analysis of the Backus plan, his supporters showed it to Backus himself: "Out of fairness, two members of the group who had easier entrée to Mr. Backus [one of these was Minneapolis businessman Welles Eastman] submitted this work to him. They wanted to be sure its content was accurate. I don't know how thoroughly he looked at it, but Backus claimed there was no truth to it whatsoever. It was all, I believe he said, 'a damned lie.'

"'What in particular do you object to?' they asked. 'Would you show us?'

"'It's all a damned lie.'

"'Well, what *in particular* do you object to? Would you show us? How about *this* statement?'

"They read it to him, then read its reference, what he had said in testimony. He waved it all aside. No importance whatever. Well, the group authorized the printing of the analysis, which must have cost quite a lot of money. I think they printed 5,000 copies on the first run, and I believe they finally published no fewer than 25,000 copies. They distributed it all over Minnesota, to libraries, to every kind of organization. I don't know the details, but these young men raised the necessary money for the printing and distribution."

The document the young men distributed, "Conservation or Confiscation," was subtitled "An Analysis Of The Water Storage Projects Proposed by Mr. E. W. Backus As Affecting International Boundary Waters Particularly in Quetico Park and the Superior National Forest." Its seven pages contained a sketch map of the Rainy Lake watershed and thirty-three subject headings in bold print, each followed by an explanatory paragraph. The margins included page numbers referring to source material in the transcript of the International Joint Commission's Rainy Lake reference hearing. Much of the document was practical in tone and included headings such as "Fire Hazard," "Effect On Fish," and "Monopoly Dangers Unlimited." But, under "Damage Includes Intangible Values," was the sentence, "Because the region is largely in a state of nature, Mr. Backus assumes that it is valueless; but that is exactly what constitutes its value for the public." And near the end of the analysis Ober wrote, "*This is one of the rarest regions on the continent, if not the world.* Nowhere else is there to be found so precious and picturesque a combination of water, rock and forest, all linked together in a single maze of bewildering beauty."

Backus was now quite aware that he had a serious fight on his hands: "We began to hear from some of his lawyers," said Ober, "and from his engineer, Mr. Adolph Meyer. Mr. Meyer began speaking before various groups. Our people attempted to answer, and Mr. Hubachek joined in the debate.

"Our group then decided they had to go much further in their publicity campaign. One of our members was Jeff Jones [of the *Minneapolis Journal*], and the *Journal* decided on a campaign, an actual campaign of opposition to Mr. Backus's proposal. All of a sudden an editorial appeared, very forthright and very definite in its opposition to the Backus program, stating why they felt this project wasn't in the public interest. The following day, as Jeff Jones told it, his door opened and Mr. Backus came in and said something decorative like:

"'What in hell do you think you're doing?'

"'What?'

"'That editorial that appeared last night. Don't I sell you my newsprint?'

"'Oh, yes, we've had very friendly relations, Mr. Backus, but that can't decide our editorial policy. I'm sorry you've gotten into this situation. I hope we've done you no injustice.'

"He was very conciliatory, but Mr. Backus had now mounted his war horse, and he went out just fuming. And the battle was on. The *Journal* continued to publish editorials against the Backus plan, a whole series of them. Every time Mr. Backus or Mr. Meyer would open their mouths, there'd be a new editorial in response. And there were debates before various organizations."

Up on the boundary lakes, the dams Backus already had in place were once again decimating shorelines. During the winter of 1926 and 1927, water levels and snow depth made it clear to Ober that conditions were ripe for another serious flood. In a letter to Tyng written on March 12, 1927, he complained that it had become "evident that there is no authority in the United States to whom to appeal for regulation of the levels." The Canadian Department of Public Works, on the other hand, "is supposed to call a halt when the 497 mark is reached. Theirs is the only supervision so far that has had any effect whatever but even that is not precautionary. It does nothing to prevent preliminary conditions that are bound to result in flood." Ober then continued:

> The Backus company is quick to profit by this chaotic situation. They are absolutely without authority of any sort, except what may be inferred from their permit to build the dam, but they are equally without restraint. So they just run amuck until such time as the two governments get together by treaty and impose the strong hand of law, if that should ever be. . . .[1]

Ober now made it a priority to combat Backus on the flood issue. He did this, first, simply because lake dwellers and shorelines suffered from such flooding, and, second, because it drew attention to why Backus should not be given control of the water levels of the entire vast lake-land region. Ober began with a letter-writing campaign to selected individuals and organizations on both sides of the controversy. With the intention of pressing a lawsuit against the Backus companies, he organized a coalition of those who had suffered flood damage in the past. And finally, with the help of his newfound lawyer friends, he began to put pressure on the Minnesota attorney general for not moving forward on flood damage suits against Backus that had been pending for years. Legally, Backus managed to hold his ground against these Oberholtzer-inspired efforts, but Ober did manage to bring considerable public attention to bear on Backus's ruthless indifference to shorelines and those who inhabited them.

The flood that Ober feared in 1927 did indeed arrive. In a June 3 letter to the secretary of the International Joint Commission, Ober's tone, usually respectful when addressing this body, smolders with anger:

> As foreseen and predicted last winter to your Commission, to various Departments of the government, and to Mr. Backus himself, a very serious flood has developed on Rainy and Namakan Lakes. The damage to property is already great and the loss to business transacted on the lakes considerable. With the water still slowly rising the flood promises to develop into a real disaster. Some smaller farmers and resort owners are threatened with complete ruin.
>
> It is useless to advise these property owners, already ruined, to seek redress by law from a vast corporation, which has long ago demonstrated its disregard for law and its assurance of immunity....
>
> The present flood has vastly prejudiced in the public mind Mr. Backus's claim for consideration from your commission.... We feel that Mr. Backus has given conclusive proof of his disregard of the public welfare and of his unfitness not only to deserve further concessions but to operate his present dams. Coming as the climax of a long series of public abuses, this present violation of trust is too flagrant to be overlooked in the determination of any large public policy.
>
> How your own Commission will regard what we consider Mr. Backus's attempt to attain by force the 500 [foot] level on Rainy Lake, for which he is petitioning, I would not of course presume to predict. I am merely taking the liberty to point out the general impression, namely that, pending your decision in this important matter, Mr. Backus has perpetrated an unpardonable piece of arrogance....[2]

Despite whatever influence Backus may have had within the commission, its members were not immune to the power of public opinion, and Ober, believing Backus had proved himself a bad citizen, was insisting the ijc take this into consideration.

The Minneapolis group now made a request of Ober that would place him at dead center of the struggle for decades to come. The group believed it was necessary to offer the International Joint Commission a constructive program for the Rainy Lake watershed as a counter to the Backus plan, or, as Ober would later write, "a conservation program of our own ... to replace the narrower industrial dream."[3] It would be a serious mistake, they believed—Ober and Tyng had already reached this conclusion—to let the situation rest as the Backus plan or nothing at all. They asked Ober to create this constructive program, and he plunged into it with great intensity:

"In order to develop my vision for this project," he explained, "I went back over all I knew from my years up here, my college studies in landscape architecture, and my knowledge of the forest service." Ober saw Quetico Provincial Park and Superior National Forest as core areas and, to some degree, structural prototypes for a larger program that would cover the entire watershed. His study of the watershed led him to understand that it was what is now called a bioregion: "Analysis showed that this watershed was a unit; that it was of the same type throughout its length and breadth, regardless of boundaries." It should therefore, he concluded, "be managed as a single unit."

Though Ober gave credit to his studies in landscape architecture, it should not be assumed that his single year in graduate school, in preparatory classes he found distasteful, was the source of the plan he was now developing. His studies did, however, provide him with a background familiarity with such planning and, in addition, acquainted him with the key concept his plan would be based on: zoning. When talking about the plan he would develop, Ober most often returned, not to his more advanced study, but to the undergraduate paper he wrote on the best use of the pond that provided fresh water for Cambridge, Massachusetts, in which his "chosen remedy was not simply a wilderness remedy." The writing of this paper established an attitudinal paradigm that remained fixed in Ober's mind, a seed experience that now began to blossom. Ober, a creative and quick-witted intuitive able to make much of little, had been placed at the center of an emerging situation for which he was asked to provide a healing solution. His formal education had provided him with the necessary basics, but it was his knowledge of the region and the conflicting interests of the people who lived and worked in it that provided the substance for his solution.

Despite considerable popular opinion to the contrary, Ober was adamant that the conservationists not over-reach: "I knew," he said, "that timber products and mineral products were the basis of local industry. Practically everyone earning a living up here did it in relation to these two industries. It would have been an extremely difficult thing—even if desirable—extremely difficult to stop all that kind of exploitation of natural resources. Mining, up to that time, had been on a very small scale, but there were very substantial timber interests, especially on the U.S. side. The Weyerhaeusers were operating northwest of Duluth, and north up to here, and they were very big. And Backus was already taking out great amounts of pulpwood fairly close by. And there were the Shevlin-Clarke large saw timber operations in Fort Frances. We acknowledged that we couldn't shut these down without doing great damage.

"What we sought instead is that these [timber interests] be operated under modern forestry principles acknowledged by the forest services of both countries. And to make sure that any further utilization would maintain the beauty of these lakes, their shores, beaches, islands, the waterfalls, and rapids. If you could maintain the natural beauty and then carry on the logging operations under a modern, sustained-yield basis—including game and fish, everything—you'd have established an ideal approach. You could then permit continued logging on this improved conservation basis, so as not to wreck the country. Recovery times would be long, but you'd have a sustained yield on the basis of what the country could produce, and industries would be geared to that level of production."

Forest Service thinking had been for some time cautiously moving in the direction of the multiple-use approach that Ober was now envisioning, but it had been held in check by already established commitments largely in support of the lumber industry. Ober, quick to grasp the possibilities in the dawning situation, was unfettered, free to create something new that expressed the emerging broader vision of the use and value of wilderness areas. The plan he was developing would provide a first concrete model for this new vision.

As a means of integrating multiple, previously conflicting goals, Ober developed a large-scale zoning plan. Zoning, said Ober, was the same "principle that cities recognize for their own good. You would apply this to the whole watershed in order to prevent the entry of all kinds of conflicting interests into the heart of this wilderness. Aside from the industrial uses I've mentioned, you wouldn't permit roads, railroads, settlements, resorts, or homes in distant, hard-to-reach areas. These things would be kept outside the heart of the area, kept on lakes like Rainy, which were already in contact with roads and railroads. You might, a little farther in, still close to facilities, permit a little such development, but without doing a lot of road-building.

"But the inner part was to be kept absolutely wild and undisturbed in terms of what you'd be able to see while traveling through [on the water]. That was the key principle in this zoning approach. Since the region was unified in terms of its resources and uses, it was clear that it would be highly desirable for all the relevant governmental agencies in both countries to agree on this program. It would be carried on under their separate jurisdictions, but with adherence to the same basic principles."

Writing for *American Forests and Forest Life* in 1929, Ober looked back on the development of what came to be called simply the Program. He knew it must not be seen as the work of a single man and therefore wrote that it "grew by careful study of all aspects of the situation and by negotiation with officials and organizations of both countries. It carried the contributions of many minds."[4]

The fulfillment of the Program depended a great deal on the support of the Canadians, and Ober's ongoing tactic would be to give them credit whenever and wherever he could. Early in the article, he revealed that his old Canadian friend and mentor Arthur Hawkes had come "to St. Paul in 1908, urging that, if Minnesota and the United States would cooperate in creating a game and forest preserve in northeastern Minnesota, Ontario would match it across the border. Thus came into being both Superior National Forest and Quetico Provincial Park." Later in the article he wrote that, "In the autumn of 1927 Arthur Hawkes of Toronto renewed his service to the region by a striking news article, in which he pointed out the incalculable advantages to be gained by final official action between the United States and Canada. He suggested a treaty, laying down a uniform policy for the use and perpetuation of all the resources, economic, recreational, scientific, and historical, in the Rainy Lake watershed."[5]

As to the possibility of a treaty establishing and maintaining policy, Ober heartily agreed with Hawkes, and the two had surely discussed this approach in private. Indeed, as the years passed, Ober became increasingly bound to the idea of a treaty as the best, most permanent solution to the long-term stewardship of the region. In the same article, he proposed that such a treaty "with the consent of the Province of Ontario . . . be adopted between the United States and the Dominion of Canada, promulgating the following four principles to apply to the Rainy Lake watershed and adjoining timber lands of like nature:

1. That park-like conditions, free from logging, flooding, draining, and all other forms of exploitation, be established and maintained on all visible shores of lakes, rivers, and islands under public control.
2. That all the hinterlands, not visible from the waterways, be administered under modern forest practices for the continuous production of a maximum timber supply.
3. That all game, fish, fur-bearers, and other wild life be managed for maximum natural production.
4. That these ends be pursued under the guidance and direction of an international board, representing forest, park, and biological authorities from both countries.

"It will be evident at once," continued Ober in the article, "that the resulting reservation would partake of the nature of both a park and a forest, as the terms are distinguished in the United States. So far as the lakes and streams are concerned, it would establish what would be virtually a vast international park, four times as large as Yellowstone and excluding all economic exploitation. So far as the untraveled interior, back from the waterways, is concerned, it would establish an international forest, protecting water sources, sheltering game, and yielding timber for permanent industry. But it would transcend both park and forest. Its principal function would be to preserve over the greater part of the area a wilderness sanctuary for man and beast...."[6]

Near the article's end, Ober once again tipped his hat to his old friend Arthur Hawkes, quoting his wish that the Rainy Lake watershed become "an outdoor university with a campus of 14,500 square miles." John Muir had written of the wilderness as a university years before, and the idea as expressed by Hawkes now caught Ober's fancy: "Well may it be called a university—a university of the wilderness! There is little else left of the original school that formed the character of our pioneer race. It is a museum of original America. It contains the larger half of wisdom—the part that cannot be taught within-doors."[7]

Though large concessions in terms of the area to be so protected would in time have to be made, the program Ober developed was to become the Magna Charta for the Quetico-Superior conservationists through most of their long struggle. It broke new ground and its concepts continue to be useful in forest planning today. Sixty years later, Charles Kelly would rank "Ober's working out a management plan for the Quetico-Superior" as one of the two most significant achievements of the entire Quetico-Superior struggle. "But that was his achievement," said Kelly, "that whole program was Ober."[8] R. Newell Searle would write as well that Ober's plan "foreshadowed the subsequent development of the Quetico-Superior region. His was a truly prophetic vision, one with few known precedents."[9]

The Twin Cities group heartily approved of the Program, and they raised money so that Ober might travel and convey its content to individuals and organizations whose support would be necessary to bring it to fruition. In October of 1927, Ober traveled by train to conferences in Chicago, Washington, D.C., New York, and Toronto. This series of cities was a round that, with slight variations, was to become a continuing and exhausting part of his life. Most importantly, on this first trip, Ober hoped to sell the Program to the U.S. Forest Service. He well knew how to move in the old boy network, and in the oral history interviews he explained that, immediately on arriving in Washington, he went to see his lawyer friend Harold Ickes, now working in the capitol:

"Ickes sent me to see his friend Gifford Pinchot [the influential first director of the U.S. Forest Service]. No longer a forester, Pinchot was living in his summer home up in the mountains of Pennsylvania. He sent me back to the Forest Service in Washington with a letter of support.

"The chief of the Forest Service was absent, so I saw his assistant [Leon Kniepp], and it was apparent from almost the start that I was a busybody who had come to criticize him and the things the Forest Service had done. I finally disabused his mind of the idea that I'd been sent to lambaste him, and he began to listen to the plan. We read the whole thing, and he raised points that he thought were debatable or that might prove difficult."

Kniepp saw that the Program's multi-use approach had something to offer the Forest Service's evolving vision of itself, and as was often the case, Ober's intelligence, wit, and charm won the day: "By the end of our first long session together," said Ober, "the assistant forester had taken a very different attitude, and he asked me to come again. He said he was going to give the plan very careful consideration, and he did. He was very thorough, and he finally provided us with a great many constructive ideas."

Like Sewell Tyng, Kniepp told Ober that to make the plan a reality the conservationists would have to organize extremely well in both the United States and Canada. In the oral history, Ober described Kniepp's thinking: "He said, 'If we are to approve a program of this sort, which seems to us logical, you will have to have large public support. You will have to have an organization. You should gain the support of these people.' And he gave me the names of a great many people, mostly in the United States. And he said we needed more help in Canada.

"He finally agreed to have his chief go over the plan very carefully. They would restate it in their language, and in view of all *their* principles. There were some things he was reluctant to agree upon. The margin along the shores, you see. I thought it should go up to the skyline. I didn't feel there should be any place that didn't appear fully forested to someone traveling by water. The forester said they couldn't do that. In some places, the skyline would be half a mile up the shore. There would be too much economic loss.

"'Oberholtzer,' he said, 'if you have two hundred feet, you'll never be able to tell from the shore whether there's been cutting going on in there. It's all going to be selective cutting, and you can't see that unless you go right up into the area.'"

Kniepp promised to have Secretary of Agriculture William Jardine's restatement of the plan available for an international forestry conference to be held in Duluth, Minnesota, on November 29, 1927. After leaving Kniepp in Washington, Ober traveled to Toronto where he met with the Ontario minister of Lands and Forests, who assured him that the province would be happy to send a representative to the upcoming conference.[10]

The international forestry conference in Duluth was organized by the Minnesota Conservation Council, which was made up of a number of organizations concerned about the Backus threat to the boundary lakes. It included delegates from the Arrowhead Association, the Izaak Walton League, Ober's Rainy Lake Association, the American Legion, the Game Protective League, the Women's Association, and the Minnesota Farm Bureau. There were also a number of delegates from Canada.[11] Though he was ever cautious about saying so, Ober was the central figure at this conference, which had been convened to give a hearing to and create support for his alternative multiple-use plan for the future of Quetico-Superior, the Program.

"Well," said Ober, "the rewritten plan [from the secretary of agriculture] came in time, and we felt this 'reply' to be a highly favorable one. As written, it preserved a certain decency of independence [for the Forest Service]. It restated things, but they amounted to the same. Some of our language, we thought, was more direct, but it seemed a wholehearted acceptance of our principles to everybody who went over it. It recognized the need for coordinating our policies with those of Ontario, the need for zoning on a large scale, and the importance of eliminating uses that conflicted with the Program, like the proposed [Backus] dams."

In the same article quoted from earlier, published in *American Forests and Forest Life*, Ober wrote, "The time was ripe. The international forestry conference had already been called under the auspices of the Minnesota Conservation Council and with the support of the Izaak Walton League of America. . . . A complete and carefully prepared program was then adopted, with the agreement that a temporary new organization should be set up for the sole purpose of fostering a treaty and of mustering the support of all friends in both countries. The result was the Quetico-Superior Council."[12]

Within the Izaak Walton League—the most powerful conservation organization in the country and one which had already invested much in support of the Quetico-Superior wilderness—there was resistance to allowing this new council to take the lead in the battle for the border lakes. In the end, however, those closest to the situation believed that an organization with a single focus and headed by Ernest Oberholtzer would prove more potent than a national organization with many items on its agenda. Nevertheless, the support of the Izaak Walton League and its huge membership was essential, and in its printed material the new council would describe itself as the "Quetico-Superior Council Associated With Izaak Walton League of America."

At the conference, when Ober was asked to lead the new organization, he showed reluctance, at least outwardly. Possibly he saw his life of relative freedom in the wilderness slipping rapidly away. More likely, his reluctance was an expression of his caution not to over-reach, not to be seen as grabbing a position of power. Deep down, he surely felt some ex-ultation at being chosen to lead this important movement, to finally have found a significant role that fit. Then, too, the presidency of the new council was to be the movement's one paid position. Ober was to receive $5,000 a year, and though conflicted about accepting money for such work, he must have felt that even a small steady income that would allow him to remain connected to the wilderness was an answer to his prayers.

"Anyway," he recalled, "our program was approved with the consent and support of the secretary of agriculture [whose department included the U.S. Forest Service]. I was then asked to head up our organization and to find a name for it. I suggested we call it the Quetico-Superior Council." Ober was proud of the new name he'd coined, but characteristically cautious: "If anyone had a suggestion for another name . . ." he would have been happy to accept another's choice. This was, however, to be Ober's organization and his to name. "I reluctantly agreed," he continued, "to go out from here—for six months—to get the organization started."

Many years later Ober would write, "It happens that I was called upon in 1927 to take charge of this movement. This I agreed to do for only 6 months, but that was nearly 30 years ago. It was a night and day affair with no rest for the weary."[13] Surely there was a rueful smile on Ober's face when, in his mid-seventies and still involved with the struggle, he wrote of his six-month commitment.

[14]

Entering the Political Arena

Oberholtzer was now president of the Quetico-Superior Council, and he was to be the first and only president of this long-lived organization. Over the decades, he would receive other titles, but this one was to be the most permanent and the one that best defined his contribution. The organization held its first meeting on January 27, 1928, in Minneapolis. Its members included Seth Gordon, O. L. Kaupanger, and Harry Denney of the Izaak Walton League; W. G. Door and Frank Hubachek of the Minnesota Conservation Council; Arthur Hawkes of Toronto, Jules Prudhomme of Winnipeg; James Harper, Fred Vibert, and Rollo Chaffee of the Arrowhead Association; J. F. Sutherland of the American Legion; Sam G. Anderson of the Minnesota Game Protective League; Dr. Nellie W. Nelson and Mrs. Willard Bayless of the State Federation of Women's Clubs; and Mr. J. F. Reed of the Minnesota Farm Bureau.[1] This was an exceptional group, and many of its members would again and again prove helpful, but, with the exception of Frank Hubachek, these original council members would be peripheral to the core group of activists that had already formed around Ober. The council described itself with the following words:

> The Quetico-Superior Council is an international organization associated with the Izaak Walton League of America for the sole purpose of obtaining, with the consent of the Province of Ontario, a treaty between Canada and the United States to protect and expand the rare public values in the Rainy Lake watershed, which forms part of the international boundary between Ontario and Minnesota.
>
> It arises out of the need of coordinating the activities of all individuals and societies interested in this task and is *limited in duration* to the achievement of its present purposes.
>
> It has no commercial interests and no class, racial, or political affiliations. It is to have but one paid officer, who will devote his full time to its affairs.[2]

Despite the fact that it would be agonizingly slow in achieving its final ends, the movement that Ober, as the council's one paid officer, now headed would, through its organization, strategy, and tenaciousness, prove an exceptional example of how a great environmental campaign should be run. "So the Program was launched," said Ober. "I continued to be called down to Minneapolis to confer with F. B. Hubachek and Charles S. Kelly. I was turned over to Kelly for help in a lot of the things I did, and he followed the project closely, in detail. Mr. Kelly kept very careful track of everything that developed. They had all the letters I ever wrote after I agreed to go out on this thing."

An early irony of Ober's new situation was that in order to fight for the wilderness he had to move to the city. For several months he had worked from the Mallard, concentrating on the issue of flood damage caused by the Backus dams. Then, in March of 1928, pulling his mother (who had little more than a year left to live) behind him on a sled, he trudged across the ice of Rainy Lake, leaving his Mallard Island home behind. Ober and Rosa moved into a Minneapolis apartment at 2605 Fremont Avenue South.

The Quetico-Superior Council and the Twin Cities group—there was an overlap in membership and they worked largely as a single unit—had begun a campaign to raise funds. "We didn't have any funds," said Ober. "We just did the best we could. If there was some printing that had to be done, the Twin Cities group took care of that. I immediately began receiving invitations to talk to organizations like the Rotary Club. There was not any such group that I didn't talk to around the Twin Cities. Meanwhile, debates were going on more and more frequently with Mr. Backus and Mr. Meyer." In a note written to himself during this period, Ober reveals one strategy he intended to use in the ongoing debates: "Make Backus ridiculous if possible by words out of his own mouth."[3]

In order to gain respectability and broad support, Ober began a campaign to recruit a prestigious national board of advisers for the Quetico-Superior Council. "One of the things everyone felt," said Ober, "and this had been urged on us by our adviser in the Forest Service as well, was that we should have a large national board of advisers. So I started out to get these people, and we had a very impressive list of supporters when we finally got all the answers. It was remarkable how well they responded."

Over the decades Ober would write many thousands of letters in support of the Program, and the writing of letters—courteous, warm, informative, and stylish—was now his means of recruitment. He made it clear that he would not have been able to recruit so well without the secretarial help of Clara Martin: "There was so much correspondence that I couldn't manage it alone, and I used to bring some of the most important of this material to Mrs. Clara Martin, who had a letter service in the Vendome Hotel. She proved to be a remarkably capable woman. To save time, I would dictate directly to her. No taking it down in shorthand first. I could sit right behind her there, and she could type it out almost as fast as I could talk. I'd spend half a day there and get out a huge number of letters. We did that for quite a while and her price was very reasonable and she seemed to like it very much. This was different from any other kind of dictation she had ever taken. It wasn't just business talk. This was very different, and apparently our mission appealed to her like everything. She entered into it with great enthusiasm, and we turned out vast numbers of letters."

The council's National Board of Advisors recruited by Ober included Kermit Roosevelt and other members of the Teddy Roosevelt family; the governor of Hawaii; Ober's mentor in landscape architecture, Frederick Law Olmsted; poets Vachel Lindsay and Carl Sandburg; environmentalists and writers Mary Austin, Ernest Thompson Seton, Robert Sterling Yard, Carlos Avery, and Aldo Leopold; social worker Jane Addams, baseball commissioner Judge Kenesaw Mountain Landis; future secretary of the interior Harold Ickes; and dozens of other distinguished Americans. "We had artists like Lorado Taft," said Ober, "scientists of all kinds. And not just forestry scientists, but every kind of scientist, the very highest among them, and they all entered into this enthusiastically. We promised not to bore them too much, but, when we felt their advice was of particular importance, we would ask them for it. One was Karl Compton [physicist and future president of M.I.T.]. He spent his honeymoon up here at the island, and he never forgot it."

The results of its fundraising efforts allowed the Quetico-Superior Council to rent a small office, and its official address now became 1218 Flour Exchange, Minneapolis. "I think," said Ober, "the rent was ten dollars a month. Just a little cubbyhole on the top floor. Then they also authorized hiring a stenographer. Without any hope that I ever could get her—she had a large business of very faithful clients—I asked Mrs. Martin if she would take the job. She came along enthusiastically, at a very small salary. I don't think it was more than thirty dollars a month. I may be wrong. I hope I am. Everything was a lot less expensive then than it is now. And she threw herself into her work with great fervor. She turned out beautiful letters. I think that's one reason we got such a good response. They were so nicely typed, clear and fine, never a mistake. If there were the slightest little mistake in it, she wouldn't let the letter go out. Some nights she'd stay long after work to get the letters ready."

Ober recalled that a businessman with an office down the hall once said, "You must be a real lady-killer, Ober. How else could you get Clara Martin to work on into the night the way she does?" The comment was intended humorously, but it has often been noted that Ober did have a magnetism that drew women to him, and since he showed little if any interest in conventional man-woman relationships, this sometimes translated into support for his cause.

Ober and the young conservationists who surrounded him lacked funds and political power, but it has been written that in their struggle with

Backus "they burned with a righteous fire and . . . were willing to fight the tough old tycoon with any weapon . . . at hand." Minnesota blazed with their publicity. They delved into the tax records of the Backus enterprises, and, with the help and advice of the group's young lawyers, they maintained legal pressure on Backus for flood damage caused by his dams. Council members hauled "cross sections of dead trees into court, describing them with fiery eloquence as 'these silent sentinels of God, withstanding for 200 years all the ravages of nature'—until killed by high waters backed up by Backus' dams."[4]

Edward Backus responded to these challenges with his usual aggressive vigor. He had connections with powerful individuals who agreed that a wilderness should be seen as a collection of natural resources for the use of humans and to be exploited for profit. "Banks suddenly called notes, to the embarrassment of the council's less opulent members. Corporations bluntly warned their young men to get out of the Quetico-Superior Council or be fired."[5] Some received threats of physical violence. Council members feared for Ober's life. The demands of that life kept the forty-four-year-old president of the Quetico-Superior Council working from early morning till late at night.

Ober had been the Program's visionary, and he now became its central advocate, lobbying for support of it and, over and over, in letters and articles, talks and testimony, telling its story. He traveled throughout Minnesota and made frequent trips to Ontario and key distant cities in the east. With the help of Clara Martin, he also did most of the council's day-to-day detail work. From the beginning, the young lawyers Hubachek and Kelly used their growing web of connections and political acumen to develop strategies and generally advise Ober as to how to proceed. Increasingly, as the years passed, since they were the fundraisers and background organizers, Ober answered to these two. The harmony among the three was exceptional, but, as the decades wore on and Ober wore down, there would be times when he groaned under the pressure of their demands.

The third lawyer from the Twin Cities group who worked closely and constantly with Ober was Fred Winston. Less adviser and more servant, Winston, like Clara Martin, was a project angel. He helped whenever and however he could. Perhaps most importantly, he often stood side by side with Ober in times of crisis.

Winston, a veteran of World War I, was a member of the American Legion, and he believed that this broad-based, relatively conservative organization could become a significant ally to the Quetico-Superior program. A battle over the issue would rage within the ranks of the legion from 1927 to 1929. Interestingly, the head of the Minnesota American Legion, Rufus Rand, had been one of the original members of the Twin Cities group that met at the Tussler home. "Winston," according to Ober, "was very influential with all the top officials of the American Legion in Minnesota just after the war. There were a number of very fine fellows among them. One was Pat Cliff from Ortonville. I never saw a man so able to stand up to someone like Chet Wilson [eventual Minnesota conservation commissioner]. When they'd just get violent, ready to cut each other's throats, he would just stand there and take it and give it. And win. Fred found people like that, and they were always people you could absolutely depend on when Fred got through with them. They just stood fast. Fred didn't like to work in the foreground. He'd have other people do that. It would be agreed upon in advance.

"'Ober,' he'd say, 'don't worry about this. Pat Cliff's going to take care of it. You wait for Pat Cliff.'

"And when the moment came, Pat Cliff would leap in like a lion. Well, we had a lot of good men like that. They were generally lawyers."

According to Ober, the members of the American Legion "had been spending most of their time on the question of a servicemen's bonus, and some men, like Fred, thought they ought to be concerning themselves with more constructive things like our program. Some of their leaders were very strong in support of it. So they dragged me up to Hibbing to speak before an enthusiastic crowd of legion fellows, and they adopted a resolution that had been prepared for them, condemning the Backus project.

"Well, this was an awful blow to Mr. Backus, having the legion against him. He was used to the Izaak Walton League and all being against him, but the American Legion! He was very much troubled, and he never quit trying to break up that original resolution. It was taken to the state body and approved by them as well, then to the national body and approved by them. The resolution that the national body finally passed was written by Fred Winston. It was a beautiful piece of work. A masterpiece."

Winston's resolution concluded with the following words:

WHEREAS, we believe that such a common enterprise would form a fitting tribute to the century of peace that has existed between ourselves and our great neighbor to the north,

Now, therefore, be it resolved, that the American Legion, in convention assembled at Louisville, Kentucky, September 30th to October 3rd, 1929, endorses, whole-heartedly this program;

Be it further resolved, that it is the sentiment of the American Legion that this great undertaking, being conceived in the spirit of international friendliness and good will, should accordingly be done in the name of peace and dedicated as a memorial to the service men of both countries who served as comrades in the Great War.

The fight to pass Winston's resolution was a bitter one, and the gentle Oberholtzer, who was not a veteran, who had never been able to pass a military exam, found the in-his-face rage of opponents rather frightening. He did not lose his courage in these situations, but he was not entirely comfortable doing battle, either. "Oh, they would just go for me like everything, some of those state officials especially, and Backus representatives who were legion men. But I always felt a sense of relief and power when Fred was along. He always had something ready, when you thought it was all over."

Winston's resolution was endorsed not only by the Minnesota and U.S. national bodies of the American Legion, but by the national body in Canada as well. Ober spoke of the resolution with a quiet pride: "It has stood all these many years, though governors and many others have tried to tear it down. Oh, my, yes, and the Minnesota conservation commissioner! He'd go to all these conventions, and come up with all the reasons in the world why they should never have adopted such a fool thing. But it's still there. And then it was taken to the Canadian Legion, and the whole national body approved it up there as well. Of course, those seemed like big victories. They didn't bring us anything in particular, and they haven't been stressed in these later years. They've been talked down, kept quiet, but they're still with us."

Winston asked in his resolution that, if and when the Canadian and United States governments created the wilderness sanctuary envisioned in the Program, it be dedicated as a peace memorial. It was to be dedicated "to the service people of both countries in World War I," said Ober. "Later they added World War II. The service men and women of both world wars. Not a monument, but the established region as a memorial to these survivors. We thought this would be a finer type memorial than anything else you could possibly do."

Oberholtzer's story reveals relatively unknown heroes in the struggle for preservation of the Quetico-Superior region. One example is Clara Martin, and, in the oral history interviews, Ober makes clear that Fred Winston was another: "Fred supported us strongly through all the years. He was all for doing his share, helping with money, or any other way that he could. When we had our office in Minneapolis and I'd be away for a long time, in Washington or whatever, he'd go to the office, conduct all the business, take care of the correspondence, meet the people—we used to have many people stop by—and send me whatever he thought I might need. And he'd do the filing. We managed to get a great deal of newspaper publicity. Well, we had scrapbooks of clippings from an agency. Fred paid for this himself. He thought it was very important to us.

"Fred was a very quiet worker. He never threatened. He never blustered. He was always very forthright when he talked to people. He didn't provide a long introduction. He just very quickly told people what he was up to. Fred didn't attempt in any way to interfere, or to guide, particularly. He was there to help. If ever he thought we were taking the wrong step, he'd say so. But he was purely and simply a wonderful friend of the Program. He could always be depended on in an emergency, and often found a solution when nobody else had one, which was very nice.

"There were other people with whom I had to go—some very good people whom I liked very much—who were awfully shaky when they got into a political situation where it suddenly appeared that there was conflict between their ideology, maybe Republican ideology, and something you were trying to accomplish. There'd be an argument from the governor or someone else, you see, and they'd cave in."

Though many of the members of the Minneapolis group and the Quetico-Superior Council were Republicans, Ober himself was a Democrat. By nature, however, he was equivocal, and he had many wealthy conservative friends, Republicans who just happened to be conservationists as well. It is notable that the Quetico-Superior movement was able to bring together fervent supporters from both sides of the aisle. One must wonder if environmental ideologies were less finely drawn than they are at present. Politically, as elsewhere, Ober's complexities and enigmatic nature have allowed others to find in him what they would like. His long-time friend Ray Anderson once said he thought Ober may have been a socialist, but, on reflection, Anderson amended this to something more like the tribal sharing Ober admired among Native Americans. Mostly, according to Anderson, Ober hated those who exploited and despoiled for profit.

That other long-time friend of Ober's, Ted Hall, told of an event that occurred during the era of Franklin D. Roosevelt's New Deal. Ober had attended a gathering at the home of his friend Major Horace Roberts on Atsokan Island, where he was surprised to discover a photo of Roosevelt on the mantelpiece. When the party warmed up, Roberts, a conservative and no friend to Roosevelt's policies, stood before the president's photo and spat on it. Others apparently followed suit. Ober was shocked and angered by this, and not too long after invited the same group to a gathering at his Mallard Island home where he also had a photo on the mantelpiece. This one, however, was not of President Roosevelt, but of Major Horace Roberts. Ober did not spit on the photo of his old friend, but he seems to have made his point.[6]

The Quetico-Superior Program, as Ober had envisioned it, would require a great deal of central or federal control on the part of two governments, and as the years passed, he would see unbridled private enterprise as a threat. "Private enterprise," he wrote, "has run riot like a bull in a botanical garden. It would look as if we could appreciate our blessings only after we stamp them out." He then, however, shifted the responsibility to the general public: "To berate or bewail is useless. The responsibility rests ultimately upon the public and upon the public alone. How they meet it may mean more for unborn generations in the two nations than many an issue of war or peace."[7]

Though clearly liberal in his personal politics and strongly against those who chose profit over the well-being of the environment, Ober was more complicated than his politics and was able to find friendship and support among those who held opposing political views. In the end he understood full well that in one way or another all must bear the burden of responsibility.

However valuable the publicity gained in a campaign such as that with the American Legion, Ober and his conservationist friends knew that political action would be necessary to halt the Backus plan and launch their own. It was at this point that they discovered they had a friend in U.S. Senator Henrik Shipstead, Farmer-Laborite of Minnesota. He had followed the controversy over the Backus plan and had begun writing a bill that would stop alteration of border-lake water levels on federal lands without congressional approval. Representative Walter Newton of the Minneapolis district was also strongly in support of such control, and he would eventually sign on as the co-author of what would originally be known as the Shipstead-Newton bill.

"Newton," said Ober, "was of a very different persuasion from Shipstead. But this gave us additional strength, you see. We had a liberal and a conservative. And Newton was very close to people like the Heffelfingers and other wealthy people who were helping us.

"Going back to Shipstead's original bill, he didn't contact us at all when he first wrote it. Of course, he knew about our fight with Backus, but the first I knew about his move was when I received notice that he'd filed his bill. I got a copy and discovered that all it provided for, I believe, was that there should be no further alteration of lake levels along the boundary without the consent of Congress. We went to him and asked him to permit us to make additions to the bill, those that covered the main provisions of [the Program]. He was quite hesitant, and we had to work hard to get just exactly what we wanted. Not because he was hostile to us, I'm sure, but because he had pride in authorship. He also understood the necessary strategy for getting a bill passed, and he felt it might get too complicated and there'd be too many enemies. But he finally consented."

The Quetico-Superior Council continued to receive good publicity: "There were frequent editorials in the *Minneapolis Journal*," said Ober. "We also had editorial support outside the Twin Cities. The Ridder papers gave us good support. The *Minneapolis Tribune,* which was a fine paper and was putting on a marvelous campaign for agriculture, kept very quiet. It was whispered around that they favored Mr. Backus, but, as it turned out, that wasn't true. I think that Mr. Murphy, the *Tribune*'s editor, felt, well, it's the *Journal*'s baby. And when they took over and began pounding away, the *Tribune* didn't want to come in and play second. A lot of people interpreted the *Tribune*'s silence as meaning they were friendly to the other side. I eventually met Mr. Murphy, and I thought he was a high-grade gentleman, that fellow, and very capable. He put on this marvelous campaign for agriculture, with very able writing. We asked him to appear at a fundraising dinner, and he appeared and gave us one of the largest checks of all. I think he gave us five hundred dollars, and he wrote a beautiful editorial, just beautiful. That was his reply to those who doubted his support."

Strategists Hubachek and Kelly believed the council should till the ground for the Shipstead-Newton bill by getting an advance joint resolution in favor of this national bill from both houses of the Minnesota legislature. According to Ober, Hubachek was especially fond of such strategies: "He loved it, and he had all kinds of ideas. I don't know where the idea originated, but it was agreed that we should get a joint resolution from the Minnesota legislature favoring the Shipstead-Newton bill which was pending out in Washington. I was being sent over to the legislature [in St. Paul] every once in a while. Backus would be there and men like [his chief engineer Adolph] Meyer and some of their lawyers.

"We did have a certain advantage there, because of my knowledge of the region. I'd have been very stupid if I hadn't known this watershed. I felt I knew it better than any man living, probably than any man who'd ever lived, because I don't think any other man that ever lived would waste so much time on it. It had been my business to travel all over this watershed, to know everybody in it, you see, to know as many of the Indians as possible, and certainly to know about the game.

"In any case, we took up the effort to get the Minnesota legislature to pass a resolution of support for the Shipstead-Newton bill with a good deal of vigor. A joint resolution was prepared and introduced in both houses, and this led to a great number of hearings, hot debate, and very strong feeling. A very determined effort was made to block this resolution, and some pretty bitter things were said about the people who were trying to push it through.

"The *Minneapolis Journal* was still supporting us. And many other organizations. The women's clubs and pretty nearly all such organizations were over there at various times speaking to their representatives and appearing at hearings. Still, it looked pretty hopeless. I think the senate was blocking it."

The chairman of the lands committee in the house, Ed Chilgren, was a Backus man who attacked Ober, who later seemed to relish telling the story: "He was chairman, and so we had to run his gauntlet. He made one choice speech. We'd appeared before his committee in the morning, and I had spoken for what we wanted. In the afternoon, he, as chairman of the committee, spoke the mind of the committee for them. His face was very red, and he made an eloquent speech as to why the Minnesota legislature should never take federal business in its hands. Then he gave his peroration. He stood way up on tiptoe, and after enough indictments to put me in prison for many years, he said:

"'He's a—He's a *hermit!*'

"I *was* a hermit. I've told you that. Anyway, it brought the house down. We all laughed. Even I laughed. What his conception of a hermit was, I don't know, but it was certainly a terrible thing. There was no question about that."

The head of the house rules committee, Roy Dunn, was also a Backus man, and it took Fred Winston's quiet but potent powers of persuasion to get the resolution out of committee for a vote:

"Roy Dunn was the czar of the house," said Ober, "and he would not let our resolution out, you see. Of course, he was all for the company. Fred dealt with him, and Fred was always fair.

"'Well, Ober,' he said, 'I'm going to go and see Roy Dunn. I think he's a fair shooter, no matter what it seems like to us. Otherwise, he couldn't hold his position. He's fair with everybody, even if he is very conservative.'

"And so he went to see Roy Dunn, and Dunn finally realized that it was hopeless to resist any longer. He threw in the sponge and let the resolution out to be voted on in the house. It was duly embossed and sent on to be acted upon by the legislature, and the result was overwhelming in our favor.

"It was a very long, drawn-out procedure before we got the final vote, and it was right at the end of the session that it finally went through. When it did, it went through by a large majority. The opposition was pretty well played out. As I recall it, they were left in a very lonely position."

Only days later, Ober was asked to appear before a joint session of the South Dakota legislature. Ober could not remember the source of their motivation. Perhaps his contact legislator had himself on occasion left his prairie home to paddle a canoe among the boundary lakes.

"A member there," said Ober, "had written Hubachek and assured him that, if we came, we could get the same sort of actions passed by a joint session of the legislature in South Dakota, of all places. After what we'd been through, this sounded too easy, and I went there reluctantly. But the legislator met me, and everything was properly laid out. I never saw anything so smooth in my life. There was a joint session sitting when I went in. I spoke my little piece, and they passed the resolution the same day and sent it right on to Washington. And so we now had two states in support of the Shipstead-Newton bill. I went away the same afternoon. Our supporter there had it all in hand. Apparently he was an unusual fellow in an unusual legislature, where there hadn't been a lot of controversy, and he was influential enough to simply say they just passed this in Minnesota, so it must be good. And how could anybody *here* object to it. Of course, I didn't use that kind of argument at all. I simply described the value of our program for all the people."

The Quetico-Superior Council was now functioning smoothly, and the conservationists had gained significant publicity and backing. With two state legislatures on record in support of them, they were ready and eager to do their part in the effort to pass the Shipstead-Newton bill now pending in the U.S. Congress.

Political Maneuvering

The Shipstead-Newton bill was introduced in the United States Congress in the spring of 1928. Hearings began in the Senate on April 30, in the House on May 4. For much of the next two years Oberholtzer would be in Washington working to pass the bill. In *Saving Quetico-Superior,* R. Newell Searle wrote that, "Although the Izaak Walton League, the General Federation of Women's Clubs, the Farm Bureau Federation and other organizations fought hard for the measure, it was Ernest Oberholtzer who bore the burden of testimony."[1] Through the long months of struggle for passage, Ober lobbied, wrote countless letters, sought publicity, and in general coordinated the effort among its various constituents. Interestingly, Fred Winston had somehow found a way to shift his law practice to Washington as well, and once again his support in times of crisis would prove to be magnificent.

On May 1, 1928, a story headlined "Backus Files Objections to Shipstead Bill" appeared in the *Minneapolis Tribune.* It reported that Backus had not known of the proposed hearings soon enough to prepare objections. In truth, he had already filed a brief opposing the bill in which he claimed it would "injuriously affect vast industries in the region and in adjoining regions in which many millions are invested. [In that Backus employs] from 8,000 to 10,000 people, with an annual payroll of approximately $8,000,000, he suggests there should be a 30 day delay." Despite these impressive figures, the Backus request was not granted. The *Tribune* article went on to say that the hearings would continue the next day but would be briefly postponed because of the absence of Ernest Oberholtzer.[2]

In a letter of May 1, Ober wrote that he had been expected in Washington to testify, "but was prevented from going by critical illness of my mother."[3] At the end of the month he would write that she had been in the hospital for five weeks. "After a night of great distress and spitting blood she went in."[4] Despite the depth of his connection to his mother and the seriousness of her illness, Ober could not now stay to care for her. Seth Gordon of the Izaak Walton League telegraphed that it was impossible to postpone the hearings and that he was sorry that Ober and other Minnesotans had been unable to attend. Ober immediately telegraphed Sewell Tyng:

Hope you can attend continued hearings Thursday and Friday next week Stop shall treat subject from all angles as exhaustively as committee permit Stop . . . Newspapermen should attend Stop Appreciate help from you and Bake [John Bakeless].[5]

Apparently Tyng and Bakeless were unable to attend the hearing, but Ernest Oberholtzer was no longer the young man who had failed so miserably to fill Sven Hedin's shoes in the Liverpool lecture of eighteen years before. Ober was now a man with graying hair of whom his opponents often said, "Don't let him speak or he will surely wrap his listeners around his little finger." His opening testimony before Congress on Friday, May 11, was based on the vision contained in the council's Quetico-Superior program. He argued against turning a vast wilderness into a series of storage basins and recommended instead a balanced approach to its development, one that would preserve its wilderness character while still allowing for wise human use of its resources. One of Ober's greatest assets in giving such testimony was his ability to evoke the awesome beauty of the region and then to connect it to a need increasingly felt in the hearts of the American people. He pointed out that 25 million people lived within 500 miles of the Quetico-Superior region to which they were becoming increasingly attracted.[6] He concluded by stating that, "The average citizen of the country, who cannot afford a summer camp of his own is to be presumed by declaration of this policy to have [ownership] rights in this last wilderness sanctuary of mid-continent."[7]

Ober's argument was amplified in early August when Congress formed a joint committee of seventeen members of the Senate Committee on Agriculture and Forestry and twenty-one members of the House Committee on Public Lands and traveled to the border lakes region. During their six-day stay, committee members were housed in army tents on Lac la Croix and flown over the region in airplanes. Lakes and streams, ancient rock, and tall and fragrant pines were allowed to speak for themselves. Through this gentle but persuasive lobbying, lawmakers actually experienced the spiritual and aesthetic values that Ernest Oberholtzer had described, and many were moved to support the conservationist's bill.[8] There was, however, competition for the minds of these observers. An August 14 telegram to Ober from Seth Gordon signaled with alarm that Backus was himself entertaining thirteen of the visiting committee members.[9]

During the early months of 1928, conservation-minded Republicans in Minnesota were in a struggle with Backus for control of their party. Frank Hubachek for one believed that Backus's grip on the party had to be broken if the Quetico-Superior program was ever to become a reality. Backus had chosen to support Frank Lowden for Republican presidential candidate that year. Though Backus claimed to back Lowden because he would provide aid to struggling farmers, the conservationists doubted Backus's sympathy for farmers. They believed it clear that Backus supported Lowden because of Hoover's good conservation record. The state director of the Hoover campaign charged that Backus was trying to gain control of the delegates to the Republican National Convention from Minnesota so that through them he could claim broad public support for his boundary waters plan.[10]

In a tactic he would use again and again, Backus asserted that his opponents were not conservationists but supporters of a rival lumber company. On March 12, he made public a letter that he claimed proved his rivals were financing the campaign against his plan. It had been written by Deane Rundlett, state president of the Izaak Walton League, and was addressed to Walter Quigley of the *Minnesota Leader*. Its first paragraph described large anti-Backus mailings the Izaak Walton League was making; the second stated:

> Mr. E. E. Smith and F. H. Carpenter are vitally interested in this. In fact they are paying for these circulars and are keeping in touch with Mr. Kaupanger and myself on this almost daily.[11]

According to Backus, "'Big Ed' Smith, Minneapolis politician, and Fred Carpenter, lumberman . . . are conspiring with one or more local officials of the League in financing and promoting the wide distribution of this false propaganda."[12] Smith and Carpenter denied any knowledge of the conservation campaign, and Rundlett denied having written the letter's second paragraph.

Rundlett had been wounded and gassed in World War I, and he suffered from tuberculosis and near-blindness. Quigley visited him during a hospital stay after Rundlett had complained to him that the *Leader* had not given the Izaak Walton League enough credit for its boundary waters campaign. Quigley asked that Rundlett write him a letter describing the league's work, which he would then publish. Because his eyes were bandaged, Rundlett dictated the letter to Quigley who typed it on a typewriter Rundlett kept in his hospital room. As Rundlett told it, "I then raised the bandage slightly from my good eye and signed the letter, presented to me by Mr. Quigley."[13]

The published letter raised a fury of charges and countercharges. No one knew how it had gotten into Backus's hands. Rundlett signed a formal affidavit in which he declared the letter "either a forgery or the result of a contemptible deception played on a man who could not see."[14] On March 14, a fiery debate between Backus and Mel Nyman of the Izaak Walton

League was held at the Nicolett Hotel in Minneapolis. Nyman claimed that the letter was a "stench bomb, prepared to affect the [Republican] caucus vote." Backus threw the meeting into turmoil by shouting: "How do you know it's not the [real] letter? Were you there?" Nyman responded that he believed Rundlett's affidavit. Backus shot back that the public should be the judge of this. Hoover supporters in the crowd shouted that "the public *had* judged," and the meeting was thrown into turmoil with continued shouting.[15]

The struggle among Minneapolis Republicans now focused on delegates to the National Convention in Kansas City, and Backus's partner, state senator William Brooks, was expected to be re-elected as a delegate. Hubachek's Twin Cities group of Republican conservationists contested his election with two candidates of their own. In *Saving Quetico-Superior*, R. Newell Searle wrote that Brooks found himself trapped between his better instincts and his loyalty to Backus. In the end, he withdrew his candidacy "in a gesture of harmony.... When he tried to moderate the views of his senior partner, quarrel followed quarrel."[16] A letter found in the Backus files of the Koochiching County Historical Society reads:

> "I ... can remember the day Sen. Wm. F. Brooks stormed out of the office for the last time. I believe he died that night of a heart attack. I don't know whether he and E. W. had a falling out, rumors were to that effect."[17]

It seems that, for all practical purposes, the death of William Brooks liberated the Minnesota Republican Party from the powerful grip of Edward Backus.[18]

In the oral history interviews, Ober recalled that Backus tried "every known device to defeat the Shipstead-Newton bill." One such had to do with a "conservation" group Backus pulled together called the Minnesota Outers Club. Through it, he hoped to give the appearance of grassroots support for his boundary-lakes plan. He made it easy to join:

"It cost only a dollar to belong," said Ober. "Its three main officials were also officials in Mr. Backus's company, and they got together a great many one-dollar memberships all of a sudden. I was in Washington presenting our position to a committee, and I handed a list of our supporters to the committee chairman.

"'Well, Mr. Oberholtzer,' he said, 'what about the Outers Club? Here's a telegram I received just this morning.'

"The telegram stated that the outers had pretty nearly a thousand members, representative citizens of Minneapolis, and that they were bitterly opposed to this piece of legislation.

"'Well,' I said, 'I'll have to tell you frankly that I have never heard of them. They are something new. But I promise to get you information on them as soon as I possibly can.'

"I went back to Minnesota, and we found out that the club's officers were all members of Backus's organization and that they hadn't consulted their rank and file membership at all as to their attitudes about the bill. They had simply taken it on themselves to wire that this organization, with so many members, was unalterably opposed.

"We asked for the right to go before this new club. We had heard that there were members of the group who were absolutely surprised when they found out what had happened. They said that, if you can present your side before an open meeting, we'll support you to the limit.

"Well, we asked for an open meeting and got it, and the man on the *Journal,* whose business it was to follow these things, went with us. He was a live wire in reporting on our issues. When we got there, we couldn't get into the meeting. The doors were locked. We were told that they were in an executive session, and we would have to wait upstairs. Waiting up there, we could hear this great thumping and bumping and yelling—loud excitement below us. After about an hour, we were asked to come down and present our story.

"Meanwhile, some of those members who were for us and hadn't known how they'd been used had discovered what had happened in their name. Oh, they just raised Cain. And so the rest of them, the Backus officials, were pretty well subdued. We were asked to speak, and we presented our side quietly. We told of our surprise when this organization, new in conservation, had taken its action against us. When we finished, there was an overwhelming and thumping vote in our favor."

The *Minneapolis Journal* article of the following morning recounted that Ober and the heads of the Izaak Walton League and the Minnesota Game Protective Association had been barred from the meeting by the club's officers. After two hours of battling between officers and membership, the doors had been opened and Ober had been allowed to make his presentation. Immediately following it, a "resolution opposing 'private exploitation' of the Rainy Lake watershed and supporting the plan for an international playground on the Minnesota-Ontario boundary, proposed by the Quetico Superior council, was adopted without a dissenting vote . . . by 57 members of the Minnesota Outers Club."[19]

Up on the border, Backus was employing yet another strategy. He bought a magazine called *Trails of the Northwoods,* through which he editorialized his position and in which he offered free advertising to resort and tourist people who supported him. "Its manager," said Ober, "had a plane in which he flew to Winnipeg and points all over the area where

people were living. He flew up here while I was away and visited most of
our supporters. He called on a resort owner I knew named Mrs. McPeek,
and this is the way she said he operated:

"'Do you know Mr. Oberholtzer?'

"'Oh, yes, we've known him a long time.'

"'He's working down in the legislature now, isn't he?'

"'Yes.'

"'But Mrs. McPeek, do you realize how he's representing your interests? Did you know that he's against you entirely? I know he doesn't seem
to be. I know he seems like a credible fellow, but you should hear what he's
saying down there. What he's saying about these resorts.'

"'Why I can't believe that. I don't think that could possibly be true.'

"'Well, it is, and you're supporting him. Your name is on a list of resort
owners up here that want this bill to go through.'

"We found out he was going to resorts and such and offering them free
advertising in the magazine. Then he flew to Winnipeg, and the next thing
we knew there was quite a piece in the paper there telling how the mayor
of Winnipeg was for Mr. Backus's project."

Backus and others would continue to make false assertions about Ober
for years, claiming that he wanted to end all financial enterprise in the region and even that he was accepting under-the-table payments for his environmental stance. In the end, these tactics were not without success,
especially in Ontario.

Meanwhile, working in support of the Shipstead-Newton bill in Washington, Ober discovered that electric power interests had influence in the
Senate: "There *were* senators," he said, "who were 'available' to electric power
interests. The Minnesota Power and Light Company were opposed to us,
because our plan ran counter to a project of theirs they called Gabbro-
Bald Eagle, up northeast of Duluth. They had acquired the area through
an arrangement with the Weyerhaeusers. The Weyerhaeusers were in the
habit of giving their cutover lands to Minnesota Power and Light in exchange for stock. And Minnesota Power and Light would then have a
flowage area for water storage, you see.

"Well, when we were working on our bill in the U.S. Senate, the man
who represented the power industry came to me one day early in the sessions and introduced himself. A nice-looking gentleman. The fellow put
his arm around me immediately and said:

"'Now, young man, Minnesota Power and Light is all for your goals, of
course. I represent them as well as certain other clients of very high character. Now, we'd have no objection to this bill of yours, if it weren't for this
conflict. If we can't go ahead with this project we've started, it's going to

mean a million-dollar loss for Minnesota Power and Light.[20] I think you can appreciate this. And we started the project before you introduced your bill.'

"It's true that they'd started their project. They'd put in the first dam, only five feet high or so, but it would flood the shoreline. And they said they had to have, in order to complete their project, ten feet more or they would lose some million dollars. Well, we didn't know anything about this project when we introduced the Shipstead-Nolan bill. It came to our attention through them, when they asked us to make an exception of their project. We said we hadn't known anything about it, and that we'd have to go up and investigate the situation. We couldn't make an exception unless there was a real difference between their project and what Mr. Backus had planned.

"'Anytime you want to come and have a look, we'll be ready,' he said. 'We'll take you right up. We'll have a man ready winter or summer.'

"And so, during a relaxed interval, I came back that winter and went over to Duluth and was taken up. It was, oh, a very cold day, just frightfully cold. I looked the situation over, got all the facts, made the measurements. After our assessment, we had to write and tell them that we were sorry, but we couldn't agree with them. We found their project unacceptable. If we made this exception, our bill would be worthless. There was no difference whatsoever between their project and those outlined by Mr. Backus.

"The only argument they had was that they had already started their project. That is, they'd put their dam in. But they had no authority to do so. Nobody ever gave them authority. The state hadn't. The federal government hadn't. They tried to make it appear that at least some forest supervisor in the area had winked in their direction, but they had never been given any actual authority, whatever this supervisor's attitude might have been. Anyway, we couldn't, with any consistency, say, well, yes, what you're doing is all right, and then continue to oppose Backus.

"So then they said they'd like to have us come to dinner. They'd have a meeting of their directors and invite us to dinner. Fred Winston and I went, and the dinner was beautifully appointed. Oh, it was excellent—the food, wine, everything. When the dinner was over, an introductory speech was given. The *Duluth Herald* was a company stockholder, and the publisher was there. He was one of the directors. One of the Weyerhaeusers was there. He was one of the directors. Men of that sort were on the board, you see, very substantial citizens.

"I had to get up and explain to this group how I had gone up to their project area, that we'd found they hadn't a shred of authorization for what they'd done and now intended, either from the state or the federal governments, and that it would place us in a very difficult position if we were to openly say their project should be excluded. Oh, my gracious! After they had provided such hospitality. They talked as if we were just a bunch of bums. Oh, they thought we were terrible, but we could never consent to what they wanted.

"Shipstead was sensitive to this situation. He had a lot of supporters there in Duluth. The company boasted that quite a large percentage of families in the area owned stock with them, you see, and they would lose income because of us. Shipstead said there was a question of fairness here, and no matter what, he always wanted to be fair to everybody. He finally insisted on this. He thought the best approach would be to write an amendment leaving the question to the state, since state lands were involved. It would give the state the opportunity to adopt a waterpower philosophy."

The conservationists were unhappy with this concession, but an amendment was written into the bill: "It didn't approve what Minnesota Power and Light had done," said Ober, "but it excluded from our provisions any enterprise started before such-and-such a date, before our bill had been launched. That was an easy way of handling it."

In northern Minnesota, significant grassroots resistance to the Shipstead-Newton bill began in 1929. Not all of it was stimulated by Backus supporters. Local governments feared loss of tax revenue. Others in the affected region thought the area to be protected was just too large to give

Shoreline damage caused by the lumber industry

over to outside control. Ober, who never ceased to dream of protecting the full 14,500 square miles of the Rainy Lake watershed, making of it a vast ten-million-acre wilderness sanctuary, may have misunderstood the grassroots nature of this resistance. Local people, holding to independent frontier values, wanted control of their own ground, and, fed misinformation by Backus supporters, they poorly understood the balanced, long-term, multi-use economic approach advocated in the Program. Ober, however, found it hard to believe that resistance to the plan came from other than a few selfish and powerful individuals. Some believe that his underestimation of local resistance proved a long-term hindrance to the Quetico-Superior program. Others have held that his continuing insistence on protecting the entire watershed led to considerably more of it being protected than could otherwise have been the case. There is likely some truth to both viewpoints.

It has been said of Ober that he could never compromise, and final, more conciliatory negotiations would usually have to be made by other, more pragmatic conservationists. In an oral history interview, Ober's longtime friend Ray Anderson stated that he once asked a question of Ober:

"'Aren't you asking for all of this, Ober, so you'll be sure to get something?'

"'No,' he said, 'I want it all. That's the way I want it.'"[21]

In any case, Ober found little time to languish in his home region, absorbing grassroots opinions. Even when at the Mallard, his work continued to arrive by the bagful in the mails, and he would then be off on frequent reconnaissance missions, canoe trips during which he monitored the environmental impact of dams, logging, and other commercial activities on the Rainy Lake watershed. The photographs and descriptive stories he brought back gave him exceptional authority as he argued for the Quetico-Superior program. It is believed that he paddled an average of 500 miles a year on such trips. And when each trip was completed, he would likely step from his canoe and board a train to St. Paul, Chicago, and Washington, D.C., then on to New York, Ottawa, and Toronto. This was a circuit, often traveled in ill health, that would continue for decades. There was satisfaction for Ober in knowing with clarity what he must do, but his inner being often groaned with longing to return to a more personal life, one closer to his heart's desire, among the pure waterways and pine-scented portages of his home country.

[16]

The Shipstead-Nolan Act

In 1929, the bill in support of the Quetico-Superior program became known as the Shipstead-*Nolan* bill. Its original sponsor in the U.S. House of Representatives, Walter Newton, resigned to become Herbert Hoover's secretary and was replaced by William Nolan. Although Nolan had also agreed to support the measure, conservationists were uncertain about him:

"Nolan had once been lieutenant governor of Minnesota," said Ober. "He was known to be a close personal friend of Backus. In terms of the things he'd supported, we thought his legislative record was poor. Many of our people, therefore, were dreadfully opposed to him, but, when he was running for election, Fred Winston went to see him and got him committed to our program. Nolan spoke very frankly:

"'Yes, I was a friend of Backus, but I don't stand with him at all on this project. I can assure you, Fred, that this is true.'

"'Would you be willing,' Fred asked him, 'to give me your written pledge that if you are elected you will give us your utmost assistance?'

"'I surely will.'

"Fred accepted him at his word, and throughout the campaign we did not attack him in any way. Nor did we do an awful lot for him. But we didn't attack him, and he was vulnerable because of things he'd done and supported in the past.

"'Ober,' Fred said, 'he told me absolutely that he would protect our plan.'

"And you know, when he was elected, the first thing he did was write me. Fred and I went over to see him, and Nolan made categorical commitments as to the various points we wanted upheld in the plan, [points] that were in danger, where we were running into difficulties. And he never failed us. He stuck when many others turned against us."

Despite an earlier record that was less than stellar from the conservationist's point of view, Nolan was simply and staunchly against the massive destruction to the natural character of the boundary lakes that would inevitably result should the Backus plan prevail.

Late in the summer of 1929, Tyng and Hubachek arranged an interview for Ober with newly elected President Hoover: "Sewell Tyng had been his secretary just after the First World War," said Ober. "With the backing of

Hubachek, who had a good deal of political influence, Sewell arranged for us to meet with Hoover during the campaign for our bill. Of course, we got a lot of publicity out of this. This was in the summer of 1929.

"'Now, Ober,' Sewell warned me, 'don't be disconcerted when you get there in front of Hoover. He has the trick of seeming to not be listening to you at all. While you're talking, he'll probably just draw lines or something, and not ask any questions, not seem to be listening. But, whatever you've got to say, just say it to him. Over in Europe, while he was listening, I often saw him write on a piece of paper: p-h-o-o-l. His way of spelling *fool:* P-h-o-o-l. Don't mind that.'

"It was awfully hot weather. A lot of discomfort in Washington that time of the year. The papers were just flaming with this reception the Quetico-Superior Council was receiving from Hoover. We were met by newspapermen outside, and they went in and got the president's interpretation of our project. We, of course, didn't make any comments ourselves, but we'd left written material with the secretary when we'd gone in. Some of this was published. It all sounded very favorable for us. Of course, we made the utmost of the publicity. So Hoover didn't do anything to harm us, but I don't think our goals were very close to his heart.

"When I came back, my mother asked me what I thought of the interview, and I said, 'Well, I tell you, I found it discouraging. I don't think he has the slightest interest in the world in what we are after. But I suppose it was worthwhile doing.'"

It was at this point, in the midst of the struggle for passage of the Shipstead-Nolan bill, that Ober was to suffer perhaps the greatest personal loss of his life. Rosa had been living with heart problems for years, and during the summer of 1929 she became desperately ill. In a June 27 letter to a Davenport friend, Ober, who had returned to Minneapolis, wrote:

> My mother has been with me here in Mpls continuously for the past year and a half, part of the time in the hospital and part at our rooms. She has been an invalid all that time....[1]

Rosa's condition continued to worsen. Though believing that her doctor, George Douglas Head, was "one of the best heart men in the northwest," Ober, in desperation, wrote duplicate letters to two Davenport doctors, former family friends, asking for suggestions that might prove helpful. He described Rosa's situation in detail:

> My mother has had pneumonia twice in the past year, with resulting pleural effusion, which she has managed both times with great difficulty to absorb. The last spell was in February of this year and she has had a nurse ever since.... [Doctor Head] says the whole difficulty is due to the heart and poor circulation....[2]

The Davenport doctors were able to offer little more than sympathy. Meanwhile, the demands of Ober's leadership role in the struggle for Quetico-Superior continued to grow. In a July 13 letter, he wrote:

> ...I have never worked so hard in all my life, not even at Rainy Lake. There I at least varied my work. Here it has been only one thing day and night for nearly two years. We are up against bitter and powerful opposition, and of course as with all public movements have had a deuce of a time financing ourselves....[3]

On July 31, Rosa received flowers in the mail. They had been picked the day before by their International Falls friend, Dr. Mary Ghostley, who some believed had been kept from a relationship with Ober by Rosa. In her letters, however, Ghostley expressed a warm friendship for Rosa as she did for Ober, but nothing more. Gossipy conjecture to the contrary, it may well be that there never had been even a brief budding of romance between Dr. Ghostley and Ober. In any case, Ghostley was now married, and in her note she wrote as an afterthought, "Oh, I have a baby—a dear little girl."[4]

On August 12, to pay medical bills, Ober drew $500 from a stock account held with Harris, Winthrop and Company of Chicago. And then, in a letter dated August 14, 1929, Ober wrote to a friend: "Lost my dear mother late today."[5]

Immediately after this date in the Oberholtzer papers there appears a list of Rosa's virtues written by Ober in preparation for her eulogy:

> A keen sense of humor. Sympathy and imagination.
> A careful and shrewd observer of people. Excellent judge of character.
> A woman of deep and tender feeling.
> Never asking anything for herself. Sensitive.
> Developing an ever richer philosophy and charm. Becoming daily richer.
> Shared in all activities on the lake and in those for protection of region now in progress. Had made a deep sacrifice.
> Spontaneous, never studied, and evoked the same qualities in others.
> Ready to make any sacrifice for those she loved.
> Able to play part of both father and mother.[6]

The following from an obituary article in the Davenport paper, most of which certainly came from Ober, reveal more of the gratitude and love he felt for Rosa:

> She met every demand upon her courage, her energy and her sympathy, [and] was a woman of deep and tender feeling. She was a friend of all dumb creatures and a lover of all sorts and conditions of people. She liked best the intimacy of the home and made a fireside sanctuary wherever she went. Her

devotion to her friends and particularly to her family knew no bounds. No sacrifice was too great. And she inspired the same devotion in others. . . .

The article also describes an abundance of floral tributes to Rosa at her funeral, many from organizations such as the Izaak Walton League of America. It then adds:

> The casket bore only one remembrance, a bunch of lilies of the valley from her son Ernest. . . . Interment was made in the evening light in the E. S. Carl lot at Oakdale cemetery. The body was laid to rest between the parents and the deceased son, Frank. . . .[7]

With Rosa's death, Ober had lost the most important person in his life, the woman that some had called "Mrs. Ober." As mentioned before, Ober was strangely moved to have a death mask made of Rosa's face. His friend Kit Bakeless thought this "the most gruesome thing. I couldn't understand why he wanted to do that, but it was very important to him."[8] According to Ted Hall, Ober had smaller replicas made of the mask as well: "I never saw the original. These were, say, half-scale. And one was plaster, and it hung over his little writing space up on the top floor of the Bird House for years. And there was another that had been cast in bronze. They were rather grim looking."[9]

Throughout his life, Ober had been supported and empowered by Rosa. In response to those who believe that she was too much present in his life, it must be remembered that her presence was, perhaps more than anything else, the matrix of his life, the source of what he became. If her continuing closeness limited the normalcy of his development, it at the same time reinforced much that was exceptional in him. Those who admire the son should admire the mother. Rosa was a great mother, with all the psychological implications contained in the term. In a letter to William Hapgood written shortly after her death, Ober wrote that, if he had nothing else, in Rosa's life he had "a very precious and inspiring memory."[10]

Flooded with letters of sympathy, Ober now had to deal with medical and funeral bills and an estate that included Rosa's Davenport house at 35 Oak Lane, much in need of repair. There were problems with its tenants as well, and with the onset of the depression, it could not be sold. Its rental value fell from $60 to $25 a month. Then it was sold for back taxes. Later, however, Ober's financial situation had improved enough that he was able to redeem it before the termination date.[11] In addition to his mother's house, Ober had inherited a commercial building he called "the old Market." This modest-sized building stood at 422 West Second Street in Davenport, just a couple blocks up from the waterfront of the Mississippi. The old Market was to be Ober's one stable source of income through most of the rest of his life. It was of Civil War vintage, and income from it was by no means high—a 1932 letter enclosing payment from the Crescent Meat Market shows the rent to have been $110 a month—but it continued steady and was the financial thread by which he would often hang.[12]

Meanwhile, shortly after Rosa's death, the Internal Revenue Service was wondering why Ober had not been paying taxes. In an October 25 letter, he explained that they had received no statements from him because he had been without income, but that he was now earning $5,000 a year. The source of this income, his position as president of the Quetico-Superior Council, could now allow him no time for mourning. It was essential that he return to Washington, D.C., and give his all to pushing the Shipstead-Nolan bill through Congress.

Ober's work—Billy Magee would have called it a hard portage—was now clear before him, and from morning to night he threw himself into testifying, lobbying, and spearheading a nationwide campaign to sway public opinion in favor of the bill. In January of 1930, with the help of Assistant Chief Forester Leon Kniepp—the forester to whom he had first "sold" the Program—Ober reluctantly worked out several small changes in the bill. These were adjustments that the Forest Service and congressional committees thought would be useful in support of timber utilization in the region.[13]

Then, on January 22, Backus supporters tried to derail the Shipstead-Nolan bill by introducing another of their own, written by Representative William Pittenger of Duluth: "This was supposedly a bill similar to ours," said Ober in the oral history interviews, "but described as more temperate, more logical, and yet would achieve the same goals, you see. It was supposed to take out objectionable features without lessening the value of the bill, but, when you read it carefully, you discovered that it authorized the very things that our bill forbade. It *authorized* them. How he could ever hope to get such a thing through was difficult to see. I guess it was a device to delay and confuse. Oh, we had a dreadful time. Pittenger was the man, above all others, who played Mr. Backus's game in the House."

In a Quetico-Superior Council publication written later, Ober analyzed this alternative bill and the strategy behind it. Pittenger, he wrote, claimed that the "essential purposes of the two bills" were the same. "If so," Ober asked, "why the substitute?" He continued with his detailed analysis:

> The essential purposes of the Shipstead-Nolan bill were two-fold—to forbid the logging of federal shore lines and to forbid, except by consent of Congress, the alteration of lake levels affecting federal lands.
>
> *Neither of these prohibitions could have been accomplished by the Pittenger bill.* Instead of the first, the Pittenger bill substituted the meaning-

less phrase: "Logging of all such shores shall be done only as permitted by and under the supervision of the Forest Service"—doubtless pleasing to the lumbermen but laying down no policy whatever. [Nor would] this bill guard shores, islands, beaches, rapids, and waterfalls against flooding, since it specifically left federal lands, which are the basis of the legislation, open to "appropriation" *and entry as mineral lands.* This could have but one result—to make it possible for private interests to acquire easements and ownership over present federal shore lines.

...The revised boundaries in the Pittenger bill would in themselves have omitted two-thirds of Superior National Forest, hundreds of the best lakes in the area, and the whole of the beautiful and historic section in the vicinity of Grand Portage. But what is more important, the language of the bill itself, as indicated above would have undermined the entire purpose of the Nolan bill. Backus would have been free to proceed with the border lakes; the Minnesota Power and Light Company, with the tributaries.

Nor was this all. Section 1 of the Pittenger bill contained an amendment, taking away the present discretion of the Forest Service with respect to roads and [made] it mandatory upon them to grant rights of way for railways and highways. This would have resulted in time in the complete destruction of the character of the region.[14]

As Ober had written, the Pittenger alternative was a "device to delay and confuse." In the end, a small, face-saving amendment was written into the Shipstead-Nolan bill for Pittenger—it excluded a small number of peripheral lakes from the region to be covered by the terms of the Shipstead-Nolan bill—but Pittenger's alternative bill did not win the day.

Edward Backus was also now in Washington, D.C., giving testimony before Congress in support of his boundary plan and against the Shipstead-Nolan bill. His principal argument was that it was not the U.S. Congress but the International Joint Commission that must make decisions affecting the boundary waters. To ignore the IJC, he contended, was the same as ignoring Canadian rights on the boundary waters. Backus hammered away on this theme, and as an extension of his argument, he sprung a surprise on the conservationists. Having considerable influence in Ontario, he had gone there and arranged for what he hoped would be a significant roadblock to the Shipstead-Nolan bill. On February 7, 1930, he announced in a congressional hearing that he had heard something about a coming protest from the Canadian government.

"They called it a protest," said Ober. "Mr. Backus advertised it as a protest from the Dominion government. All that had happened, really, was that Backus had been powerful enough to get Ontario officials to say that they feared our bill was going to hurt their interests, and the Dominion government, in fairness, had had to send this message to our Department of

State. This was easily handled by our writing an amendment which read: 'Nothing in this bill shall be interpreted as in any way interfering with existing rights or agreements between the two governments.' We didn't lose anything by this, and it removed the false objection that Backus had managed to raise.

"The day before the Canadian 'protest' arrived, newspapermen frightened us by asking: 'Do you know what's coming tomorrow? Mr. Backus has this supporting protest from the Dominion government. This is very serious. How can you hope to get your bill through now?'

"I was alarmed. I went over to a big nearby hotel to telephone Mr. Tyng, the New York lawyer who'd been supporting us, to tell him about this new threat. As I was going through the revolving door, here came Mr. Backus, whom I'd been meeting in the hearings, you see, but in a formal, cold manner. He looked as if he were going to the finest party—a brand new suit, brand new fedora hat, and a cane. He was all smiles, so happy with himself over this coming protest from the Dominion government the next day, which was causing me so much anguish. He saw me and stopped.

"'How do you do, my boy. Well, nice to see you here in the Willard.' Then he said, 'So you're still climbing the tree?'

"'Oh, yes,' I said, 'pretty tall tree, isn't it? I don't know, maybe I'll get up there yet.'

"'Well, we'll see,' he said, and went on through the door."

The Shipstead-Nolan bill made it through the U.S. Senate, but, as with the resolution in support of it in the Minnesota legislature, Backus managed to get the bill stranded in committee in the House of Representatives:

"Shipstead hadn't had much trouble getting it through the Senate," said Ober. "He had wonderful allies there who helped him, you see. The House had taken it up, but we couldn't get it out of the rules committee. A man named [Bertrand] Snell from New York State was in charge of that committee. He'd held that position for years and was quite famous at the time. Legislation that wasn't favored by old-liners who were for the big companies wouldn't be let out of committee for a vote. And Snell was doing this to us."

Apparently, Snell's refusal to release the bill was at least in part an effort to discipline Minnesota Republicans, especially Nolan, who had deviated from the party line. The refusal was also seen as a reward for Pittenger, who had not deviated.[15] Ober, however, was soon to discover that the principal roadblock was within the *Minnesota* Republican delegation, in which a powerful group of representatives were committed to the Backus plan, perhaps because of financial contributions, perhaps because their philosophies were more closely tied to ideas of industrial growth than environmental preservation. The congressional session was almost over, and the bill was going nowhere. This was just the sort of crisis in which Fred Winston shone most brightly:

"Fred had lots of courage," said Ober. "He never hesitated when something like this came up and you couldn't get anywhere. He'd go right to the man and demand to be heard, you see. He was very fine in this way. He did this in the Minnesota legislature, and he did it in the U.S. Congress. I hesitated to go to Snell. I didn't know him. I didn't know anything about him. But we knew he had us stymied. And so Fred, who always felt that such men had a better side, that if you appealed to them in the right way you could get a good and truthful response, went to him.

"'I know the sort of thing Snell does,' he told me, 'but I think he, too, is a straight-shooter. I think you can count on him to do what he says he will. He says he can't let this out because there's a delegation that opposes it. He didn't say who this is, but he won't let it out for this reason.'

"There were only a few days left in the session. It had gone through the Senate, and Shipstead told us, 'If you can get this to a vote in the House, even if they make some small amendment that will require further action by the Senate, I guarantee to hold the Senate in session long enough to act on this.' Otherwise, it would have had to go to an entirely new Congress, you see, and we had worked like everything on this thing. So Fred went to Snell again and Snell said:

"'Mr. Winston, if you will get a resolution from the Minnesota delegation asking me to let this out of committee, I'll do it. It will be available immediately for a vote.'

"Fred came to me and said, 'I've already gone to see the chairman of the Minnesota delegation.'

"This was a Minnesotan named [August] Andresen from down around Red Wing who'd been in Washington a long time and was very influential on farm matters. We knew he didn't stand with us. I wasn't pleased at all by much of his performance. He didn't seem to be being entirely honest with us. He'd always have reasons why he couldn't do something with us, and there was always a sort of snarl in his voice. He didn't like us. We were a nuisance to him. And yet he was a very influential man, the chairman of the agriculture committee, as well as being on this House committee of lands. Well, Fred went to him and asked him for a session that afternoon.

"'You can't have it,' Andresen said. 'You can't have it, Fred.'

"'Well, why not?'

"'We're too busy. These are busy men. We're approaching the end of the session here, and they've got all kinds of business that has to be done. We can't fool around with this now. Why didn't you come to me three months ago?'

"Well, the situation hadn't arisen then. But Fred said, 'Now, look here. We want this *this afternoon.* Are you telling us no? Here's our portfolio of favorable newspaper commentary.' Fred always had all these things right with him. 'Are you, in the face of all of this and in the face of our favorable Senate action, are you going to let this bill be lost because you can't get together here for ten minutes and decide whether or not to ask Snell to let it out?'

"Andresen was firmly in support of the Backus plan, but this was the sort of pressure that politicians must take seriously. Andresen says, 'I'll see what I can do.' And he got the Minnesota delegation together.

"'Now, we're going to meet at two o'clock in the afternoon,' Fred said to me, 'and you're not to come, Ober. But come with me anyway. You can wait outside the door.'

"I didn't want to come, but did. Fred went in there. He never minced words when he did these things. He just told the delegation point-blank:

"'This is something that the state is absolutely determined to have, and you know it, and you know why. And we all know why you're opposing it. Now, do you want the whole story to go back to the newspapers in your home constituencies? Is that the way you want it to be? Or are you going to do the right thing and urge Snell to let this out of committee this evening?'

"They took an affirmative vote on it right then and there. When they broke up, the first man coming out of the door was Andresen. He walked up to me. He was just frothing at the mouth.

"'Oberholtzer,' he said, 'I'll be damned if any such outrage will ever again happen in this committee.'

"Oh, he was so enraged he just didn't know what to do. He was one of those who'd been opposing our bill, but now it was too late. Anyway, the day after we got the consent which freed the bill to be voted on in the House, the American Forestry Association laid a booklet on the desk of every senator and representative in Washington. The American Forestry Association had edited it beautifully. It was illustrated, largely in colors. The frontispiece was a picture of a great tall young fellow with a huge muskie. It was a very effective piece of printing and illustrating. The American Forestry Association had just gone the limit to give us everything they could, and they had one of these booklets lying on the desk of every member of Congress before the vote was taken.

"Our bill was acted on and passed at half-past eleven on the last night of the session. It went immediately over to the Senate where Shipstead was waiting. There had to be one slight change, and he got them to accept that at once. There had been bitter opposition, but, when the vote was cast, not one member in either [the House or the Senate] dared to vote against the bill. A certain number of people absented themselves. Not a great many, though. Pittenger did. But nobody in the whole of Congress, House or Senate, voted against it, which was very unusual. If it hadn't passed on *that* night, we would have had to start all over again with the next Congress."

After many months of unrelenting, sometimes heroic effort by Ober, Winston, and others, the Shipstead-Nolan bill passed without a single dissenting vote on July 3, 1930, at the midnight hour of the last day of the congressional session. President Hoover signed it into law on July 10. Before the bill had even passed the Senate, Ober was on his way back to Minnesota. A telegram from Winston caught up with him in Detroit on July 4: "Senate concurred in final hour of session hurrah for Shipstead."[16]

Congratulations poured in on Ober from all quarters, and he was surely exhilarated by his part in the success, but in the statement he quickly sent to six Twin Cities newspapers, all honor was given to those who had supported him:

> Felicitations to the conservationists of Minnesota and of the whole country.... Too much praise cannot be given to the loyal men and women all over the country, many of them unrecognized, who gave of their best in the public interest. The cooperation from individuals, associations, and the metropolitan press was brilliant. No previous conservation effort in America has had anywhere near comparable support.[17]

Fred Winston of course had been the first of all those who would go largely unrecognized for their contribution, and in a July 9 letter to him, Ober wrote:

> Where would I have been this winter without you and [your wife] Elizabeth and what hope would there ever have been for our movement without the essential [financial] backing you secured it back in Minnesota?[18]

In its support of wilderness values for federal lands, the Shipstead-Nolan Act was the first legislation of its kind, and Ober believed correctly that it would remain the foundation of their continuing efforts. He wrote that the essential purposes of the act "were two-fold—to forbid the logging of federal shore lines and to forbid, except by consent of Congress, the alteration of lake levels affecting federal lands."[19] In truth, in a historical sense, the Shipstead-Nolan Act accomplished far more than this. Foreshadowing the Wilderness Act of 1964, it was something new in United States history. For the first time, Congress had legislated that federal lands should be preserved as wilderness. Such lands, wrote Ober, would link "us with the primeval past... promising sanctuary for all time to unborn multitudes."[20]

With Ober at the helm, the conservationists of the Quetico-Superior movement had guided the U.S. Congress into new legislative waters, a region of shimmering environmental consciousness that for the first time officially recognized and mandated wilderness values.

[17]

Return to Harvard

Back in May of 1930, with the Shipstead-Nolan bill still inching its way through Congress, Ober traveled north from Washington carrying letters of introduction to Lawrence Winship of the *Boston Globe* and F. Lauriston Bullard, Esq., of the *Boston Herald*. He hoped to gain editorial support from these papers, but he had a personal agenda for the trip as well. It had been more than twenty years since he had returned to Harvard, and there were three old friends whom he dearly hoped to visit: Samuel Morison, Conrad Aiken, and Charles Copeland, a noted English professor under whom he had studied. In the oral history interviews, Ober revealed how emotional this reunion with his old friends was for him. He began by recalling his difficult final parting in Scotland with Conrad Aiken so many years before:

"My thoughts have often returned to that incident. I wouldn't have lost Conrad Aiken as a friend for anything in the world. I had had no correspondence with him. Once in a while I'd send a card, and I'd get a card back. No letters. I never expected letters, but the cards were always friendly and nice.

"I decided to go up on the Fall River Boat, which always used to be a very lovely trip from New York to Boston. You rode the boat overnight. As I was getting close to Boston, I began to think, well, what do I want to do when I get there? Whom do I want to see? It was Conrad Aiken. I sure wanted to get in touch with him. And I wanted to see Sam Morison, if I could, and Copeland, under whom I had studied English. Those three people above all. I wired them in advance, hoping they would be there."

Such reunions make one acutely aware of what he or she has become, and Ober was anxious as to how these old friends would now perceive him: "Well, if possible, I wanted to meet with these three, but I felt great diffidence. I had led this life that was so absolutely different from theirs. Possibly they didn't approve of my life. I didn't know, you see, for they'd never said. They would undoubtedly have expected me to do very different things. They might even scorn the life I was living out here, like a wild man, such a physical life. I didn't know, and of course it would have been an awful blow to me if I'd come into contact with these people and they were no longer interested in me or even friendly. That would have hurt me terribly."

Ober's first stop was at the home of Samuel Eliot Morison, who was on his way to becoming one of America's foremost historians. Morison, who had already done substantial work, was to write more than twenty-five books, two of which, *Admiral of the Ocean Sea* and *John Paul Jones,* would win Pulitzer Prizes. In 1942, President Franklin Delano Roosevelt would commission Morison to write a history of U.S. naval operations during World War II, a project that resulted in fifteen volumes published between 1947 and 1962.[1]

As many have noted, Ober loved to develop a fascinating narrative from the slightest situation. He discovered, for instance, as he was walking to Morison's home, that he did not know the way, but his legs did!

"As I approached Boston that night," said Ober, "I was thinking, let me see, where did Sam Morison live? I knew he lived on the hill near the capitol, near Beacon Street. His place was called Brimmer, on one of the oldest streets in Boston. I went there every day for a year, tutoring his brother, and I often walked quite a distance. And I thought, how do you get there now? I was going to see Sam first, you see. When I began walking, it was a very strange thing. There's something automatic, I guess, that underlies our movements. I didn't think about it anymore. I just let my legs go, and they walked me straight to Sam Morison's house. I can't tell you how it ever happened.

"I rang his bell that morning, and Sam came down to the door. The boat had got in quite early. We shook hands and went up to his office.

"'Sam,' I said, 'it beats all, but some things seem to have just been inbred into my bones. I could never have told anybody how to get to your house, and yet here I came, directly. I came around the corner to your house, and there was the parrot, hanging out of a corner window, seeming to be the same parrot that was there every single morning twenty-five years ago, when I came to tutor Bradford.'

"'What parrot?' asked Sam.

"'Why, the parrot that was always there when I came to tutor Bradford.'

"Sam paused a while. 'You know, Ober, that parrot has never entered my mind. It's been there all these years. I never even knew it was there. You're the first person to ever call my attention to it. I guess those people did have a parrot all this time.'

"Wasn't it strange that Sam should be so oblivious? But then he was concentrating on his work all the time. And I, of course, had entered a new environment and such a thing would have impressed me."

Ober took pride in the often impressive accomplishments of his friends, and he tended toward hyperbole in telling of them. Such is the case as he reminisced about Morison. When they were in college together, he had predicted that Sam would be offered the presidency of Harvard: "Usually,

I never saw much of Sam, because he was always studying. He was always absolutely devoted to his studying. One day, when I was in his room and he seemed a little freer, I said to him:

"'Sam, one day you're going to be president of Harvard.'

"And, sure enough, he *was* offered the presidency. But he didn't take it. That wasn't scholarly enough. He didn't want administrative work. He was a scholar. And probably Harvard has never had a greater scholar. I can't imagine anybody that would be more meticulous about his scholarship than Sam Morison. He regarded it as absolutely unforgivable to slip up. But, of course, out of the huge amount of material he has gone through, it would be remarkable if he hasn't slipped up somewhere. This would be forgivable, out of such a mass of manuscripts. I think often of all he's accomplished, especially as we can see it now in these later days, when he's completely ripe.

"Well, then, I'd passed through that gauntlet. With Sam, it was the same as it had been years ago, as if I'd walked into his room back then, when we knew each other so well. I couldn't see the slightest difference. Sam, of course, had always been reserved and dignified. He was a scholar above all else, you see. He's had a marvelous record. He's a marvelous man, and here I was leading the life—in some ways, of a recluse. Some called me a hermit, you see. But, of course, I was anything but a hermit. Though I lived alone on the island, hordes of people were coming up here all the time. Still, my life was anything but scholarly. I wasn't reading. I was always traveling by canoe, mingling with the Indians, had great numbers of Indians as intimate friends. There was nothing scholarly about my life, but nevertheless Sam and I were perfectly at ease with each other, as if it were our old college days, as if there were no difference whatsoever in our lives."

Surely Ober's life must have seemed strange to Morison, but just as surely Ober and the open-air life he had led and the movement he now headed must have seemed a breath of fresh air to Morison, even inspiring, just as Morison's life was inspiring to Ober.

As Ober explained, when Morison welcomed him warmly, he felt as if he had passed through a gauntlet. His approach to Conrad Aiken proved a second such trial. Aiken had already published twenty respected books, mostly of poetry, and in the year of Ober's visit his *Selected Poems* would win the Pulitzer Prize. In 1953, his *Collected Poems* would win the National Book Award. Much of Aiken's fiction is based on psychoanalytic theory, and Sigmund Freud would acclaim his book *Great Circle* to be a masterpiece of analytical introspection.[2]

"I didn't know how it would be with Conrad Aiken," said Ober. "He had told me I should telephone him, and he told me where he lived in Harvard Square. So, because the time was short, I telephoned from Sam's about coming to his house.

"'Yes, come out and have dinner with me,' he said. Then he added, 'I don't know whether you know that my wife and I have separated.'"

Aiken, whom Ober had characterized as the shyest, most sensitive man he had ever known, had become something of a Don Juan and had just divorced the second of his Loreleis.

"That was his second wife," said Ober, "and he was warning me in order to avoid any embarrassment. He didn't say anything about a third wife. I went out to his place in an old hall in Harvard Square, a very well known place."

Technologically incompetent as ever, Ober could not operate the hall's elevator: "I found it to be one of the very first of those that had been made automatic, and I didn't know how to operate it. They'd come in since I'd left city life. So I had to whistle up through the tube, and I heard back:

"'Is that you, Ernest?'

"'Yes,' I called back. 'How do you get up one of these things? I don't know how to do it.'

"He told me what to do, and so I went up to his floor, where it stopped automatically. And there, standing at his door, [was] a man who at first sight I believed I had never seen before: stocky, heavyset, sort of sagged and tired looking. But it was Conrad. When I looked into his face and heard his voice, it was Conrad, unquestionably. So we shook hands, and by the time we'd entered his room, I felt exactly the same with him as I had back in our college days, just as free and everything else. I had that feeling instantly."

Whether or not he was aware of the possibility, Ober does not mention that it was likely his own magnetic enthusiasm that made reunions with these often difficult men so remarkably easy and alive.

"Then we sat down and began to talk," said Ober, "and I looked at him closely. He had light hair, and it had changed—it was somewhat faded. And he had this very stocky appearance, overweight. But there was the same expression in his eyes that he'd always had, but now it had become emphasized. It was a sort of repressed pain in his eyes—far back—a look of sadness.

"'Ernest,' he said, 'I'm sorry, but my wife can't come tonight. She works for one of the Boston newspapers, and she won't be able to come here and prepare dinner. I'd like to go to such and such a place.'

"So he took me out to this modern place in the suburbs, where we stood around on a sort of balcony. There was a poorly lit dance floor—purposely, you see—and you could get good food and watch the dancers. Or dance if you wanted.

"Well, we sat up on our platform there, ate supper, and just talked until midnight or one o'clock, until they closed. And this talk just flowed on. There was no trouble about it. We just continued right on as if it were the old days. There was no reference made to our difficult parting—none whatsoever. I never mentioned it to him, except once, I think the last time I saw him. Maybe I was a little indiscreet.

"'Conrad,' I said, 'you know there is nothing I'd like better than to have you come out to Rainy Lake for a visit sometime with your wife. If you'll come, I promise you—if you wish—you will be left entirely alone. Nobody will speak to you.'

"I shouldn't have said that. I wasn't referring to our time together, only to what I knew to be true, that he would like to have such freedom from intrusion. But he's so sensitive; he might have thought I was making some reference.

"After that first return meeting, I saw him two or three times. Every time I went to Boston I looked him up, but our correspondence has never been more than the occasional post card. Yet I feel very close to him, and apparently he does me now, too. He was certainly very demonstrative when he saw me. We had a very, very nice time, and it was hard to leave. Once a friend drove me from Albany to Conrad's home out on Cape Cod, which he called The House of the Forty-One Doors. It's an old tumble-down place where they live. They haven't got any money. He had a competence left him, but it wouldn't have been satisfactory for these days. It provided for him very well when he was at college. His brother and sister were adopted by some very fine Philadelphia people, so whatever estate there was could go to Conrad.

"I can't imagine that any book he's ever done has brought him any worthwhile return. They're not popular books. His poems are read by the poets; he's a poet's poet. He's written short stories, which I think are the most wonderful things he's done. They've been collected, and some of them are as fine as I've ever read in my life. He's an absolute master of the short story. Then he wrote this autobiographical book, *Ushant,* and three or four books of fiction, some of which I've read. Most of them, frankly, I found difficult to read. They exist in a sort of no man's land and are a little hard to follow, but they do contain his extreme sensitivity.

"I was characterized in *Ushant.* I didn't read it all the way through. The references that I recognized were set mostly on the boat we took over to England in our youth. I'd like nothing better than to sit down and read that book, but I just can't turn aside for it now. It was made up of recalled feelings or sensations that were related, not in time or substance, but by the flow of his mind and the way he was affected by them. It was stream of consciousness, a supreme example of stream of consciousness in autobiography. It's the only place I know of where it was used in autobiography."

Though he would never be as comfortable with Aiken as with Morison, Ober would remain fascinated by the troubled and enigmatic character of the man for whom, many years before, he had provided a "certain protection against the clash of the world around him." One can only wonder what the complex and self-involved Aiken might have thought about Ober and the life he led.

Then there was Charles Townsend Copeland, a man famous for public recitation of poetry and as a mentor of writers. Over the years, students in his Harvard writing course would include such writers as T. S. Eliot, Bernard De Voto, Malcolm Cowley, Oliver La Farge, and John Dos Passos. For his students, Copeland held legendary Monday evening socials that often included such unannounced guests as John Barrymore, Robert Frost, and Ernest Hemingway. He was so loved by his former students that they formed an alumni association for him that endured for thirty years.[3]

"Copey was the final one of the three I visited that first time I was renewing old Harvard acquaintances," said Ober. "I'd had no correspondence with him during that time, but he, too, responded at once. He had little idiosyncrasies that made him most interesting. He had lived on the top floor of the building where I'd lived for two years. He said he lived up there closest to the angels.

"'Now, Ernest,' he said. None of them called me Ober. 'When you come, I would like you to come to the corridor exactly as the clock strikes nine in the yard, and then climb the stairway, and I'll be waiting to see you.'

"That was my second evening there, I guess. When Conrad heard I was going over there the next evening, he said, 'Come to my place first, and I'll walk over there with you. It's only a short distance.'

"So, at exactly 9:00, we were there. The time really didn't have any significance, except *that* was Copey. Anyway, Conrad took me to the door, and as the clock struck 9:00, I stepped into the hallway, and at the same time, I heard a footstep on the third floor. As I went up, I could hear footsteps coming down. Wasn't that lovely? It was Copey, and he met me halfway and shook my hand, put his arm around me, and led me up to his room. Wasn't that wonderful?

"Copey was easy to caricature. His very appearance led in that direction—his large head and small body, his dry smile when he knew he had something funny to say. As an actor, his assumed timidity alone, when he stepped on the stage, caused a laugh. His dry comment caused still more a moment later. He was a born actor, even when he commented on his students' themes. He wanted to get a rise out of them, one way or another, and took secret satisfaction in doing so.

"He was sometimes sharp in his comments, especially when he thought they weren't being appreciated, but he was never malicious. He was the heart of kindness, but not always frank. It was hard for him ever to be completely impersonal. He favored students more for personality, as revealed in their themes, than for any final merit. He often recognized something that he considered worth encouraging.

"The actor likes attention. So did Copey. There is nothing wrong in this, but it rubs some students the wrong way. And it did so with Copey. It would have helped in these cases if the student had realized that Copey was above all an actor. He was only a greater reader because he was less an actor. He would have been an actor if he could. If his stature had been as good as his voice, he might easily have been among the great actors of his time. In fact, he became famous the country over. A little more and the same fame might have been his as an actor."

Copeland questioned Ober about his life: "'What have you been doing? Oh, how interesting that is. Ernest, I want to write a note for you to Perkins.'

"Max Perkins had been in our class, and had now become the head of Scribner's. I'd known him in college. I served on the *Advocate* with him for a while, but I didn't know him well. He wasn't a personal friend.

"'Ernest,' Copey said, 'I want to give you a note to Perkins, so you can publish some of these experiences you've had.'"

Maxwell Perkins of Charles Scribner's Sons was perhaps the most important book editor of the early twentieth century and the editor and publisher of Copeland's well-known anthology *The Copeland Reader.* This may have been a significant moment of opportunity for Ober, the frustrated author, but he chose not to accept his old professor's offer:

"'Oh, no, I don't want to do that,' said Ober.

"'Why not?'

"'Well, I have a sort of feeling against doing anything of that sort. Years ago, when I read Tolstoy, I couldn't help agreeing with his feeling that most of this writing business is overdone. It's just sort of an indulgence and not beneficial to the world to have all of this writing.'

"So I didn't have him write that note. Well, Perkins was the fellow that got behind the novelist Thomas Wolfe, a Harvard man who came after me."

Ober's notebooks and journals reveal that an amazing amount of his life was spent in thinking about and preparing to write something that would justify his existence and solve his continuing financial difficulties. A writer as good as he with such stories to tell would surely have received at least an interested reading from his old college acquaintance Perkins. Why then refuse such help? His doubt of the value of most writing was in truth a sort of minor theme in his thinking, and he would later write in a letter to Sam Morison that he had "what amounts to an absolute prohibition against adding to the world's [literary] burden . . . unless it had rare value."[4] Ober, however, found endless numbers of books to be of rare value to him. He was a great lover of books, and in the coming years, he would collect many thousands of them—surely not the pastime of one who doubted their value. Books were a passion with him. If anything, it seems more likely that he over-valued writing, and was frightened, overwhelmed, by the possibilities contained in Copeland's offer. One will recall that Ober's response was somewhat similar when Arthur Hawkes sent him letters of introduction to the editors of English periodicals: his "not wanting to take advantage of the other fellow." In any case, as president of the Quetico-Superior Council, Ober's work was now unrelenting. There would be little time for extraneous writing for many years to come.

"I saw Copey two or three times after that," said Ober. "He was getting older and older. He lived to be over ninety, and the last time I visited him he didn't recognize me. His mind was going. It wasn't long after that that he died."

In the end, Samuel Morison would become by far the closest friend of the three Ober visited on that trip. Unlike Conrad Aiken, who would not accept Ober's invitation, many years later, in the autumn of 1962, Morison and his wife did visit Ober on the Mallard:

"Sam was extremely responsive," said Ober in an interview conducted less than two years after Morison's visit. "We were just planets apart in our experience, our achievements and all, but there was something there that united us. Apparently, it continues. And finally, Sam came out to see me two years ago. It will be two years next autumn. He was only here two days. He had his wife with him and was on a university speaking tour. That renewed our association, and since then I've been hearing much more from them. Of course, he has the aid of his wife who writes occasionally. When they don't hear from me often enough now, she writes to inquire about me. And finally they invited me to come and live with them. That wasn't too long ago. Sam said he'd take care of all the expenses of my moving there and everything, which was surely generous. He said that, if I didn't mind climbing all the stairs, I could be on their third floor, with a whole suite of lovely rooms.

"I've stayed there before. I'd have a fireplace, my own bathroom. It's an opportunity such as I've never had in my life, if I wanted to do written work. It couldn't be finer, except that I'd be out of my locale, you see, and away from all the people who have been my life. I couldn't do it. I'll probably have to die up here. And I hope I do. I hope I don't die just yet. I hope I can spend my last days up here, and that I won't have to be in an institution for a long time."

Ober continued to hope that he and Morison would somehow yet be able to spend extended periods of time together, but these wishes were not to come true:

"I'd like to see Sam often. I wish he could come out with his wife and spend quite a long time. But he probably never could. I'd like to be able to go to Boston once in a while to see both of them. Well, of all the people I knew, those were the three who were closest to me at Harvard. And I'd managed to see all three of them at one time. They were just as different as any three people could be."

Ober would never cease to treasure his Harvard experience and the friends he made there. That experience, those friends, were continuing presences by and against which he measured the value of his overall life.

[18]

Tragedy and Triumph

With considerable pride, Oberholtzer would one day write that passage of the Shipstead-Nolan Act "was one of the great landmarks of United States conservation. It placed Congress solidly on record for preservation of the wilderness character of the main lakes and streams on the Minnesota side of the Rainy Lake watershed. It not only broke the back of the ill advised private project of Mr. Backus, but opened the way toward at least equal opportunity for the many-sided and far-seeing Quetico-Superior program."[1] R. Newell Searle, whose book *Saving Quetico-Superior* is the principal source for those who would understand the early struggle for preservation of the border lakes region, was in agreement with Ober when he wrote that the "Shipstead-Nolan Act of 1930 embodied most of the principles of the [matured and comprehensive] Wilderness Act of 1964."[2] Ober pointed out that those "who were hostile have now realized [the act has] never hurt them in the slightest. They can't show a single way in which they've been hurt. We got quite a lot of mail after the bill first passed, but then almost immediately the depression came along, and we didn't have even enough money for stamps. We could hardly make it back from Washington. And then we went into the doldrums for quite a while."

In fact, however, on first returning to Minnesota, Ober continued to be terribly busy. In a July 8, 1930, letter to Fred Winston, he wrote, "The amount of work here stuns and irritates me. I don't know how we are ever going to take care of it."[3] In a second letter written the following day, he added, "I just can't keep up the pace and yet neither can I find any way so far to avoid the many requirements of the situation."[4] With the depression, however, the stream of donations that had funded the Quetico-Superior Council's efforts dried up, and the Program did indeed go into the doldrums.

Hubachek and Kelly had moved their law offices to Chicago when Household Finance Corporation, one of their firm's major clients, moved its headquarters there. Along with Fred Winston, these two were the Program's most important fund-raisers, but, not yet being well connected in Chicago, they found the town to be less than generous toward their cause. According to R. Newell Searle, the council's work was now almost entirely supported by Hubachek and Kelly, Fred Winston, his twin brother Don, their mother, and two families with environmental leanings that were prominent in the Minnesota grain trade and who greatly admired Ernest Oberholtzer: the Andrews and the Heffelfingers. Despite its small circle of support, the council was slowly able to pay off a debt of $4,000 incurred during the struggle to pass the Shipstead-Nolan Act.[5]

Ober had returned to Mallard Island, and, refusing to accept salary from the council's meager funds, he continued the work of the Program. On September 2, in irritation, Fred Winston wrote to him:

> Ober, it makes me sore to hear that you have asked Mr. Byam to hold up your monthly salary check. If the Council is up against it that bad, I can get them another $1,000 from Mother without the slightest trouble. That your salary should be held up is the last thing in the world that ought to happen. Don't be foolish, Ober, please.[6]

Not until 1933 did the Quetico-Superior Council begin to move out of the "doldrums." Forest lands and waterways owned by the state of Minnesota were not under the protection of the Shipstead-Nolan Act, and as described earlier, powerful interests had long been at work with projects that altered water levels and natural shorelines. As Ober told it, during the legislative session of 1933, because of "the exception that had been made for Minnesota Power and Light [due to their pre-existing Gabbro-Bald Eagle Project], we introduced the *state* Shipstead-Nolan bill into the Minnesota legislature. It contained the same language, was for the same purposes, and was just as bitterly fought. The opposition had one of the highest paid lawyers in Duluth. He came down [to St. Paul] to see me during legislative sessions.

"'Oberholtzer,' he said, 'you're butting your head against a stone wall. You've got very few friends in Duluth, and when we're through with you, you won't have a single one.'

"Well, that was largely true, too. Oh, my, how that was fought. What a time we had. [There were big headlines in support of us] that read: 'Shall we permit trespass on state lands?'"

According to Ober, Minnesota Power and Light had entered state lands without proper authorization and built dams. The conservationists posted their headlined stories outside the doors of legislative chambers. "We also," said Ober, "had printed matter which went into the situation at greater length. It seemed there was a danger our printed matter might be destroyed, so we had a young man named [Winston] Schmidt guard our table there at the entrance to the legislature. He sat there guarding our material every day."

Public opinion was strongly in favor of this state bill, which contained the same ideas that had proved overwhelmingly successful in Washington. "This was for the same purposes," said Ober. "It wasn't asking the state to do anything more for its own good than the federal government had, you see. Our terms were almost identical, except that they applied to *state* lands and forests. The bill included the provision that what Minnesota Power and Light had done up to that point would be accepted. But they would have to clean up the land, the flowages, so there would be no sign of their activities. They were given a time limit to do this in, and they were forbidden to raise the lake any farther. It was considered fair. We felt it was fair. We didn't demand that lakes be restored to their original levels. Maybe that was a mistake."

In the end, opposition to the bill was completely crushed. The lawyer who had told Ober he wouldn't have a friend left in Duluth came to visit him. "'We acknowledge we're beaten,' the lawyer said. 'We've got to accept this, and we're going to accept it with the best grace we can. We want you to meet with us here on Sunday to draw up a final agreement concerning this bill.'

"So the agreement was drawn up. The president of Minnesota Power and Light was there, and he would flare up every once in a while and say:

"'I object to that!'

"And his lawyer would say, 'Now look, didn't we have an understanding?' I was surprised. He put the president of the company right in his place. 'There is nothing else we can do,' he said. 'We have to accept this.'

"Anyway, we got the state bill through, and it's an excellent piece of legislation. It put the state on record for all the essentials of our program, things to do with forestry, flooding, ownership, and zoning. It doubly assured our official protection against Mr. Backus's program. It would be extremely difficult for him to get authorization [for his project from both the U.S. Congress and] the State of Minnesota. So we were doubly strengthened. The program that we thought ought to be applied to lands of that sort had been made officially the program of both the state and the federal governments."

The Minnesota Shipstead-Nolan Act, officially called "An Act to Protect Certain Public Waters and Lands Adjacent Thereto Owned by the State of Minnesota," was passed by the Minnesota legislature on April 19, 1933, and it did indeed provide the same set of protections for state-owned lands as the Shipstead-Nolan Act had provided for those owned by the federal government. In a letter to the emerging environmental figure Sigurd Olson, who would one day take over Ober's leadership role in the movement, Ober was jubilant over the passage of the bill:

> If the bill becomes law by signature of the governor [and it did on April 22], it really will do more for us than the Shipstead-Nolan Act of Congress. It will

be an overwhelming victory and should once for all settle the dispute with the Duluth power company and leave us free to deal with Backus alone. It was a bitter campaign and the tactics of the Duluth company were utterly shameless. They [smeared] my name at every opportunity.[7]

Though the relationship between Ober and Olson would in time become edgy and competitive, Olson responded now with equal enthusiasm:

Accept my congratulations for the splendid piece of work you put through, and I say *you,* because without your personal unquenchable enthusiasm and fearlessness in the face of unlimited and unscrupulous opposition, we would never have a chance of winning....[8]

Meanwhile, though he was slow to grasp it, Backus's struggle with the conservationists was becoming less than half his problem. He had not been tending to business as he once had, and the Great Depression arrived for "the forceful and fortunate Mr. Backus" just as it had for the Quetico-Superior Council. And in spades. During the boom years of the twenties, that dangerous decade in financial history, Backus chose to begin a program of rapid expansion. He increased the size and productivity of his existing mills and invested heavily in new plants in Tennessee, Ontario, and Finland. In 1926, he began construction of three large power dams on the Seine River in Ontario just above Rainy Lake. By the late 1920s, the Backus-Brooks companies, for the most part owned and controlled by Backus, were estimated to be worth $100 million. It may be, however, as was sometimes suggested in newspaper accounts, that Backus, in order to expand his credit potential and perhaps for egotistical reasons, inflated this figure by about $20 million.

To thoroughly understand the crisis in which Backus now found himself requires some background. In *Saving Quetico-Superior,* R. Newell Searle wrote that the depression had in fact arrived two years early for the pulp and paper industry, and even as the expansion of Backus's empire gathered momentum, the bottom was beginning to fall out from under his markets. Throughout the decade, to attract investment from the United States, the Canadian government had offered huge grants of timber and waterpower to industrialists, and Backus like the others accepted the grants and invested in new mills in Canada. By the mid-twenties, paper production was outstripping the market and competition had forced the price of paper downward. Then, with the onset of the depression, the worldwide demand for paper fell.[9]

The conservationists of the Quetico-Superior Council watched the growing crisis in fascination. They studied and clipped articles from the financial pages. They paid for a small focus-study of their own, in which their statistician reported that the paper industry was "suffering from over production, from low prices, from foreign competition and from uncontrollable competition of a drastic nature."[10]

In June of 1928, a number of newspaper stories on the crisis were published. One told of Backus's new plant in Fort William, Ontario, having to shut down. On June 23, the *Sault St. Marie Star* "pointed out the need of a 'dictator' to regulate the production of the Canadian mills and save the industry from cut-throat competition."[11] It is believed that one reason the industry could not come together under such a controlling figure was that other industrialists were unwilling to work with Backus.[12] Then, to add to Backus's financial woes, newspaper magnate William Randolph Hearst filed suit against a number of Canadian mills for alleged breach of contract over shipment of three million tons of newsprint. The suit totaled $24,750,000. Hearst was suing Backus's Fort Frances Pulp and Paper Company for $1,200,000, his Kenora Paper Mills, Ltd., for $900,000.[13]

In an August 2, 1928, letter, Charles Kelly wrote incisively and a bit incredulously of Backus's growing difficulties:

> "He apparently is devoting his entire time to politics, letting his business take care of itself and it apparently is not competent to do so. We are continually getting reports to the effect that his high-handed tactics at the labor hearing at International Falls and elsewhere are reacting against him and I have reason to believe we are in the best position we have been at any time. The news print industry as a whole, logically should be opposed to the granting of any additional [water] power rights or timber concessions to augment the already glutted condition of the market....[14]

Backus's financial situation was indeed becoming grim, but, in his struggle for the right to dam the border waterways, even after the Shipstead-Nolan legislation was passed, he had one card left. The International Joint Commission, which had long been considering his plan and with which he had considerable influence, had yet to make its decision. Should the commission decide in his favor, both the federal and state versions of the Shipstead-Nolan legislation would, at the least, be weakened.

Ober explained that Backus argued, "'Well, you've gone into a treaty in which you authorize the commission to investigate [and recommend settlement of] these problems, and before [the commission could make its decision] Congress says, no matter what you decide, you can't raise water levels without our consent.' That's how Backus got Ontario to make its protest."

In letter after letter during that period, Ober and other members of the Quetico-Superior Council reiterated the importance of gaining the support of the Canadians, especially the citizens of Ontario, necessary partners in the Quetico-Superior program. Fully two-thirds of their hoped-

and planned-for wilderness sanctuary lay in Ontario, and they saw that support in Ontario had increasingly become the key to the Program's success. Though technically it was not true that the United States was bound by treaty to go along with ijc findings—they served only as recommendations to the two governments—Ober felt it extremely important to respect them. Not to do so would be to disrespect the citizens of Ontario, whose support was essential.

In April of 1932, the ijc aired the results of an engineering survey it had ordered in an effort to discover the best use of the Rainy Lake watershed. As might have been expected, the engineers did not take a broad, visionary approach to the future of the region. Instead, in narrow engineering terms, they had studied the region's waterways as to the feasibility of the Backus plan. And yes, they thought it could be done, and they then went on to describe how they would do it. Even though the ijc engineers made no definite recommendation, Ober and his conservationist friends were angered and frightened by what read like a pro-dam report.

In a countermove, Ober turned to the Minneapolis Engineer's Club and asked its members to examine the report of the ijc engineers. Through the summer of 1932, Ober exchanged numerous letters with the president of the club, M. D. Bell, who would prove to be yet another untiring servant in support of the movement to preserve the border lakes wilderness. Apparently unemployed due to depression cutbacks, Bell set up in the Quetico-Superior Council's office at 1220 Flour Exchange in Minneapolis and worked full time organizing a committee to respond to the ijc engineer's report. In a letter to Ober, Clara Martin wrote, "You have no idea the effort Mr. Bell is putting in to get the committee together, answer the questions, and give them the whole background of everything that has happened to date. I can hear him talking it from morning till night. It isn't that the engineers are unwilling but that the job is so big."[15] In that the ijc engineer's report was 4,000 pages long, the job of responding to it was "big" indeed.

Ober's work continued as well. He told of it in a letter to Raymond Ickes:

> It was up to me to either accept defeat [from the ijc engineer's report] or to try to tide over in the hope that we may somehow outlast our opponents.... All summer engineers, lawyers, and state officials have been here on the island. I have had from two to nineteen people the season through and have done all the cooking and house-keeping.[16]

In the end, in a written response, the committee of Minneapolis engineers argued cogently for wilderness values instead of the development of unneeded waterpower. Members of the ijc had long been under pressure from the Backus forces, but it had become clear where U.S. public and political opinion stood, and they carefully read and took into account the counter-arguments in this technical response to their study.

As the report of the ijc engineers was being reviewed and argued over, Sewell Tyng arrived for an extended stay with Ober on Mallard Island. This was an interesting and complex period in the history of wilderness preservation, and the presence at this moment of the brilliant, life-loving, and self-indulgent lawyer Sewell Tyng was to prove no small matter. Not many would contribute more than he to the establishment of the protected areas along the Minnesota-Ontario border. As described earlier, Tyng visited the region regularly, staying on the Mallard, and he and Ober each found joy in the depth, brilliance, and humor of the other.

In 1932, however, Sewell Tyng's life had taken a downturn that Ober described in detail in the oral history interviews. Tyng had become embroiled in a romantic scandal that had begun as a canoe trip from the Mallard with an attractive woman Ober had taken to be Tyng's secretary. It was at this point, according to Ober, that Tyng's wife, Ruth, became incurably insane. Tyng's wealthy mother sent Ruth to C. G. Jung's clinic in Switzerland, but Jung was unable to help her. According to Ober—this was no doubt metaphoric—Ruth spent the rest of her life "rolling balls of colored yarn up and down a hallway."

Ober recalled that one day in 1933 he answered a telephone call from Tyng's mother: "Ober, Sewell isn't very well. He's in trouble. Do you think you could take him at your place for a year?"

Tyng needed somewhere in which to become quiet and heal emotionally until the storm of his scandal died away. He also wanted to plunge into the writing of a book he had been planning. When he arrived on the Mallard, he was not able to look Ober in the eye. By mistake, Ober opened a telegram meant for Tyng that revealed the extremity of Tyng's emotional state. In it, a friend pleaded that he not commit suicide. Once again Ober took on the role of caretaker, and in time he and the Mallard proved healing for Tyng, who then plunged into the writing of his history of the World War I Battle of the Marne. Through the deep cold of the border winter, he worked, hunched and nearsighted, between a pair of kerosene lamps. His humor came back, and in the evenings he strode the narrow aisles of the kitchen boat, waving his arms and loudly holding forth on whatever came to mind, while Ober cooked their supper. Tyng often forgot and lit a second cigarette, and both would dangle and bob from the corners of his mouth as he talked, their ashes falling over kitchen surfaces and the food that Ober was trying to prepare. After a hearty meal, he would wipe the silverware, one great handful at a time, talking, joking, and jibing while unknowingly prancing, first on one end of the drying towel, then the other.

According to Ober, Tyng's book, *Campaign of the Marne 1914*, though highly specialized, proved to be a masterpiece. At the outset of their long stay together, Ober had told him, "Don't expect me, now, Sewell, to listen to you talk about this book. There's nothing I'm so little interested in as military affairs." In the spring, however, he relented and let Tyng read much of it to him. Ober was deeply impressed.

Upon completion of the book, Tyng returned to New York City, where he quickly found a publisher in Longmans, Green and Co. Then, presidential-candidate-to-be Thomas Dewey brought Tyng on as his assistant in his much publicized efforts to prosecute Mafia figures. According to Ober, Tyng was suddenly "all the rage" in New York, and dowagers of his mother's vintage competed to have this romantic figure on their guest lists.

On a shelf in Ober's Mallard Island office can be found the copy of *Campaign of the Marne 1914* that Tyng gave to Ober and in it a handwritten message: "To Ernest C. Oberholtzer, whose friendship in difficult days, made this book possible." Signed, "Sewell Tyng, June 13, 1935."

Remembering Tyng, who was to die at the age of fifty-two, Oberholtzer said, "He really was a wonderful character, a remarkable person, and I'd say he was the ablest fellow we ever dealt with during our Quetico-Superior struggles. He was on the edge of genius, at least on the edge.... Sewell Tyng was just one of the world's free spirits, floating around in the ether."

For the conservationists of the Quetico-Superior program it was a synchronistic piece of good luck that Sewell Tyng spent much of 1933 on the Mallard, for it placed him side by side with Ober during the ever-so-important final hearings of the International Joint Commission on the Backus proposal to build dams and raise water levels within the Rainy Lake watershed. These two final hearings were held in October of 1933, the first in Minneapolis, the second in Winnipeg. Both sides in what had become an eight-year struggle now made their final preparations.

At the Minneapolis hearing, proponents of the waterpower plan included not only Backus and representatives of the Minnesota and Ontario Paper Company, but four other witnesses from the Rainy Lake area: the mayor and city attorney of International Falls, the county attorney of Koochiching County, and a worker representative of the pulp, sulfite, and paper mills workers' union. The Great Depression was now at its height, and testimony given by these men as to the importance of the thousands of jobs provided by the Backus industries must have made a significant impact. City Attorney J. J. Hadler "asserted that 'these people have the right to earn livings, if people from other regions have the right to come to the border and play.'"[17]

Representing the Quetico-Superior Council, Sewell Tyng called an impressive array of witnesses, which included Congressman William Nolan, co-author of the Shipstead-Nolan bill, W. E. Neal of the U.S. Junior Chamber of Commerce, and M. D. Bell, president of the Minneapolis Engineer's Club.[18] But surely the most important witness called by Tyng that day was a young guide and writer who was to become the bard of the boundary waters. He was just beginning his involvement with the Quetico-Superior movement, but some fourteen years later he would inherit its leadership from Ernest Oberholtzer. His name was Sigurd Olson, and years later, in the *Saturday Evening Post*, Harold H. Martin would write that Olson "stood up and talked of lakes and portages and trees and rocks... of a land that should be not one man's resource, but a people's heritage.... [They] say as he spoke... you could see the long light shimmering on the lonely lakes... and hear the mournful calling of the loon."[19] It has been said that, on this day in Minneapolis, Olson discovered something of his power to move others in support of wilderness preservation.[20]

Ober made his appeal at the final hearing in Winnipeg. In Minneapolis, Sigurd Olson had spoken spontaneously. In the Oberholtzer files, twenty-

*Sewell Tyng and Ober at International Joint Commission
hearing in Winnipeg*

six legal-sized pages of close-set handwritten notes testify to Ober's typically anxious over-preparation. In *Saving Quetico-Superior,* R. Newell Searle wrote that, at the hearing, "Tyng's incisive cross-examination" of Backus's chief engineer, Adolph Meyer, gave Ober confidence, and he went on the offensive.[21] He argued that the Minnesota and Ontario Paper Company, *even to continue with the operation of its present dams,* needed to upgrade its approach to property and the environment. With precision and clarity, he made the case for the positive plan he and others had developed for the region at the onset of their long struggle. He then tried to convince the ever-so-important IJC representatives from Ontario that the Program's multi-use approach to resources would, in the end, offer the most, even economically, to the people of their province. Sadly, for Ober's dream of a huge ten-million-acre wilderness sanctuary, this was an argument, however sound, that would find only limited favor with the majority in either Ontario or Minnesota. The final hearing adjourned and the conservationists could now only wait through the long northern winter while the commission made its decisions and wrote its final report.

Meanwhile, the financial circumstances of Edward Backus had continued to worsen, and during the concluding hearings of the International Joint Commission, he had become less a factor than could ever have been imagined. In April of 1927, Backus's Minnesota and Ontario Paper Company had issued $5 million in bonds to finance the industrial expansion he had so unwisely embarked upon. A $3.5 million payment was to come due in 1931, and, over-invested in a dying market, he was caught in a downward spiral. To stay afloat, he raised $2.4 million with promissory notes, and he began to shift funds from one of his corporate subsidiaries to another. These exchanges—for that time the figures were huge—were complicated and desperate. It is interesting here to compare the Quetico-Superior Council's debt of $4,000, which its members found so difficult to repay, with the $40 million debt that Backus is said to have accrued. Late in 1930, Backus went to New York in an effort to refinance his $5 million bond issue, the first payment on which was soon to come due. The New York bankers refused him, and from that time on Backus would blame his financial difficulties on a conspiracy between eastern bankers and unnamed competitors in the pulp and paper industry.[22]

It can be said that in 1931 Edward Wellington Backus, that old admirer of Napoleon, met his Waterloo. Given the financial quagmire he was now in, it was deemed necessary to remove him from control of his empire. On February 28, 1931, the Minnesota and Ontario Paper Company and sixteen subsidiaries passed from Backus's control into receivership.[23] Edward Backus now stood uncertainly on the far side of the river from the thumping machines and belching smokestacks that had for so long been the source of his pride.

As Ober told it, "For a period of three or four years Backus had been doing almost nothing but fight this public movement. He'd bought the outdoor magazine. He'd sent a man around in a plane. He'd organized the Outers Club. He [built a club called] the Nanibijou Club and presented memberships in it to all kinds of people he thought could help him—judges, industrialists. . . . He spent an awful lot of money. More than that, he had used up his energies and his time at a most critical moment in the financial history of the country."

Backus was originally retained as one of the receivers assigned to manage his former financial empire, but his presence proved a stumbling block to reorganization, and he was driven out. The new receivers, Clive Jaffray and R. H. M. Robinson, soon became the target of Backus-inspired accusations of incompetence and mismanagement. Then, on April 8, 1934, the *Minneapolis Journal* reported that Jaffray and Robinson, after a lengthy examination of Backus's affairs, had filed suit against him, charging that he had, just before losing control of his companies, "extracted approximately seven million dollars from the Minnesota and Ontario Paper Company and subsidiaries for himself and associates." Some of the missing money had supported Backus's efforts to carry on his enterprises, but it was asserted "that much of this money went into personal stock market operations."[24] Backus responded immediately with a two-million-dollar libel suit against the receivers in which he charged that the suit against him was part of the eastern bankers' plot to destroy him. Though the courts had long been a useful tool for Backus, they now seemed less and less willing to serve his ends.

Through the broad circulation of two letters, Backus had begun a campaign to regain his empire. In one, addressed "To my *Old Loyal Employees*," he stated that he had "brought suit to remove Mr. Robinson and Mr. Jaffray from the position they now hold as Receivers for Minnesota and Ontario Paper Company and as managers of all its subsidiaries." He warned that the incompetence or worse of the receivers would lead to a situation in which they would not "be able to even pay the workers." He then alleged that the two were part of "a conspiracy on the part of Big Eastern Bankers to take from me these properties which I have spent my whole life—with your help—in building up." The plot, as he described it, was to turn over all his properties "to the big competing company which is working with the Conniving Bankers. . . ." He wrote that, since all his former executives had thrown in with the receivers, "I must rely entirely on my old loyal workers."[25] There was no mention of what he hoped these workers might do for him.

The second letter, dated January 5, 1934, was a carefully crafted, seven-page argument addressed "To the Bondholders of Minnesota and Ontario Paper Company." In this letter, after describing the plot between powerful money interests and certain industries that competed with him (and the bondholders), he asked that the bondholders "withdraw their securities from the hands of the present [receivership Protective Committee]; revoke its authority to act in your behalf, and stand firm in the independent exercise of your own rights." On page two of the letter, Backus wrote, "All idea of personal gain was wholly foreign to my underlying purpose during the upbuilding of these companies." On the final page, he told once again the story of his 200-mile snowshoe trek to the border, of his arrival there "one beautiful moonlight night after midnight with the thermometer at 40 below zero. I viewed the wonderful water falls there and decided to do some constructive pioneering." In conclusion, Backus evoked the Democratic New Deal by asking the bondholders to work with him in the spirit of "our worthy leader President Roosevelt."[26]

These letters were a sad and desperate effort that moved very few to support Backus's increasingly hopeless cause.

In April of 1934, on the strength of his unrelenting campaign, Backus got a hearing before a skeptical United States Senate Banking Committee in Washington, D.C. His purpose was to convince the committee that a conspiracy of bankers had indeed plotted to take his holdings from him. The old tycoon, once so deeply respected in financial circles, was shown the door.

According to Ober, Backus claimed that the preservationist efforts of the Quetico-Superior Council were also part of the plot to ruin him: "When he seemed to be losing, Backus made a plea before Congress that [the Quetico-Superior program] was nothing but a conspiracy against him by very wealthy interests that wanted to see him put out of business. He didn't name any of them, but he said his business enemies were back of all this and that if it could be investigated it would be found in time that the entire movement was a thing that had been turned up by his business enemies who were eager to bankrupt him.

"Of course, it was an absurd thing to think that our entire movement, all the people associated with it, could have been fostered by business enemies. But he told very heartfelt, forlorn stories in Congress about these attempts to block his progress in great public works for the benefit of the people of the region. I don't think too many people believed him. I don't know how much sympathy he got. There isn't any question that he had vast numbers of enemies who were anxious to see his downfall, but none of them had anything to do with us. They never contributed a penny that I know of to anything we did. I know who some of them were. The Shevlins [the Shevlin-Clarke Lumber Co.] were very much opposed to him, but they never did one single thing for us."

During the final hearings with the International Joint Commission, the Minnesota and Ontario Paper Company receivers, Jaffray and Robinson, had believed it prudent to press the commission to accept a plan for waterpower development that was less extreme than Backus's, but that would provide power for future expansions as needed. Ober saw this as very dangerous to the Quetico-Superior program, for it might seem a reasonable middle ground alternative to the commission, when it too would end up drowning rapids, waterfalls, and shorelines. Receivership had cost Backus control of his industries, but he still controlled all the dam sites of importance in the watershed and therefore continued to be a player in this game for the future of the region.

The International Joint Commission's final report came out in the summer of 1934, and, advising a wait-and-see approach, it appeared not to fully settle anything. "The 'final report,'" said Ober, "[described the Backus] proposals as undesirable for that day, uneconomic, and not required in the interests of the M & O Paper Company. It stated that it was conceivable there might some day be a situation where more water power would be called for, but in the meantime they hoped that nothing would interfere with the program of the Quetico-Superior Council for an international forest and wilderness area."

Sewell Tyng was disgusted by the unresolved nature of the final report. Ober, on the other hand, rightly believed that, with federal and state protection provided by the Shipstead-Nolan legislation, the ijc's inconclusive report marked the end of the industrial dream of turning the boundary waters into a power basin. On June 19, 1934, a headline in the *St. Paul Pioneer Press* read: "The Border Playground Saved." The article went on to say that the ijc had done "far more than settle an immediate controversy over power development." The commission had found that no additional power was needed, "and that ends the debate." The writer of the article admitted that "the door is not absolutely closed" to future power development, but that "the Commission plainly considers recreational interests paramount." Ober and the other conservationists who had struggled so long for this moment must have been deeply moved to read that "the area's present status is well assured."[27]

"That was a very big gain for us," said Ober. "For ten years we constantly had had that problem to deal with. The Shipstead-Nolan Act had placed

Congress on record as opposed to any further development, or any further change, of the natural water levels along the border between Minnesota and Ontario, without the consent of Congress. If the Backus proposal had been approved by the IJC, that [could have created problems]. For instance, if Canada had objected, having agreed to the reference, then it was possible that some question might arise as to the legality of the Shipstead-Nolan Act. So the commission's decision removed that danger and was naturally a great source of satisfaction to all those who had labored on the side of conservation through those years, along the border."

As the years passed, the telling of the story of the final IJC hearings made the conservationists' victory seem more and more decisive. A 1948 *Saturday Evening Post* retrospective revealed that, as Backus testified before the International Joint Commission, he "pleaded, almost in tears, for the chance to crown his years of building with this one last great enterprise." The one-time baron of industry had, however, lost his power to persuade: "The commission heard every plea, pondered at some length, and turned Backus down."[28]

The *Post* article also described a "joyous celebration" held by the young men of the Quetico-Superior Council. One wonders if Ober would have been involved. He was older than most of the others and, though sometimes a prankster himself, this seems a bit crude for him. It has been written that Frank Hubachek was behind it. In any case, the victorious young men went to Backus's home in Minneapolis, and "bore by night quantities of singularly repulsive fish, such as shovel-nosed sturgeon, eels, gar and lawyer-fish. These they tossed alive and flopping, over Backus' garden wall into his swimming pool."[29]

In this narrative of the struggle over the fate of the Quetico-Superior region, much of the worst side of Edward Backus has shone through, and it is easy to take satisfaction in the image of his pool squirming with a wonderful collection of nature's bottom-feeders. This, however, is perhaps the last moment in which a sensitive soul might take joy in contempt for the old baron. Aristotle, who set down the rules for tragedy, would surely agree that Backus's fall fulfilled most of them, that his was indeed a grand and sad American tragedy.

Ober was certain that Backus, even at the end, was far from broke: "Of course, he wasn't a poor man, I'm convinced of that. His family were very well-to-do. His wife was probably a wealthy woman. But he wasn't a hundred-million-dollar man any more. He might have had a million. He might have had five hundred thousand."

Whatever his remaining financial worth, it was not enough to satisfy Edward Wellington Backus. And certainly simple wealth was not the goal for a man who had once wielded such power. He was a fighter, and once again he went to New York in hope of financing a new beginning. His dream was to start afresh and create yet another lumbering empire, this time in the Pacific Northwest and Alaska. In his dream of Alaska as his final frontier of hope, one is reminded of that perhaps most pathetically tragic figure in American literature, the salesman Willy Loman. Beyond his new dreams, Backus, like Willy, now had little more to bring to the financiers than his smile and the shine on his shoes.

Backus, of course, failed to find backing for his new venture, and on October 29, 1934, at the age of seventy-three, alone and friendless, he died of a heart attack in his rooms in the Vanderbilt Hotel. His wife was in France. His daughter-in-law took the train north from Florida to take charge of his remains. Among his personal effects found in the hotel were 213,500 shares of stock, dividends checks totaling $37,000, and an envelope containing three wills. These might suggest he knew his end was near, but, belying those who believe he committed suicide, he had summoned a house physician five minutes before his 5 A.M. death.[30]

One can only imagine the emptiness this once great capitalist felt during his final lonely effort to begin again. As for Ober, though Backus had been his enemy and their struggle the focus of his life for almost a decade, he seemed to recognize that they had simply played opposing roles in a single great drama. In *Saving Quetico-Superior*, R. Newell Searle quoted from an Oberholtzer letter of the time in which he had elegantly written, "I'll miss E. W. One cannot be in harness with a team mate so long without missing him."[31]

In the oral history, Ober further described the complex of feelings that rose in him in response to the fall and death of Backus: "When Mr. Backus finally crashed . . . well, you can imagine what that must have meant to a man of his particular character and disposition. It must have been most tragic, an overwhelming situation for a man who had had everything his own way, who just overrode everybody, and then suddenly found himself bereft of all this property that he'd built up through the years, by his own genius and force. No one knows for sure how he died. He died very suddenly in his [hotel rooms] in New York one night. . . . I heard of it suddenly. Two or three telephoned me—joyously. It didn't affect me that way at all. I felt the other way. Of course, I said jokingly to people, 'Well, now we have lost our very best friend, because we haven't got [anyone to quarrel with] now.' . . . But, I don't want anybody to think I'm so inhumane as not to appreciate his state of mind. What an awful thing that was [for him], you see. It was enough to kill anybody."

Though Backus's personal life ended in disaster, his most important enterprises survived, evolved, and thrived. They continue to provide power, an array of forest products, and employment for thousands. Those whose sympathy lay with industry rather than the environment eulogized Backus for his extraordinary vision as a developer of natural resources. They even argued that he was "greater and more powerful than he ever realized."[32] There are very few, even among his supporters, however, who doubt that character flaws in Backus himself, more than anything else, had led to his fall. He had arrogantly over-reached; he had created enemies; he was not psychologically prepared to deal with setbacks; and he was not tending to business as he once had. In short, he was in no way prepared for the situation that brought him down.

When Ober described Backus as his teammate and the Quetico-Superior program's best friend, he was expressing not just whimsy but insight into the way culture evolves. That Ober and the Program should have an archenemy at once so powerful *and* so vulnerable could hardly have been better luck. If history is the enactment of myth, as has often been observed, then an individual such as Backus who had had it all his way for so long was surely ripe for his fall. Early twentieth-century American consciousness was moving beyond the vision of the empire builder and beginning to take stock of what had been lost in the recent selfish scramble. Backus's arrogant and heavy-handed efforts to deny and turn back the burgeoning tide of environmental consciousness provided an almost perfect symbolic situation for Ober and the other conservationists. Their struggle was a great drama played out in town meetings, newspapers, legislative sessions, and the halls of Congress, and its plot and characters permeated the rapidly emerging environmental consciousness.

Because Backus, at the outset, was a formidable opponent whose plans truly threatened the wilderness of the Quetico-Superior region, Ober and his friends in conservation rose in an equal and opposite response. More than equal. Theirs was a necessarily heroic response. It was a morality play, and the right—for that time—won out. Without the Backus threat—and his extremes—there would have been no Quetico-Superior Council. Ober would not have developed the compensatory positive program for the region, and Quetico-Superior would be far less pristine than it is today. And, too, the life and legacy of Ernest Carl Oberholtzer would have been far different without his teammate, "the forceful and fortunate" Edward Wellington Backus.

In the year of Backus's death, Ober turned fifty. Under his leadership, the conservationists had enjoyed an almost unbroken but hard-earned string of successes. The nine-year struggle had honed and toughened him, and a sense of authority shone from the articles and the thousands of letters he would write in the coming decade. The struggle had conditioned all the conservationists in and around the Quetico-Superior Council. They were now an efficient and cohesive group, some of whom would continue on in the struggle for yet another forty years. The council would maintain three active centers: Ober would be in control on the Mallard, Fred Winston in Minneapolis, and Hubachek and Kelly in Chicago. Though there were some differences in philosophy among these men, it is remarkable how they managed to work together so closely for so long a time.

"There was this bond of enthusiasm among us," said Ober.

Nevertheless, Ober would continue to be divided about his unending commitment to the struggle. In a 1942 letter to Samuel Eliot Morison, he wrote, "so much has been put into it that, regardless of its value, I do not like to throw it over. Giving up may bankrupt me spiritually as going on has long ago bankrupted me materially." He then whimsically added: "I still cling to the hope of finishing and turning to something else more nearly my own."[33] In truth, the struggle to establish the Program was Ober's fate and more nearly his own than he realized, and he would continue on with it, decade following decade.

Though Ober's role in the ongoing Quetico-Superior struggle could easily fill yet another volume, it is not within the scope of this work to tell of it. Through its first two decades, Ober was the hub around which the wheel of the Quetico-Superior movement revolved. After the death of Backus, however, the story would become increasingly less Ober's and more and more that of many individuals and organizations. The Program could now move forward only slowly and across a very broad front, and the rights and wrongs of its various issues were less and less clear. The story of this broader movement has been told in a number of other works, perhaps most fully in *Saving Quetico-Superior: A Land Set Apart* by R. Newell Searle, *Canoe Country: An Embattled Wilderness* by David Backes, and *Troubled Waters: The Fight for the Boundary Waters Canoe Area Wilderness* by Kevin Proescholdt, Rip Rapson, and Miron Heinselman.

With the damming threat to the border lakes over, the agenda for the conservationists shifted. They took the offensive in their effort to establish their positive program for the Quetico-Superior region. The energies of Ober and the other conservationists were now focused on bringing as much as possible of the targeted area on the United States side under federal ownership, and, having proved the good faith of the United States by doing so, to then join in a treaty with Canada to preserve and govern the planned-for and dreamed-of vast, ten-million-acre wilderness sanctuary, the entire Rainy Lake watershed. Their opposition now would be not a few powerful individuals, but a complicated coalition of grassroots interests and representatives of the governments of Minnesota and Ontario, all fighting for local, state, or provincial control of land and resources.

Well into the 1940s, Ober and the other members of the Quetico-Superior Council would write as if they were but a year or two from a treaty with Canada and the complete realization of the Program, the entire ten million acres of it. In letters, articles, and informational releases, they wrote of their unbroken string of victories with pride and excessive confidence. One council pamphlet was titled "On to the Next Victory in the Fight for the Border Lakes!" By the end of World War II, however, the tone of the conservationists had become more subdued, and some of the council members, if not Ober himself, now knew full well that the entire ten million acres would never be theirs. In the end, fewer than three million acres would be protected, but, to their immense credit, the resolve and effort of the conservationists never seriously wavered, even as they woke to the realization that they might not see an end to the struggle in their lifetimes. At age eighty, Ober predicted that the struggle would never be entirely over. One must wonder if the tenacity of the group could have held without the disciplined effort of that original central figure who had no other career, was married to nothing else, and was willing to work unrelentingly, year after year, often without pay.

Succeeding the death of Backus, there would be key moments along the way to the present-day status of protected areas within the Quetico-Superior region. In 1934, inspired by Sewell Tyng, the President's Quetico-Superior Committee was established by executive order of Franklin D. Roosevelt. Its program was the same as that of the Quetico-Superior Council, but from a federal perspective, and Ober was its chairman for the first twelve years of its existence. In 1947, Sigurd Olson succeeded Ober as the spearhead figure of the Quetico-Superior movement. Ober nevertheless continued untiringly as one of the movement's key figures—and its elder statesman—until late in the 1960s. In 1949, by executive order, President Harry S. Truman banned float planes from landing in the roadless areas, and the Canadian Quetico-Superior Committee was established. In 1957, instead of a treaty between the United States and Canada, a formal exchange of letters between the two countries established an agreement on mutual protection of the Quetico-Superior region. In 1972, Quetico Provincial Park was given full wilderness protection, and Voyageurs National Park was established. And, in 1978, the Boundary Waters Wilderness Act was passed, extending full wilderness protection to much of the Boundary Waters Canoe Area.[34]

In that it is not a fully protected wilderness—motorized traffic is allowed in certain zones—the Boundary Waters Canoe Area Wilderness is a special case among designated wilderness areas. In part, these exceptions are due to the multiple-use approach contained in the original Quetico-Superior program developed by Ober, which, through the years, had become hard-wired into negotiations. Unlike his compatriots Hubachek and Kelly, Ober, in the end, opted for a pure wilderness designation. This was not to be, however, and Ober's many grassroots opponents, who for years vilified him as an extremist, have him in part to thank for the variances they now enjoy.

Since 1978, there have been many political and legal challenges to the Boundary Waters Wilderness Act, and, as Ober predicted, it seems all but certain that the struggle will never be entirely over. The Quetico-Superior region was never to become a peace memorial dedicated to the war dead of the United States and Canada, as Ober, Fred Winston, and the other conservationists of the Quetico-Superior Council had long dreamed. The established protected areas within the region, however, should surely be seen as a memorial, a truly fitting one, to the many conservationists who have struggled with undying dedication for so many years to make such protection a reality.

III

Atisokan

[19]

The Mallard Spreads Its Wings

Until the death of Edward Backus, Ober's life moved with something of the direction and pace of a plotted novel. The young man's search for self and health and career, directionless as it often seemed, led inexorably to his defense of the wilderness and his nine-year conflict with the last of the great lumber barons. Until that point Ober's story could be compared to the stem of a plant. Most of the remainder of his life, then, was to be the blossoming.

Depth psychologist Carl Jung taught that linear development largely ceases somewhere in one's middle years and that increasingly one simply circumambulates that center of the psyche he termed the Self. Such surely was the case with Ober. For him, after age fifty, linear development, linear time seems to have been replaced by something else. Having come to rest somewhere near center, his life seems more and more to have taken on a steady-state quality, repetitive as the seasonal rounds. For the most part, therefore, the telling here of his later life, the blossoming, will be approached, not as linear narrative, but in impressionistic strokes and stories that illustrate his life over broad periods of time.

Between the mid-1920s and the mid-1930s, Ober spent more than two years in Minneapolis and Washington, D.C., and on his circuit of travel in support of the Quetico-Superior program. Nevertheless, even as the environmental battle raged, he somehow managed to maintain and expand a rich personal lifestyle on that narrow 1,100-foot spit of rock, moss, and pine, Mallard Island. Ober's development of the Mallard and his lifestyle there seems to have been an inevitable expression of his inner self, something he could not keep from doing. The mind of Ernest Oberholtzer, haunted by death in youth, immersed for decades in the lakes and forests of the northland, immersed in study, music, and story, cast an image of itself onto the rocks of Mallard Island. Most who have been there agree that, with the help of skilled craftsmen, especially that wonderful alcoholic carpenter Emil Johnson, Ober's creative imagination turned his island into a tiny paradise.

There are those who go further and say that the Mallard became and continues to be a sacred place. In a 1993 article titled "A Home For the Spirit," Robert Franklin of the Minneapolis *Star Tribune* wrote:

Mallard Island belongs to the spirits, they say. It is sacred to the Rainy Lake Ojibwe Indians. It is a mystical place whose spell may have influenced the course of history and the preservation of the Canadian border lakes country.

Franklin noted that Ted Hall, who has spent time on the Mallard since he was nine, told him that "the island has long been a spiritual place for Indian visitors. 'The island provides a place where they can ... be in communication with the spirit families.'"[1]

Hall, the former correspondent and deputy New York bureau chief for Time-Life, was mentored by Ober in his youth, and the two continued to be close friends throughout Ober's long life. In 1972, Hall returned to Ober's country and started his own newspaper, the *Rainy Lake Chronicle*. During the open-water season, Hall lives much of the time in a houseboat, once Ober's, on nearby Gull Island, one of the four narrow, closely aligned islands known as the Review or Japanese Islands, of which the Mallard is one. Though often cautious in his discussion of Ober's spiritual dimension, in an informal interview Hall expanded on the notion of the spirit families:

"Ober never felt that he *owned* these islands," said Hall. "He believed he was only a caretaker for the spirit families." Once again, then, Ober emerges as caretaker, as keeper. Hall continued: "I once asked an Ojibwe woman named Nancy Jones if Ober was a member of the spirit family.

Atisokan

"'Oh, yes,' she said.

"Ober's still running the place then," concluded Hall.

Ray Anderson, another long-time friend of Ober's whose words, like Hall's, have often enriched this story, is also cautious in his discussion of the spiritual. Ray is a photographer and former mail carrier along the shores of Rainy Lake. Due to blindness in one eye caused by shrapnel wounds, he wears a black eye patch. Before entering the service during World War II, he had seen the Mallard only once, but, while lying blinded from his wounds in an olive grove in Sicily, an image of Mallard Island hovered continuously before his mind's eye. In his interview, Anderson drew no conclusions as to why his unconscious should have presented this image, but the suggestion hung in the air that, in this moment of deep crisis, something sacred and healing was given him.

Individuals who in their youth built a tree house or a fort in the woods and found it to be a magical place, a place in which they felt connected to the deep source of things, will rediscover old emotions when they step onto the Mallard. In many, an archetype is awakened that releases an ancient joy at finding human shelter so in continuum with nature. There are, of course, others who snort that the island's dwellings are worn and impractical. This is an arguable point, but, in any case, those in whom the archetype awakens become playful, expansive, and creative on the Mallard. They regain connection with soul.

In his formative years, Ober welcomed a broad array of influences. If something interested him, he studied it, made it part of himself, and, by not focusing on a career, marriage, and family, he did not experience so much of the repression that adulthood requires of most people. Instead, his blue eyes shone in a 360-degree circle of interest. It can be argued that what is denied and held down in an individual, the shadow area of one's repression, contains a lost innocence, a lost Eden. Many who sojourn on the Mallard recover something of what has been lost.

Mallard Island Program Director Jean Replinger aids (and allows) the island to influence people with all the dimensions of Ober's life. In a recent interview, her enthusiasm for his full circle of interest was apparent:

> It's pretty clear that he lived a wonderfully integrated life. I mean he interfaced the political world, he was a part of the musical world, he loved the Indians, unquestionably loved them in a time when [many had little respect for them].
>
> The man lived one of the most wholesome, well-integrated lives. I mean, he might have been a concert violinist, but he played that violin in his canoe with his Indian guide. He was a photographer and he used the photography, not to become rich in money, but rich in information about Indians and moose and to share that information.... He loved people, and he, wherever

he met them, invited them here to his music, his art, his Indian friends, his wilderness life. The man was an explorer. He studied deeply anything that he did before he did it. He was a rare, rare man in terms of this integration, and he is a marvelous model for us today. And I think that this is what we have to offer on the island. When people come, this is what they find. It's like self-discovery for them as to what life can really be like. We tend to think we have to be a musician, an artist, or a storyteller, and that has to be our main way of functioning, but Ober put it all together.

People come here and are interested in the man ... because [he exemplifies a] hidden desire in themselves. The world they live in isn't integrated, and they don't feel like integrated persons.[2]

Ober supervised the evolution of the Mallard's architecture. Small buildings constructed of native materials were, one after another, fitted along shorelines and onto rock outcroppings. The Wannigan or Kitchen Boat, Cedar Bark, and Japanese House, a lovely little building set out over the water at the island's west point, were in place by the mid-1920s. To these were added the two-story Front House near the island's east point; Winter House, an insulated cabin that Ober moved into during periods of deep cold; and a strange, tall building which Billy Magee christened Bird House, on the top of which, in warm weather, Ober often slept. North of the Kitchen Boat, near the island's east-side channel, a work shed was built, used mostly for the repair of canoes and the boats that were moored along extensive landing docks. The buildings were often sided or trimmed with rough slabs of orange-hued cedar bark. Some had fireplaces; almost all had wood-burning stoves. Their windows offered long shining views of the lake.

In the late 1950s, at the top of a bluff on neighboring Hawk Island, Ober organized the reassembling of an elegant, perhaps 35-foot-tall tepee, originally sided with birch bark. Built by Emil Johnson in 1923, it had been part of the Bror Dahlberg estate on nearby Jackfish Island. The tepee, which had fallen into disrepair, was apparently given to Ober who, as previously described, had supervised the construction of Dahlberg's central building, Red Crest, in 1924. During those early years, jutting upward from a shoreline bluff, the tepee could be seen from the Mallard. At that time, it housed a luxurious circle of red velvet cushions and a grand piano, and story has it that Sinclair Lewis wrote part of *Elmer Gantry* in it while a guest of the Dahlbergs.

It is surprising to some that Ober kept his island more carefully groomed than it is today. His natural bent, coupled with his studies in landscape architecture, led him to appreciate an integration of nature with civilization, and this integration is apparent in many places. Much of the island's shoreline, for instance, was built up in low rockwork walls. A small

Ober's Big House

Cedar Bark House, said to have been a brothel before being installed on the Mallard

*Front House,
where Frances Andrews
and Barbara Thomas
stayed during the
summer of 1955*

*The dwelling
christened
Bird House
by Billy Magee*

Ober on path from Big House to Kitchen Boat

rockwork bridge made Japanese House accessible during periods of high water. In the mortar between its rocks, the track of a small dog can be discovered, almost certainly that of Ober's terrier Snippy. On a shore just west of the bridge, one can also find the paw print of a bear in old concrete. Surely there was a smile in the eyes of an Ojibwe craftsman as he pressed this signature into the wet cement.

Here and there around the island, rockwork steps lead down to the water, drinkable directly from the lake until quite recently. In the winter, with the help of local workers, Ober cut blocks of ice from the channel between the Mallard and The Crow—the third of his islands—and stored it in a small sawdust-insulated icehouse for summer, when he often made homemade ice cream. He also loved to make and serve small custards. Being extremely health-conscious, however, he quit eating these foods when he became aware of the risks of cholesterol.

As a young man Ober had smoked. But again, in the 1950s, with increased awareness of the health risk, he quit cold. His strategy was to take up small tasks such as the cleaning of windows whenever he had the urge for a cigarette. As for exercise, some thought him inconsistent. No one, they claim, paddled a canoe or carried it over a portage with more endurance than he, and in warm weather he frequently swam around the entire 1,100-foot Mallard. Nevertheless, he avoided shoveling snow or helping to push stuck cars for fear of damage to his heart.

Ober loved gardening and did much of the work of maintaining fourteen small vegetable and flower gardens. As needed, he had barge-loads of soil and manure hauled onto the island and spread over its thin soil. One of his gardens, a sixty-by-ten-foot strip at the southeast corner of the island, was called "Little Iowa" because its crop was sweet corn, a favorite food of Ober's. A rock ledge on one side and a somewhat protected channel of water on the other held enough heat to give this crop a chance to ripen. It is said that, due to the northern climate, Ober's stand of corn seldom reached full maturity, but, year in and year out—staying in character—he kept trying. Again surprising to some, Ober transplanted to the island many of his favorite flowering plants and shrubs from his childhood home in Iowa. They say it was heaven to be there during the blossoming. It continues to be so.

Ober's circle of interest was not quite complete: on the island one does not discover the pelts and stuffed heads and bodies of animals so common to the region. Though he did sometimes fish for food and accepted food presents of game, late in life he claimed never to have killed an animal or bird during his fifty years on the island. Instead of rods and guns and the taxidermist's art, paintings and photographs and native artifacts decorate the walls of island buildings. Such surroundings make a special impact on visitors there. The Minneapolis *Star Tribune* article quoted from above recounts that island visitor, writer Marsha Chall, "was struck by the sophistication of intellect that just permeates everything."[3] Writer-musician Bill Holm has elegantly zeroed in on the evidence of Ober's passion for music:

> Though he was a bachelor, his private mistress was music. The place is piled with scores of chamber music, keyboard music, violin sonatas, scores of symphonies and operas, American ballads, old hard bound editions of songs by Mendelsohn, Schubert, Sullivan, a whole shelf of Bach cantatas, 4-bound arrangements of overtures and quartets to [wile] away a winter night. To play [there are] 2 pianos, miscellaneous flutes and strings and who knows what else. And when the sound is done for the night, and the music has begun floating out over the dark cold lake full of shadowy islands, more thousands of books to read—biographies and letters of composers, first-rate 19th century music criticism and several complete old Grove's dictionaries to check the facts and savor the bouquet of the prose. However austere the surface of Oberholtzer's life, no man who had accumulated a music library of this size was not a sensualist of the most perverse . . . and enthusiastic kind. . . .[4]

And then of course, as Holm mentioned, there are the thousands of books. Through the mails, Ober built a truly marvelous collection of secondhand books, an island library of huge proportions. Everywhere among his papers one discovers correspondence with secondhand booksellers in London, Toronto, San Francisco, and New York. In time, the walls of all the dwellings on the island were covered by more than 11,000 volumes, very likely the finest private collection in the north country. Ober's interests were broad, but the collection is especially strong in literature, art and music, natural history, exploration, anthropology, and ethnography. The collection thoroughly reveals his intense interest in Native American peoples. Beyond these obvious interests, quality was clearly his most important criterion for selection.

No one knows the book collection better than Island Program Director Jean Replinger who, when she first arrived on the island in the early eighties, several years after Ober's death, discovered what she considered to be a great treasure in books, and she has since supervised the cataloging of them all. It was through reading the abundant exchanges between Ober and secondhand book dealers that she became fully aware of just how much time and energy Ober put into searching out his books. In an interview, Replinger expanded on the ordering process:

> A lot of people today insist that Ober just blindly bought bags full of books. But I have just page after page after notebook full of carefully thought through orders that he made, many of them to England, many to Toronto. . . . He

> would order them very carefully with specific wants and dislikes: I want this volume with this kind of plates, this kind of binding and not this.... He was a very careful orderer of books....[5]

The island was and continues to be imbued with the spirit of Ober's wonderful collection of books. They are a reflected image of the man and his range of thought. "It would be hard to help people understand the man without the books," said Replinger. Ober's long-time friend Bob Hilke, another whose words have added much to this story, stated that to Ober books "were like friends and almost like family."[6]

Though some claim and complain that Ober never read his books, that he was too busy to do so, abundant margin notes in his handwriting make clear that he read considerably, at least during the winter. In a 1937 report to his Harvard classmates, Ober touched on his interest in books and reading. "My hobbies and recreations," he wrote, "include wilderness travel, Indians, music, and second-hand books. I seldom have a chance to read, but enjoy good books of any kind, especially such fiction as Tchekov, Gorky, Rolvaag, Hamsum, Jim Tully, Liam O'Flaherty, Mark Twain, Hawthorne, Emily Bronte, Jane Austen, and accounts of early American travel, especially of Indian life."[7]

There is a secondary value as well for a well-educated person living within the surround of such wonderful books: their names on the bindings, what one knows of their content and their authors' lives, imbues one in a subliminal, background manner with their stored power. They serve as a continuing reminder of the best in human thought and imagination, a reminder too that all are part of a great evolving pattern of thought, imagination, and story.

One cannot discuss Ober's books without thinking of him as teacher. At the end of Ober's life, boundary waters writer Sigurd Olson wrote that Ober was "always a canoe man." Olson well knew the immensity of Ober's lifelong canoe journey. However, Ted Hall, who knew Ober better than did Olson, wrote that, "Atisokan was, above all, a superb if unaccredited teacher."[8] Other former island habitués agree: Ober was always a teacher. One of these is Marnee Monahan. Though far older than she and her husband Hugh, Ober was the best man at their wedding, and over the years she and Hugh spent many months on the Mallard. In an interview, Marnee remembered that, for Ober, teaching, often through storytelling, was his central mode of relating to others. She says that there was an indescribable magnetism around Ober that she had been fortunate enough to witness over and over again around Ober's kitchen table.

A written summary of Marnee's interview tells that, since Ober was physically small, stature had nothing to do with his magnetic power. Marnee believed instead that it was his voice:

> [According to Marnee], he would open his mouth and be powerful and influential. Marnee remembers him as a man of great humor, but not intimacy. She never saw anyone touch Ober, pat him on the shoulder, give him a welcome bear hug. His reserve amidst the humor was a barrier plain and simple and meant to be there as a personality trait to respect. It perhaps heightened his influence and his ability to teach. For teach he did.... [People listened] to Ober talk about wildlife, water, land, and the abuse of all of these by the ruthless lumber business. Ober made clear to other influential people, that [such] treatment of this wilderness was wrong. He taught appreciation of Rainy Lake to anyone at the table. Marnee remembers good hour after good hour listening to him talk and knowing that the audience at the table ... were using Ober well, and learning from him, a marvelous but impractical man who loved the lake she loved as well.[9]

It goes without saying that the Mallard became a force in support of the Quetico-Superior program. Those who went there, often people with influence, were charmed by the place and experienced the magnetic power in Ober, and many of them became supporters of Ober's wilderness vision and the Program. Marnee seems to believe that Ober's integrated complexity expressed itself and was the source of his magnetic power:

> ... it was a fine synthesis of objective knowledge, passion and performance ability that held so many of their own free will, at [Ober's] table, for so many years.... [People] came to Ober's aid unasked. Everyone loved to help him and get close to him for his talk.... A small man who spoke beautifully.... What she does remember of Ober so clearly is that he gave her an education. "Timeless," she says.[10]

Ober taught by example as well as through talk. According to Marnee, his respect for nature included even the abundant mosquitoes of the north: "'The mosquitoes were horrible,' she said. "But Ober refused to use spray against them. "'Bugs don't like that,' he would say."[11]

When Ted Hall was a boy, Ober taught him an object lesson he has not forgotten. They were on a canoe trip together, and on setting up camp one evening, Ober asked Ted to catch a fish for supper. Ober had always told him never to take more fish than they could eat, but that evening, at the foot of a beautiful waterfall, walleyes hit at nearly every cast, and Ted carried a heavy string back to Ober, who said nothing. Instead, he made a large and delicious kettle of chowder from the fish, and day following day they ate nothing but walleye chowder until it was gone. Apparently, this culinary monotony sank deeper into Ted's young mind than had Ober's verbal admonition.

In his youth, Bob Hilke found that Ober taught far more than conservation and wilderness lore. He taught him to know people as well. Hilke met people from all over the world on the island. Ober also taught him appreciation of nature, that standing beside a mature pine tree was an experience of grace. In an oral history interview, Hilke expanded on this teaching:

> I just saw Ober's real affection for these things, and I liked him so much that I found that I got to where I could appreciate a little lichen or a piece of moss growing on a rock a whole lot. Before, I took those things for granted, even though I noticed them and liked them. But it became something very special later because Ober treated those things that way and talked about them that way.[12]

As proof that Ober had learned from one of *his* teachers, Billy Magee, Hilke said that Ober taught him patience as well. When on a canoe trip together, should Ober observe, say, an interesting ridge of pines a considerable distance up from shore, he would often insist that they stop and hike up to that ridge. Like most teenagers, Hilke wanted to push on toward a destination, but the hike, the view, the grove of singing pines were always worth it. These side-hikes often turned out to be the high points of their trips together.

Many who knew Ober best, then, think of him first, not as a wilderness figure—a canoe man and preservationist—but as a teacher.

The question is frequently asked how Ober, so often financially on the edge, could afford the development of his island home. As described earlier, his three islands—Mallard, Hawk, and Crow—were the largest portion of his settlement from William Hapgood after the breakup of Deer Island, Inc. As to the island's many buildings, it must be understood that they are slight and simple and were often secondhand structures scavenged or bought cheaply, as was the case with the houseboats. They were then redesigned, improved, added to, made one with the island. This work was done with the help of the not-so-expensive skilled craftsmen available in the 1920s and 1930s. The one exception to the above description of the island's buildings, Ober's Big House—also called Old Man River House or simply Ober's House—is a substantial, log-beamed structure of three stories built into a rock bluff at the island's highest point. This building was not completed until 1940 and was apparently paid for by the sale of the house in Davenport Ober had inherited from Rosa.

Though unwilling or unable to curtail his creative development of the Mallard, Ober was indeed often under financial strain. It seems that the rent from the Davenport commercial building he had inherited, the old Market, never rose much above $100 a month, and often there was no money in the Quetico-Superior Council fund to pay his salary. A 1927 letter written to his legal adviser Judge John Brown reveals that he is desperate to realize money from the Mallard. In it, too, is a reminder of his resale agreement with his former partner William Hapgood:

> It may be necessary in the near future for me either to sell or mortgage the "Mallard." I would rather mortgage for two reasons. In the first place I would have a chance to recover the property after my necessities become less. Secondly, I think I could raise at least as large a sum by a mortgage as by a sale. If I sell to Mr. Hapgood as by agreement, I have to let him have the property at cost. The cost I believe to be far below present values, for all improvements have been made economically and with a thought of the beauty of the island. Altogether the property constitutes a unique establishment, which would have a high selling value on account of its ideas.[13]

It may be that the unpleasant clause in Ober's agreement with Hapgood is all that kept him from selling the island during the depression. A second letter to Judge Brown, written in Washington, D.C., in 1930, discloses that Ober is planning to give the island to Harry French in payment for his growing debt to him. The contents of this letter also express a sense of the tremendous strain Ober is under due to the Quetico-Superior struggle. Surely thinking of his heart, he hints at anxiety as to his survival:

> What I'll probably do before long, as soon as it can be arranged, is to turn over all my property on Rainy Lake to Harry French of Davenport. I may be tied up in my work for a considerable time yet and therefore not able to make any other more satisfactory adjustment with Harry French. He would be perfectly willing to let matters stand as they are, but I do not like to leave them hanging in the air. I am all alone now and under a very great strain and no one can ever tell what may happen. . . .
>
> I think you have never yet perfected my deed to the Mallard under the present survey. I hope that can now be done promptly, for that will be the main item to be included in the transfer to Harry French. I have had that understanding for a number of years but, like all my own personal business affairs, it has had to be utterly neglected.
>
> I hope to see Harry French before many weeks more and to discuss with him exactly what final arrangements I can make. He has been wonderfully considerate with me.
>
> I miss the lake and my old life more than I can say. It is very difficult for me to understand why it should have fallen to my lot to carry on the battle for this region, where I was always such a quiet and unobtrusive sojourner. . . .[14]

Though Harry French would have none of the above plan, Ober's financial plight was not to go away. The struggle for preservation of Quetico-Superior had become his fate, and yet he often felt he could not accept pay from the depleted resources of the Quetico-Superior Council. In a 1935 letter to his historian friend Samuel Eliot Morison, one to whom Ober seemed able and willing to bare his soul, he is again trying to derive income from the Mallard. In it, Ober provided his description of the island, and his pride in its development as well as his desperate financial circumstances are apparent:

> ... I am writing you now, because I am trying to find some way this summer to capitalize my island at Rainy Lake and my long years of experience there. You may just happen to know someone who would be interested.
>
> I have never been able to extricate myself from the Quetico-Superior Council.... We are ... in sight of the goal and yet on the point of collapse. This is my fourth year without income with the result that the taxes on my island and on my mother's home in Davenport, which still cannot be sold, are long delinquent and I am heavily in debt.
>
> There is no question what I should do and must do soon, judging by my own necessity. But that will mean the complete loss of all we have struggled so hard for in the border lakes region. So I am still fool-heartedly clinging to the red hot iron.
>
> We still have an office address in Minneapolis but no help there. My official headquarters for a number of years has been at my island. This summer I want instead to rent the island or find some other way to get a return from it.
>
> The island is a very attractive place. It lies seven miles from town by boat. We were 15 years building it up to its present condition. There are four main cabins, one of them used exclusively as a kitchen and dining room, the rest as living quarters; and several smaller buildings. Also docks and all other facilities. There are no modern improvements, such as electricity and running water; but each house has its own sink and pump. The houses are simply built and furnished in the style of the country but extremely comfortable and pleasing. I have never seen any other place like it anywhere.
>
> The problem of renting is not so easy. I must get at least $500 for the season to make it worth while. This includes wood and ice, which are now on the island ready for use. I must also reserve one of the cabins, in which I have my office and personal effects. There is ample room in the rest for a large party, say up to a dozen, or a small party with occasional guests would be very happily situated.
>
> ... It is not particularly a place for sportsmen, though excellent fishing can be had in neighboring lakes and of course there are unlimited canoe routes.... The boating and swimming are excellent. It is well suited to a family with a variety of interests and needs. Each one can have a place to

himself. Or it would be an excellent place for musical people. We have a good piano, beautiful phonograph records and quite a library of well-selected second-hand books. Visitors would not have to bring anything but their personal effects and perhaps some linen and blankets. There are first-class stores in town and fresh farm supplies, including milk and poultry, are easy to get.

... I have also thought of taking one or two boys, just as I took Secretary Ickes' son [Raymond] back in 1925 and 1927 but that would be more difficult, since I could not very well do anything else, especially if I undertook to go canoe cruising with them. The Quetico-Superior work is ever-present and very insistent and, while I plan to reduce it to the minimum this summer, it is a constant problem.

I hope you will not mind my writing you thus in detail about a personal matter. Unless you know someone to whom these plans may appeal do not give them another thought. On the other hand, if you do hear of someone misguided enough to want any such outing, just refer him to me. I can send photos of the island and the various cabins.[15]

Despite his financial predicament, Ober often refused payment from the Quetico-Superior Council, even when funds were available, when he felt his salary would cut into the ongoing work of the Program. At times, other members of the council found this simply unacceptable. The following pair of notes from council treasurer, J. G. Byam, vice president of the First National Bank and Trust Co. of Minneapolis, give insight into the situation:

As your account here showed an over-draft of $150, I have placed to your credit today $200, representing the salary you declined to withdraw for the month of September, which will take care of the over-draft. Of course you know that it is strictly against the rules of the bank to permit over-drafts, and I hope you will avoid having them in the future.

It is, in my opinion, only fair to you that while the treasury has cash on hand, there should be paid to you each month the small salary you have drawn during the past year.[16]

And again:

As requested in your letter of the 23rd, we have placed to your account to-day $25, in connection with your recent expenses on the Canadian trip, and duplicate deposit slip is enclosed.

Also, I have much pleasure in advising you that $3000 has been placed to your credit, by instructions of the Executive Committee, and a duplicate deposit slip for this is enclosed. This amount represents salary which you declined to draw in the past, and the Committee wish me to advise you that an additional $2000 will go to your credit the First of next year. ...[17]

Blessed relief!

All who knew Ober point out that his wealthy friends sincerely wanted to, and often did, provide financial support for him and his causes. These generous friends included Harry French, Fred Winston, and Frances Andrews, the woman-friend who in the 1930s became an increasingly important part of Ober's life. Ober experienced an underlying sense of guilt over this dependence, and his book-writing fantasies were often connected to the idea that a good-selling book would allow him to pay back what had been given him.

It was not only the wealthy, however, who appreciated and wanted to help Ober. In 1931, a handwritten note sent to the Quetico-Superior Council included a $10 bill and these words:

> Some day I hope all of our people will appreciate the years of unselfish service rendered by Mr. Ernest C. Oberholtzer in connection with this great project. He is a great citizen. With best wishes for success....[18]

During the summer, guests arrived on Mallard Island as regularly as the waves to its rocky shores, and they often paid for their stay. The names of certain visitors, appearing over and over in the Oberholtzer archives, suggest they had become part of an island family. Correspondence with these people, often artists and writers from the east, was heavy over the years, and there are stories and wilderness trips that go with each. There were of course the Hapgoods and Sewell Tyng, and a man not yet introduced in the foregoing pages, a New York medical researcher named Gilbert Dalldorf, originally from Davenport. Then there were Ober's other Davenport friends who built summer homes on nearby islands: Harry French and his wife, Virginia, and her father, Major Horace Roberts. New York writers John and Kit Bakeless and a Duluth and Greenwich Village visual artist, Penelope "Pep" Turle, were also frequent visitors during those golden years on the Mallard.

Then there were the sons of an International Falls medical family, Hugh and George Monahan, and their wives, Marnee and Gene. Something of Marnee's experience on the Mallard has appeared in the preceding pages. As a youth, George, who would become a military man in later life, spent much time on the island and on canoe trips with Ober. Gene was a visual artist, and after George's retirement from the military, they spent their middle years in Greenwich Village, then returned to International Falls. In the 1960s, George would conduct several oral history interviews with Ober, and after Ober's death Gene served as an unofficial island caretaker and is responsible, it seems, for much of the early phase of preservation of the Oberholtzer papers, so important to the telling of this story. Ober was the godfather of George and Gene's daughter, Jean, and one of their sons, Laird, would for a time be a caretaker for Ober in his old age. Another of their sons, Robin, also became a friend of Ober's. A lover of the wilderness, he would one day take on the challenge of retracing much of Ober's Hudson Bay canoe journey.

In a 1970 letter, Kit Bakeless recalled a camping trip she was on with Ober in the 1930s. At the time she wrote, Ober's memory was failing, and Bakeless reiterated the word "remember," hoping that Ober would recall just how fine those days—and he himself—were:

> Yes—many memories—and wonderful memories.... [On the trip, the party experienced] one of the worst long-drawn-out rains in a depressing burnt-over area, with no complaints. That rain went on and on, Ober, HARD for several days, and intermittently for eight. It was hard work for you, because with it all you kept us in firewood with a little fire going constantly—I could never understand how you could chop out dry wood in that sopping wet place. You did all the work.

As ever, Ober was the kindly caretaker for the party. Two of its members had to return to civilization for the beginning of the school year:

> So we camped a few miles below Atikokan, and you took them back to Fort Francis [*sic*] by train. Pep [Penelope Turle] and I stayed two nights alone in the fine big fly you put up for us. After we saw you off on the train, Pep and I went into Atikokan's store to get materials to make you a new jewel-case. (You remember the Tyngs always called their camp knives, forks, and spoons, the *jewels*.) And your old canvas case was pretty worn out and ripped and torn. Pep and I sat in the fly that whole day sewing up your new jewel case for a surprise. Then you came back with George Monahan, and the weather turned gorgeous. Clear beautiful sunrises, sometimes a little frost, beautiful campsites—and Billy and the Indians on Wild Potato Lake. There we stayed two nights—you cooked a bang up meal of baked beans and corn bread and invited Billy and his wife to dinner, remember? When she held out her plate for a third helping of your delicious food, Billy grunted and made her pull back her plate.... Wonderful experience for us. Then after dark we went over to the Indians' camp, and they were having a ceremony by the medicine man to preserve the life of the old dying mother-in-law of the chief—whom we had seen lying against her wigwam that noon, wrapped in a rabbitskin blanket—remember? Later I asked you if she had lived and you told me that she lived through the next winter. Incredible.
>
> After that wonderful paddling down Seine River—we came to a blueberry paradise where we camped and you gave us a breakfast of blueberry pancakes!!!!! Then later that very morning was the lovely little spot of white water, and you asked me if I would like to run down them in the canoe with you. Did I JUMP at the offer! You warned me to sit low and not do anything. But when I saw a big rock coming at us, I just tapped it to avoid it, and thereby caused a rush of some water into the canoe. You didn't scold me,

and of course you would have avoided the rock but it all went so fast. It was certainly thrilling. And I'm still thanking you.[19]

Ted Hall has described Mallard Island life during Ober's mature years as a continuing salon. Jean Replinger agreed:

> There was a time when there were two or three Chautauquas going on here at a time. I mean, the New York people lived on one section of the island and Washington people on another, and they would put on plays for each other at night. The island was a microcosm of and a metaphor for a very integrated artistic-realistic world. . . .
>
> Ober was a part of that wash of wealth that came to the Rainy Lake area, but he was known as the fellow who came in tennis shoes and his wool shirt and whatever hat he had on. He never changed as a person to be acceptable; he just was acceptable as he was. A lot of people from around this area sought him out; a lot of people came to him from his political arena. He would invite people back to this place in which he was not political.[20]

There was another kind of visitor about which Ober's old friends love to tell. During his travels, in support of the Quetico-Superior program and on personal trips, usually by train, Ober would frequently talk to strangers, tell them stories, then invite them to visit him. His magnetism and sincerity were such that many of these people did appear on the island. In one case, a husband and wife and five children arrived one day, brimming with enthusiasm for their visit. As a matter of course, Ober installed them in available housing, but he had no idea who they were. Finally, after several days, he felt he had to ask the man where they had met and was told he had invited the man when he helped Ober with his baggage.

Ober worked hard at maintaining friendships. Though he left many of his own gifts untouched, even unopened, his Christmas gift list was truly lengthy, and it is said that, on the island, he spent half of each day writing letters. Many of these were in support of the Program, but, by volume, half of this writing must have been devoted to personal correspondence. Letters were his way of keeping his many distant friendships alive. Ober did not write books, but after his death some 54,000 letters and reports would be turned over to the Minnesota Historical Society. At his best, Ober was a master of the letter, but there was a problem. As the years passed, his handwriting grew so difficult to read that, out of necessity, he often turned to a small mechanical typewriter. Changing its ribbon, however, seems to have been a serious technical challenge for him. But, in order to maintain his friendships, scores and scores of letters had to be written, and it is said that "he lived for the return mail" and would risk thin ice to get it.

With his mother's death, a new possibility (and perhaps need) opened in Ober, and, shortly thereafter, Frances Andrews entered his life. Their early letters discussed brief meetings and mutual enthusiasm for the wilderness and native peoples. There followed a friendship, a love, apparently platonic, that was to last the rest of their lives. In a 1934 letter to Sewell Tyng, Ober wrote that Miss Andrews wanted to become the island cook that summer, and apparently she did at least help in that position. Frances was mesmerized by Ober—his person, his talk, his work as a wilderness preservationist—but, it seems, his physical reserve, whatever its source, was never to be relaxed.

Some believe that the relationship between Ober and Frances was one of the most interesting stories of Ober's life, and it may be that it deserves its own book. Frances was an attractive woman of about Ober's height. She was an environmentalist, the daughter of a well-to-do Minneapolis grain merchant, also an environmentalist. She had been engaged to a pilot who was killed in World War I, and later, as Ober had cared for Rosa, Frances cared for her father, who lived on into his nineties.

As the years passed, Frances became an increasingly permanent part of Ober's life. She continued to own a fine home in the Minneapolis suburb of Golden Valley, but she began spending summers in Front House on the east point of the island, carefully distanced from Ober's House. She tended flower gardens and, though she seldom cooked, developed the

Ober and Frances Andrews on Mallard Island dock

menus for island employees and guests, often totaling ten or fifteen people. She supported Ober in his environmental struggles, her "man" George chauffeuring her to the sites of many of his meetings, and she often provided financial support for endeavors that went beyond Ober's means. When apart, their correspondence was abundant, and Frances's letters often ran to an enthusiastic five or ten pages. Ober's letters to her during this period, sensitive and touchingly warm, often provide a clear picture of his activities on the Mallard.

According to a number of accounts, Frances loved Ober dearly, and it was her wish that they be married, but, though Ober clearly loved her in his own way and treated her with tender respect, with him there was no question of marriage. It is said that Frances sometimes broke into tears before friends because she could not be married to Ober. It must sometimes have been hard for her. Once in an International Falls store, after she had rinsed her white hair blue, a not-so-sensitive old fellow with a brogue yelled at her: "You'll never get Ober with that god-dammed blue hair!"

In an oral history interview conducted by George Monahan, Ober said that he had once thought about taking an Indian wife. Frances was present during this interview, and Ober's awkwardness at its end was surely at least partly due to her being there: "I looked that situation over [marriage], but decided not to join in. Expensive. I was limited in a way that the Indians weren't. They could live on moose meat, and I didn't even shoot moose. So I didn't undertake—I thought about it a couple of times, about taking an Indian wife. They told me up in Mine Centre:

"'You want to study Indians? You know the best way to learn the language?'

"'No, what's that?'

"'To get a sleeping dictionary.'

"At first I was puzzled. I didn't instantly comprehend, but, as I turned around to go, I suddenly knew what they meant. But, even though it would have been a nice way to learn the language, it involved an expense that I didn't want to take on. Even now, well, I, it's the same thing. I can't involve myself in that kind of a deal. So, well, this isn't getting on to what you want is it, at all? It goes back almost to the time when I was born."

Ober's hint that the source reason(s) for his not marrying went back to the time of his birth was repeated in one of the 1960s columns that Jim Kimball wrote about him: "Asked if [Ober] ever wished he had married and raised a family, he said, 'No, I have always been quite self sufficient and was born in the wilderness.'"[21] One must wonder if the word "wilderness" in this context might not have been code for something inborn that kept him from a conventional family life, that is, his sexual orientation. As was mentioned in chapter ten, Ober's usual prohibition against touching seems not to have applied to his young male friends, one of whom has said that on a cold night in a tent Ober might even cuddle up to him. Such hints fuel the conjecture that Ober was indeed a repressed homosexual.

Beyond Ober's immediate circle of friends, rumor has spread and expanded till there are many who now assume that he was actively homosexual. There are even some who suggest he may have been inappropriate with the boys and young men he mentored. It must be made clear that a complaint of this nature has never been made. Those who knew Ober well say that there is no indication he was actively homosexual, and some argue that it is a stretch to claim he was homosexual at all. Whatever his sexual orientation, then, it seems to have been repressed, and one can only guess at the degree of effort this required and the inner burden it may have created.

In the late 1950s, Frances Andrews bought a home on the mainland, a short distance across the water from the Mallard, on land that Ober had once owned. Ober would eventually inherit this house from Frances, and some say she originally meant it to be a present for him—she apparently hoped they would live in it together—but Ober refused to live in it at all until long after Frances had died.

Ober often described his Deer Island project with William Hapgood as a ten-ring circus. If so, his life on the Mallard was at least a three-ringer, and

Ober and Frances Andrews

he needed helpers. One such assistant was Oscar Gilbertson, who had come to the island to do some stonework and never left, serving as an all-around island handyman. Another was Barbara Thomas (now Breckenridge), a nineteen-year-old student at the University of Minnesota, who took on the formidable job of island cook during the summer of 1955. Frances Andrews hired her, paid her $100-a-month salary, and brought her north in June. A series of letters from Barbara to her mother provide a lively picture of island life during her stay. She was immediately impressed by Ober, who was now seventy-one. She expected to see someone who looked old but found him to be very agile, very active: "He isn't much taller than I am [five feet five inches], if any, with very broad shoulders. He has white hair. He is very funny. At night, after we finish eating, we sit and he tells story after story. He'll say the funniest things and keep the straightest face all the while."[22]

In an oral history interview, Barbara expanded on such moments of mirth:

> I always say he was a pixie of a man. He had a twinkle in his eye, always, and he loved to tell stories. We would sit two hours in the evening, and he would tell stories. He would have us just laughing until we cried sometimes. But you never knew how much to believe of the stories he told.
>
> Yes, he had great charisma, and he was so welcoming to everyone. I think the big influence both he and Miss Andrews had on me was that they treated everyone as equals, whether it was a research doctor from New York or a viola player from England or an Indian family that had stopped by—everyone was welcomed.[23]

Barbara was struck by Ober's courtesy and kindness, and she noticed something else that others have noted: "I don't remember ever seeing him angry." There are some who have, of course, but to see him angry was a truly rare experience.

In the letters, Barbara noted that Frances, too, was about her height "and probably about the same weight with white hair and a round face. She's very nice and I think we are going to get along fine." As for the interior of Front House where she stayed with Miss Andrews, Barbara writes: "My room is on the second floor with windows on every wall and no matter which way I look I can see water and other islands. Our little house is very homey looking. The outside is of weathered wood. The inside is decorated with bark. Much of the furniture is made from weathered logs. Really rustic, but very comfortable.... The outhouse for our house is even luxurious. It is papered with pink and green flowered wallpaper with the boards painted green."[24]

Barbara offers insight into the relationship between Ober and Frances and the magnetism of Ober's personality: "Ober and I get along fine. Miss

Andrews is sometimes rather forgetful, but Ober winks at me, and we let it pass. We understand each other. He's a fascinating man, Mom. Must be 70, but is very, very active."[25]

Barbara's letters also reveal the continuing presence of music on the Mallard. Beyond Ober and his violin, there was Buddy Friday, the Indian youth who worked on the island and who "used to sing over the radio station at the Falls and can play any string instrument plus the accordion. Speaking of music, I am playing the piano again. Have been playing at least half an hour every day." And it was in the summer of 1955 that Harry French's daughter Alice Virginia arrived with her new husband: "I met a pretty famous man last night. *Sir* William Primrose, said to be the world's greatest viola player."[26] It seems that Ober backed away from the opportunity to accompany Primrose in a string duet. Ober often promised that they would listen to recordings of violinists, but the island had no electricity—its appliances were gas-driven—and characteristically he could never get the generator to work.

As to conduct on the island, Barbara wrote her mother, "I'm sorry you worried about my being alone on the island with just men. If you knew them, especially Ober, you wouldn't have to worry. Nobody does anything wrong on this island. They are good people, whether Indian or white, if they are going to stay on Ober's island."[27]

Near the end of the summer during which Barbara Thomas cooked in

Music was a continuing presence in all seasons

the Kitchen Boat, a young man arrived. Ober had met him on a train and he became a canoeing partner and long-time friend. "The photographer arrived yesterday," wrote Barbara. "His name is John Szarkowski, he's 27, quite tall and lots of fun."[28] The tall young man, it seems, arrived with a homegrown eggplant in each pocket of his coat, and Barbara had no idea how to prepare them. Szarkowski, now recognized as one of America's most influential photographers, was later to become director of the Department of Photography at the New York Museum of Modern Art. His admiration for Ober and his support for projects that further the Oberholtzer legacy continue even to this day.

Over the years, conservation meetings were frequently held in towns surrounding the Quetico-Superior region, and Ober was often a central figure at these. Since he did not own a car and could not drive, he employed young men to drive for him. Many of them had already come under his mentorship and would continue to be his lifelong friends. One was Winston Schmidt, the son of a Rainy Lake commercial fisherman who ferried Ober about the region in an old seven-passenger Caddy with jump seats. They traveled to meetings and to visit resort owners, south to Crane Lake, northeast into Canada to Atikokan, then on to Fort William–Port Arthur. Schmidt, a man of few words, said that he seldom attended the meetings: "They talked about dams," he said. As for Ober, however, "*He* was interesting to be with."[29]

As mentioned earlier, Ober also traveled extensively by canoe each summer. These trips were surely healing escapes, but their underlying purpose was to monitor effects on the region of logging and other exploitative intrusions. His claim that for four decades he paddled a minimum of 500 miles a year is unquestioned, and it is believed that, overall,

Ray Anderson in his youth on a canoe trip with Ober

his canoe travel amounted to enough miles to circumnavigate the planet. Sometimes he paddled alone. More often, he traveled with friends, Indian or white, or the sons of these friends, some of whom were sent to the Mallard to learn at the feet of the man who had become recognized as a wilderness master.

In the oral history interviews, there is a section in which Ober told of three boys who accompanied him on canoe trips. Two, who will be discussed in the following chapter, were Ojibwe. One was a young white boy named Douglas Head, son of the heart specialist who had cared for Ober and Rosa: "He was a very joyous kind of boy," said Ober, "and he would often break into song. He had a lovely soprano voice, but he'd break into song at the most unexpected moments, maybe at a point when I was hoping to photograph a deer or moose. So I had to ask him to wait until we got ashore at night, and no sooner would we get ashore than he'd break forth in a luxuriant amount of song."

One day, as they paddled together, Ober was able to provide Douglas, who would one day become the attorney general of Minnesota, with an especially interesting experience. They saw a big buck deer swimming across a lake about two miles ahead. Ober knew that they had a chance of overtaking him, and in fact, with the help of a blinding sun, the joyous young boy was able to lay his hand on the antlers and back of a swimming buck deer.

Indeed, there was quite a long line of those who, as boys and young men, absorbed the teachings of Atisokan. In the Oberholtzer papers, there is a letter from Harry Henderson, a psychiatrist with Native American blood, who in 1954 wrote to thank Ober:

> ... In retrospect, looking back on the years of your strengthening influence upon me, with the cherished memories of [my] youth ... traveling beside you in the lake country, I deeply thank you for all of it. Impossible it will be for you to actually understand what you have done for me and the hopes you have kindled.
>
> Of all the boys you helped to learn the love of the wilderness, I was probably the poorest material to work with and the one for you to be most discouraged over. Yet twenty years have passed and although you have not been physically present beside me, you have been constantly with me as a guiding light. ... My life has been filled to over flowing and knowing "Ober" has made much of my happiness possible. ...[30]

Later in life, Henderson bought a small area of oak forest and native prairie in Nebraska that he named, for Ober, the Atisokan Wilderness Area.

Letters implying the power of Ober's teaching are abundant in the archives. Some of the young men who learned from him maintained a lifetime correspondence, but none more so than Gilbert Dalldorf. Shortly after his return from Hudson Bay, Ober was briefly the assistant scoutmaster for a Davenport troop Dalldorf had joined, and that was the beginning of a lifelong friendship that frequently brought Dalldorf and his family to the Mallard. Dalldorf was to become head of the New York State Research Laboratory and was the first to isolate the polio virus, thus making possible the vaccine. Ever one to make the most of his friends' successes, Ober always argued that Dalldorf received far too little credit for this achievement. Dalldorf in turn idolized Ober, gave him great credit for whatever he had become, and maintained a special room at his home devoted to Oberholtzer memorabilia. It was a dream of Dalldorf's that one day a U.S. postage stamp would honor Ober.

Bob Hilke not only went on canoe trips with Ober, but, as described earlier, also listened to sonatas and played violin duets with him as northern lights flashed and ice cracked in the deep cold of Rainy Lake winter nights. In an oral history interview, Hilke expanded on how Ober had taught him appreciation of classical music:

> I had a lot of respect for Ober [as a violinist], because he could play a lot more difficult things than I could, and yet he had patience. If I started to play, he'd help me. We both understood the difficulty of these pieces. I guess part of my thrill was to see how much Ober enjoyed this. And when we listened to music we listened totally. We didn't have anything else bothering us at all. I mean, it was just that music. We could sit there for a long time and just really listen to it.[31]

Until recently, Hilke was the owner and captain of the Voyageurs National Park tour boat, *The Pride of Rainy Lake,* and the talks he gave during his tours owed much to Ernest Oberholtzer. He also has a room in his house that he thinks of as his Oberholtzer room.

Ted Hall went a step further. As mentioned earlier, he lives much of the time in Ober's former houseboat, the *Frigate Friday,* and after Ober's death, he was a central figure in a legal fight to forestall the sale of the Mallard so that it might be preserved as a living memorial to his old friend and mentor. Later, photographer Ray Anderson, with his wife, Ruth, spent an entire winter on the Mallard archiving Ober's more than 5,000 photographs, again creating a fine memorial to the man and his works. Ray's younger brother, Leo, who had worked on the island as a teenager and gone on many canoe trips with Ober, became a journalist and magazine publisher and, later in life, canoed the entire length of the Mississippi, certainly to some degree a tribute to Ober's influence.

Ober loved people from all walks of life, and, when not overwhelmed by financial problems and Quetico-Superior demands, he was, according to those who knew him best, a delightful companion. Many who have gone to live in nature have done so in denial of human community and culture. Though he loved to paddle beyond the reach of civilization, Ober was not of the sort who go to the wilds to get away from people. The lifestyle he created on the Mallard was a rich blend of natural simplicity and cultural sophistication. There is in western civilization a nature-culture division that has become our sad heritage. Within himself and through the lifestyle he developed on the Mallard, Ober did much to solve, dissolve, and transcend that division.

Friendship with the Ojibwe

Ober continued to dream of a life given to the study of the culture of native people, especially that of the Ojibwe he had come to know in his youth. It may be that this dream was the expression of a desire for a free and deep immersion in the natural world while still living in a culturally rich human community. As it hovered in his mind, it was surely compensatory to the long Quetico-Superior struggle in which he often felt trapped, the "red-hot iron" he could not put down. Though this dream was never to be fully realized, the lifestyle Ober evolved on the Mallard owed much to his fascination with Indian ways, and his relationship with the Ojibwe grew deeper and richer with the passing years. In a 1996 interview, in answer to the question "Has any other white been so close to your people as Ober?" his Ojibwe friend Harry "Pinay" Boshkaykin responded, "He's the one, the only one. . . ." But then, on reflection, he remembered the Mine Centre trader Edgar Bliss: "That store man in Mine Centre, he's dead now long ago. Called him Iceman. . . . Liked to enjoy Indians, too, that man."[1]

When time allowed, Ober traveled by boat and canoe to Indian communities north of him in Ontario, especially the Seine River and Red Gut Reserves. And when he paddled the region by canoe to monitor environmental impacts, he often traveled with Indian companions. With increasing frequency, Indian people also came to the Mallard to be near Ober. They maintained a summer camp on The Hawk, but a stone's throw across a channel from Ober's House. They, too, often enjoyed the cooking in the Kitchen Boat, and some were given work. There was always work to be done on the Mallard.

Ober's charitable support of Ojibwe people during a hard transitional time is well known. He bought bundles of clothing that were kept on the Mallard and given to Indians who needed new pairs of pants or shirts. There is a letter from Ober to Frances Andrews—Ober had apparently asked her to purchase clothing for this stock—in which he gently scolds her for sending a bundle of "designer" outdoor clothing she had ordered from L. L. Bean. While on the island and traveling by canoe, Ober himself wore simple clothing, usually high-topped tennis shoes and often a checked flannel or woolen shirt. Some thought his dress a little innocent, even a little funny. A young Ojibwe whom Ober had mentored, Maurice Perrault, wrote of the first time he saw Ober: "He was dressed in a canvas hunting jacket and what I would call hunting pants and wore tennis shoes. And he wore a funny hat. The sight of him [made me want to] laugh." But then, "The more I talked to this quaint old gentleman [the more] I knew that he was no ordinary man."[2]

When Ober was unable to provide needed support for Indian people from his own resources, he often found others willing to help, frequently Frances Andrews or his old friend of the European tour, Harry French. For twelve-year-old Allen Snowball, born with a seriously defective hip that kept him from walking, Ober found a Winnipeg surgeon and a financial donor, apparently Frances Andrews. As a result, Allen was able to walk almost normally through his adult years. Until his recent untimely death, he often came to the Mallard, where he talked to visitors about Indian ways and the life of Ernest Oberholtzer.

An extended series of letters written to Ober by the man the Ojibwe called Iceman, Mine Centre trader Edgar Bliss, is part of the collection held on the Mallard. The letters, containing extraneous exclamation marks meant no doubt to express enthusiasm, reveal that, though Billy Magee had often proven an elusive friend, Ober had taken on considerable responsibility for him and his family's material well-being. Ober maintained an account with Bliss for this purpose, and Bliss's responses to Ober's letters provide a sense of their financial arrangement and Ober's solicitousness. It seems that at some point in 1937 Billy suffered a stroke, and, although Quetico-Superior work and travel prevented Ober from visiting him, the plight of his old wilderness traveling companion was seldom far from his mind. On November 19, 1937, Bliss wrote:

> Your very kind letter with enclosure received. Well now! Mr. Oberholtzer, yesterday I made up my mind to personally visit Billy. Although the lakes have been recently frozen over. . . . But: I reached Billy's quarters at the mouth of big Turtle River *and*! repeated to him contents of your letter. With me! I took over Tea, Sugar, Box Matches & couple Pkgs of Tobacco. I found Billy pretty good, considering! Although he tells me he cannot work hard, also, not able to trap, *neither* can he smoke but very little. He is getting quite thin but insists that he is able to walk as far as the store (about 3 miles). . . . Billy seemed to understand [it was] the lady Miss Frances Andrews of Minneapolis who was so kind & generous and I wish you to assure Miss Andrews that the cheque will be properly spent to the very best advantage for Billy Magee's benefit! and also! I will furnish you whenever you wish "A Statement" of goods given.[3]

Three days later Bliss wrote to tell Ober that Billy had walked into Mine Centre with his wife. It had taken them four hours to walk the three miles. "I noticed that Billy was practically OUT." Ober was working on Quetico-

Superior concerns in the nation's capital, but he responded immediately to the Bliss letter. The Bliss return states:

> Your letter from Washington arrived. Quite agree with you as regard Billy Magee doing any walking or packing & I gave Billy to understand this....[4]

On April 26, 1938, Billy suffered a second stroke. Four days later Bliss wrote to Ober:

> I deeply regret to inform you that Billy passed away 1:20 a.m. May 1st. There were some Indians here Saturday noon, & explained to me that Billy was very sick. I hired one of them with canoe. Took some few things & spent the afternoon in Billy's wigwam. I realized Billy had not long to live & it was impossible to do anything for him apparently in a coma & had been since he took what "I judged from the Indians" a stroke some four days ago.

Billy Magee shortly before his death

Billy Magee's sister [Notawey] is also very, very low. It seemed that she has given up hope. I done all I possibly could to explain to Johnnie White-fish & other Indians, that! if she would eat something nourishing she would still be all right. . . . I don't believe any of them had eaten since Billy took sick. I am writing the Indian Agent to try & assist these other Indians. You possibly know their ways. When one of [them is] very sick, nobody works. . . .

Billy was buried opposite the Headlight Portage. I gave them a nice flag to hang up along side of Grave. I am sending the account So! you will know exactly how money was dispensed. Thanking you for your great kindness to Billy Magee.[5]

The exchanges between Ober and Bliss persisted for yet another fifteen years, as Ober continued to help with the support of Billy's sister, Notawey, and her cousin, Johnny Whitefish.

In the oral history interviews, Ober told of two Ojibwe boys he mentored and who accompanied him on canoe trips. The first of these was Bob Namaypok, and his story was a tragic one. "He was out on the waters with me," said Ober, "at the age of fourteen, one of the most wonderful people I ever went out with, a remarkable boy, very talented and eager to please." At one point in their travels, Namaypok pleaded with Ober to take him home to the Mallard: "Ober, if you will take me to your cabin this winter, I will scrub your floor every day."

Recognizing the boy's abilities (not as a scrubber of floors), Ober hoped that he could stay with him so he could work to develop his budding genius as a visual artist: "He could draw and paint just beautifully. Oh, it was wonderful. I was told this before we began to travel together, so I brought along large sheets of paper, and I'd give him one of these every evening to draw on."

Bob, however, went back into the wilderness that winter to help on his uncle's trap line, and he ended up with an advanced case of tuberculosis. Later, while cutting pulpwood, he hemorrhaged and nearly bled to death. Ober was called to the hospital in Fort Frances, where he found the boy dozing and could see that he had bled terribly during the night.

"Just as I was laying the book on the table he opened his eyes and looked right at me. 'Now, Bob,' I said, 'don't say one word. One word might start it again.' I put the book there beside him, said, 'Here's a little money in case you need it. We're going to do everything possible to get you through this. I'm going right over to see the doctor.'"

Bob did die, however, and, as it turned out, Ober's next youthful traveling companion was to be Bob's younger half-brother, Pinay. Ober, looking for someone to paddle with him to check on water levels, was talking to the parents of the boys. It seemed there was no one available. "But all the while we were talking," said Ober, "a little boy had been jumping up and down in front of me. You never saw a more expressive face in all your life. Jackie Coogan [the then-famous child actor] wasn't even in it compared to that face."

As a joke, Ober said: "Well, I guess I'll take *him*."

To Ober's surprise the father said, "Yes, that's what he wants. He wants you to take him."

"Oh, I couldn't take that little fellow. Why, he might get sick."

"No, he never sick."

And Ober did, in fact, take Pinay with him on that trip, and thus began another lifelong friendship of which Pinay, in shy and uncomfortable English, told in the interview quoted from above. Pinay is a sturdy man of more than sixty without gray in his hair. As he told it, he was not as enthusiastic to go along on that first trip as Ober had remembered:

> I tell you, I tried to run away from him, because I never see a white man before, so close to me. Was a little scared of him. . . . Every summer he would come again, looking for me again. So I began to know. I realize I can go with him anytime. That was the beginning.[6]

Ober began to teach Pinay English, perhaps the only such lessons Pinay would ever receive:

> He talked to me some days, some evenings. I didn't understand what he said. Great to listen to quite a lot of that from him. He began to tell me the words, to tell me the stories, tell me to speak English. . . . That was quite interesting, eh? That's the way I was. Didn't speak English at all. . . . He give me a pencil and paper and make me write notes, but I couldn't do it. He said to me big words. He put my hand, put that pencil on me, eh, to try to make a word, not a picture, but a word. So I did, I made those words, that sign. "All right, he said, you done good."

It pleased Pinay that Ober would give him a pat on the back for his efforts:

> Yeah. That was very interesting about him. After some time, I began to know him. When I grew up, I always come over here [to Mallard Island]. I do lot of work here for him, cutting wood, kept working every day. I never stop. Sometimes I was tired though. Sometimes I go in those cabins, I see a bed, I lie down for a minute. But he'd start looking for me, "Hey, where you are? Run away from me so you can dream, eh? Come on, I'll show you what to do." Always wish to show me what to do. Every summer. Always do things over here, a lot of things to do, never stop. . . . Sometimes I'm very tired. But I kept going, had to finish that job first, before dark, eh? So that's the way it was.

Ober, now about age seventy, had become an elder, and, though he continued to push himself when he and Pinay traveled together, he too sometimes became exhausted: "Oh yes, he does," said Pinay. "I see him lying down on the ground some days, toward evenings.

"'I don't get up,' he says.

"'I don't care,' I says, 'you don't get up.'

"I thought maybe he has us go to wash. Oh, no, he has us lying down. I see him lying down there. He tired, eh? Tired from paddling all day like that."

Pinay tells of a canoe trip, when he was around fifteen, on which he may have saved Ober's life:

> We had a canoe trip to White Otter. We stopped at the railroad station there. A man across the lake had a resort. He took us all the way over there with his truck, with all that we have, maybe about nine miles, in his truck. "Son of a bitch," he says, "I don't care anything, we'll just go." Oberholtzer says to me, "That man, that talking dirty man." We paddled White Otter. When we come to it, we are afraid to go cross the lake. It was cold weather, eh? It began to snow. I know that's cold water too. We have to go to that little island right in the middle of the lake. Ober said, when we get to the island, "I'm going to take a pee." So I hold that canoe [so he can] get out and take a pee there, before we cross again.

In getting out of the canoe, Ober slipped and fell into the water.

> So I catch hold of him there, one arm. And I pull him out. He was shaking cold like that. My, he was cold. Was almost freezing, you know. Well, I was scared myself, how come he does that? I see a place for a fire. I run over to the place, get wood very quick. While he settled down, I brought all the stuff there to be by him. I moved the blankets to him too, so he can sit in the blankets. We just sit there. "Make some soup," he said. "We've got some crackers. Make yourself tea." I make a little more fire, you know. He's still cold. He say we better stay here because we can't get out anywhere in this cold air. It was a north wind too, cold. But he seemed to sit there, was cool, eh? I was so scared about that. That's the only time I was so scared.

However, Pinay does tell of another time when he was scared while paddling with Ober:

> Ober never had a gun either. He told me all his life he never had a gun. All he has are hatchets, little hatchets. I'd be scared. Sometimes a moose can run over you. But never done to us at all. If you talk bad things about animals, they hear you, what you say about them, and that's why they come after you.
> When we see a moose, Oberholtzer tried to say something with the moose sounds. I was scared. "Don't say that," I say. He made sounds like a moose. The moose is looking at us, big, you know, in front of the canoe. I paddle behind. A bull moose come over close. Yeah, he learned that, he learned to make the sounds of a moose. The moose was looking at us. Then he came

Ober photographing from canoe

Pinay

Pinay giving Ober a haircut

Ober and Pinay paddling

toward us, about ten feet away. Oh, boy, Oberholtzer really laughing. He's joking and laughing. He waited for another [moose, a] cow, another picture. He laughs. He say, "That will make a nice picture. That was nice of you." He say to the moose, yah. I think he does talk to animals, try to say something. Oh, yes, I think so.

Ober and Pinay went on trips that lasted as long as a month and a half. There was fun in it for the young Ojibwe, but hard work too:

Yeah, that was a long trip we had. Sometimes we'd make a portage, some-times we'd make a trail, eh? Take the packs there and make the trail which way we want to go. That's hard work, you know. Oh, yes, yes, we do that since I know him. I know that he be paying me good too. After this one—that's why I change—he buy me, too, buy me clothing. I like it very much that he buy me clothing.

Perhaps a measure of the closeness that grew between the two is con-tained in the fact that Pinay liked to play tricks on Ober:

Yeah, I did. I did too. Tricks on him. Tell something, yeah. Oh, yes, I tell him other stories [than] what I heard, eh? Story or joke, joke on him. When he sore at me, he say, "Believe me, I'll kill you later, honest." That was good, eh? That was good story. I tell lots of jokes. He tell me lots of jokes too.

In February of 1964, as part of the Minnesota Historical Society's series with him, Ober participated in an oral history interview conducted by a student of Ojibwe culture, Evan Hart. Ober's customary interviewer, Lu-cille Kane, was also present. In this session, Ober told of his long experi-ence and friendship with Ojibwe people. He spoke in praise of native peo-ple and their traditional ways, which he believed should be studied as an extension of the wilderness itself. He also talked of Indians losing their culture and their story. It has been said that, in later years, Ojibwe friends sometimes came to Ober to retrieve a story he had originally gotten from their grandparents.

This interview reveals that at age eighty Ober was still dreaming of finding a way to collect Ojibwe stories. Hart, noting that he had heard that Ober now has a tape recorder, asked, "Wouldn't it be a fine thing if you could get some of these older Indians in your area just to come in and record stories?"

"Well," responded Ober, "that's what I'd love to do, and that's what I was doing. I didn't have a recorder way back, but I was recording them by hand, which was pretty hard. I finally did borrow a recorder. It was at the time [probably the early 1950s] that I'd said to Mr. Kelly: 'Well, now, I can't go ahead with any more of this Quetico-Superior work.'

"I saw all my old Indian friends were disappearing. I had these old In-dians friends, they'd tell me almost anything, in spite of the prohibitions against these things, you see. They don't like a lot of publicity, and they've got dignity and respect for themselves. They think that this thing that Americans admire so—they wouldn't put it into words—but this terrific notoriety that everybody seems to want, oh, they don't like that at all. If they thought you would give them that by taking down their words, you wouldn't get very far. But now the old people that could tell you these things are nearly all dead. Oh, that's the thing that's heartbreaking. I'd like nothing better than to devote part of whatever strength and energy I have left to going around all through the Ojibwe country trying to find the relics of things I once knew and record them."

Ober told Hart of his early friendship with Frances Densmore, the famous collector of Indian songs, whom he and his mother hosted on the Mallard in the early 1920s. He thought she was a wonderful woman but despaired over her avoidance of the "pagan" Indians to whom he hoped to introduce her. For fear of obscenity, she interviewed only Christianized Indians in a chaperoned setting. "Most of the places where Miss Densmore had been," said Ober, "the Indians were getting religion, and the material was pretty restricted. So my mother wrote her and invited her to be our guest, to come up and talk the situation over. She spent about a month with us.

"But, oh, no, she couldn't risk that at all. The thing was that these were Indians that hadn't changed any, you see. They danced in the old way. They held the original *mide* ceremonies, and they had their medicine men, and the *tchisiki-winini*. These men were, of course, magicians, but *tchisiki-winini* is a being—a magical being. And these men were in close communion with these beings—these *tchisiki-winini* beings—when they carry out their medicine. Now, as to how you would translate . . . these [were] mythical creatures that you can talk to—spirits."

Ober went on to discuss the Ojibwe legends called *Atisokan:* "They call [the Nanabozho legends] *Atisokan.* That's also what they call me, Atisokan. It means story, but that particular kind of story. The Indians always sort of elided the 'i' and said *Atsokan.* That's one kind of story that's not a *tepatchimowin.* A *tepatchimowin* would be something you could tell at any time. [Not just in winter.] It's based on an experience that's happened—maybe in the teller's own time—that people have talked about. *Tepatchimo* is to speak about it, and *win* is a noun. But the *Atisokan* go way back. They are old, old legends, particularly those of Nanabozho."

Pinay remembered why Ober got his Indian name:

Yeah, yeah. Because he go all over to the Indian people, asking about *Atisokan.* That's vision story. That's what he been call by those people, Indian people. "Tell me *Atisokan.*" That's what he'd ask people, that's what they'd give him. . . . Yeah, he begin to call him[self] this too. And so, what do you know, old people, they'd tell him religion stories, especially old people. That's why he'd go over there. He'd hold tobacco in front of them every time. Yeah, bag of tobacco, he handed it to them, "Will you guys tell me a story? *Atisokan.*" Those guys would turn around and look what they have, eh? And tell him that. Enjoy sitting down together. Indian words, eh? I don't know how he does that. Gets a paper and he write those words those people said. I never seen it before. Telling in Ojibwe letters there. From the people, yeah. He tell me how he made those notes that he made. He said very slow, some of those words. I understand what he say and what he's writing there. That's strange, eh? A white man writing those Indian words. That's interesting. I told Ober, "I don't know how you did that, write those notes like that."

In the interview, Hart commented on Nanabozho, saying that he "was a dual sort of personality. He did much good for his people and at the same time was a trickster. There are almost two categories of the stories. Some are sort of ribald."

"Oh, I should say so," responded Ober. "That's what Miss Densmore was afraid of. She was afraid they were going to tell one of those stories, *Atisokánan.* The story about Nanabozho and the wild rice, when he couldn't find any wild rice and talked to a duck. Well, it is hardly a parlor story."

According to Ober, the Ojibwe elders were the ones who passed the *Atisokan* along to the children: "The grandparents were the ones that did most of that sort of thing, grandmother, or grandfather sometimes, but grandmother, particularly. They'd get the children early, and they'd still be devoted to the grandmother. Oh, yes. I've always thought of it as being simply due to the venerable nature of the old person and the intimate relationship they have with the little children for a long time. They certainly took very great pleasure in telling the stories."

In notes Ober made for a story he hoped to write about Billy Magee, he recounted that Billy had told him "the *Atisokan* used to be told to children of from 6 to 16 years. Especially in the autumn when the first snow came. All the children would go to bed after supper and then an old man after smoking his pipe a while in silence would begin to talk while the rest listened in rapt attention. . . . When he stopped, they would all go to sleep without a word."[7]

In the Hart interview, Ober commented on the importance of such storytelling: "Of course, the children had nothing to guide them but these stories. There was nothing printed. They had these exceptionally good memories as a result. Those Indians up there where I worked—I was surprised—were so familiar with these stories that when you went back and made little corrections by reading them back to the one who gave them to you—Well, another Indian would come along, and you'd say, 'Well, how does this sound to you?' And you'd read it back to him. Pretty soon, he'd be repeating it himself, word for word."

In his notes for his never-completed Billy Magee story, Ober wrote that "Nanibojou [*sic*] was the grand medicine man, initiating all into the mysteries. All the magic is destroyed for children if they do not believe these things. I prefer credulity to skepticism. But now the Indian children have lost their fantasy and will not hear the *Atisokan*."[8]

Ober often bemoaned the fact that Ojibwe children had quit learning their old songs and stories, their language. In the Hart interview, he said, "In school, they're taught almost to scorn them. When I get hold of one of these kids or their fathers, I say to every one of them: 'Oh, don't give up your language, whatever you do. Hold on.'"

Ober loved the sound of the Ojibwe language, the beauty of its names. The word *Ojibwe*, he explained, means "the real people." "*Anishinabe* [another name the Ojibwe have for themselves] means the real people, too," he continued. "I think that's a nice name, Anishinabe—musical. Yes, it's a beautiful language to hear. And it hurts me to think of the scorn with which it's treated, even by some geographers. You have these beautiful names clinging to these places in the north, and then they give them some perfectly commonplace name. I think that's awful. Maybe there's some man in the legislature over there in Canada . . . and they name it for him. Some temporary minister of lands or forests. They use a name like Finlayson, when they already had a wonderful name like Kabetogama or Anishinabe or any of the beautiful old Indians names, you know, soft and lovely, with a significance that goes way back."

Ober felt that modernity had proved to be a poison for the Indians he had known. "But," he continued, "when one way gets them the money to live, it's easy to give up the other. And when the Indian girls go to the movies and see all these modern things, you know, they are just aghast. It's such a gap. They just think, 'oh, what we've been missing. Just think what we could be doing.' I feel sorry for them, because it's all illusion. What we've got to offer them is mostly just poison. Of course, they want entertainment. They are a people full of the love of hospitality and gaiety. They're never great people to laugh the way we do. I don't know whether you ever hear them go 'ha, ha, ha.' But they have a fine sense of humor. They're making fun all the time. A group of men may be just joshing and joking for hours, but you never hear them bombard your ears in the fashion of some of these white men with their ha-has."

Ober then told Hart of that time when he "finally did borrow a recorder" with which to record the stories of his old Ojibwe friends. It was an ancient model, driven by a gasoline engine. He hauled it to a winter camp in the woods to record Billy Magee's ninety-six-year-old sister, Mrs. Notawey, and her cousin, Johnny Whitefish. "Mrs. Notawey," said Ober, "was one of the greatest women I ever knew in all my life. She was the oldest sister of Billy Magee. They were this marvelous old family. She was as talented as

Sarah Bernhardt. She had long arms something like Sarah Bernhardt. And when she told you a story, you would see all the things she was talking about vividly. She would make little wigwams and little canoes with her hands as she was talking. You'd see them coming together right there before your eyes. And her voice would change. It would go way down when she spoke in the voice of some of the men, and up again for the women. A wonderful quality, a rich voice.

"Mrs. Notawey," said Ober, "was living a mile and a half from the village of Mine Centre, on the Canadian side, forty miles from where I lived. You could go there on the train. She was living with her cousin, Johnny White-fish, who was ten years younger than she was.

"It was frightfully cold weather. It went down to fifty-four below zero while I was there, and I was all alone. I got hauled over to this place on a truck. I had the recorder along and a motor to operate it with, which I had borrowed at Mine Centre. It was an old thing, and I didn't know very much about it. I had a tepee tent, and I dug down three feet through the snow. Oh, I went to great trouble. I had about a week before I had to go to a meeting in Chicago. I dug down through the snow to the ground. This tent was about fifteen feet in diameter, a great big nice tent, and I had brought a stove, an airtight heater. I got boughs, and did it the way the Indians did, put the boughs down on the ground, set up the stove, cut some wood, and got a nice fire started.

"First, I invited Johnny to come down. I wanted both of them to come, but the old lady was very, very old, and they said if I tried to take her down there, she might die on the way. So, I got all set up for Johnny, cooked a meal, had it nice and comfortable in there, warm, with this nice stove, and fragrant boughs on the ground, and he didn't come down. I couldn't understand that. He was only about a quarter mile away. When he hadn't come by noon, I went up there and said:

"'Why, Johnny, you said you were coming down. You were going to tell me the story of my trip to Hudson Bay the way Billy told it to you.'

"That was Billy Magee, his cousin, who had died. I was anxious to get Billy's version, his point of view on our trip, you see. I thought I'd get many rich morsels from such an interview. For one thing, because they loved to make fun of you. The second thing was that he would have seen things I wouldn't have. I wanted to hear what had impressed him, see how it differed from my memories."

Johnny did not come on the second day, either, and, as Ober told it in the oral history, he was soon to find out that the problem lay with a group of "lumbermen with whom we had been struggling over Quetico-Superior issues. They had come to Mine Centre and were staying in a little hotel in the place. They didn't like the fact that we had friends among the Indians, you see. They had prejudiced a lot of other people in the region against us as well. In an anguished voice, Johnny told me what they'd said:

"'White man, he say, pretty bad, Johnny. You go down there, you maybe sure die. You know that man, he send your picture all over the country. He make lots of money—you die.'

"The old lady was sitting there. She heard all of this.

"'Johnny,' I asked, 'did you ever know me, over all the years, to do anything to hurt you?'

"No, he never had.

"'Now,' I said, 'I'm not getting a single cent for any of this. Johnny, I don't want to see you go away forever. I may never see you again, and I'd like to hear your voice sometimes. Just like your picture, I like to have that. You used to be afraid that I had your picture, afraid that I took you away. I'm not taking you away. Recording your voice is just like having these pictures. I'd like to keep you. I'd like to have this.'

"Pretty soon he was nearly crying, and the old lady says: 'Johnny, you go. You go. Atsokan, he want. You go.'

"'All right,' says Johnny.

"And he came down the next two days and told me everything he possibly could, all that he remembered that Billy had told him about our Hudson Bay trip. He told me some things I had forgotten and didn't believe at first. It took me quite a while before I was convinced that I had done what he said."

It seems that Ober and Johnny were not alone during this session. Pinay remembers that, as a boy, he and others were also there. "Tapes . . . always a long talk, yeah. Johnny Whitefish. He'd tell the stories from old time, stories from Hudson Bay. . . . We hear him [tell] very much of a story, but I always liked that. I was tired and lying down on the ground, listening to him tell the story. Sometimes I fell asleep there. Those guys sitting all around there listening to that story. That was nice. Great story too."[9]

Ober may have gotten a great story from Johnny, but he was reluctant to leave without at least capturing Notawey's voice on tape: "As I've said, she couldn't come down to where I'd set up. Even if I hauled her on the toboggan, it would have been too dangerous. So, on the last day, I moved everything up to their wigwam. There were other wigwams nearby, other Indians outside. The children were playing and yelling, the dogs barking and fighting. I had to put the wires down in the snow under the wigwam, fix up a place in the old lady's wigwam.

"'Now, I want you to tell me something,' I said to her. 'You don't have to talk very long.'

"She was lying down. It was pretty hard for her to sit up—poor, old, frail thing. You could see every bone in her hands. But this wonderful face—the expression—oh, my! Then, just as I got the machine started and we were going to talk, here came a wagon from Mine Centre with a message that had just come in telling me that they wanted me to take the train for Chicago that afternoon, for the meeting. I turned the microphone off for the moment.

"'Just wait a little,' I said. 'Let me do this recording; then you can haul this equipment back with you.'

"We got the old lady sitting up and she asked, 'What would you like me to tell you?'

"'Tell me,' I said, 'how it happened that Billy Magee was called Tay-tah-pa-sway-wi-tong.'

"Billy was her younger brother. So she sat up as well as she could, and then in this beautiful, wonderful voice she told of how her mother was

Notawey

holding Billy in her arms and of a sudden there was a flash, and a vision came, and a voice gave her this name, which means far-distant echo. And I looked down, and the microphone wasn't attached. She was lying down again. And this rich, beautiful voice. Oh, this marvelous voice! And I said:

"'Oh, my gracious!' They were waiting outside for me. 'I want you to tell me that again,' I said.

"She couldn't do it again. She had used every bit of strength that she had, and that was the last opportunity I ever had to record the voice of that wonderful old mind."

Throughout his adult life, Ober was fascinated by and explored as deeply as he was able Native American spirituality. His own spirituality was highly developed, even his sense of the presence of God, but he seems not to have been comfortable with Christianity. According to Pinay, he once said, "I know I'm not going to church at all. I like to live Indian way."[10] Ober often complained of what he considered the destructive effects of Christianity on native peoples and their traditional ways. He used the word "pagan" with a sort of relish, and it would seem that, if he ever found a spiritual home in an established religious tradition, it was in that of the Ojibwe. The religious pluralism of his Unitarian upbringing and his study with William James and other psychologist-philosophers at Harvard would also surely have, early on, opened his mind to this possibility. An important aspect of the Ojibwe spiritual tradition, similar to that of Unitarianism, is an honoring and caring for the interconnected web of life. In addition, with the Ojibwe—and this would have been important to Ober, whose health had so often been shaky—it is believed that such honoring sustains one's own life.

In response to questions about Ober's spirituality, Pinay recalled that Ober smoked the medicine pipe with sincerity:

Yes, he used to have a pipe here. Originally made out of stone, eh? Big brown one. Well, it could be the old people [taught him how], from long ago. I don't know, nobody been telling me how he knows that. He was teached from the old people. Whenever comes wrong, bad on you, like thunder, lightning, that's the time to put tobacco in that pipe there, light it. That's all he does. Didn't say a word at all, just kind of smoke the pipe, that's all, and put it away. Maybe that's a good way to do that, too, without saying anything. Maybe that's the way to do it. Yes, just remember what it's going to be to you.[11]

In his interview with Hart, though sometimes showing caution—keeping his personal convictions "in the closet"—Ober argued aggressively for the value of the Native American spiritual tradition:

"There is no question," he said, "that . . . they had pretty profound intuitions about things, about a lot of things that we might be right on the edge of, psychologically. I believe William James had a better approach than most scientists, because he never turned anything down. He was ready to investigate. I would see and hear all these things among the Indians, and I often think that they have a wisdom that we don't have. If we ever had it, we've forgotten it. We've been reared entirely on the idea that nothing is true unless you can prove it in a concrete way—two and two are four. . . . We shut our minds to many spiritual things. We dismiss them. But the Indians are very alert and sensitive to all such things. I think we may find in time—maybe this is just a pipe dream—that some of these very remarkable things they seem to know, that can't otherwise be explained, that these things indicate they have a sensitiveness they have not thrown away, almost like a telephone system. And a lot of us might have that. Maybe all of us once had it. If we hadn't grown up with the idea that it was impossible, you see, and absurd.

"Dreams are a great thing with them. I've seen them when their faces were darkened, when they went off and stayed, sometimes quite a ways. Other times they wouldn't be very far away. They would often go up into a tree and stay there. They were not supposed to eat or drink then until they had a dream that was to be a guide for their lives. Often they pick their own personal god from what they have seen in the dream. They interpret what they've seen and heard, you see.

"I guess anyone is likely to have those vivid dreams if they starve enough. That's the physical basis for it, you see. They know a lot of such things. . . . They feel you have released a spirit by not clogging it with a lot of food. Oh, I think these things are tremendously interesting. I think we're just on the edge of understanding these primitive thoughts and impulses.

"Well, I have never shut my mind to these ideas. I have never had the slightest feeling of ridicule toward any of it, no matter how ridiculous it may seem—never. There is always a good basis for these beliefs. This is one thing I believe. These men were sincere. Sometimes, the *tchisiki-winini* aren't, because they get paid. They perform for money. In character, the *mité* is the highest type among these medicine men. They're more like a Masonic order, something of that sort. You have to go through a long training. You have to go through a long training for each thing. They are not fakers.

"Sometimes the *tchisiki-winini* are fakers to this extent: they want to scare the patient so that he'll pay money, or maybe win the favor of the patient so he'll pay money. I know some of them like that. They're simply imposters, but they're not all that way. Oh, no. Some are real doctors. They're like our psychiatrists in a way. They've had elaborate training.

And I'm convinced that they feel they are dealing with the spirits, supernatural creatures. There's one up at the Seine River named Charlie Friday. He's that way. He built a chimney for my house. I went away, and when I returned, I found it had turned out bigger than I thought it would be.

"'Now, Charlie,' I said, 'that's big enough for the U.S. Steel Corporation.' He smiled. He saw whatever joke there was in that. And then I said to him, just for fun, 'Charlie, you know, I don't believe I'm going to live in the house. I believe I'll live in the chimney.'

"Smiling, he looked at me and said: 'I could.' At first I expressed astonishment, but he repeated: 'I could.'

"Then I knew what he meant. He believed that his spirit could enter and be in such a place, and he knew how to put it there, you see, at the right time. He had had that kind of training. He could dwell in there."

Story has it that when Charlie Friday died his spirit did reside in the chimney he had built for Ober. It had been an addition to a large houseboat, since named *Frigate Friday,* that had been grounded on the mainland property where Frances Andrews's house, Wildcroft, stood. Friday's chimney had been part of a retrofitting that turned the houseboat into Ober's cold weather home when he became too old and infirm to winter

Fireplace room in Ober's Big House. Charlie Friday's spirit has been ritually placed in the round stone on the bottom left corner of the fireplace.

on the Mallard. After Ober's death, the *Friday* was moved, and when a new owner of Wildcroft decided to tear down the now free-standing chimney, a single round stone was taken from it, and in a ritual process that took an entire day, this stone, containing Charlie Friday's spirit, was moved by Ojibwe medicine men and set in concrete on the bottom left side of Ober's fireplace in the Big House on the Mallard.

The fireplace room in Ober's Big House also contains an Ojibwe ceremonial drum. Both the Seine River and the Red Gut communities claim to have given it to Ober many years ago, and it is now frequently visited and blessed by native people. According to Ted Hall, "The gift of a drum is not a casual thing to the Ojibwe, for a drum has a spirit, a soul of its own." In giving this drum to Ober, continued Hall, the Ojibwe "demonstrated their respect, their admiration for their friend, Atsokan."[12] At one point after Ober's death, the drum was taken from the Big House and kept in the county historical society. Ojibwe people borrowed it back for a ceremony they were holding on the Mallard, after which word spread that bad things would surely happen to anyone who took it off the island again. It has remained there ever since.

Ober kept the drum tied between a pair of log rafters perhaps seven feet above the floor, and, well into his seventies, this man who was now less than five feet six inches tall practiced leaping into the air and kicking it. His island cook for the summer of 1955, Barbara Thomas Breckenridge, told of this feat:

> He did demonstrate kicking the Indian drum which hung from the ceiling while I was here. Well, he said that it was a tradition that everyone who came here had to do it. He didn't insist that I try, but he could do it. He could still jump and kick the drum with one foot. I don't remember ever seeing anyone else doing it while I was here.[13]

Ted Hall described the feat a little differently: "Ober would just step over like a ballet dancer, just reach up and tap it with the toe of his canvas shoe."[14]

Once when Hall, as a boy, was cleaning the beams that held the drum, he retied it a bit higher than it had been, just enough so that Ober could not kick it, which apparently frustrated him considerably. Hall claims it was an accident, but Ober afterward loved to tell of this practical joke young Teddy had played on him.

In the Hart interview, Ober further discussed those spiritual presences, the *tchisiki-winini:* "They have certain favorite voices. I'm trying to think of some that appear when a *tchisiki-winini* is talking. They suddenly come here and have their say about things. At times, there'll be quite an argument."

Ober continued by telling more fully a story Kit Bakeless touched on in the letter shared in the previous chapter: "One [such argument] that I remember was very impressive. There were some white people visiting me. We'd been up Seine River and were approaching this Indian village called the Wild Potato Indian Reservation, about fifty miles from my home. There were a couple women, a man, and a boy. We camped near the reservation that night, but it got dark too early for us to go over. We were going to go over in the morning, but I could hear off afar that there was something going on over there—one of these *tchisiki-winini*—and I told the people about it. They'd never seen it.

"'Well,' I said, 'do you suppose we should go over there?'

"It was a nice night. So, after supper we very quietly went over, and there was a hillside from which we could look right down on them. There was grass down there. It was extremely dark, but we could see there was one of these tall *tchisiki-winini* tents, and there were people sitting around on the ground in a circle, as if they were in church. And you could hear this *tchisiki-winini* inside—this one man—talking in his own voice, and you could hear some of the responses. And the Indians sitting around there would say: ai-uck, ai-uck, ai-uck. As if in church.

"It was very quiet and nice, but then we heard a good deal of commotion. There was something lying in a pack. It looked like a pack. Well, I found out later that it was this old woman who was sick. She was unconscious, wrapped in a rabbit-skin blanket. Lying there, she didn't know anything that was happening. She was supposed to be close to death. There was an argument. The medicine man was saying to her that she must live, that they wanted her. They didn't want her to die. They all needed her. You could hear this feeble old voice say:

"'Oh, no, I'm too tired. I can't. I've got to go away.'

"Well, then, you'd hear Quakadus. That's the name I've been trying to think of. Quakadus took part in this.

Kicking the drum

'Oh, no,' he'd say, 'it's too soon for you to go. Your people all need you very much. You are very dear to them. They need you.'

"And: ai-uck, ai-uck. So this argument went on. Sometimes there'd be two or three of them going at it, you know. My people were just thrilled beyond words. We withdrew and got away, and they never heard us. Well, that was nice, and the next spring, when I went back up there, to my surprise the old lady was going all around the village. She was old, but she had recovered."

It is likely, of course, that the healing focus of much Ojibwe spirituality played a considerable part in attracting Ober to it, especially the secrets held by the Grand Medicine Society, the *Midéwiwin*. As quoted in chapter one, in his fiftieth anniversary report to his Harvard classmates, Ober wrote that "a severe bout with rheumatic fever at 17 made more difference than anything else, for it put a premium on health throughout college and for long afterwards."[15] Given the overall breadth and intensity of his interests, this is a weighty statement, and one can well believe that the healing tradition of the Ojibwe, whom he so admired, would have fiercely attracted him. The elaborate healing ceremonies of the *Midéwiwin,* which it seems have to do with enhancing the flow of life forces through the vital centers of the body, may have proven of significant value to Ober.[16] According to Allen Snowball, many Ojibwe believe that Ober's immersion in their healing tradition was the reason he lived to such an old age, despite his heart condition.

In the opening of a 1936 letter to Frances Andrews, Ober wrote, with perhaps half-humorous intent, that "I'm a sort of witch doctor or ought to be after my long association with the Indians."[17] Though the story here grows shadowy, concrete evidence and Ojibwe testimony provide confirmation that Ober entered into the Ojibwe Grand Medicine Society, the *Midéwiwin,* and became an initiate himself. Years after his death, a bundle containing the accoutrements of a medicine man was found in his effects, and his attainment, thought to be in the mid-range of possible developmental levels, has since been verified by several Ojibwe people. Recently a woman elder from Emo, Ontario, told Mallard Island Program Director Jean Replinger, "It was that old man Dan Namaypok who taught him. It was that old man Dan Namaypok who carried on those ways. The bundle of a medicine man usually goes with him when he dies. Ober left his behind so people would know of these things he had done."

Just how deeply Ober became involved with the *Midéwiwin,* the Society of *Mide* or Shamans, will perhaps never be known. Such knowledge is not much talked about by those in the know. Indeed, it is considered somewhat improper for an initiate to openly identify him- or herself as such.

An initiate is expected to selflessly give his or her all to the well-being of the greater whole. Surely Ober lived up to that aspect of the tradition. And, likely, such a spiritual secret, held within, would have sustained and empowered him. Though he was very able to compartmentalize, one would imagine this secret might also have distanced him in some ways from the white world. Certainly it would have brought him closer to the Ojibwe people, and to the degree that they knew of his involvement with the *Midéwiwin,* they would have offered him the greater respect he seemed to enjoy from them as the years passed.

As to Ober's friendship with and profound admiration for the Ojibwe people and their culture, there can be no question. Shortly after Ober's death, Sigurd Olson would say of him, "He was a great lover of the Indians, and it would be impossible to tell all of the good things he did for them. They considered him kind of a saintly individual."[18]

When asked why Mallard Island had become a spiritual nexus for Ojibwe people, whether this had to do with the island itself or with Ober, Pinay, who had been a pallbearer for Ober, answered that it was Ober: "Yeah, it's because of him. He knows more about people in the past. That's why people are so interested.... We stay behind and we try to build what he was. Just like that. That's the way it is."[19]

There are others who believe that the Mallard had been held sacred by the Ojibwe for many generations preceding Ober's caring for it. Whatever the case, a biographical sketch in the Minnesota Historical Society's holdings states that following Ober's death, "the children and grandchildren of his old Indian friends gathered at his Mallard home, made medicine, and placed a protective and reverential spell over the island."[20]

[21]

Legend

In the early 1960s, in the fullness of his maturity, Ober was thought of by those who knew him as a wilderness sage, a teacher, a teller of stories, of legends, as a legend himself. More and more often, even his white friends called him Atisokan, especially when talking about him. Increasingly, however, he was beginning to experience the losses that inevitably accompany the aging process. In July of 1961, his dear friend Frances Andrews died. Ober, now seventy-seven, was terribly troubled by her passing, and six months later, in his Fifty-fifth Anniversary Report to his Harvard classmates, he wrote of his sadness over this loss. In the report, he described Frances as his "generous hostess":

> Lacking family, the void has been filled all my life by a wide assortment of close friends, both men and women, including Indians. And here, more and more, like the rest of you, I am suffering grievous losses, none greater than this last July, when my generous hostess, Frances Andrews of Minneapolis, on whose property my present winter home is located, died here after a brief illness.
>
> These are sobering events that are forcing me at last to look backwards a little, instead of planning a thousand years ahead for all that I would still like to do. Instead I go back to my senior year [at Harvard], when I was studying violin under Willy Hess, concert master of the Boston Symphony, and late at night I fiddle a little.[1]

There was yet, however, one adventure that Ober was planning ahead for, a return to the then-unexplored territory he and Billy had passed through in 1912, a return to Nueltin Lake. The Nueltin Lake–Hudson Bay expedition, according to Ober, had been the single most powerful experience of his life, and in that same report in which he told of Frances's death, he wrote that the expedition was "more myself than anything I've ever done."[2] As was argued earlier, the Nueltin Lake–Hudson Bay journey was also the achievement that above all else had established him as a wilderness figure, both personally, in a psychological sense, and in the eyes of the world. Until nearly the end of his life Ober dreamed of writing a book about the experience, but he seemed never able to find the time and the focused will to do so. In many ways it had turned out to be a spiritual journey, not something to exploit economically. It was a story in which he had played a heroic role, and it seemed that something deep in him blocked his efforts to so celebrate himself. Still, his desire to write of the journey persisted, and in the oral history interviews he often mentioned this subject:

"I have always hoped to make a record of it myself. All my life I've hoped to do this, but...."

"I think I must do this, write this, in justice to the old Indian...."

"I couldn't just sit down and go into this story. Thoughts of it just shook me. Whenever I thought of it, it was just a landslide, you see."

As well as hoping to write of the expedition, Ober had long dreamed of a return to that far-north point at which he and Billy had felt most lost, the high promontory on Nueltin Lake that he had named Hawkes Summit. There, in a tin can protected by a stone cairn, he had left a message to the world before continuing on into the vast unknown of the Arctic barrens. For years his dream had been to fly in, then proceed by canoe to Hawkes Summit, but there was never the time and the cost was prohibitive. And then, in his seventy-ninth year, nearing the end of his active life, he found a way and the will to return. He discovered that a permit had been granted to commercial fishermen at the south end of Nueltin. "Of course, I was sorry to hear about that," he said, "but you could fly up there from a new terminus of the Hudson Bay Railway, in one of the planes that hauled out the fish. And at a very much lower rate than that of a charter plane. But they couldn't haul anything larger than a seventeen-foot canoe. This would make it impossible to travel such a lake by canoe, as I had wanted, to carry the necessary load in those big waves."

Nevertheless, Ober went ahead with the plan. "I thought, well, I must go. I may never get another chance. We'll see what we can do." As com-

"And late at night I fiddle a little"

panion and helper, he brought along his young violin-playing friend Bob Hilke, who, like others, thought of Ober as a second father: "I took Bob Hilke with me—a white man who had been out with me many times before—young, but with very good judgment."

Ober and Hilke were flown in to the fishing camp, some twenty miles up from the south shore of the lake. "We landed there with our equipment and this little bit of a canoe. The fishermen just wondered about us. There were two white men and a boy and a dozen Indians who raised the nets. That very first night they had us over to dinner—white fish.

"'Take all the fish you want,' they said. 'Have all you want.' They were catching tons and tons of fish."

It was then that Ober suffered a severe fall on the shoreline rocks. "It's a wonder I didn't break my leg. It was just purple from the hip down for a couple of weeks. After a few days, though, I was able to hobble around on it, but we couldn't get away because we didn't have a large and heavy canoe."

In an oral history interview, Hilke recalled that at this point Ober told him, "Now, Bobby, if something happens to me up here, I don't want to be taken out. I want to just be buried under these rocks up here someplace."[3]

Ober and Hilke knew they could not safely paddle up the lake without a large and heavy canoe. Perhaps it was the magic of Ober's story and his telling of it that fired the imaginations of the men in the fishing camp: "One day the owner of the camp came to me," said Ober. "Oh, they were awfully anxious to help me. They were generous, nice fellows who were calling me 'Ober' by this time.

"'Ober,' he says, 'I tell you, we've got an extra steel boat.' These boats were about twenty-two feet long and about five feet deep. They raised the nets with them. 'And we have a fifteen-horse motor. If you want to use them, and think you can make it up the lake. There are reefs, you know.'"

There was no question in Ober's mind as to whether or not he wanted to use the boat: "I don't like motors at all, but Bob knew how to handle them. He sat high in the rear, with a big rain suit on. I sat under a tarp in a chair in the front, with the map I had made fifty-one years before." For Ober it must have been a strange experience to be so easily moving up the immense stretch of water that had been his and Billy's labyrinth so long before in his youth. Nueltin is one hundred and twenty miles long, and Ober and Hilke traveled nearly seventy miles up the lake that day. "For the final twenty miles," said Ober, "we could see this great eminence looming before us. It was the one I had climbed with Billy." This eminence was, of course, Hawkes Summit, which Ober believed to be at least twenty miles wide at the base. They arrived at its foot that evening.

The next morning they prepared for their ascent: "Before Bob and I began our climb, I looked very closely at the rim above. In my notes, I'd said, 'the highest point.' I felt that I just didn't want to miss anything." With his injured leg, Ober found it hard to climb, but he knew he was on the right track. He told Hilke to go ahead of him, told him to find the can with his note. "But I was only joking, you see. Then I saw him standing up there about two hundred feet away, waving something. When I got closer, I could see that it was exactly the right shape.

"'Ober,' Bob said, 'I didn't open it.' That was very nice of him. 'I wanted you to do that. But your note isn't in it. You can see through the bottom. It's got little holes in it, little rust holes.'"

A later explorer, P. G. Downes, who would follow after Ober and eventually become his friend, has written that in 1939 he interviewed a trapper named Cecil "Husky" Harris who told him that in 1924 he had found the note and taken it with him, leaving the can behind.[4] During the interview with Bob Hilke about Ober's return to Nueltin, the very can that had held Ober's note to the world and which had lain on Hawkes Summit for fifty-one years lay on the table between us, rusted and with little holes, but still solid. It had been a remarkable closure for Ober, we thought. So near the end of his outward adventure, to have returned to that high point in his life. A circle had been completed there on the summit, "at the end of the earth." Though Ober had years yet to suffer and honors to receive, it could be said that that moment of high return marked the end of his great outer story.

In 1963, the same year that Ober returned to Nueltin Lake, Lucile Kane and Russell Fridley of the Minnesota Historical Society, along with various of Ober's friends, recognizing the importance of Ober's life and story, began the series of oral history interviews that make up so important a part of this book. He was soon to be recognized in many other ways as well. During the 1960s, as one of North America's foremost conservationists, Ober received several significant awards, and, as he was proud of the honors that came to many of his friends, he was also proud of those that came to him.

On June 12, 1966, Ober was awarded the Honorary Degree of Doctor of Humane Letters from Northern Michigan University, "with all rights, privileges and immunities appertaining thereto,"[5] given in recognition of his unrelenting work to preserve North American wilderness. Photographs of Ober in a dark academic gown show him to be very happy on that day. In a letter to Samuel Morison, Ober thanked him warmly for his role in the award.

On March 22, 1967, when Ober was eighty-three, the United States secretary of the interior, Stewart Udall, presented him with "the highest honor within the power of the Department of the Interior to bestow upon a private citizen": the Department of the Interior Distinguished Service

Award. It was given in recognition of his outstanding service in the field of conservation. This award was presented in Tucson in April at the annual meeting of the Wilderness Society, which Ober had helped to found more than thirty years before. In his award statement, Udall wrote, "I congratulate you on your highly productive life and your accomplishments

Ober with powdered milk can in which he'd left a message to his mother
and the world fifty-one years before

which have greatly benefited the field of conservation."[6] The presenter of the award in Tucson was Sigurd Olson, who over the preceding two decades had taken Ober's place as the figurehead conservationist in the Quetico-Superior movement. Though there had earlier been tensions between Ober and Olson, it would seem that, by the time of this ceremony, these had largely dissolved.

On July 14, there was a second presentation of this award in Fort Frances, Ontario, that may have been even more important to Ober than the Tucson presentation. In a letter of thanks to Udall, Ober, whose health had begun to fail, wrote:

> The gracious donor was your own Fred C. Fagergren, regional director of your Omaha office, who helped me to the platform. Many of my old Indian friends were among those who came up afterwards to offer their simple congratulations. I was deeply moved as you may imagine.[7]

This was Ober's year for awards. Another, called the Capitaine International Honor Award, was given to him in Grand Marais, on the north shore of Lake Superior, on July 19. A letter from Ober to his long-time friend and supporter Peavey Heffelfinger describing his attendance in Grand Marais offers a sense of his failing health and the impact of the previous week's award ceremony on him:

> The Forest Service provided me a plane with a pilot and a forestry guide to make sure that all went well. I was gone just six hours altogether. I didn't think it well to try any more. I don't get round well and broke down completely at a similar presentation from the Department of the Interior, though there too I had a guide. There were many old Indian friends present and, when they crowded round me on the platform after the presentation, that was just too much for me.[8]

Among the smaller awards given to Ober at this time, the language in one received from the Natural History Society of Minnesota is the most interesting. The presentation was made by the society's president, Clayton Budd, on January 6, 1967, "In Recognition of the Dedicated, Untiring Effort of Ernest Carl Oberholtzer in behalf of the Wilderness Canoe Country and the entire wilderness estate of the United States of America, we members of the Natural History Society of Minnesota honor him. In paying our respect to him we appreciate the fact that he more than any other individual is responsible for the perpetuation of our wilderness canoe country."[9]

There are so many who gave so much that the canoe country would be preserved—it is unnecessary to claim that one individual was first among them—and yet it may at least be true that no other gave so much of himself to the long struggle as did Ober.

When it came to self-evaluation, Ober seldom awarded himself much praise. According to some who knew him late in life, he often spoke of himself as a failure. In this declaration are humility, humor, and a degree of true dissatisfaction, not so much with himself or his life as with his accomplishments. It is clear that, even in old age, he dearly wanted to write and publish books. In his notebooks for 1953 and 1954, when he turned seventy and was wintering alone on the Mallard, he wrote:

> Have a sketch book, write something every day, whenever the spirit moves— a sketch or tour de force.... Effortless. Let it write itself.
>
> Very simple stories of the people of this country, both Indian and white.
>
> Waste no time. Keep the goal in mind. This is the time of times. Save The Program. Save yourself. Money. Fulfillment. Reward friends. Relieve them of responsibility. All these interests come together.
>
> We never know our powers until we put them to the test.... Written work essential to everything. Someone said: "I shall not have lived in vain if I keep one heart from breaking."
>
> Do not disgrace Copey, your college, your friends, including the Judys and Mrs. Tillinghast and Mr. Griggs and your family.[10]

And then, given the knowledge that his book was never to be written, there is this rather heartbreaking note to himself:

> At last in the dark early in the morning of Dec. 2, when waking, I had the vision of what the book really would be. Write with delight and emotion. Swiftly produced. When it's all over I'll wonder how I ever could have made such a fuss about it.[11]

In connection with his failure to write and publish books, Ober well into old age would experience a sense of failure for his inability to earn money. His position with the Quetico-Superior Council provided little more than subsistence support, and, given the richness of his life experience, his communication skills, his connections, and his flair for story-telling, writing seemed the obvious answer to his felt need for more income. There is little evidence that late in life he looked elsewhere for opportunities to earn.

As for the unending Quetico-Superior struggle, until the end of his days Ober felt keenly the fact that fewer than a third of the original ten million acres he had envisioned were to be protected under anything like the program he had developed. The Boundary Waters Canoe Area Wilderness has become the largest wilderness area east of the Rockies and is now the most visited wilderness area of all, but, with luck in dealing with the governments of Minnesota and Ontario, much more of the region might have been protected, and Ober was to forever feel pain for what might have been.

Such self-criticism, however, was but one facet of Ober's complex personality. In general, he was a positive man of good humor who easily lost himself in the moments of his days. In his Thirtieth Anniversary Report to his Harvard classmates, he wrote: "I'm one of the erring brothers who thinks the world is growing and subject to improvement; in other words, that man, by taking thought and acting with courage, can improve his lot. The present world ferment seems to me not fatal, but full of promise. All is not yet lost. And I always remember with gratitude a classic expression heard years ago in a London musical comedy, where the hero reminded a particularly doleful companion: 'Cheer up, Quicksilver. You'll soon be dead.'"[12]

And in Ober's Fiftieth anniversary report to his Harvard classmates—written just in advance of a grand reunion in Cambridge—one discovers considerable pride in himself and joy in the life he has led. The report begins with a touch of characteristic humorous self-deprecation, but builds through several pages toward a crescendo:

Close friends of all sorts have occupied a large part of my life and still do. Whatever the other interests—and there have been many—these friends know my incurable slant toward primitive people and wilderness, particularly Indians and Eskimos and the sub-arctics of America. The Indians, who love droll caricatures, could probably give a more "vivid picture" of me at this late date than I. . . .

There have been times in my life at Rainy Lake when I have been entirely alone for long periods. In summer the situation is often just the opposite. Whatever has happened, even in the worst times, I have thought I was enjoying myself. Many of my intelligent friends are unhappy. I have a suspicion that only the ignorant are happy but am willing to accept the onus. In worldly wealth I have much less than at the start, but I am richer in health and friends of every sort, many of the best of them Indians who never had a day in school. I have never had a car or driven one but have lived on a big wide-open stage and seen a whole pioneer era pass—probably the last. I have my heart set now on that fiftieth anniversary in Cambridge, even if I have to slip in by way of the Charles in a battered birch-bark canoe.[13]

At the end of a typed copy of this report found in Ober's office on the Mallard there is a scrawled, handwritten note:

He made it, and stopped in N.Y. to see the Monahans, arriving with a jaunty boater hat, and stick with (1957) flag, and carried his 20 yr. old god-daughter Jean E. up the stairs of our old brownstone in Greenwich Village, exuberantly.
                    —George Monahan

On three occasions in this chapter, quotes from Ober's reports to his Harvard classmates mention the importance of friends in his life. And indeed his multitude of warm friendships must be considered one of the greatest achievements of his life. A vital person like Ober, connected with his deep self and the natural world, vitalizes and vivifies the lives of those around him. As island "salon-keeper," as guide, mentor, friend, it is clear that Ober was a magnet around which life swirled abundantly, and people loved him for it. Having, in his youth, lived out so many of his own dreams, he validated the dreams of others, made them seem real and possible and exciting again.

When one lifts others to a higher plane, they respond with love and try to give back. Such was the case with Ober. People chauffeured him to distant environmental meetings and paddled deep into the wilderness for him, in order to be with him, to hear his talk and to see the world through his eyes. Ober was always giving himself, and people responded to him in kind, gave him whatever they could. His wealthy friends—Harry French, Fred Winston, Frances Andrews, and many others—were forever offering to and often did ease his financial burdens. If he had asked for such help, it may have been different, but because he seldom did, the giving was spontaneous.

In his later years, Ober took pride in his continuing agility and extreme physical flexibility. As mentioned in chapter one, throughout his life he had been able to sit and put both feet behind his neck. Ted Hall described the last time Ober achieved this pose. He was over seventy, and "there came a day when he did this, and he had trouble getting unlocked, and that scared him. He said he really thought he was going to die."[14]

In 1964, Ober suffered a stroke that nearly did take his life. In a 1965 *Minneapolis Tribune* column, one of several he devoted to Ober in the mid-60s, Jim Kimball wrote that Ober was "80 now and recently... sick enough to spend 6 weeks in an oxygen tent."[15] Kimball concluded, however, by writing that, after the interview, Ober chose to walk rather than ride the two or three miles back to his home. Ober was to live twelve more years, but, as time passed, he would suffer increasingly from ill health, memory loss, and mental confusion.

Ober inherited Wildcroft from Frances Andrews. In addition, she left him $55,000, and his circumstances were then such that in 1965 he could establish a modest charitable trust, the Ernest C. Oberholtzer Foundation. The purpose of this trust was to aid continuance of his life's work, especially in support of Native American culture and the preservation of wilderness areas.

With his inheritance from Frances, Ober felt relatively secure, but his health was now rapidly failing. In 1967, though he had long fought the shift to modern comforts, he surrendered and moved from his beached houseboat, the *Frigate Friday,* up to Wildcroft where, for about a year, he managed to live alone. Then, however, the man whose life had been so full of care taking needed care himself. From 1968 to 1973—during which time he also spent six months in the International Falls hospital—he was helped by a series of live-in caretakers, sometimes individuals, sometimes married couples. Often the people who lived on and around Rainy Lake took care of him as well. One such was Charlene Erickson, the wife of a Rainy Lake commercial fisherman. Ober's enthusiasm for correspondence continued to be intense, and he knew that if he sent letters he would receive them. In an interview, Erickson explained how she helped Ober produce his letters:

> Someone passed the word to me that he wanted help writing letters, so I was home at the time, not working steady, so I agreed to let him come to my house. He would just come and sit in a chair across the table and dictate. And I would type as he would talk. Many times it would be repetitious, and we'd start over. Many times he would fall asleep while he was talking. Ted Hall has told me that many times I had a little sentence on the bottom kind of explaining what Ober was trying to say, or else saying that we knew it was repetitious, but Ober was extra tired.
>
> Lauren [Charlene's husband] actually knew him long before I did. Ober was always a generous man. At Christmas he would bring books and sometimes little china cups and saucers. He loved to give gifts. Sometimes [with his letters] he would stick in a picture of a moose or someone in a canoe or something, and say, "I would like to send this along to them. I think they would appreciate it."
>
> He was a likeable person. I think everybody liked him that knew him, and in his later years you kind of tried to help look after him a little, you know, when he was getting feeble. He would stay sometimes, and if he was there through lunch hour, then I'd fix lunch for us. He loved soups and things like that, so he would usually have a little bite to eat before we took him on home. But he was a warm, gentle person, a nice person to know.[16]

In 1969, after two years of debilitating illness, Ober, hobbling along with two canes, found himself able to venture out into the world one last time. As advisor and honored elder, he attended a meeting of the President's Committee on Quetico-Superior in Chicago and meetings of the Wilderness Society in Florida and British Columbia. Then, in 1970, at the age of eighty-six, without family and no longer capable of managing his affairs, Ober was declared a ward of the state. Ferdinand Hilke (the father of Bob, who had accompanied Ober on his return to Nueltin Lake) was named his personal guardian. The First National Bank of Minneapolis became the guardian of his estate. At this time, the value of Ober's property was assessed at $119,501 and he had $73,447.50 in negotiables.[17]

On January 4, 1973, Ober became a resident of the Falls Nursing Home in International Falls. He was apparently having recurrent minor strokes that limited his ability to speak, and, according to Ted Hall, there would be days when he "simply could not articulate. He'd get very frustrated and angry at you for not being able to pull the words out of him." This frustration and anger due to his limitations, especially his inability to communicate, grew in Ober during the final years of his life, a strange sight to those who had almost never before seen him angry. There were, however, better moments. Hall told of a day when he was pushing Ober along an International Falls street in his wheelchair. "The whole morning there hadn't been a word you could understand. He just communicated by signs. And as we were crossing the street, an Indian woman called out to him and started a conversation. It wasn't until she left that I suddenly realized that in Ojibwe Ober was completely, absolutely articulate. Then [when she was gone], he couldn't get a word out."[18]

On October 10, 1973, a ceremony in honor of Ober was held on the Mallard. The event originated in the mind of the world-famous medical researcher and lifelong friend of Ober, Dr. Gilbert Dalldorf. Dalldorf designed a bronze casting about two feet in diameter on which the following was inscribed:

> This island was for fifty years the home of Ernest Oberholtzer, pioneer in the effort to save the wilderness, devoted Atisokan to the Indians and cherished friend and companion. 1973

Seventy-five of Ober's friends came together at the ceremony during which the plaque was installed in rock on the highest point of the island. Eighty-nine years old and confined to his wheelchair, Ober was in attendance, but Atisokan's marvelously sensitive and alive storyteller's mind was no longer much present. However, when the tale of his return to Hawkes Summit and recovery of the can was told, he waved his hand and yelled:

"And that's the truth!"

Everyone clapped.

In the years just before and after Ober's death, Ted Hall published a flurry of articles about him, often in his own newspaper, the *Rainy Lake Chronicle*. In one, he wrote that most of Ober's years in the north country had been glorious ones. He had survived beyond expectations and "moved from one north country adventure to the next." And these adventures each "seasoned" him a little more, until "in his sixties he had that presence sometimes encountered in older men who have vision that make them grow steadily younger in spirit."[19]

Later in the same article, sensing how rapidly memory of Ober's contributions would fade, Hall described a gathering of the Voyageurs Park Association in the International Falls Holiday Inn. The group had met, wrote Hall, poignantly and a trifle bitterly, "to praise one another for their contributions to conservation." And as they did so, "an old man named Ober dozed in his chair in the nursing home next door, dreaming at the far end of his dream."[20]

Ober spent his final years in the Falls Nursing Home, often visited by long-time friends. He had occasional moments of clarity and once stated, "I probably look like a surprise fairy tale." Near the end he refused food. On June 6, 1977, the long-troubled, great heart of Ernest Oberholtzer quit beating. He was ninety-three years old.

Memorial services were held for Ober in both International Falls and Davenport. He was buried alongside his mother, brother, and grandparents in their family plot in Oakdale Cemetery in Davenport. Oakdale was the same cemetery in which, eighty-five years before, the gravedigger Tom Burke had opened the book of nature to Ober's bright young eyes. Some have wondered why Ober's ashes were not scattered on the Mallard, but Ober himself had chosen to be buried with his family. During his final trip to Davenport, he had stopped by the cemetery and made his arrangements with the caretaker there. The following words were carved on his headstone:

Ober
Ernest Carl Oberholtzer
Atisokan
His Indian Name for Storyteller
Feb. 6, 1884 — June 6, 1977

Sigurd Olson gave the eulogy at the International Falls service. He titled it "A Defender of Wild Places," and in it he stated that those who had visited Ober on the Mallard would remember "the twinkle in his blue eyes, his ruddy skin, his violin, the 'Bird House' he built high above the treetops from which he could look over the water, his hanging gardens growing in soil he had brought from the mainland to the cliffs of his rocky home. The Mallard," said Olson, "was a delightful, dream-planned place."[21]

He then told of Ober as a canoe man and storyteller: "He learned the legends of the Indians who accepted him as one of their own. They understood him, and he understood their way of life. No one who heard his tales will forget them—tales of the Black Sturgeon, the Manitou and Nanabozho, spirits who dwelled in the depths of the lakes he knew so well. He spoke [Ojibwe] fluently and the Indians called him Atisokan, a teller of legends.... Listeners were always enthralled by his stories, for as he spoke, a strange light came into his eyes—and he became part of the Indians' spirit world...."[22]

Many who knew Ernest Oberholtzer continue to tell of him to fascinated listeners, and as they do, they are imbued with something of the old storyteller's power, and a light comes into their eyes. The story of Ernest Oberholtzer's life is in itself one of his finest legacies. In an interview given after the funeral, Sigurd Olson said, "In a way he was a legend."[23]

It seems that when, early in the twentieth century, the Rainy Lake Ojibwe gave Ober the name Atisokan, meaning legend or teller of legends, this naming contained a touch of humor, but it had nevertheless hit the mark. By the time of his death, Ober and his story had grown to fulfill the dimensions implied by his Ojibwe name.

Notes

By far the richest source of information on the life of Ernest Oberholtzer is to be found in the collections of the Minnesota Historical Society in St. Paul. The microfilm edition of the Ernest C. Oberholtzer Papers consists of fifty-two rolls of microfilm, each containing hundreds of pages of carefully organized information. The scores of boxes of Quetico-Superior Council Records housed in the History Center in St. Paul are another vast source of information on Oberholtzer, specifically in relation to his work as a wilderness preservationist. In addition, for those who would hear the Oberholtzer story in his living voice, an extensive collection of taped oral history interviews can be found at the History Center as well. (See note below on the oral history and my use of it.) All in all, the Minnesota Historical Society's abundance of Oberholtzer material was enough to prove daunting as I began work on this book.

The Koochiching County Historical Society in International Falls, Minnesota, holds a limited number of loosely organized, interesting folders relating to Oberholtzer and his environmental foe Edward Backus, which also were valuable to my research.

Oberholtzer's long-time home on Mallard Island, now maintained by the Ernest C. Oberholtzer Foundation, proved a very rich source of content for this book. I continue to wonder how and why materials so often appeared as needed in Ober's office in the Big House and in the nooks and crannies of the many other small buildings on the island.

Many of Oberholtzer's friends are still alive and have been generous in telling me about him and in providing me with materials from their small personal collections of letters and clippings. I also conducted oral history interviews with a number of these friends, gathering material that has greatly enhanced this work.

Many of the newspaper and magazine articles quoted from in this book are from clippings discovered in the sources described above. Some of these clippings offered little or no information as to where and when they had been published. In these notes, I've provided whatever source information is available, including the place where I found it.

A Note on My Use of the Oberholtzer Oral History Interviews

Most of the oral history interviews that make up so important a part of this book were conducted in 1963 and 1964 when Oberholtzer was turning eighty. During this time, he suffered a stroke and was hospitalized for six weeks, after which he often experienced memory problems. Therefore, in the interviews, while often speaking with that eloquence for which he was famous, Oberholtzer was also frequently confused and halting. Perhaps because of this, the interview transcripts were never fully edited, and I have therefore rather heavily edited much of the material I've selected. In addition, in order to present each sequence of events in its fullness, I have often brought together content from various parts of a given interview or two or more interviews. In this editing and arranging, I have been extremely careful throughout to maintain Oberholtzer's intent while, to the best of my "ear" and ability, maintaining the eloquence that was the voice of Ernest Oberholtzer at its finest.

Notes to the Introduction

1. Bob Hilke, interview by the author, tape recording, Sept. 3–4, 1996.

2. Ernest Oberholtzer in Lucile Kane, "Biographical Sketch," Ernest C. Oberholzter oral history interviews, Minnesota Environmental Issues Oral History Project, Minnesota Historical Society (hereafter, MHS), St. Paul.

Notes to Chapter 1

1. Oberholtzer in Kane, "Biographical Sketch." Much general information in this chapter came from this sketch.

2. Ernest Oberholtzer, "Harvard College, Class of 1907: Fiftieth Anniversary Report" (1957): 464. At five-year intervals, Oberholtzer's Harvard class privately printed these reports, written by the individual class members. Copies of this and other five-year reports are in Oberholtzer's office on Mallard Island.

3. Charles Skrief, "Backus' fame came from Ober conflict," *The Daily Journal* (International Falls, Minn.), Feb. 27, 1981, Progress Edition, 6G.

4. "Harvard College, Class of 1907: Fiftieth Anniversary Report" (1957): 460.

5. Edith Rylander, "All the Different Obers," *Oberholtzer Foundation Newsletter* 8 (1994).

6. F. H. Griggs to Ernest Carl, Feb. 6, 1884, Ernest C. Oberholtzer Papers, MHS, 52:0290.

7. Marnee Monahan, interview by Alicia Johnson, Dec. 16, 1997. Quotation from a summary of the interview, provided by Johnson.

8. Much of this information is from Kane, "Biographical Sketch," and from Clerk of Court Divorce Packets, 1st Series, Scott County, Iowa, microfilm, roll 1653817.

9. Marguerite Carl Holland to Fritz Hilke, Aug. 5, 1977, private collection.

10. Oberholtzer in Kane, "Biographical Sketch."

11. Ibid.

12. Ibid.

13. Ernest Oberholtzer, "Notes for a Davenport Story," n.d., Oberholtzer Papers, 24:0518.

14. Oberholtzer in Kane, "Biographical Sketch."

15. Ernest Oberholtzer, "Hudson Bay Canoe Trip Journal," Sept. 16, 1912, in the possession of the author.

16. Ted Hall, interview by Margaret Robertson, tape recording, Feb. 5 and 8, 1987, Minnesota Environmental Issues Oral History Project, MHS.

17. Ibid.

18. Oberholtzer in Kane, "Biographical Sketch."

19. Jim Kimball, "'Ober' Recalls Lifelong Battle for Wilderness," *Minneapolis Tribune*, Apr. 28, 1967, 23.

20. Ibid.

21. Oberholtzer, "Notes for a Davenport Story," 24:0515–0528.

22. Ibid.

23. Oberholtzer in Kane, "Biographical Sketch."

24. Ibid.

25. Ernest Oberholtzer in Quetico-Superior Council, "Quetico-Superior: A New-World Peace Memorial" (flyer), in the possession of the author. Using almost the same wording, Oberholtzer made this comparison on a number of other occasions.

26. Oberholtzer in Kane, "Biographical Sketch."

27. Hilke, interview.

28. Katherine Bakeless, interview by Margaret Robertson, tape recording, Feb. 6, 1987, Minnesota Environmental Issues Oral History Project, MHS.

29. Oberholtzer in Kane, "Biographical Sketch."

30. "Harvard College, Class of 1907: Fiftieth Anniversary Report" (1957): 460.

31. Oberholtzer in Kane, "Biographical Sketch."

32. Oberholtzer, "Notes for a Davenport Story," 24:0515–0528.

Notes to Chapter 2

1. See section on the Oberholtzer oral history interviews in the introductory comments to these notes.

2. Unknown writer to Mr. Max Smith, Sept. 19, 1910, Oberholtzer Papers, 1:0263.

3. Ernest Oberholtzer, Canoe Trip Journal, vol. 7, Aug. 4–17, 1906, Oberholtzer Papers, 28:0584. All journal entries that follow in this chapter are from this source, dates included in the text.

Notes to Chapter 3

1. Ernest Oberholtzer, England Trip Journals and Notebooks, vols. 56–57, July 8–Sept. 3 and Sept. 3–Oct. 8, 1908, Oberholtzer Papers, 30:0001.

2. Conrad Aiken, *Ushant* (New York & Boston: Duell, Sloan and Pearce–Little, Brown, 1952), 47. In the oral history, Oberholtzer seems to overstate his presence in this book. My reading of *Ushant*, a rather difficult book, reveals little of the repetition he has suggested.

3. Ibid., 59.

Notes to Chapter 4

1. Jean Replinger, "Chronology: Mallard Island," in the possession of the author.

2. Ted Hall, "KCHS Presents: A Look at the Life of Ernest Carl Oberholtzer" (radio transcript), n.d., Oberholtzer folders, Koochiching County Historical Society, International Falls, Minn.

3. Ernest Oberholtzer, "The International Forest" (1909), Oberholtzer Papers, 25:0341.

4. Kimball, "'Ober' Recalls Lifelong Battle."

5. Ernest Oberholtzer, "The Rainy Lake District of Ontario" (material for lecture), 1912, Oberholtzer Papers, 25:0404.

6. Ernest Oberholtzer, "Canoe Trip Notes" (1909), found in Oberholtzer's Mallard Island office.

7. Ibid.

8. Ibid.

9. Ibid.

10. Oberholtzer, "The Rainy Lake District of Ontario."

11. Oberholtzer, Canoe Trip Journal, vol. 8, Aug. 19–Sept. 22, 1909, Oberholtzer Papers, 28:0613. All journal entries that follow in this chapter are from this source, dates included in the text.

12. Ernest Oberholtzer, "Portage Philosophy" (pamphlet), Quetico-Superior Council, reprinted from *American Forests*, n.d., in the possession of the author.

13. Oberholtzer, "The Rainy Lake District of Ontario."

14. Arthur Hawkes to Oberholtzer, Aug. 23, 1909, Oberholtzer Papers, 1:0220.

Notes to Chapter 5

1. Oberholtzer, Canoe Trip Journal, vol. 13, May 22–June 13, 1910, Oberholtzer Papers, 28:0893. All journal entries that follow in this chapter are from this source, dates included in the text.

2. Don "Buck" Johnson, interview by the author, tape recording, May 30, 1997.

3. Ernest Oberholtzer, "In Domestic Circles" (narrative essay), n.d., Oberholtzer Papers, 25:0589.

4. Ernest Oberholtzer, "Photographing Wild Moose," *American Photography* (Aug. 1915): 468–73.

5. Oberholtzer, "In Domestic Circles."

Notes to Chapter 6

1. Ernest Oberholtzer, England Trip Journal, vol. 58, July 3–Sept. 19, 1910, Oberholtzer Papers, 30:0099. All journal entries that follow in this chapter are from this source, dates included in the text.

2. Oberholtzer to Rosa Oberholtzer, Aug. 28, 1910, Oberholtzer Papers, 1:0256.

3. Arthur Hawkes to Oberholtzer, Mar. 16, 1911, Oberholtzer Papers, 1:0281.

4. "The Top of the Continent" (publicity flyer for Oberholtzer lecture), Nov. 14, 1910, Oberholtzer Papers, 1:0266.

5. Oberholtzer entry, Mar. 2, 1960, Oberholtzer Papers, 28:0519.

Notes to Chapter 7

1. R. H. Cockburn, "Voyage to Nutheltin," *The Beaver* (Jan.–Feb. 1986): 5. Cockburn's article in this Canadian magazine is extensive, scholarly, and richly detailed.

2. "Harvard College, Class of 1907: Fiftieth Anniversary Report" (1957): 460.

3. Ernest Oberholtzer, "Among the Canadian Reindeer," found in Oberholtzer's Mallard Island office. This nine-page discussion of the beginning of the Hudson Bay journey was probably used as a script for a photographic slide show.

4. Calvin Rutstrum, *North American Canoe Country* (New York: Macmillan, 1964), 27.

5. Oberholtzer entry, Mar. 2, 1960, Oberholtzer Papers, 28:0519.

6. Ibid.

7. Ibid.

8. Ibid.

9. Wallace W. Morgan, "He's Spent 60 Years On Voyageurs' Trails," *Duluth News Tribune*, July 2, 1967, second news section.

10. Oberholtzer, "Hudson Bay Canoe Trip Journal." All journal entries that follow in this chapter and the next are from this source, dates included in the text.

11. Cockburn, "Voyage to Nutheltin," 7.

12. Ibid., 10.

13. Rutstrum, *North American Canoe Country*, 129.

14. Cockburn, "Voyage to Nutheltin," 16.

Notes to Chapter 8

1. All journal entries in this chapter are from Oberholtzer, "Hudson Bay Canoe Trip Journal," dates included in the text.

2. Morgan, "He's Spent 60 Years On Voyageurs' Trails."

3. Cockburn, "Voyage to Nutheltin," 24–25.

Notes to Chapter 9

1. Arthur Hawkes, "Oberholtzer Who Has Gone North," *The British News of Canada*, n.d. The clipping in my possession was surely published in early summer, 1912.

2. Oberholtzer to Hawkes, Nov. 14, 1912, Oberholtzer Papers, 1:0345.

3. J. B. Tyrrell to Oberholtzer, Nov. 16, 1912, Oberholtzer Papers, 1:0347.

4. Oberholtzer to J. E. Chalifeur, Dec. 2, 1912, Oberholtzer Papers, 1:0350.

5. Oberholtzer to J. E. Chalifeur, Dec. 29, 1913, Oberholtzer Papers, 1:0454.

6. Oberholtzer to Reynolds, Mar. 13, 1913, Oberholtzer Papers, 1:0467.

7. Arthur Hawkes to Oberholtzer, July 16, 1912, Oberholtzer Papers, 1:0339.

8. Oberholtzer to Arthur Hawkes, Feb. 13, 1913, Oberholtzer Papers, 1:0364.

9. Oberholtzer to Franz Boas, June 14, 1913, Oberholtzer Papers, 1:0424.

10. "Harvard College, Class of 1907: Quindecennial Report" (1922): 401.

11. "Harvard College, Class of 1907: Fifty-fifth Anniversary Report" (1962): 105.

12. Oberholtzer, Canoe Trip Journals, vols. 15–16, June 26–Aug. 7, Aug. 8–Dec. 3, 1914, Oberholtzer Papers, 28:0978. All journal entries that follow in this chapter are from this source, dates included in the text.

13. "Harvard College, Class of 1907: Quindecennial Report" (1922): 401.

14. Ibid.

15. *Youth's Companion* to Oberholtzer, Jan. 19, 1912, Oberholtzer Papers, 1:0303.

16. Oberholtzer to Dr. Truman Michelson, May 8, 1915, Oberholtzer Papers, 1:0464.

17. Truman Michelson to Oberholtzer, May 22, 1915, Oberholtzer Papers, 1:0465.

18. Oberholtzer to Michelson, May 28, 1915, Oberholtzer Papers, 1:0468.

Notes to Chapter 10

1. Oberholtzer, Canoe Trip Journal, vol. 18, Feb. 21–Apr. 1, 1916, Oberholtzer Papers, 29:0001.

2. Ibid.

3. Ted Hall, "Atisokan: His Rainy Lake," *The Rainy Lake Chronicle* (Ranier, Minn.), 5 (Oberholtzer Papers, 1:0036).

4. Oberholtzer to William Hapgood, Mar. 6, 1917, Oberholtzer Papers, 1:0479.

5. R. Newell Searle, "Ober's Long Shadow," *Living Wilderness* (Jan.–Mar. 1978): 6.

6. Acting Sec. of Agriculture Carl Vrooman to Canadian Minister of Lands, Forests, and Mines, Feb. 4, 1918, Oberholtzer Papers, 1:0480.

7. Oberholtzer to Uncle Henry, Oct. 3, 1920, Oberholtzer Papers, 1:0533.

8. Ray Anderson, interview by the author, tape recording, May 30, 1996.

9. Monahan, interview.

10. Ibid.

11. Grace Parkhurst to Oberholtzer, Aug. 8, 1934, Oberholtzer Papers, 4:0261.

12. Deer Island Articles of Incorporation, July 28, 1920, Oberholtzer Papers, 1:0527.

13. John Brown to Oberholtzer, Mar. 31, 1922, Oberholtzer Papers, 1:0582.

14. Ted Hall, "The Queen Buys Sand Point," *The Rainy Lake Chronicle* 3:43 (Aug. 29, 1976).

15. Ernest Oberholtzer, list, 1922, Oberholtzer Papers, 1:0496.

16. "Harvard College, Class of 1907: Quindecennial Report" (1922): 402.

17. Ibid.

18. Oberholtzer to Deputy Collector, U.S. Internal Revenue, Dec. 22, 1923, Oberholtzer Papers, 1:0649.

19. "Harvard College, Class of 1907: Quindecennial Report" (1922): 402.

20. Ernest Oberholtzer, "Program for Summer, 1923," Oberholtzer Papers, 1:0619.

21. Harry French to Oberholtzer, Jan. 30, 1924, Oberholtzer Papers, 1:0683.

22. Harry French to Oberholtzer, Jan. 31, 1924, Oberholtzer Papers, 1:0684.

23. Bror Dahlberg to Oberholtzer, Oct. 31, 1924, private collection.

24. Kane, "Biographical Sketch."

25. Ibid.

26. Hall, interview.

27. Oberholtzer to William Hapgood, Oct. 26, 1929, Oberholtzer Papers, 2:0665.

28. Bakeless, interview.

29. Ibid.

30. Oberholtzer to Sewell Tyng, May 3, 1924, private collection.

Notes to Chapter 11

1. Ernest Oberholtzer, "The Lakes of Verendrye: A University of the Wilderness" (Quetico-Superior Council, n.d.), 1. This publication is a sixteen-page trilogy of articles originally published in the September, October, and November 1929 issues of *American Forests and Forest Life* under these separate titles: "A Lakeland Archipelago," "The Ancient Game of Grab," and "A University of the Wilderness."

2. Much of the above information on the history of the Quetico-Superior region was drawn from R. Newell Searle, *Saving Quetico-Superior: A Land Set Apart* (St. Paul: MHS Press, 1977), 1–33.

3. Oberholtzer, "The Lakes of Verendrye," 9.

4. Ibid.

5. Ibid., 10.

6. Ibid., 9–10.

7. Ibid., 10.

8. Oberholtzer to Secretary of War, Feb. 23, 1917, Oberholtzer Papers, 1:0478.

9. "The Last of the Barons" (anonymous manuscript), n.d., Backus folders, Koochiching County Historical Society.

10. Searle, *Saving Quetico-Superior*, 35.

11. "The Last of the Barons."

12. "The Inception of the Company's Paper Manufacturing Activities," *Daily Mail & Empire of Toronto*, July 1, 1927.

13. "The Last of the Barons."

14. Skrief, "Backus' fame came from Ober conflict."

15. "The Last of the Barons"

16. Anonymous newspaper clipping, Oct. 30, 1934, Backus folders, Koochiching County Historical Society. The paper was likely *The Daily Journal* of International Falls.

17. Searle, *Saving Quetico-Superior,* 39.

18. Minnesota and Ontario Paper Co., "Outing Party" (flyer), Sept. 5–11, 1927, Backus folders, Koochiching County Historical Society.

19. R. Newell Searle, "A Clash of Giants," *The Rainy Lake Chronicle* (June 19, 1977): 5.

20. Oberholtzer to Welles Eastman, Sept. 12, 1959, Oberholtzer Papers, 43: 0014.

Notes to Chapter 12

1. Much of the information on early stages of the political struggle for the future of the border lakes region was drawn from Searle, *Saving Quetico-Superior,* 42–59.

2. Sewell Tyng to Oberholtzer, Sept. 19, 1925, Oberholtzer Papers, 36:0523.

3. Sewell Tyng to Oberholtzer, Oct. 14, 1925, Oberholtzer Papers, 36:0537.

4. Harold Ickes to Oberholtzer, June 1, 1926, Oberholtzer Papers, 36:0644.

5. Kevin Proescholdt, "Tall Pines and Wilderness: The Legacy of Frank B. Hubachek," BWCA *Wilderness News* (winter 1987): 6.

6. Oberholtzer to Orville Freeman, 1965, private collection.

Notes to Chapter 13

1. Oberholtzer to Sewell Tyng, Mar. 12, 1927, Oberholtzer Papers, 37:0047.

2. Oberholtzer to William H. Smith, June 3, 1927, Oberholtzer Papers, 37:0049.

3. "Harvard College, Class of 1907: Fiftieth Anniversary Report" (1957): 461.

4. Oberholtzer, "The Lakes of Verendrye," 13.

5. Ibid., 11.

6. Ibid., 13–14.

7. Ibid., 16.

8. Charles Kelly, interview by Margaret Robertson, tape recording, Sept. 24–25, 1986, Minnesota Environmental Issues Oral History Project, MHS.

9. Searle, *Saving Quetico-Superior,* 66.

10. Oberholtzer to Welles Eastman, Sept. 12, 1959, Oberholtzer Papers, 28: 0014.

11. Ibid.

12. Oberholtzer, "The Lakes of Verendrye," 13.

13. "Harvard College, Class of 1907: Fiftieth Anniversary Report" (1957): 462.

Notes to Chapter 14

1. Donald Hough, "An International Playground," *Outdoor America* (Jan. 1928) (Oberholtzer folders, Quetico-Superior Council Records, MHS).

2. Quetico-Superior Council, "Program of The Quetico-Superior Council" (flyer), in the possession of the author.

3. Handwritten note by Oberholtzer to himself, Oberholtzer Papers, 37:0001.

4. Harold H. Martin, "Battle to Save Wilderness Called Successful," excerpted from *The Saturday Evening Post* (Sept. 25, 1948) and reprinted in *The Daily Journal* (International Falls, Minn.), Feb. 27, 1981, Progress Edition, 2G.

5. Ibid.

6. Hall, interview.

7. Oberholtzer, "The Lakes of Verendrye," 10.

Notes to Chapter 15

1. Searle, *Saving Quetico-Superior,* 74.

2. "Backus Files Objections to Shipstead Bill," *Minneapolis Tribune,* May 1, 1928.

3. Oberholtzer to Thomas Watson, May 1, 1928, Oberholtzer folders, Quetico-Superior Council Records.

4. Oberholtzer to Grace Parkhurst, May 29, 1928, Oberholtzer folders, Quetico-Superior Council Records.

5. Oberholtzer to Sewell Tyng, May 5, 1928, Oberholtzer folders, Quetico-Superior Council Records.

6. Searle, *Saving Quetico-Superior,* 75.

7. Quetico-Superior Council Bulletin, May 11, 1928, Oberholtzer folders, Quetico-Superior Council Records.

8. Oberholtzer to Welles Eastman, Oct. 21, 1958, Oberholtzer Papers, 43:0001.

9. Seth Gordon to Oberholtzer, Aug. 14, 1928, Oberholtzer folders, Quetico-Superior Council Records.

10. "Bowen Raps Backus' Republicanism And Magnus Johnson Plea," *Minneapolis Journal*, Mar. 8, 1928.

11. Charles B. Cheney, "Backus Offers Letter To Prove Dam Fight Is Politics; 'Hoax', Is Reply," *Minneapolis Journal*, Mar. 12, 1928.

12. "E. W. Backus Replies to Isaac Walton League," *International Falls Press*, Mar. 5, 1928.

13. "Rundlett Takes Oath Letter Was Forgery Or Trick," *Minneapolis Journal*, Mar. 13, 1928.

14. Ibid.

15. "Heated Debate At Political Meeting," *The Daily Journal* (International Falls, Minn.), Mar. 14, 1928.

16. Searle, *Saving Quetico-Superior*, 72.

17. Carl Holmer to Director of Koochiching County Historical Society, Dec. 12, 1982, Backus folders, Koochiching County Historical Society.

18. Searle, *Saving Quetico-Superior*, 72.

19. "Outers Members Object to Dams, Despite Officers," *Minneapolis Journal*, June 15, 1928.

20. In Searle, *Saving Quetico-Superior*, 76, the Minnesota Power and Light investment is said to be $314,000.

21. Anderson, interview.

Notes to Chapter 16

1. Oberholtzer to Mrs. Perry Richardson, June 27, 1929, Oberholtzer Papers, 2:0545.

2. Oberholtzer to Dr. J. W. Watzek, July 13, 1929, Oberholtzer Papers, 2:0559.

3. Oberholtzer to F. I. Skane, July 13, 1929, Oberholtzer Papers, 2:0562.

4. Dr. Mary Ghostley to Oberholtzer, July 31, 1929, Oberholtzer Papers, 2:0572.

5. Oberholtzer to August E. Steffen, Aug. 14, 1929, Oberholtzer Papers, 2:0597.

6. Oberholtzer's eulogy notes, Aug. 14, 1929, Oberholtzer Papers, 2:0598.

7. Obituary article, n.d., private collection.

8. Bakeless, interview.

9. Ibid. Hall was present and an occasional participant in the Bakeless interview.

10. Oberholtzer to William Hapgood, Oct. 26, 1929, Oberholtzer Papers, 2:0665.

11. Oberholtzer to Clara, Nov. 3, 1933, Oberholtzer Papers, 4:0125.

12. Crescent Meat Market to Oberholtzer, Mar. 23, 1932, Oberholtzer Papers, 3:0637.

13. Searle, *Saving Quetico-Superior*, 81–82.

14. Quetico-Superior Council, "The Issue of Conservation," n.d., Oberholtzer Papers, 37:0436.

15. Searle, *Saving Quetico-Superior*, 88–89.

16. Fred Winston to Oberholtzer, July 4, 1930, Oberholtzer folders, Quetico-Superior Council Records.

17. Oberholtzer press release, July 1930, Oberholtzer folders, Quetico-Superior Council Records.

18. Oberholtzer to Fred Winston, July 9, 1930, Oberholtzer folders, Quetico-Superior Council Records.

19. Quetico-Superior Council, "The Issue of Conservation."

20. Oberholtzer, "The Lakes of Verendrye," 16.

Notes to Chapter 17

1. Morison, Samuel Eliot [Columbia Encyclopedia online], Mar. 1, 2001. Available: http://kids.infoplease.lycos.com/ce6/people/A0834048.html.

2. Conrad (Potter) Aiken (1889–1973) [Books and Writers online], Mar. 1, 2001. Available: http://www.kirjasto.sci.fi/caiken.htm.

3. Copeland, Charles Townsend [Britannica.com online], Mar. 1, 2001. Available: http//www.britannica.com/seo/c/charles-townsend-copeland/.

4. Oberholtzer to Samuel Morison, Feb. 2, 1955, Oberholtzer Papers, 23:0071.

Notes to Chapter 18

1. Oberholtzer to Welles Eastman, Sept. 12, 1959, Oberholtzer Papers, 43: 0013.

2. R. Newell Searle, "Ernest Oberholtzer: border wilderness architect," *Minnesota Historical Society News,* n.d., found in the Book House on Mallard Island.

3. Oberholtzer to Fred Winston, July 8, 1930, Oberholtzer folders, Quetico-Superior Council Records.

4. Oberholtzer to Fred Winston, July 9, 1930, Oberholtzer folders, Quetico-Superior Council Records.

5. Searle, *Saving Quetico-Superior,* 94–95.

6. Fred Winston to Oberholtzer, Sept. 2, 1930, Oberholtzer folders, Quetico-Superior Council Records.

7. Oberholtzer to Sigurd Olson, Apr. 18, 1933, Oberholtzer folders, Quetico-Superior Council Records.

8. Sigurd Olson to Oberholtzer, Apr. 25, 1933, Oberholtzer folders, Quetico-Superior Council Records.

9. Much of the preceding information is from Searle, *Saving Quetico-Superior,* 91–92.

10. Statisticians Report to Quetico-Superior Council, July 27, 1928, Oberholtzer Papers, 37:0178.

11. "Canadian Manufacturers of Newsprint Paper are Planning to Have Dictator," *Sault St. Marie Star,* June 23, 1928 (Oberholtzer Papers, 37:0152).

12. Searle, *Saving Quetico-Superior,* 93.

13. "Breach of Contract Alleged by Hearst," *Manitoba Free Press,* June 20, 1928 (Oberholtzer Papers, 37:0146).

14. Charles Kelly to Rollo Chaffee, Aug. 2, 1928, Oberholtzer Papers, 37:0185.

15. Clara Martin to Oberholtzer, n.d., Oberholtzer folders, Quetico-Superior Council Records.

16. Oberholtzer to Raymond Ickes, Dec. 30, 1932, Oberholtzer Papers, 3:0795.

17. "Backus to Testify in Lake Case Today," Oct. 12, 1933, Backus folders, Koochiching County Historical Society.

18. Ibid.

19. Martin, "Battle to Save Wilderness Called Successful."

20. David Backes, *A Wilderness Within: The Life of Sigurd F. Olson* (Minneapolis: University of Minnesota Press, 1997), 100.

21. Searle, *Saving Quetico-Superior,* 100.

22. Ibid., 91–94.

23. Ibid., 92–93.

24. "Backus Took 7 Million, Two Declare," *Minneapolis Journal,* Apr. 8, 1934.

25. Backus to Old Loyal Employees, Jan. 9, 1934, Backus folders, Koochiching County Historical Society.

26. Backus to Bondholders of Minnesota and Ontario Paper Company, Jan. 5, 1934, Backus folders, Koochiching County Historical Society.

27. "The Border Playground Saved," *St. Paul Pioneer Press,* June 19, 1934.

28. Martin, "Battle to Save Wilderness Called Successful."

29. Ibid.

30. "Death of Founder of Local Industry Recalls Ambitions," *The Daily Journal* (International Falls, Minn.), Oct. 30, 1934.

31. Searle, *Saving Quetico-Superior,* 104.

32. "Backus found prosperity by setting sights high," *Blandin Broke Pile,* Aug. 1951, reprinted in *The Daily Journal* (International Falls, Minn.), Feb. 27, 1981, Progress Edition, 2G.

33. Oberholtzer to Samuel Morison, May 9, 1942, Oberholtzer Papers, 23:0036.

34. The following is a list of key moments leading to the present-day status of protected areas within the Quetico-Superior region:

1934: The President's Quetico-Superior Committee was established by executive order of Franklin D. Roosevelt. During its first meeting, the Quetico-Superior program was endorsed as the official program of the committee and Ober was elected its chairman, a position he would retain for twelve years. After Ober, Tyng (briefly) and then Charles Kelly would be committee chairmen.

1935: The Wilderness Society, one of America's most influential environmental organizations, was founded by president's committee member Bob Marshall. Over the years the society would take strong interest in Quetico-Superior issues. Ober was one of eight founding members of the society, a member of its governing board till 1968, and an honorary vice president from that time till his death.

1947: Sigurd Olson succeeded Ober as the spearhead figure of the Quetico-Superior movement.

1948: The Thye-Blatnik Act was passed. In an attempt to eliminate fly-in resorts in the heart of the wilderness, this act authorized and provided funding for the Forest Service to acquire resorts, recreation lands, and private holdings in the Superior National Forest roadless area. It also established federal compensation rates to county governments in northeastern Minnesota for properties taken off their tax rolls.

1949: By executive order, President Harry S. Truman banned float planes from landing in the roadless areas.

1949: The Canadian Quetico-Superior Committee was established.

1957: Instead of a treaty between the United States and Canada, the two countries established an agreement on mutual protection of the Quetico-Superior region. Shortly thereafter a six-member Quetico-Superior International Advisory Committee was organized, with three representatives from each country.

1958: The name of the Superior Roadless Areas was changed to the Boundary Waters Canoe Area (BWCA).

1964: The Wilderness Act was passed by the U.S. Congress. This act established the National Wilderness Preservation System. The BWCA was included in this system, but it was considered a special case and some logging and motorized travel was allowed to continue.

1972: Quetico Provincial Park received full wilderness protection.

1972: Voyageurs National Park was established.

1978: The Boundary Waters Wilderness Act was passed, extending full wilderness protection to much of the Boundary Waters Canoe Area.

Notes to Chapter 19

1. Robert Franklin, "A Home For the Spirit," (Minneapolis) *Star Tribune*, Sept. 6, 1993, 1E.

2. Jean Replinger, interview by the author, tape recording, May 29, 1996.

3. Franklin, "A Home For the Spirit."

4. Bill Holm to Jean Replinger, 1983, in the possession of the author.

5. Replinger, interview.

6. Hilke, interview.

7. "Harvard College, Class of 1907: Thirtieth Anniversary Report" (1937): 92.

8. Hall, "Atisokan: His Rainy Lake," 5.

9. Monahan, interview.

10. Ibid.

11. Ibid.

12. Hilke, interview.

13. Oberholtzer to John Brown, Mar. 28, 1927, Oberholtzer folders, Koochiching County Historical Society.

14. Oberholtzer to John Brown, Apr. 11, 1930, Oberholtzer folders, Koochiching County Historical Society.

15. Oberholtzer to Samuel Morison, May 11, 1935, Oberholtzer Papers, 23:0022.

16. J. G. Byam to Oberholtzer, Nov. 9, 1937, Oberholtzer Papers, 37:0821.

17. J. G. Byam to Oberholtzer, Dec. 29, 1937, Oberholtzer Papers, 37:0864.

18. Arch Coleman to J. G. Byam, Oct. 16, 1931, Oberholtzer Papers, 37:0805.

19. Kit Bakeless to Oberholtzer, June 3, 1970, private collection.

20. Replinger, interview.

21. Kimball, "Oberholtzer Recalls Lifelong Battle."

22. Barbara Thomas (Breckenridge) to her mother, June 28, 1955, found in Oberholtzer's Mallard Island office.

23. Barbara (Thomas) Breckenridge, interview by the author, tape recording, May 29, 1996.

24. Barbara Thomas (Breckenridge) to her mother, June 22, 1955, Oberholtzer's Mallard Island office.

25. Ibid.

26. Ibid.

27. Ibid.

28. Ibid.

29. Cathy Janson, "Ernest Oberholtzer: 'He and Backus never got along on account of the dams,'" *The Daily Journal* (International Falls, Minn.), Feb. 27, 1981, Progress Edition, 1G, 9G.

30. Harry Henderson to Oberholtzer, Jan. 9, 1954, Oberholtzer Papers, 14:0022.

31. Hilke, interview.

Notes to Chapter 20

1. Harry "Pinay" Boshkaykin, interview by the author, tape recording, Sept. 2, 1996.

2. Maurice Perrault, "Adventures with Atisokan: The Most Unforgettable Person I've Known" (manuscript), found in Oberholtzer's Mallard Island office.

3. Edgar Bliss to Oberholtzer, Nov. 19, 1937, found in Oberholtzer's Mallard Island office.

4. Bliss to Oberholtzer, Nov. 22, 1937, Oberholtzer's Mallard Island office.

5. Bliss to Oberholtzer, Apr. 26, 1938, Oberholtzer's Mallard Island office.

6. Boshkaykin, interview. All Boshkaykin quotations in the following sequence are from this interview.

7. Ernest Oberholtzer, notes for a story, Oberholtzer Papers, 24:0607.

8. Ibid.

9. Boshkaykin, interview.

10. Ibid.

11. Ibid.

12. Hall, "KCHS presents: 'A Look at the Life of Ernest Carl Oberholtzer.'"

13. Breckenridge, interview.

14. Hall, interview.

15. "Harvard College, Class of 1907: Fiftieth Anniversary Report" (1957): 460.

16. Alice Palmer Henderson, "Midewiwin Record On Birch Bark" [The Philosophical Research Society, online], Mar. 2, 2001. Available: http://www.prs.org/books/book448.htm.

17. Oberholtzer to Frances Andrews, Oct. 29, 1936, found in Oberholtzer's Mallard Island office.

18. Jim Bluebaugh, "Environmental Pioneer Dies," *International Falls News-Tribune*, June 1977.

19. Boshkaykin, interview.

20. Gregory Kinney, "Biographical Sketch," *Guide to the Microfilm Edition of the Papers of Ernest Oberholtzer* (St. Paul, Minn.: MHS Division of Library and Archives, 1989): 4.

Notes to Chapter 21

1. "Harvard College, Class of 1907: Fifty-fifth Anniversary Report" (1962): 106.

2. Ibid., 105.

3. Hilke, interview.

4. Cockburn, "Voyage to Nutheltin," 5.

5. From framed diploma found in Oberholtzer's Mallard Island office.

6. This and preceding quotation from Stewart Udall, "Department of the Interior Award Statement," found framed in Oberholtzer's Mallard Island office.

7. Oberholtzer to Stewart Udall, July 14, 1967, private collection.

8. Oberholtzer to Peavey Heffelfinger, July 29, 1967, private collection.

9. From Clayton Budd, "Natural History Society of Minnesota Award Statement," Jan. 6, 1967, found framed in Oberholtzer's Mallard Island office.

10. Oberholtzer notes, Oberholtzer Papers, 26:0317–0322.

11. Oberholtzer notes, Oberholtzer Papers, 44:0002.

12. "Harvard College, Class of 1907: Thirtieth Anniversary Report" (1937): 92–93.

13. "Harvard College, Class of 1907: Fiftieth Anniversary Report" (1957): 460, 464.

14. Hall, interview.

15. Jim Kimball, "He's Lived 45 Years on Island," *Minneapolis Tribune,* Jan. 10, 1965, 11H.

16. Charlene Erickson, interview by the author, tape recording, Sept. 4, 1996.

17. Newspaper clipping, *The Rainy Lake Chronicle,* Dec. 7, 1975 (Oberholtzer folders, Koochiching County Historical Society).

18. Hall, interview.

19. Ted Hall, "A Man and a Dream," *The Rainy Lake Chronicle* (Feb. 10, 1974).

20. Ibid.

21. Sigurd Olson, "A Defender of Wild Places," *Living Wilderness* (Jan.–Mar. 1978): 11.

22. Ibid.

23. Jim Bluebaugh, "Environmental Pioneer Dies."

Index

Illustration Credits

Keeper of the Wild was designed by Will Powers at the Minnesota Historical Society Press, set in Kepler by Allan Johnson at Phoenix Type, Milan, Minnesota, and printed by Maple Press, York, Pennsylvania. The Perfection Eggshell paper is made with thirty percent recycled post-consumer waste.